The authors

Duran Seddon is a barrister with a London set of chambers who specialises in immigration and welfare law. He has trained and written widely on these subjects, having contributed to other CPAG publications as well as to *Macdonald's Immigration Law & Practice* (5th edition) and *Halsbury's Laws of England*. He is also the editor of the 2002 edition of the *JCWI Immigration, Nationality and Refugee Law Handbook*.

Pamela Fitzpatrick is a policy adviser at the Family Rights Group Black and Ethnic Minorities Project, a co-author of CPAG's *Welfare Benefits Handbook* and a welfare rights trainer.

Mick Chatwin is a solicitor and barrister with over 20 years' experience in immigration and related areas of law.

Acknowledgements

The authors would like to thank everyone who has contributed to this book. We would, in particular, like to thank Belayeth Hussain, Eileen Bye and Arnie James for their invaluable comments. Thanks go too to Simon Cox for his contribution to the book and to Duncan Lane for his advice.

Thanks are due to Pascale Vassie and Alison Key for editing and managing the production of the book, Kay Hart for the index and Mary Shirley for proofreading the text.

Contents

Glossary of terms used

Adjudicator The person who hears and decides an immigration appeal in the first instance.

Administrative removal A form of enforced departure used to remove those who have breached their conditions of leave, overstayed their leave or who have obtained leave by deception.

Applicable amount A figure representing your weekly needs for the purpose of calculating your benefit. For income support your applicable amount is the amount you are expected to live on each week. For housing benefit and council tax benefit it is the amount used to see how much help you need with your rent or council tax. For working families' tax credit and disabled person's tax credit it is a fixed amount. For full details, see CPAG's *Welfare Benefits Handbook*.

Application registration card The form of identification for those who have claimed asylum, replacing the standard acknowledgement letter.

Association agreement A treaty signed between the European Community and another country which gives nationals of the other country (mainly business and self-employed people) preferential access to the countries of the European Economic Area.

Asylum A place of refuge; allowing a person to stay in one country because of the danger s/he would face if returned to the country from which s/he has fled.

Asylum seeker A person who makes a claim to the immigration authorities to be a refugee, as defined in the United Nations Convention on Refugees 1951. The status of asylum seeker ends when the person is given permission to stay in the UK, or when any rights of appeal against refusal some to an end. For benefit and asylum support purposes, someone who claims that removing her/him from the UK would violate rights under Article 3 of the European Convention on Human Rights is also treated as an asylum seeker.

Asylum support Support given to asylum seekers instead of welfare benefits and support under the National Assistance Act 1948. An 'interim' system of asylum support administered by local authorities was introduced in December 1999 (and still applies to some asylum seekers). A more permanent scheme administered by the National Asylum Support Service was introduced in April 2000. This *Handbook* only looks at asylum support in outline as it is not part of the welfare benefits system.

Certificate of entitlement A certificate of entitlement to the right of abode demonstrates that a person has the right of abode (right to travel freely to and from the UK). British citizens have the right of abode and can demonstrate this by producing their passports. However, a few Commonwealth nationals also have the right of abode and can obtain a certificate of entitlement, endorsed in their own national passport, to demonstrate this.

Certified case There are many different 'certificates' used in immigration and asylum law – eg, some claims for asylum are 'certified' on the grounds that the asylum seeker can be sent to a safe 'third country' of asylum. The new Nationality, Immigration and Asylum Bill 2002 proposes to allow 'clearly unfounded' certificates to be issued in asylum cases which will deny those asylum seekers a right of appeal until after they have left the UK. At present, the term is most used to describe certificates used to prevent asylum seekers and those making human rights claims from appealing beyond the first tier of appeal to the Immigration Appeal Tribunal.

Common Travel Area The UK, Republic of Ireland, Isle of Man and the Channel Islands, between which there are no immigration controls. Following the events of 11 September 2001, however, some airlines are demanding to see travel documents/passports.

Commonwealth countries Antigua and Barbuda, Australia, Bahamas, Bangladesh, Barbados, Belize, Botswana, Brunei Darussalam, Cameroon, Canada, Cyprus, Dominica, Fiji Islands, Gambia, Ghana, Grenada, Guyana, India, Jamaica, Kenya, Kiribati, Lesotho, Malawi, Malaysia, Maldives, Malta, Mauritius, Mozambique, Namibia, Nauru, New Zealand, Nigeria, Pakistan, Papua New Guinea, Samoa, Seychelles, Sierra Leone, Singapore, Solomon Islands, South Africa, Sri Lanka, St Kitts and Nevis, St Lucia, St Vincent and the Grenadines, Swaziland, Tanzania, Tonga, Trinidad and Tobago, Tuvalu, Uganda, Vanuatu, Zambia, Zimbabwe.

Deportation (order) Sending a person out of the UK under an order signed by the Home Secretary after the person has been convicted of a serious criminal offence, or because the Home Secretary has decided on public policy or national security grounds that the person's presence is 'not conducive to the public good'. The person cannot return unless and until the order has been revoked.

Enforcement A term used to refer to any of the different ways in which a person can be forced to leave the UK for immigration reasons: having been refused entry at port, having been declared an illegal entrant, or having been notified that s/he is someone who is liable for administrative removal, or who is being deported.

Entry clearance officer An official at a British post overseas who deals with immigration applications made to the post.

European Community (EC) In this book we refer to the legislation of the European Union (previously known as the European Community and before that the European Economic Community) as EC law.

European Convention on Human Rights An international instrument agreed by the Council of Europe. The rights guaranteed by it have now largely been incorporated into UK law by the Human Rights Act 1998.

European Convention on Social and Medical Assistance (ECSMA) An agreement signed by all the EEA states, plus Malta and Turkey, requiring that ratifying states provide assistance in cash and kind to nationals of other ratifying states, who are lawfully present in their territory and without sufficient resources, on the same conditions as their own nationals. It also prevents ratifying states repatriating lawfully present nationals of other ratifying states simply because the person is in need of assistance. If you are a person who is covered by the Convention you are not a 'person subject to immigration control' for means-tested benefits.

European Economic Area (EEA) covers European Union states plus Iceland, Liechtenstein and Norway. EEA nationals have free movement within these and all European Union member states. From 1 June 2002, the right to free movement also applies to Switzerland

European Union (EU) member states are Austria, Belgium, Denmark, Finland, France, Germany, Greece, Ireland, Italy, Luxembourg, the Netherlands, Portugal, Spain, Sweden and the UK (the UK includes Gibralter for this purpose).

EU/EEA national In this book we use this term to describe citizens of EU member states and EEA countries.

Exceptional leave Used in two senses: either to refer to any leave given to a person outside the immigration rules or to the leave given to a person who is refused asylum but is allowed to stay in the UK under the European Convention on Human Rights or for other humanitarian reasons.

Family For benefit purposes, under British law your family is yourself, your partner and any dependent children who are members of your household (for definition of household, see CPAG's *Welfare Benefits Handbook*). Under EC law, family members include a wider range of relatives.

Great Britain comprises Wales, Scotland, England and adjacent islands (but not the Isle of Man or Channel Islands).

Habeus corpus A legal remedy to protect personal liberty by requiring that a person who is being held in custody is brought before the court/judge giving the grounds for the detention. The court/judge can then test the legality of the detention and, if appropriate, direct that the person be released.

Habitual residence In order to be entitled to income support, income-based jobseeker's allowance, housing benefit and council tax benefit, a claimant must be habitually resident in the Common Travel Area. Some people are automatically treated as habitually resident and are exempt from the test. The term 'habitually resident' is not defined in the benefit regulations and will therefore be determined by looking at all the circumstances in each case. Habitual residence has a different meaning in EC law.

Illegal entrant A person who immigration officials decide has *entered* the UK in breach of the immigration law – this could be by deception.

Immigration Appeal Tribunal The second tier of the immigration appellate authority to which people can appeal against decisions of immigration adjudicators.

Immigration appellate authority The courts, tribunals and adjudicators that make decisions in immigration and asylum appeals.

Immigration officer An official, usually stationed at a British port of entry, who decides whether to grant or refuse leave to enter. Immigration officers also, however, have responsibility for enforcing immigration control.

Immigration rules Rules of practice made under the Immigration Act 1971 which set out the requirements for granting or refusing entry clearance, leave to enter and leave to remain to people applying in the various different categories.

Indefinite leave Leave which has no time limit.

Lawful presence This is not defined in social security law. However, for housing law it has been decided that a person is not lawfully present if s/he has been given temporary admission to the UK. It has yet to be decided whether or not this applies to social security.

Limited leave Leave which is given for a certain period of time only.

Maintenance undertaking A formal statement signed by a sponsor in the UK that s/he will support a relative or other person applying to come to or stay in the UK. The relative is not eligible to claim non-contributory welfare benefits for five years after it was signed, or after the person has been given leave to enter or remain in the UK on this basis (whichever is the later), unless the sponsor dies.

Ordinarily resident You must be ordinarily resident in Great Britain to be entitled to working families' tax credit, disabled person's tax credit, disability living allowance, attendance allowance, invalid care allowance, severe disablement allowance and Category D retirement pension. There is no definition in the benefits regulations of ordinary residence. This means that 'ordinary residence' should be given its ordinary and natural meaning.

Partner A wife, husband or cohabitee (of the opposite sex) who is, or is treated as, a member of the same household as the claimant for benefit purposes.

Person from abroad A statutory definition that refers to a person who has failed the habitual residence test. It is not linked to a person's immigration status and even a British citizen can be termed a person from abroad for social security purposes.

Person subject to immigration control A social security term. A person subject to immigration control is excluded from entitlement to most social security benefits.

Public funds For immigration purposes these are: housing provided by local authorities – either as a homeless person or allocated from its housing register; attendance allowance; severe disablement allowance; invalid care allowance; disability living allowance; income support; working families' tax credit; council tax benefit; disabled person's tax credit; housing benefit; income-based jobseeker's allowance; child benefit.

Refugee A person who satisfies the definition of those who need international protection under Article 1A(2) of the 1951 Convention relating to the status of refugees.

Removal The final procedure for sending a person refused entry, or who is being treated as an illegal entrant, or who is subject to the 'administrative' removal or deportation process, away from the UK.

Right of abode The right to enter, remain, leave and return freely to the UK without the need to obtain 'leave' from the immigration authorities. All British citizens have the right of abode. Some Commonwealth nationals also have the right of abode.

Settlement/settled status Defined in immigration law as being 'ordinarily resident' in the UK without any restrictions on the time the person is able to remain here. Those with indefinite leave are generally accepted as being 'settled' in the UK.

Social Chapter The 1961 Council of Europe Social Chapter has been signed by all the EEA countries, plus Cyprus, the Czech Republic, Hungary, Latvia, Malta, Poland, Slovakia and Turkey. If you are a national of one of these states and you are lawfully present you are not a 'person subject to immigration control' for means-tested benefits.

Standard acknowledgement letter These letters (SAL1 and SAL2) are now being replaced by application registration cards as the document which confirms that a person is an asylum seeker.

Subject to immigration control People often use this term to refer to those who need 'leave' to enter or remain in the UK – and this is the definition given in the Asylum and Immigration Act 1996. However, the Immigration and Asylum Act 1999 gives the same phrase a different, narrower, definition, which is used to exclude people from non-contributory welfare benefits and certain services provided by local authorities' social services departments. In this book, we use the term as it is defined in the 1999 Act for welfare purposes.

Temporary admission A temporary licence given to people to be in the UK while they are waiting for a decision to be made on their immigration status or while they are waiting to be removed from the UK. The alternative to temporary admission, used particularly where a person is waiting to be removed, is detention.

Third country Usually used to refer to a country, other than that of which an asylum seeker is a national, to which the Home Office wishes to send an asylum seeker in order for her/his claim to be decided there, rather than in the UK. Third country nationals is also used to refer to nationals of a country, other than an EU/EEA state, who do not (unless they are family members of an EU/EEA national) enjoy EU rights of free movement.

The United Kingdom comprises England, Wales, Scotland and Northern Ireland.

Unmarried partners A term used in the immigration rules to refer to couples (heterosexual or same sex) who have been together for two or more years, who are in a relationship 'akin to marriage' and who cannot marry according to the law (eg, because they are of the same sex or one of them is already married). The immigration rules give unmarried partners some rights to enter and remain in the UK where one partner is settled in the UK or has limited leave to enter or remain here.

Visa nationals People who always need to get entry clearance in advance of travelling to the UK, for whatever purpose they are coming here, unless they are returning residents returning within two years or are returning within a period of earlier leave granted for more than six months, or certain refugees and all asylum seekers. For a list of countries covered, see Appendix 8.

Work permit A formal document issued to employers allowing them to employ a named individual in a particular job. They are issued by Work Permits (UK), which is part of the Home Office. This is different from the Home Office 'granting permission' to work, for example, to an asylum seeker. When the immigration authorities do this, technically they simply remove the condition on the asylum seeker's temporary admission prohibiting her/him from working.

Abbreviations

AA	Attendance allowance	GB	Great Britain
ARC	Application registration card	HB	Housing benefit
BDTC	British dependent territories citizen	HRT	Habitual residence test
		IB	Incapacity benefit
BL	Budgeting loan	ICA	Invalid care allowance
BNO	British national (overseas)	ILR	Indefinite leave to remain
BOC	British overseas citizen	IND	Immigration and Nationality Directorate
BOTC	British overseas territories citizen		
		IS	Income support
BPP	British protected person	JSA	Jobseeker's allowance
BS	British subject	MA	Maternity allowance
CAB	Citizens advice bureau	NASS	National Asylum Support Service
CCG	Community care grant		
CL	Crisis loan	NI	National insurance
CSA	Child Support Agency	NICO	National Insurance Contributions Office
CTA	Common Travel Area		
CTB	Council tax benefit	NINO	National insurance number
CUKC	Citizen of the United Kingdom and colonies	PFA	Person from abroad
		PSIC	Person subject to immigration control
DfES	Department for Education and Skills		
		REA	Reduced earnings allowance
DLA	Disability living allowance	SAL	Standard acknowledgement letter
DPTC	Disabled person's tax credit		
DWP	Department for Work and Pensions	SDA	Severe disablement allowance
		SEF	Statement of evidence form
EC	European Community	SF	Social fund
ECHR	European Convention on Human Rights	SIAC	Special Immigration Appeals Commission
ECtHR	European Court of Human Rights	SMP	Statutory maternity pay
		SSP	Statutory sick pay
ECJ	European Court of Justice	TCO	Tax Credit Office
EEA	European Economic Area	TWES	Training and work experience scheme
ELE	Exceptional leave to enter		
ELR	Exceptional leave to remain	UK	United Kingdom
EO	Employment officer	VOLO	Variation of Leave Order 1976
EU	European Union	WFTC	Working families' tax credit

About this *Handbook*

This *Handbook* is intended to bridge the gap between guides on welfare rights and those on immigration. It is designed to be used by migrants and their advisers wanting advice on benefit entitlement. By 'migrants' we mean people who have come or returned to Great Britain from abroad and people who have left Great Britain to live abroad or are temporarily abroad.

The *Handbook* covers the benefit rules that are most likely to affect migrant claimants and their families, and the practical problems they are likely to face. It is not a complete guide to the benefit rules and should be used together with general guides such as CPAG's *Welfare Benefits Handbook*.

How to use this book

Your benefit rights may depend upon your immigration status. In Part 1 we outline the immigration system and explain the terms used in immigration law which appear in the rest of the book. Part I aims to provide welfare rights advisers with a framework of immigration law. In some cases Part I may contain enough information for you to use the rest of the handbook to work out your benefit entitlement. However, if you are unclear about your immigration status or the effects of claiming benefit, you should if possible ask a specialist immigration adviser for immigration advice.

If your immigration status is clear, you should use Part 2 to work out your benefit entitlement. Use the chapter relevant to your immigration status.

If you are abroad, use Part 3. If you are planning to go abroad, use Parts 2 and 3.

Part 4 deals with European Community rules as they affect benefits here and in Europe. Part 5 deals with international agreements with certain other countries that can be used by their nationals and residents.

The law covered was correct at 1 April 2002 and includes regulations laid up to that date.

Part 1

Immigration law

Chapter 1

Immigration control

This chapter covers:
1. Immigration control (p4)
2. The effect of immigration control (p6)
3. How immigration control operates (p11)

There is not space in this book to set out and explain the conditions which need to be satisfied under the immigration rules (see p15) under which 'leave' (permission) to enter or remain in the UK may be applied for and granted; nor the criteria applied when deciding whether to grant a work permit; nor the general grounds for refusal of leave. The intention of Part 1 of the book is to set out the framework and mechanics of immigration control so that the system of control can be understood and so that welfare advisers can more readily identify and understand a person's immigration status and advise on her/his benefit entitlement. The criteria contained in the immigration rules for admission as a refugee (Chapter 3) and as a student (Chapter 4) are given as examples only. If you want to know more about the criteria for the different admission categories, they are set out in the immigration rules in accessible language (the immigration rules are not legislation).[1] The criteria applied when determining whether a work permit can be issued to an employer for someone who wishes to obtain leave to enter and remain is updated regularly. Information, including guidance notes on making applications, can be found at http://www.workpermits.gov.uk

The requirements of the rules which relate to 'maintenance and accommodation without recourse to public funds' (which apply to many of the categories to which leave can be granted) are, however, explained in Chapter 4. These requirements are included because they are relevant to the immigration consequences of claiming (or trying to claim) benefit.

In addition, a list of all the categories of entry, together with the specific 'maintenance and accommodation' requirements which apply to each one, can be found in the tables in Appendix 4 and Appendix 5.

1. **Immigration control**

The term '**immigration control**' refers to the system by which people's ability to enter, stay and live in the UK for different purposes is restricted and regulated by the government. Control takes place by examining passengers at ports of entry into the UK and continues to operate after a person has been admitted to the country. The body largely responsible for immigration control is the Immigration and Nationality Directorate (IND), a part of the Home Office. The IND describes its role as being to 'regulate entry to and settlement in the UK in the interests of social stability and economic growth, and the facilitation of travel by United Kingdom citizens'.[2]

However, in many cases, immigration control begins overseas at designated posts, for example at British embassies and high commissions. Visa sections at these posts are regulated by 'UK Visas'. UK Visas is a joint section of the Home Office and the Foreign and Commonwealth Office which was created in June 2000 (originally known as the Joint Entry Clearance Unit) and replaces the Foreign and Commonwealth Office's Migration and Visa Department.

Some people are barely affected by immigration controls and may freely come to, and go from, the UK without any restrictions. The largest group of people who fall into this category are those with the 'right of abode' in the UK (largely British citizens – see p6). Immigration control has its greatest impact on people who require specific permission (called 'leave') to come to the UK. For these people, the effect of immigration control is to allocate to them a particular immigration status. Rights, such as access to social security and employment, are very much determined by the immigration status that a person has as a result of immigration controls. There are other groups of people who are subjected only to reduced forms of immigration control or who enjoy certain advantages in relation to immigration control as a result of being nationals of certain countries other than the UK, or even the particular nature of their employment (see p6).

'Citizenship' or 'nationality' is connected, but not equivalent, to immigration status. In many countries nationality law determines whether a person may freely come to and go from the territory – ie, if the person is a national of the country s/he may freely come and go. The relationship between nationality law and immigration law in the UK is more complex because there are different classes of British national, some of which are greatly affected by immigration controls (see Chapter 2).

Who is affected by immigration control

Everyone must undergo some form of examination by the immigration authorities when they arrive in the UK, but the extent of immigration control varies greatly between different groups. There are two main groups.

- Those who require specific permission to come into and stay in the UK; this permission is technically known as **leave to enter** and **leave to remain** in the UK and that is how we will refer to it.
- Those who do not require leave.

In the past, immigration lawyers and advisers have always distinguished these groups by referring to those who are 'subject to immigration control' (meaning those who need leave) and those who are not subject to control. The Asylum and Immigration Act 1996 defines those subject to control in exactly this way.[3] However, since the introduction of the latest major change in immigration law, the Immigration and Asylum Act 1999, use of these terms has become confusing because that Act[4] introduces a special definition of '**persons who are subject to immigration control**' (PSIC). The purpose of this definition is to determine entitlement to social security benefit and access to certain community care services (see Chapter 13). The group of people who are included within this definition is narrower than those who require leave to enter/remain in the UK. For this reason, we will only use the term 'subject to immigration control' when talking about access to welfare under this new definition. For immigration purposes, we will refer to those who require, and who do not require, leave to enter or remain in the UK, but you should be generally aware that the term may be used more loosely by other people. Home Office publications, for example, may refer to people being subject to immigration control when they require leave to enter the UK.[5]

Leave to *enter* is simply that leave given when a person is coming into the UK from another country whereas leave to *remain* is that which may be given to those who have already entered.

In addition to granting or refusing leave, the immigration authorities can impose conditions and limitations (eg, access to work and time limits) on leave. They may also curtail leave and, in many circumstances, can enforce a person's departure (see Chapter 7) from the UK.

Movement within the Common Travel Area

Although leave is generally required for those people who need leave in order to enter the UK, there is one circumstance in which it is the *journey* which is taken rather than the *person* who takes the journey, which largely determines whether leave is required. This is when the journey is within the Common Travel Area (CTA). The CTA consists of the UK, the 'Islands' (Channel Islands and the Isle of Man) and the Republic of Ireland.[6] Journeys within the CTA are not subject to immigration control and, as a result, leave is not required. However, there are exceptions to this general rule of freedom of travel within the CTA. For example, people who simply pass through the Republic of Ireland on their way to the UK still need leave to enter the UK.[7] The existence of the CTA means that citizens of the Irish Republic may travel to the UK without requiring leave to enter.

2. **The effect of immigration control**

The right of abode in the UK

People who have the '**right of abode**' do not need leave to enter or remain in the UK. They are 'free to live in, and to come and go into and from, the United Kingdom without let or hindrance'.[8] They may stay in the UK for as long as they like and there are no conditions restricting what they may do while in the UK. Those with the right of abode are:[9]

- British citizens;
- certain citizens of Commonwealth countries (for list of Commonwealth countries, see the glossary of terms at the beginning of this book).

Commonwealth citizens who have the right of abode are those who, before 1 January 1983, were either:

- Commonwealth citizens with a parent born in the UK; *or*
- women who had become 'patrial' (see p20) through marriage.

For more information about nationality and the right of abode, see Chapter 2.

If you fall into one of these groups, you do not require leave to enter or remain in the UK. However, you are still required to undergo a very limited form of examination sufficient for you to demonstrate that you do hold the status claimed.[10] The passports of those who do not require leave to enter are routinely checked by immigration officers on entry to the UK.[11] You can prove that you have the right of abode by producing:[12]

- a UK passport describing you as a British citizen or as a citizen of the UK and Colonies having the right of abode in the UK; *or*
- a certificate of entitlement (see p110) issued by the UK government certifying that you have the right of abode.

People who do not have the right of abode in the UK

If you are not in one of the above groups (ie, with the right of abode), you generally need leave to enter or remain in the UK. This means that to enter or remain in the UK you must satisfy the requirements of the immigration rules. However, there are certain 'special groups' of people, some of whom do not need leave to enter or remain, even though they do not have the right of abode (see below).

Special groups

No leave required

There are certain special groups of people who do not fit easily into the division between those who need leave and those who do not. The following groups do not need leave, but their ability to enter and remain without leave depends upon their satisfying, or continuing to satisfy, certain conditions. These special groups are:

- nationals of states which are members of the European Union (EU) or a party to the European Economic Area (EEA) (see below);
- family members of EU/EEA nationals who would normally require leave to enter the UK (see below);
- diplomats, embassy staff and others (see p8);
- armed forces personnel (see p8);
- ship and air crews (see p9).

EEA nationals and their family members

EEA nationals are nationals of countries which are members of the EU (Austria, Belgium, Denmark, Finland, France, Germany, Greece, Ireland, Italy, Luxembourg, Netherlands, Portugal, Spain, Sweden, United Kingdom) and nationals of Norway, Iceland and Liechtenstein, additional countries which are a party to the 'Agreement on the European Economic Area'.[13] The source of the legal rights of EEA nationals to enter and remain in the UK derives ultimately from the EC Treaty and several EC Directives and not from UK domestic law. It is for this reason that the right cannot be made subject to the need to obtain any permission (leave) from the immigration authorities before it can be exercised.[14] Nevertheless, the government has *described* the existence of these rights in regulations: the Immigration (European Economic Area) Regulations 2000.[15]

Generally, the **family members** of an EEA national (including nationals of a non-EEA country, known as 'third country' nationals) are the spouse, descendants (ie, children, grandchildren) of the EEA national or the EEA national's spouse who are either under 21 years or, if over 21 years, dependent on the EEA national or her/his spouse; and the dependent relatives in the *ascending* line (parents, grandparents) of the EEA national or her/his spouse.[16] The immigration authorities may also, in exercising discretion, treat other extended family members as also being family members.[17]

The right to reside in the UK of EEA nationals and family members are dependent, however, upon the EEA national exercising rights of free movement which are recognized by EC law, namely as a worker, a self-employed person, provider or recipient of services, self-sufficient person, retired person, student or as a self-employed person who has ceased activity. The regulations refer to these EEA nationals as being *qualified* persons.[18] People who would otherwise enjoy these rights may be removed from the UK if they cease to be a qualified person or the family member of a qualified person[19] and they may also not be admitted to the UK, or removed, if the Secretary of State determines that such action is justified on the grounds of public policy, public security or public health.[20] Nationals of certain other countries may also seek to enter or remain in the UK in order to establish themselves in business pursuant to 'association agreements' agreed between the EU and those countries (see p418).

Diplomats and staff of embassies, high commissions and international agencies

Diplomats and certain staff of embassies and high commissions and their families who form part of their household are exempt from immigration controls and so do not require leave.[21] Unless you are actually a diplomat, you cannot benefit from this exemption unless you were out of the country when you were offered the position.[22] If you are employed by a high commission or embassy but pay local taxes (ie, UK taxes), then you are probably not within the category of staff who are exempt.[23] If you are privately employed by a member of the mission (rather than by the mission itself), the law is not clear as to whether you are exempt from control.[24] For this category of people, there are no clear guidelines as to who is a member of the family or who can be said to form part of the household. A judgement must be made on the facts of each case.[25]

There are further exemptions or partial exemptions from immigration control for:[26]
- consular officers or employees in the service of a foreign government;
- members of foreign governments or their representatives in the UK on official business;
- officials of international organisations such as the International Monetary Fund;
- people attending certain international conferences in the UK and certain Commonwealth officials.

In practical terms, if you fall into any of the above categories you are entitled to benefit from your exemption as soon as you arrive in the UK. However, the exemption only applies for as long as you retain the status for which it was granted.[27] If a person ceases to be exempt from control because, for example, s/he loses her/his job, then s/he is treated as having been granted a period of leave of 90 days from the date s/he ceased to be exempt[28] unless s/he, before becoming exempt, had an existing period of leave which would expire before the end of that 90-day period, in which case s/he is treated only as having that existing leave.[29] This provides the person with a period of grace in which to leave the UK without having remained in the UK unlawfully or to make an 'in-time' (see p38) application for further leave.

Armed forces

The following are exempt from all immigration controls except deportation:[30]
- members of UK armed forces;
- members of a Commonwealth or similar force undergoing training in the UK with the UK armed forces;
- members of a visiting force coming to the UK at the invitation of the government.

In addition, a person who wishes to return to the UK as a returning resident (ie, who had indefinite leave when s/he last left the UK) and who has been away accompanying her/his spouse on duty abroad where her/his spouse is a member of the armed forces, a diplomat or a member of the British Council, does not need to show that s/he has not been away from the UK for more than two years as other returning residents do.[31] Also, a person of any of the occupations listed above is treated as 'present and settled in the UK' (one of the requirements of the immigration rules relating to married couples) even though s/he is serving overseas, for the purposes of applications by her/his spouse for leave to enter, remain or settle in the UK.[32]

Ship and air crews

If you arrive in the UK as a member of the crew of a ship or aircraft, hired or under orders to depart as part of that ship's crew or to depart on the same or another aircraft within seven days of arrival, then you may enter the UK without leave.[33] You may also remain in the UK without leave until the ship or aircraft is ready to leave. In order to be a crew member you must be employed to carry out functions necessary to the running of the ship or aircraft.[34]

You will not benefit from this exemption if:[35]

- there is a deportation order against you;
- you have, at any time, been refused leave to enter the UK and have not since been given leave to enter or remain in the UK; *or*
- an immigration officer requires you to submit to examination.

People who require leave but have certain immigration advantages

A second group of people require leave to enter or remain in the UK but due to their nationality, place of birth or employment, enjoy certain advantages in immigration control. They are:

- British nationals who are not British citizens. Not everyone who possesses British nationality has the right of abode (see p6) which comes only with British citizenship. Other British nationals have to obtain leave but they do have certain immigration advantages (see Chapter 2);
- non-visa nationals (see below);
- nationals of certain countries (see p10);
- non-British citizen children born in Britain on or after 1 January 1983 (see p11).

Non-visa nationals

The immigration rules distinguish between **visa nationals** (who require prior 'entry clearance' obtained overseas in order to come to the UK in any category – ie, for any purpose), and **non-visa nationals** (who do not require entry clearance, unless the immigration rules for the category in which they wish to come to the UK specifically requires an applicant to obtain entry clearance). The list of visa national countries is frequently updated and is to be found in Appendix 1 to the immigration rules themselves.[36] A current list is in Appendix 8.

Nationals of certain countries

Depending upon the category in which you seek to enter, the requirements for admission can vary according to nationality. So, in certain circumstances, a national of one country may be in a better position than a national of another country. EEA nationals, of course, benefit from European rights of free movement as discussed on p7. These other circumstances are very much the exception rather than the rule.

- Admission for an au pair placement can only be granted under the rules to citizens of Andorra, Bosnia-Herzegovina, Croatia, Cyprus, the Czech Republic, the Faroes, Greenland, Hungary, Macedonia, Malta, Monaco, San Marino, Slovak Republic, Slovenia, Switzerland and Turkey.[37]
- Admission in the capacity of 'working holidaymaker' is only open to Commonwealth citizens (see the glossary of terms at the beginning of this book for a list of the countries of the Commonwealth) although the government is proposing opening up this category to nationals of other countries.[38]
- If a Commonwealth citizen wishes to seek employment, then s/he may be admitted on the basis of her/his having a grandparent who was born in the UK thereby avoiding the far more restrictive rules relating to work permits for other people who require leave to enter and remain.[39]
- Nationals of the following countries (and their dependants) may seek leave to enter or remain in the UK as people establishing themselves in business in self-employment or partnership: Bulgaria, the Czech Republic, Estonia, Hungary, Latvia, Lithuania, Poland, Romania and Slovakia. Nationals of all these countries, and in addition Slovenia, may also seek to establish themselves in a company which they control and obtain leave in that capacity.[40] The source of these rights, although they are written into the immigration rules, is EC law in the form of 'association agreements' made between the EC and those countries. There are other association agreements which give nationals of certain other countries less valuable immigration benefits and which are not referred to in the immigration rules. The most significant of these is the Turkish Association Agreement which, if certain criteria are satisfied, progressively extends the right to work in the UK, and with it the right to stay in the UK, to Turkish nationals who have otherwise obtained lawful access to the labour market. However, it provides for no right of entry for the worker concerned.[41] There are, of course, rights to enter the UK for business purposes under the immigration rules which nationals of *all* countries can use, but they are more restrictive. For example, they require that the applicant has £200,000 to invest in the business.

Non-British citizen children born in Britain on or after 1 January 1983

Since the British Nationality Act 1981 came into force on 1 January 1983, certain children (see p25) born in the UK are not automatically born British citizens. They, therefore, require leave to enter and remain in the UK. If they were to leave the UK, they would be subject to the ordinary provisions of the immigration rules if they wished to return. However, because they have never actually been granted leave to remain they cannot be:

- removed from the UK as 'overstayers' or as in breach of their conditions of leave;[42] *or*
- removed from the UK as a person who has been refused leave to enter or as an illegal entrant.[43]

These people can, however, be forced to leave the UK if they are removed as part of the family to which they belong.[44] However, at present this can only happen when their parents are required to leave the UK under the enforcement procedures known as 'administrative removal' (see p78) or 'deportation' (see p78). The Nationality, Immigration and Asylum Bill 2002 proposes to ensure that the child can be removed as part of the family in all cases.

For more details about enforcement of immigration controls, removal and deportation, see Chapter 7.

---

3. How immigration control operates

This section is relevant to people who require leave to enter/remain in the UK. It summarises the basic mechanics of immigration control, the decision making process and the personnel involved at different stages of the immigration process. Further details of relevant immigration controls and how they operate in practice are given in Chapter 3.

Types of leave

There are two kinds of leave:[45]

- limited leave to enter or remain (meaning limited in terms of time – eg, six months or two years);
- indefinite leave to enter or remain (with no restriction on time).

Depending on your circumstances, it is probable that certain conditions will be attached to your limited leave to enter or remain. No conditions may be attached to indefinite leave.[46] The conditions may relate to:[47]

- your employment or occupation;
- maintaining yourself in the UK 'without recourse to public funds' (see p92);
- registering with the police.[48]

Personnel

The main office of the Immigration and Nationality Directorate of the Home Office (IND) is in Croydon,[49] but the IND also has regional offices in Leeds and Liverpool (see Appendix 2 for details). The officers who work at these offices are all ultimately responsible to the Secretary of State for the Home Department. The following personnel play a significant part in the system of immigration control:

- **Entry clearance officers.** They are stationed in overseas posts with responsibility for control prior to entry. They are responsible for issuing entry clearance (visas) to those who wish to come to the UK. Following changes made by the Immigration and Asylum Act 1999 (see p14), entry clearance now qualifies as leave to enter when a person arrives in the UK. Entry clearance officers are also responsible for issuing family permits to family members of European Economic Area (EEA) nationals who want to come to the UK and certificates of entitlement to the right of abode (see p110).

- **Immigration officers**, including chief immigration officers and immigration inspectors. They are generally responsible for 'on entry' immigration control and are mainly to be found at the ports of entry into the UK.[50] Following changes made by the 1999 Act (see p14), immigration officers may grant a person leave to enter before s/he has actually arrived in the UK. Immigration officers also have wide powers of detention. They may detain people after their arrival in the UK while a decision is made as to whether leave should be granted and they may detain people who are in the process of being removed from the UK.[51] Connected to their powers of detention, immigration officers are also largely responsible for actually operating the process of enforcing the departure from the UK of those who cannot show that they have any entitlement to remain. There are different enforcement procedures which depend upon the category into which the case falls. Immigration officers may 'remove' those refused leave to enter (see p79), those unlawfully in the UK (see p81) and 'illegal entrants' (see p81). In a separate enforcement procedure called 'deportation' (see p79), immigration officers can make initial decisions to deport people on behalf of the Secretary of State,[52] but the later making of the deportation order itself is the responsibility of the Secretary of State. Immigration officers also have powers in relation to suspected immigration criminal offences. They may exercise powers of arrest without warrant and, with a warrant issued by a magistrate, may enter and search premises and search suspects.[53]

- **The Secretary of State** and his officers at the Home Office are, in general, responsible for immigration control after entry (see p38).[54] Applications for extensions of leave to remain in the UK after a person has already entered are generally determined by the Secretary of State.[55] The Secretary of State is also responsible for:

- considering whether there are sufficient compassionate factors to enable those who have overstayed their leave (see p80) or have breached conditions of their leave (see p81) or who are liable to deportation (see p79) to remain in the UK and for deciding whether a deportation order may be revoked;[56]
- the detention and removal of those who are being forced to leave the UK by the deportation process;[57]
- making the immigration rules (see p15).[58]

- **Officials at Work Permits (UK)** are responsible for issuing work permits under the work permit scheme and under the 'training and work experience' scheme to those who are not nationals of an EEA country and who would otherwise not be entitled to work in the UK.[59] Work Permits (UK), which is based in Sheffield (see Appendix 2), used to be part of the Department for Education and Employment and is now part of the Home Office. Work permits are not entry clearances.[60]

- **The Lord Chancellor** is responsible for the appointment of personnel of the immigration appellate authority (adjudicators and members of the Immigration Appeal Tribunal who are responsible for hearing and deciding immigration appeals[61] and for making rules of procedure for immigration appeals.[62]

- **Adjudicators and members of the Immigration Appeal Tribunal** (appointed as above), are all responsible for hearing and determining appeals on decisions of entry clearance officers, immigration officers and the Secretary of State.

- **Asylum support adjudicators**, responsible for determining appeals against decisions refusing all asylum support under the National Asylum Support Service (NASS).[63]

- **Home Office presenting officers** appointed by the Secretary of State and responsible for presenting the case for the Home Office at immigration appeals.

- **Police officers**, responsible for the registration of certain people who require leave to enter and remain in the UK,[64] the arrest of people suspected of having committed criminal offences under immigration law[65] and the arrest and detention of people who are liable to be detained in order to enforce their departure from the UK under immigration law.[66]

- **Detainee custody officers** are a class of officers created by the 1999 Act[67] who, as well as immigration officers, prison officers, prison custody officers and the police, have functions relating to holding people who may be detained in custody under immigration law and in escorting them from one place to another.

- **NASS officers**, acting on behalf of the Secretary of State and responsible for making decisions on asylum support. Similarly local authority officers are responsible for making decisions on interim support under the interim scheme of asylum support.[68]

Immigration legislation

The Immigration Act 1971 contains the basic provisions setting out the framework for immigration control. Subsequent Acts of Parliament, the Immigration Act 1988, Asylum and Immigration Appeals Act 1993, Asylum and Immigration Act 1996 and the Immigration and Asylum Act 1999 and other legislation passed since 1971 have substantially modified the 1971 Act and have added many new aspects. It was hoped that the 1999 legislation would consolidate all of the preceding legislation into one free-standing statute. Unfortunately, the 1999 Act, while long, detailed and introducing many new measures, greatly amends the 1971 Act and the other legislation without replacing it wholesale. In addition, there are a substantial number of statutory instruments and orders made under the Acts of Parliament which add further detail to the main provisions.

The **Nationality, Immigration and Asylum Bill 2002** continues to build upon the previous legislation without consolidating it. The proposals (based on the Bill's first reading, 24 April 2002) are not as far reaching as the changes made by the 1999 Act but build on that legislation in several significant respects. In particular, there are proposals to:
- abolish discrimination against illegitimate children in nationality law;
- introduce new procedures for naturalising as a British citizen, including a requirement that applicants have sufficient knowledge about life in the UK and that they take a new citizenship pledge;
- allow those British overseas citizens (see p20) who would otherwise have no right of abode in any country to obtain British citizenship. This applies to present and former residents of former UK colonies, mainly in East Africa, who have not been able to acquire the nationality of their, now independent, country of birth;
- make asylum seekers subject to a new 'end to end' procedure beginning with 'induction centres' progressing through 'accommodation centres' and, if their claims are finally determined against them, to allow them to be detained at what are to be re-designated as 'removal centres';
- provide support to asylum seekers in trial accommodation centres where, although asylum seekers will not be 'detained', they will be required to reside. If they refuse, they will not be provided with other forms of asylum support – eg, in ordinary 'dispersal' accommodation;
- allow the removal of family members of people who the immigration authorities are taking enforcement action against in *all* circumstances. At present, there is only power to remove family members where the principal member is being deported or subject to administrative removal (see pp78-83). The 2002 Bill will allow family members of those who are refused entry at port and 'illegal entrants' to also be removed. The government, in particular, wants to ensure that it can remove from the UK children who are born in Britain, but

who are not British citizens because neither of their parents are British or settled here and who the immigration authorities wish to remove;
- clarify and streamline the system for immigration appeals. The 1999 Act introduced a 'one-stop' appeals process which required all appellants to raise *all* of their grounds for being in the UK at the same time so that they could all be dealt with together at the same appeal. The process became messy and confusing and it is proposed to simplify it;
- prevent asylum seekers from appealing against a refusal of asylum under the 1951 Refugee Convention where they are instead granted exceptional leave for 12 months or less;
- prevent any in-country appeal at all in asylum cases deemed to be 'clearly unfounded';
- prevent multiple adjournments of immigration appeals by introducing a statutory closure date by which time the appeal must be determined and to prevent adjournments except in strictly defined circumstances;
- prevent judicial review of decisions of the Immigration Appeal Tribunal to refuse leave to appeal from decisions of the immigration adjudicator;
- create new powers for immigration officers to enter business premises and arrest immigration offenders and to create new criminal offences including those relating to trafficking people into or out of the UK for the purposes of prostitution, and forgery of asylum 'application registration cards'.

The Home Office White Paper, *Secure Borders, Safe Haven: integration with diversity in modern Britain* (7 February 2002) makes various further proposals which do not necessarily require an Act of Parliament but can be effected through changes in the immigration rules. Where relevant, these proposals are flagged up in the text of this Part.

The immigration rules

Decisions as to whether or not a person who requires leave:
- should be granted leave to enter or remain in the UK;
- upon what conditions and for how long; *and*
- whether s/he should be required to leave the UK;

are generally made according to the immigration rules made under the Immigration Act 1971 Act.

The 'immigration rules' are not *legislation* but rules of practice. The rules themselves are made by the Secretary of State and put before Parliament for approval.[69] The Secretary of State frequently issues statements of amendment to the rules and sometimes re-issues the whole of the rules in a different form. The last complete statement of the rules was laid before Parliament on 23 May 1994 and is referred to as 'HC 395'. Those rules came into effect, with transitional provisions for applications made prior to that date, on 1 October 1994.[70] The two latest main changes to the immigration rules came into effect on 30 July 2000[71] and 2 October 2000[72] and reflect many of the changes made by the Immigration and Asylum Act 1999 as well as introducing some new categories in which leave to enter and remain in the UK can be granted. Unlike social security regulations, which are legislation, the immigration rules are drafted in an informal style and the words used must be given their most natural and ordinary meaning.[73]

The rules set out:

- a series of 'requirements' which a person needs to satisfy in order to be granted entry clearance or leave in any particular category – eg, as a student, visitor or as a refugee (see p52 for an example);
- a set of additional general considerations for determining whether a person should be granted entry clearance or leave to enter the UK in any category;
- the length of time for which a person may expect to be admitted in any category and the conditions which a person is likely to have attached to her/his leave if granted;
- the process and criteria for deciding whether a person who has breached immigration control should be required to leave the UK; *and*
- which people are required to satisfy the 'maintenance and accommodation' requirements (see p92).

Immigration decisions outside the rules

Certain people are admitted or allowed entry outside the rules. The rules represent the minimum standard of treatment that a person may expect and must be applied by entry clearance officers/immigration officers.[74] However, the Home Office has the discretion to waive any of the requirements of the rules (and to authorise immigration officers and entry clearance officers to do likewise), and therefore to treat any person more favourably than the strict letter of the rules requires. A person who is treated in this special way, is said to be granted leave 'exceptionally'. Leave may be granted exceptionally to a whole range of people in different circumstances who cannot fit the normal requirements of the rules. Exceptional or indefinite leave can be limited. However, the term **'exceptional leave'** is also used more narrowly to describe leave which is given to a person who has applied for, but been refused, refugee status but is granted leave because the Home Office determines it would not be right to require that person to return to her/his country, and has instead given her/him some form of protection. Exceptional leave is dealt with in more detail in Chapter 6.

Notes

1 Statement of immigration rules, HC 395, parts 2-8 and 11

1. Immigration control

2 'Home Office Aim' Six cited at the head of the website of the Immigration and Nationality Directorate: http://www.ind.home office.gov.uk/
3 s13(2) AIA 1996
4 ss115(3) and (9) and 116-117 IAA 1999
5 See, eg, Immigration and Nationality Directorate website at Chapter 1, Section 1, paragraph 1
6 s1(3) IA 1971
7 For details of these categories, see s9(4) and (6) IA 1971 and I(CERI)O (as amended) and para 15 HC 395

2. The effect of immigration control

8 s1(1) IA 1971
9 s2(1) IA 1971 as substituted by s39(2) BNA 1981
10 s3(8) IA 1971; paras 12-13 HC 395
11 s1(1) and Sch 2 paras 2-4 IA 1971
12 s3(8)(a) IA 1971
13 Signed at Oporto 2 May 1992, adjusted by the Protocol signed at Brussels on 17 March 1993
14 s7 IA 1988; *R v Pieck* C–157/79 [1981] QB 571
15 Reg 1(2) and (3) I(EEA) Regs. These Regs replace and revoke the earlier Immigration (European Economic Area) Order 1994 referred to in the last edition.
16 Reg 6(4) I(EEA) Regs. However if the EEA national is a student, 'family members' are restricted to spouse and dependent children, reg 6(2) I(EEA) Regs
17 Reg 10 I(EEA) implementing Article 10(2) EEC No. 1612/68 and Article 1(2) Directive 73/148/EEC
18 Reg 5 I(EEA) Regs
19 Reg 21(3)(a) I(EEA) Regs
20 Regs 21(3)(b) and 23 I(EEA) Regs
21 s8(3) IA 1971; Diplomatic Privileges Act 1964; International Organisations (Immunities and Privileges) Act 1950; International Organisations Act 1968; Commonwealth Secretariat Act 1966 and associated Orders in Council
22 s8(3A) IA 1971 inserted by s6 IAA 1999

23 *Kandiah* (2699)
24 *Florentine* [1987] Imm AR 1
25 See for some guidance, *Gupta* [1979-80] Imm AR 52 and footnote reference to QBD decision at 52 and 78
26 s8(2) IA 1971; I(EC)O as amended
27 s8(3) IA 1971
28 s8A(1) and (2) IA 1971 inserted by s7 IAA 1999
29 s8A(3) and 8(5) IA 1971 inserted by s7 IAA 1999
30 s8(4) and (6) IA 1971
31 para 19A HC 395 inserted by para 6 Cmnd 4581
32 para 281 HC 395 as amended by para 30 Cmnd 4581
33 s8(1) IA 1971
34 s33(1) IA 1971 and *Diestel* [1976] Imm AR 51
35 s8(1) IA 1971
36 Appendix 1, HC 395
37 paras 88-90 HC 395 and para 4 HC 329, 2 April 1996 with effect from 4 April 1996
38 paras 95-100 HC 395
39 paras 186-193 HC 395
40 paras 211-223, dependants at paras 240-245 HC 395
41 Ankara Agreement, 12 September 1963 and Decisions 2/76, 1/80, 3/80 of the Association Council made under the Agreement. A useful explanation is to be found in N Rogers, *A Practitioner's Guide to the Turkey-EC Association Agreement* (2000, Kluwer).
42 s10 IAA 1999
43 Sch 2 paras 8 and 9 IA 1971
44 s3(5)(b) IA 1971, s10(1)(c) IAA 1999

3. How immigration control operates

45 s3(1)(b) IA 1971
46 s3(1)(c) IA 1971
47 s3(1)(c) IA 1971
48 paras 324A-326 HC 395; Immigration (Registration with Police) Regs 1972; and see list of countries/territories whose nationals are required to register with the police in Appendix 2 to the immigration rules, HC 395

49 For all addresses and telephone numbers of relevant Home Office Sections see *JCWI Immigration, Nationality and Refugee Law Handbook*

50 s4(1) IA 1971

51 Sch 2 IA 1971

52 *R v SSHD ex parte Oladehinde* [1991] AC 254

53 ss28A-K IA 1971 as inserted by ss136-139 IAA 1999

54 s4(1) IA 1971

55 para 32 HC 395

56 paras 364-395D HC 395

57 Sch 3 paras 1 and 2 1971 Act

58 s3(2) IA 1971

59 paras 116-121 and 128-135 HC 395

60 s33(1) IA 1971

61 Schs 2-3 IAA 1999

62 Sch 4 paras 3-4 IAA 1999

63 ss102-103 and Sch 10 IAA 1999

64 s4(3) IA 1971

65 s24(2) IA 1971

66 Sch 2 para 17 and Sch 3 para 2(4) IA 1971

67 s154 IAA 1999

68 Part VI and Schs 8-9 IAA 1999

69 ss1(4) and 3(2) IA 1971

70 para 4 HC 395

71 HC 704

72 Cmnd 4851

73 See most recently *ECO Bombay v Stanley Walter De Noronha* [1995] Imm AR 341

74 Sch 2 para 1(3) IA 1971 and Sch 4 para 21(1)(a) IAA 1999, *R v SSHD ex parte Hosenball* [1977] 1 WLR 766; *Pearson v IAT* [1978] Imm AR 212

Chapter 2

Nationality

This chapter covers:
1. Different types of British nationality (below)
2. British nationals and immigration law (p22)
3. Different ways of acquiring British citizenship (p24)

1. Different types of British nationality

There are six types of British national:[1]
- British citizens;
- British overseas territories citizens (BOTC);
- British subjects;
- British protected persons (BPP);
- British nationals (overseas) (BNO);
- British overseas citizens (BOC).

The following is an outline of how these categories evolved in the UK.

Before 1948

Before 1948 people were divided into three groups:
- British subjects – born in a territory belonging to the Crown, including the UK;
- aliens – non-British subjects;
- BPPs – aliens under the protection of the Crown.

Then, as now, the last two groups had no right of abode in the UK.

British Nationality Act 1948

With the implementation of the British Nationality Act 1948, people were divided into five groups:
- citizens of the United Kingdom and colonies (CUKC) – people born in, or connected with, the UK or a Crown colony;[2]
- Commonwealth citizens – people born in, or connected with, a Commonwealth country which became independent from the UK and who then became

••••
19

citizens of the newly independent country. CUKC status would normally be lost when the colony became independent;
- British subjects without citizenship – people who did not become citizens of the Commonwealth country in which they lived;
- BPPs;
- aliens.

Until 1962, CUKCs, Commonwealth citizens and British subjects without citizenship could freely enter the UK. It is no longer possible to become a British subject or a BPP.

1960s: Commonwealth Immigrants Acts

The Commonwealth Immigrants Acts of 1962 and 1968 affected the immigration position of CUKCs and Commonwealth citizens:
- The 1962 Act gave rights of entry to people who had British passports issued in the UK or issued on behalf of the UK government abroad, but denied Commonwealth citizens free entry to the UK.
- Under the 1968 Act CUKCs who did not have parents or grandparents born in the UK lost the automatic right of entry to the UK. One of the main effects of this legislation was to deny entry to the UK to large numbers of East African Asians who had CUKC status.[3]

Immigration Act 1971

The 1971 Act introduced the concept of '**patriality**'. Patrials had the right of abode in the UK and therefore did not require leave to enter or remain and could come and go freely. Most of the people who obtained patrial status were CUKCs, although some Commonwealth citizens also qualified.[4] Patrial status could derive from the person's ancestry, the nature and duration of their residence in the UK, how their CUKC status was obtained and, for certain women, the status of their husband. The 1971 Act separated 'nationality' from the right of abode and, with it, the right to enter the UK freely.

British Nationality Act 1981

The British Nationality Act 1981 came into force on 1 January 1983 and created three new types of nationals out of patrial and non-patrial CUKCs:[5]
- British citizens – ie, patrial CUKCs;
- British dependent territories citizens (BDTC) – ie, non-patrial CUKCs who had a connection with a place which continued to be a colony or 'dependent territory' (now BOTC);
- BOC – ie, non-patrial CUKCs whose connection was with a place which had ceased to be a British dependent territory by 1983.

Under the 1981 Act, British citizens have the 'right of abode'.[6] Until 1 January 1983, some non-patrial CUKCs were entitled to patrial status and obtained the right of abode after five years' ordinary residence in the UK.[7] Non-British citizen British nationals (eg, some CUKC, BPP and British subjects without citizenship resident in the UK for five years) have the right to register as British citizens if they satisfy certain conditions (see p26).[8]

Commonwealth citizens who were patrial on 1 January 1983
- by virtue of having a parent born in the UK; *or*
- because they were women married to patrials

were classed simply as Commonwealth citizens with the right of abode in the UK.[9] After 1 January 1983, a Commonwealth woman marrying a British citizen did not have the right of abode.

Anyone born abroad after 1 January 1983 who would have qualified for the right of abode as a result of their parentage, became a British citizen 'by descent'.[10]

Developments since the 1981 Act

Since the 1981 Act, there have been four important developments in British nationality law.
- Following the war in the Falkland Islands in 1983, legislation was introduced which converted most people born in the Falklands from BDTCs to British citizens by birth.[11]
- Before Hong Kong was returned to the People's Republic of China in 1997, Hong Kong's BDTCs had the chance to register as a new type of national, BNOs.[12] In 1997, status as a BDTC ended for those living in Hong Kong, but BNOs were able to continue to use British travel documents and were able to register as British citizens following five years' residence in the UK having achieved settled status in the UK.[13] Others, who were ordinarily resident in Hong Kong in 1997, and who would have become stateless except for their British nationality, were also permitted to register as British citizens.[14]
- The Secretary of State also registered as British citizens 50,000 residents of Hong Kong who were 'heads of households'.[15] Selection was carried out by the Governor of Hong Kong under the provisions of a well-publicised scheme.[16]
- The British Overseas Territories Act 2002 re-designated BDTCs as BOTCs and stated that all those who were BOTCs when the relevant parts of the Act came into force, would automatically become British citizens with the right of abode.[17] The result is that, anyone who was a BOTC (formally BDTC) on 21 May 2002, becomes a British citizen.[18] The dependencies themselves have been re-named as 'British overseas territories'. These territories are as follows: Anguilla, Bermuda, British Antarctic Territory, British Indian Ocean Territory, British Virgin Islands, Cayman Islands, Falkland Islands, Gibraltar, Montserrat, Pitcairn Islands, St Helena and Dependencies, South Georgia and the South

Sandwich Islands, the Turks and Caicos Islands and the Cyprus Sovereign Base Areas of Akrotiri and Dhekelia. However, BOTCs from the Cyprus Sovereign Base Areas do *not* obtain British citizenship under the Act.

A late amendment to the Nationality, Immigration and Asylum Bill 2002 proposes to allow certain BOCs to acquire the right of abode in the UK. This will apply to those BOCs who would otherwise have no right of abode in any country (see p14).

Dual nationality

A '**dual national**' is a person who is simultaneously a national of two countries. Some countries do not allow dual nationality so some people are forced to choose between being a national of one country or a national of another. UK nationality law does not prevent a person from being both a British national and a national of another country.

Loss of citizenship

You can lose British citizenship in the following ways:
- If you obtained it by registration or naturalisation (see p26) the Secretary of State can make an order depriving you of British citizenship. This can only be done if you:[19]
  - obtained citizenship by deception;
  - have been sentenced to prison for 12 months or longer;
  - have acted treasonably.
- You renounce your citizenship where you are either a dual national or wish to obtain another nationality. The Secretary of State must be satisfied that you will obtain the nationality of the other country.[20]

The 2002 Bill proposes to replace the above criteria for deprivation of citizenship (except the 'deception' criterion) with the criterion that the Home Office 'thinks that the person has done anything seriously prejudicial to the vital interest of the UK'. All British citizens can, under the new provisions, potentially face deprivation (ie, not just those who obtained citizenship by naturalisation or registration) *unless* deprivation would make them stateless. The Act also proposes that there will be a right of appeal against deprivation decisions.

In certain circumstances, the Home Office may also declare that a person has never been a British citizen. This may happen where citizenship was acquired on an incorrect basis or the authorities made a mistake.

---

2. British nationals and immigration law

British citizens have the right of abode in the UK and, therefore, do not require leave to enter or to remain in the UK (see Chapter 1). All other types of British national (see p19) require leave to enter or remain in the UK and must satisfy the various provisions of the immigration rules (certain Commonwealth citizens also have the right of abode – see p20). However, some non-British citizen British nationals enjoy certain immigration advantages. These are set out below.

Right of re-admission

British overseas citizens (BOC) granted indefinite leave to enter or remain in the UK by the immigration authorities any time after 1 March 1968 can leave the UK and qualify for indefinite leave to enter on their return. They do not have to satisfy the normal returning residents' rules which apply to those who left the UK when they had indefinite leave.[21] The ordinary returning residents' rules, which these BOCs do not have to satisfy, are that the returning resident:

- had indefinite leave to enter or remain when s/he *last* left the UK;
- has not been away from the UK for more than two years;
- did not previously receive assistance from public funds towards the cost of leaving the UK;
- is seeking admission for the purpose of 'settlement' when s/he returns to the UK.

Special voucher scheme

Until 5 March 2002, there was a special voucher scheme which applied to BOCs. It was abolished on that date without notice and applications for vouchers on or after that date will not be considered. Under the scheme, if you were a BOC, you could be admitted to the UK for an indefinite period if you had been issued with a 'special voucher' by the immigration authorities.[22] Your spouse and children were also allowed to join you if you could maintain and accommodate them without recourse to public funds (see p92).[23] Applications for vouchers could be made at either a British high commission or a British embassy. Although vouchers have been abolished there is nothing to prevent a dependant of a voucher holder still applying.

The special vouchers were introduced at the same time as the Commonwealth Immigrants Act 1968. There was an annual quota which caused long waiting lists. There were no formal rules stating who would qualify for a voucher. In practice, the applicant had to:

- have no other nationality available to her/him;
- be under pressure to leave the country in which s/he was resident (this has mainly applied to people living in East and Central Africa and people who left those countries to go to India);
- be the head of a household (married women are excluded).

Admission of other passport holders

Any national of the non-British citizen types (see p19) is entitled to be freely admitted to the UK on production of a UK passport which was issued prior to

1 January 1973 in the UK, Channel Islands, the Isle of Man or Republic of Ireland. The only exceptions are those people whose passports are endorsed to show that they were subject to immigration control and required leave.[24]

3. **Different ways of acquiring British citizenship**

British citizenship and birth

There are two main factors determining British citizenship according to birth:
- whether you were born before or after 1 January 1983, the date when the British Nationality Act 1981 came into force;
- whether you were born inside or outside the UK.

The rules relating to these two main factors are set out below. However, British nationality law is very complicated and the information provided below is only a guide and is not exhaustive. If you are uncertain you should seek expert advice.

The *way* in which British citizenship is obtained is also important as it determines whether you can pass on your citizenship to your children:
- If you were born abroad and, therefore, acquired British citizenship because of the nationality of your parents (British citizens by descent), you cannot automatically pass on your citizenship to your own children if they are born abroad.
- If you obtain your citizenship by birth, registration, naturalisation (British citizens otherwise than by descent), you can automatically pass on your citizenship to your children even if they are born abroad although this citizenship passes for one generation only (special provisions are made for children born to those living abroad who are working for the government).[25]
- British overseas citizens, British subjects and British protected persons cannot generally pass on their citizenship.

Born before 1 January 1983

Born in the UK

Children born before 1 January 1983 in the UK are British citizens, as are those who were adopted in the UK by a British parent. Only children born to diplomats and enemy aliens at times of war do not become British citizens.[26]

Born outside the UK
- Children born overseas to British fathers became British citizens if, at the time of the birth, the father was a citizen of the United Kingdom and colonies (CUKC) otherwise than by descent and the parents were married. The father must have registered or naturalised.

- Children born overseas to a British mother and non-British father (or to a British father who was not married to the child's mother) would not become British citizens, but the government has allowed such mothers to register their children as British citizens provided they do this before the child is 18. The last registrations under this provision, therefore, occurred at the end of 2000 (ie, 18 years from 1 January 1983).
- Children born in non-Commonwealth countries whose father's father was British otherwise than by descent are British provided the birth was registered at a British consulate within a year of the birth.

Born on or after 1 January 1983

Born in the UK

- Children born in the UK after 1 January 1983 are only British citizens if, at the time of their birth, one parent is either a British citizen or is settled (ie, ordinarily resident with no restriction on their stay[27] in the UK).[28] People who have indefinite leave are normally accepted as being 'settled'.
- Children adopted under an adoption order made in the UK also become British citizens if either of the adoptive parents are British citizens.[29]
- A child will be a British citizen even if the parent upon whose citizenship the child relies dies prior to the child's birth.[30]
- Children born in the UK who are not British citizens can apply to 'register' (see p26) as British citizens after they have been in the UK for 10 years or after either of their parents obtains settled status.
- Children who do not have the nationality of any other country and are not born British are stateless. For the immigration position of children born in the UK who are not British, see p26. They may also register as British citizens.

'**Parent**' for these purposes always includes the mother but excludes the father if he is not married to the mother at the time that the child is born.[31] However, the Nationality, Immigration and Asylum Bill 2002 proposes to abolish discrimination in nationality law against 'illegitimate' children (see p14).

Born outside the UK

- Children born outside the UK on or after 1 January 1983 are British citizens by descent if either their father or their mother:
  - is a British citizen by birth, registration or naturalisation (ie, otherwise than by descent);[32] *or*
  - was a CUKC and gained the right of abode by living in the UK for five years or more before 1 January 1983.
- Children born abroad to parents who are themselves British citizens by descent[33] do not generally become British citizens. These children have certain rights, but the law is complex. You should seek expert advice if you are in this position.

Applying for citizenship

You may be able to acquire British citizen status either by 'naturalisation' (see below) or by 'registration' (see below). If you register and satisfy certain conditions for registration, the Home Office must give you British citizenship. Other forms of registration are discretionary. If you apply to naturalise, the decision whether or not to grant citizenship will always be discretionary although, in practice, if you meet certain conditions citizenship will be granted.

The 2002 Bill proposes to remove the current legislation which states that the Home Office cannot be required to give reasons if it refuses to grant citizenship. The Bill will also remove the prohibition on challenging naturalisation decisions in the courts. See p14 for more details.

Naturalisation

You can apply to the Home Office to be naturalised as a British citizen if you fulfil all of the following criteria relating to settlement, length of residence, language, future intentions and good character.[34]

- You must have been settled in the UK (usually a person with indefinite leave) for at least a year prior to your application.
- You must have lived lawfully in the UK for five continuous years without absences of more than 450 days (if you are married to a British citizen, the qualifying period is three years without absences of more than 270 days) and, in all cases, not more than 90 days of absence in the last year.
- If you are not married to a British citizen, you must be able to show sufficient ability in either English, Welsh or Scottish Gaelic.
- If you are not married to a British citizen, you have to show that you intend to reside (have your main home) in the UK.
- You must be of good character. Among other matters, criminal convictions may be taken into account.

The 2002 Bill proposes various changes to the naturalisation requirements. In particular it proposes that you:
- show a 'sufficient knowledge about life in the UK';
- could be required to pass a test to demonstrate your knowledge of one of the relevant languages;
- take a new citizenship pledge. There has always been a citizenship oath which applicants had to take but the government will change the wording and wants it to be taken in public, for example at a registrar's office or at a community centre.

Registration

The following people can register:
- Non-British citizen British nationals who have had 'settled' status in the UK (see p50) for a year or more have a right to register as British citizens if they

have lived lawfully in the UK for five years.[35] During that time, they must not have been out of the UK for longer than 450 days in total nor for longer than 90 days in the last year.

- Non-British citizen children born in the UK have a right to register as British citizens if, while they are still minors, one of their parents becomes settled.[36]
- A child born in the UK, who is stateless, can be registered if s/he remains in the UK for ten years (the 2002 Bill proposes to remove this age requirement).[37]
- People born overseas to British citizens (who are British by descent) can register in one of two ways. You should seek specialist advice if you are in this position.[38]

The Home Office retains the discretion to register all other children.[39] As stated above it has been Home Office policy to register those born abroad before 1 January 1983 to British-born mothers provided the application is made while the child is still a minor. The Home Office may also register children who are 'illegitimate' and therefore did not obtain citizenship through their British citizen father. It may also register a child who has been living in the UK for a substantial period of time depending on the child's immigration status, her/his connections with the UK and her/his parents' status.

Notes

1. Different types of British nationality
1 For further details see *Macdonald* and *Fransman* (see Appendix 3)
2 s12 BNA 1948
3 *East African Asians v UK* [1981] EHRR 76
4 s2 IA 1971, now substituted
5 Parts I, II and III BNA 1981
6 s2(1)(a) IA 1971
7 s2(1)(c) IA 1971 as substituted
8 s4(1) BNA 1981
9 s2(1)(b) IA 1971 as substituted
10 s2(1) BNA 1981
11 Falklands Act 1983
12 Hong Kong Act 1985
13 s4(1) BNA 1981
14 British Nationality (Hong Kong) Act 1997
15 British Nationality (Hong Kong) Act 1990
16 Hong Kong Selection Scheme Order
17 s3 British Overseas Territories Act 2002

18 British Overseas Territories 20002 (Commencement) Order 2002
19 s40 BNA 1981
20 s12 BNA 1981 (last complete statement of immigration rules, 23 May 1994)

2. British nationals and immigration law
21 para 17 HC 395
22 paras 249-251 HC 395
23 paras 252-254 HC 395
24 para 16 HC 395

3. Different ways of acquiring British citizenship
25 s2(1)(2) BNA 1981
26 Now s50(3) BNA 1981
27 s50(2),(3) and (4) BNA 1981
28 s1 BNA 1981
29 s1(5) and (6) BNA 1981
30 s48 BNA 1981
31 ss47 and 50(9) BNA 1981
32 s2(1)(a) BNA 1981

33 s14 BNA 1981 for definition of 'by
     descent'
34 s6 and Sch 1 BNA 1981
35 s4(1) BNA 1981
36 s1(3) BNA 1981
37 Sch 2 BNA 1981
38 s3 BNA 1981
39 s3(1) BNA 1981

Chapter 3

··

Admission to and staying in the UK

This chapter covers:
1. Immigration control before arrival (below)
2. Immigration control on arrival (p35)
3. Immigration control after entry (p38)

1. Immigration control before arrival

Entry clearance

Depending upon your nationality and the reason why you are coming to the UK, you may need to obtain '**entry clearance**' (evidence of your eligibility to enter the UK) before arriving in the UK. An entry clearance will normally be issued in the form of a visa or an entry certificate.

- If you are a 'visa national' (see below), technically the entry clearance which will be issued to you is called a 'visa'.
- If you are a 'non-visa national' (see p30), technically your entry clearance is called an 'entry certificate'.[1]

Visas and entry certificates are in the form of stickers endorsed on your passport (see p109).[2] They are valid for a certain length of time and you must arrive in the UK and present the entry clearance within the period of its validity. Confusingly, all visit entry clearances state 'visa' on the sticker and other entry clearances state 'entry clearance'. The former are green and the latter are red.

People who need entry clearance

Whether or not you need an entry clearance mainly depends on your national status and your reasons for coming to the UK. The general rules are:[3]

- **Visa nationals** require entry clearance whatever their purpose for coming to the UK. Visa nationals are nationals of all those countries which are listed in the appendix to the immigration rules (see Appendix 8 for the current list). Others who need a visa whatever the reason for their coming to the UK, are:

people who hold passports or travel documents issued by the former Soviet Union or the former Socialist Federal Republic of Yugoslavia, stateless people and people who do not hold national documentation.[4]

- **Non-visa nationals** only require entry clearance (or alternatively some other documentation fulfilling a similar function, eg, a valid work permit) for entry for non-temporary purposes – ie, categories of entry which may lead to settlement, which include most working and business-related categories as well as applications for settlement for spouses, common-law partners and other dependent relatives.

Despite the above rules, however, you do not need an entry clearance if:[5]

- you are returning to the UK within the period covered by a previous grant of leave, which was granted by the immigration authorities for more than six months, as long as you are seeking to return for the same purpose;
- you qualify to be admitted to the UK in the category of a returning resident (those who had indefinite leave (see p49) in the UK when they last left);
- you are a refugee with a 1951 Convention travel document and you are coming to the UK on a visit of three months or less *and* the travel document was issued by a country which is a signatory to the Council of Europe Agreement of 1959 on the Abolition of Visas for Refugees;
- you are seeking asylum in the UK.

EEA nationals and family members

A European Economic Area (EEA) national does not require any form of entry clearance in order to be admitted to the UK.[6] A non–EEA national who is a 'family member' of an EEA national and who is coming to the UK with or to join the EEA national under community law (see p7) who is *either* a visa national, *or* is coming to the UK to live with the EEA national rather than just for a visit, must get an EEA family permit before travelling.[7] The family permit is therefore a form of entry clearance. It can be obtained free of charge from the entry clearance officer.[8]

When entry clearance is optional

It is clear from the above that, although you may not need an entry clearance in order to obtain admission under the immigration rules, you can choose to get entry clearance before travelling to be more sure of your eligibility for admission.[9] For example, the rules recommend that non–visa national prospective au pairs obtain an entry clearance.[10] In deciding whether to apply for entry clearance when this is not strictly required, you need to weigh up the additional cost and delay of getting an entry clearance against the risk of being refused on your arrival in the UK if you arrive without it. People who have had immigration problems in the past, but who do not strictly need an entry clearance, often apply for one to avoid problems on entry. You should also be aware that even if you have an entry clearance, admission to the UK on arrival is not guaranteed (see p35).

Entry clearance taking effect as leave to enter

From 28 April 2000, entry clearance operates as leave to enter the UK so that you are treated as having already been granted leave to enter when you arrive in the UK.[11] An entry clearance operates as leave to enter the UK where the entry clearance states the purpose for which it is given (eg, fiancé or working holidaymaker) and either:[12]

- is endorsed with the conditions to which it is subject (these may be any of those conditions which are referred to on p52);[13] *or*
- it contains a statement that it is to have effect as indefinite leave to enter.

For examples of these 'new style' entry clearances, see p110. If you look on the entry clearance sticker in the passport it should have a 'valid from' and a 'valid until' date. The technical term for the valid from date is the 'effective' date and the term for the valid until date is the 'expiry' date. The period of validity is the period between these two dates. The passenger must arrive during the period of validity. If s/he arrives before that time or if s/he asks for entry for a purpose other than that given on the entry clearance then the immigration officer may cancel the entry clearance altogether so that it is no longer valid.[14]

In the case of a visitor, the leave which is granted is for six months from the date of arrival if the period of validity of the entry clearance is six months or more on the date of arrival. If the remaining period of validity is less than six months on that date, then s/he is given leave for the remaining period of the validity of the entry clearance.[15] A visit entry clearance which takes effect as leave to enter may have that effect on an unlimited number of occasions during the period of its validity.[16] An entry clearance for any other purpose only takes effect as leave to enter on one occasion. The leave which is given is for an indefinite period if the entry clearance states that it is to have effect as indefinite leave to enter but, in any other non-visitor case, the leave lasts until the expiry of the period of validity of the entry clearance.[17]

It is essential that people realise that, in cases where the entry clearance gives only limited leave, they will not be treated as having leave beyond the 'valid until' (expiry) date of the entry clearance. Visitors are granted a maximum of six months from the date of entry.

Example 1

Sadhna obtains an entry clearance from Delhi to come to the UK as a foreign spouse. The 'valid from' date is 2 February 2002 and the 'valid until' date is 2 February 2003. Under the old entry clearance system, provided Sadhna arrived in the UK during the period of validity of the entry clearance (under the old system this was usually six months), she would then apply on entry to the immigration officer. If there were no difficulties, she would be granted 12 months' leave (the probationary period given to spouses) from the date of her arrival. However, under the new system, if Sadhna arrives on 10 October 2002, she is treated as given leave until the end of the period of validity of her entry clearance – ie, 2 February 2003. She does not get leave until 10 October 2003. The immigration officer will normally place a date stamp across the entry clearance, but this is only to mark her entry, it does not grant her 12 months' leave from that date.

Example 2

Anneka regularly comes in and out of the UK for business trips and she has been granted an entry clearance with a three-year period of validity marked valid for visits. It is valid from 30 March 2002 to 30 March 2005. On each occasion Anneka enters she is treated as being given leave for six months and must leave the UK within that period. She is not treated as having been granted leave until 30 March 2005 because it is a visit entry clearance which operates differently to other forms of entry clearance. Anneka can, however, use the entry clearance on as many occasions as she wishes. If, however, she enters on 8 January 2005 she will only be treated as having leave until 30 March 2005 because there are less than six months remaining on the period of validity of her entry clearance.

There are two further points to note:
- It generally does not matter that entry clearances (other than visit entry clearances) only operate as leave on one occasion because most leave (other than that granted to visitors) does not lapse when a person leaves the UK (see pp36-37). Also, provided that the leave was given for more than six months no entry clearance is required to return to the UK within the period of the leave. This applies even if the person is a visa national.[18]
- Sadhna (Example 1) should take one of two steps. If she knows that she is going to be travelling some time after the time at which the entry clearance is likely to be issued, she should ask the entry clearance officer to issue the entry clearance with a later 'valid from' (or 'effective') date. For this purpose, entry clearance officers have been given instructions to ask applicants about their travel plans. If Sadhna later delays her travel unexpectedly then she can ask the immigration officer on her arrival to vary her leave so that she gets the 12 months normally given initially to foreign spouses. No application form need be used on arrival although the immigration officer is not required to make a decision. If the immigration officer declines to make a decision where an application to vary leave is made on entry, Sadhna can apply to the Home Office instead.

It is important that people do not misunderstand the above rules relating to entry clearances. If they do, they may not make a further application for leave in time and become overstayers and 'subject to immigration control' (if they were not before) – see p39.

Obtaining entry clearance

You must be outside the UK when you make your application for entry clearance.[19] Applications are usually made to a British embassy, high commission or consulate[20] in the country in which you are living unless:

- there is no such post in that country; *or*
- you are applying to come to the UK as a visitor, in which case you may apply to any post which accepts applications for that category.[21]

You will not be considered to have made the application until you have paid the appropriate fee,[22] although it is possible to ask for the fee to be waived if you have no means to meet it. The fee should be paid in local currency.

To apply for entry clearance, you need to complete the relevant forms[23] which may be obtained either from the British embassy/high commission or from UK Visas of the Foreign Office/Home Office who have made the forms available at http://www.fco.gov.uk/ukvisas/

Often the entry clearance officer will interview the applicant and may conduct further investigations such as making enquiries of other agencies or even visiting relatives or neighbours.[24]

Entry clearance decisions

When deciding whether to grant entry clearance to a person in a particular category, the entry clearance officer takes account of exactly the same requirements as govern leave to enter in that category (see p31).[25] The requirements in the rules are applied to the circumstances that exist at the date of the decision on the entry clearance application. The only exception relates to a child applying to join parents for settlement in the UK. In this instance, the child's age is taken to be the age at the date of application rather than the date of the decision.[26] These considerations are important as there is often a long delay between making an entry clearance application and the decision on it. The fact that there may be long delays could have benefit implications. For example, the definition of 'family' for income support and jobseeker's allowance purposes is affected by the period a couple are living apart (see Chapter 12).

The immigration rules relating to each category state that leave may be granted if the particular requirements of the rules relating to the category in question are satisfied. However, even if you satisfy the requirements of the rules for the category in which you seek entry, you may still be refused an entry clearance under the 'general grounds' on which leave may be refused. Again, these rules are similar for applications for entry clearance as for leave to enter (see p31).

If entry clearance is granted then an entry clearance will be endorsed on your passport (see p110 for examples of entry clearance). If the entry clearance officer refuses to grant entry clearance and you have a right of appeal against the decision (see Chapter 7), then you will receive a written notice of the refusal which will include details of the reasons for the refusal and how you may exercise your right of appeal.[27]

Revocation of entry clearance

An entry clearance officer may revoke an entry clearance after it has been granted if s/he believes that it was obtained by false representations or a failure to disclose material facts, or that there has been a change of circumstances since it was issued, or if the person's exclusion is conducive to public good.[28] A person who has an entry clearance may also be refused leave to enter by an immigration officer before s/he arrives in the UK (see p35). Where this occurs, the entry clearance will not have effect as leave to enter.[29]

Other documents relating to entry that may be obtained before arrival

Work permits

Work permits are not entry clearances[30] so, if you intend to come to the UK for work permit employment[31] or for work for which you need a training and work experience scheme (known as TWES) work permit[32] and you are a visa national, you still require an entry clearance in accordance with the above rules in order to come to the UK.[33] Work permits for a person intending to come to the UK in this capacity must also be applied for and obtained before the person arrives.[34]

Certificates of entitlement

If you are a British citizen or other person with the right of abode in the UK, you can obtain a certificate of entitlement to the right of abode (see p110) by applying to the entry clearance officer at a British post overseas.

Granting leave to enter before arrival in the UK

In addition to entry clearances which operate as leave to enter, from 28 April 2000, it is also possible to be granted or refused leave to enter before you have even arrived in the UK. Leave may be granted or refused by an immigration officer before a person's departure from her/his own country or while s/he is travelling to the UK.[35] For these purposes, an immigration officer may examine people outside the UK, ask them questions and ask them to produce documents including an up-to-date medical report.[36] A failure to supply information or to produce such a document is a ground in itself for refusing leave to enter.[37]

These powers are used to grant leave to enter to groups which the Home Office believes are at low risk of abusing immigration controls (eg, school groups and recognised reputable tour groups) so that immigration congestion at the port of entry is avoided. Immigration officers may also be sent abroad to grant or refuse leave to enter in order to relieve certain pressure points at ports of entry where there would otherwise be large queues of people waiting to be granted entry.

Although the grant and refusal of leave to enter and remain is normally given in a written notice (or written stamp if granted),[38] in order to facilitate the grant/ refusal of leave before arrival, immigration officers can now grant leave to enter by fax or email[39] and, in the case of decisions relating to visitors, orally over the telephone with a written notice to follow.[40]

The reason for this change and the introduction of entry clearances taking effect as leave to enter (see p31) is the need to reduce the routine questioning at the ports of entry given that, on the Home Office's statistics, the amount of passenger traffic has increased by 45 per cent to 84 million people a year over the five years from the mid-1990s.[41]

2. **Immigration control on arrival**

Examination on arrival

Immigration officers carry out examinations of people on their arrival at ports of entry to the UK in order to determine whether s/he:[42]
- is a British citizen; *or*
- may otherwise enter the UK without leave; *or*
- requires leave to enter, already has leave which is still in force and, if not, whether s/he should be granted leave to enter the UK and, if so, for what period and upon what conditions.

A person who does not require leave to enter (see Chapter 1) is nevertheless required to produce to the immigration officer a passport or travel document which demonstrates her/his identity and nationality together with evidence of her/his entitlement to enter without leave.[43]

People who have leave when they arrive in the UK

A person who already has leave when s/he arrives may be examined to determine whether or not that leave should be cancelled by the immigration officer.[44] A person may already have leave before s/he arrives in the UK if :
- leave to enter was granted before s/he arrived in the UK. Where a person was given leave orally as a visitor, the burden is upon that person to show that s/he does in fact have leave;[45]
- s/he arrives in the UK with an entry clearance which operates as leave to enter; *or*
- s/he still has leave from her/his previous stay in the UK (see below).

Although the period of leave which is granted by an entry clearance is calculated from the date of entry, confusingly, for the purposes of the immigration officer, people with entry clearances are treated as having leave and are, therefore, examined to determine whether that leave should be 'cancelled' (see p37).[46]

People may still retain their leave when they depart from the Common Travel Area (CTA – the UK and the Republic of Ireland together with the Channel Islands and the Isle of Man)[47] as a result of changes to the law which were introduced in July 2000.[48] This system was introduced because it was thought to be anomalous that a person who had been in the UK (for example, for three years) might leave for a few days for a trip to the continent and then have to seek leave to enter again on her/his return. Before these changes, all leave to enter or remain in the UK lapsed when a person left the CTA.[49] However, from 30 July 2000, any leave which was given before or after that date,[50] does not lapse when a person leaves the CTA provided:[51]

- it is leave which was given by means of an entry clearance that had effect as leave to enter (other than a visit visa) (see p31); *or*
- it is a leave which was given for a period of more than six months; *and in either case*
- the leave was not varied (changed) such that it was no longer valid for a period of six months or less from the date of the variation.

If your leave falls within the above categories and it is limited leave, the leave remains in force when you leave the CTA until its natural expiry time. However, if it is still in force after you have been outside the UK for two years it will lapse at that point.[52] If the leave was indefinite leave, it will remain in force while you remain outside the UK for a continuous period of two years but will then lapse if you have not returned to the UK within that period.[53] Where leave remains in force while you are outside the UK, the conditions which are attached to the leave are suspended until you return.[54]

If your leave does not fall within the above categories, then when you leave the CTA, it will still lapse.[55] If, in these circumstances, you return to the UK within the time which was given by the original leave then, despite it having lapsed, on your return the immigration officer may well still give you leave for a period which completes the period of the original leave and upon the same conditions.[56]

Where a person arrives in the UK having been granted leave to enter before her/his arrival or with leave which did not lapse upon her/his leaving the UK previously or with an entry clearance which takes effect as leave to enter, the immigration officer may also, by notice in writing, suspend the leave while s/he is examined further to determine whether to cancel the leave.[57] If appropriate, after that examination, the immigration officer may cancel the leave[58] if any of the following conditions apply:[59]

- there has been a change of circumstances such that leave should be cancelled;
- leave was obtained by providing false information or failing to disclose material facts;
- medical reasons make it undesirable to admit the person (unless s/he is settled in the UK or there are strong compassionate factors);
- exclusion is conducive to the public good; *or*

- the person has failed to provide information or documents as requested by the immigration authorities.

If your leave is cancelled on the above grounds, you will generally have a right of appeal to an immigration adjudicator against the decision.[60] It should be noted that the same criteria may be applied by the immigration officer or the Secretary of State to cancel any leave which a person has who is outside the UK and which did not lapse when s/he left the CTA.[61] The immigration officer or Secretary of State may also 'vary' such a limited leave to remain (ie, by adding or removing conditions or altering its length) while you are outside the UK.[62]

People who do not have leave when they arrive in the UK

In deciding whether to grant or refuse leave to enter to someone who arrives in the UK without existing leave, the immigration officer must apply the criteria in the immigration rules as to whether or not the person satisfies the requirements in the category for which s/he has applied. The immigration officer must also be satisfied that none of the *general* grounds upon which leave can be refused to a person seeking entry in any category apply (eg, previous breaches of immigration control, refusal of a sponsor to give, when requested, an undertaking to be responsible for the person's support in the UK or where the Secretary of State has directed that the exclusion of the person from the UK is conducive to the public good).[63] In cases where a person has arrived in the UK without an entry clearance or a work permit there is no in-country right of appeal unless the person claims asylum or makes a human rights claim to enter the UK.[64]

Decision to grant or refuse leave or to cancel existing leave

If leave to enter is to be refused or an existing leave cancelled, then the immigration officer must first obtain the authority of either a chief immigration officer or an immigration inspector.[65] If leave is granted, you will receive the appropriate stamp in your passport (see Appendix 9).[66]

You must be given written notice of any such refusal which must also inform you of any appeal rights.[67] If leave to enter in one category is refused, there is nothing to prevent you applying for leave in another category. However, it is often unlikely that you will be able to demonstrate that you are genuinely seeking entry in the further category following a refusal on a different basis. After you have been refused leave to enter the UK and you have had the opportunity to exercise any in-country rights of appeal (see Chapter 7), the immigration officer has the power to set directions for your removal.[68]

When the immigration officer cannot make an immediate decision

In many cases, in particular where the person is seeking leave to enter as a refugee (see p58), the examination to determine whether to grant entry cannot be carried out immediately. While this examination is continuing, the immigration officer has two options: either the person may be detained pending a decision to give or refuse leave to enter or to cancel an existing leave to enter, or s/he may be granted **'temporary admission'** to the UK.[69] Temporary admission is not 'leave' to enter or remain in the UK, it is a restricted licence to be in the UK and it can be revoked in favour of detention at any time.[70] People who are initially detained under these powers may later be released on temporary admission by the immigration officer[71] or, in most cases, may seek to be granted bail.[72] Temporary admission may be granted subject to conditions (as to residence, employment, reporting to the police or an immigration officer).[73]

3. Immigration control after entry

Responsibility for control after entry

Once you have entered the UK,[74] responsibility for regulating your immigration position passes to the Secretary of State for the Home Department (the Home Secretary acting through the Home Office).[75] You have technically not 'entered' the UK while you are on temporary admission or you are detained pending a decision by the immigration officer following your arrival in the UK.[76] Therefore some people, in particular asylum seekers (see p58), may be in the UK for a very extended period but yet immigration law does not recognise them as having 'entered'. Once you have entered the UK, any application for leave is termed an application for leave to remain rather than leave to 'enter'.[77] There have been recent moves to break down this traditional distinction between the powers of the immigration officers and the Home Office and the Nationality, Immigration and Asylum Bill 2002 (see p14) proposes to give Home Office officials powers to detain which were previously exclusively exercised by immigration officers.

Applying for leave to remain

If you require leave and you have been granted only limited leave to enter (or remain) in the UK, you may decide that you want to stay for a longer period. Alternatively, you may wish to change the conditions on which your leave has been granted. These applications may be described as applications for leave to remain or applications to 'vary' leave. People who have been granted indefinite leave to enter or remain do not need to apply while they are in the UK to extend or vary their leave because:
- it is indefinite and therefore has no time limit attached to it;
- no conditions can be attached to an indefinite leave to enter or remain in the UK and so there will be no conditions that can be lifted.[78]

You should always apply to the Home Office before your current leave expires to extend your leave.[79] If your leave has already expired by the time you come to apply for further leave, then you should obtain legal advice about making a further application without delay.

Failing to apply for further leave in time

The consequences of not applying for further leave in time are serious. If you do not apply in time:

- as a person who becomes 'subject to immigration control'[80] (see p157), you may lose entitlement to social security benefits and/or support from a local authority social services department;[81]
- your application for further leave may be refused under the immigration rules;[82]
- you become liable for removal from the UK as an overstayer;[83] *and*
- you are liable to criminal prosecution.[84]

In-time applications with a delayed decision

In many cases, the application is made before the leave expires, but it is not possible for the Home Office to make a decision on the application before the leave expires. In all cases where this occurs, the person automatically continues to have leave so that s/he does not become an overstayer while waiting for a decision. This also has implications for whether a person becomes 'subject to immigration control' with consequential implications for non-contributory benefit entitlement (see p157). All overstayers are 'subject to immigration control' but a person who is awaiting a decision after an in-time application, is treated as having the same leave as previously. If the leave is subject to a maintenance and accommodation condition (or given on the basis of a maintenance undertaking), then the person is subject to control because of that condition. If not, the person *continues* to not be subject to immigration control for benefit purposes.

The law in relation to automatic extensions of leave changed on 2 October 2000 and is slightly different depending on whether the variation decision was made before or after that date (see below).

Variation decisions made on or after 2 October 2000

For variation of leave decisions which are made on or after 2 October 2000 (whether the application to vary was made before or after 2 October 2000),[85] a person continues to have leave to enter or remain where s/he makes an in-time application to vary her/his leave and no decision is taken on that application by the time that the leave naturally expires. In these cases, the leave is treated as continuing on the same conditions until the end of the period which is allowed for appealing against a negative decision on the application.[86] The time for appealing against the decision is 10 days and leave is, therefore, initially extended for this period.[87] However, if an appeal is made against the variation decision, then the leave continues on the same conditions for as long as the appeal is pending.[88] The appeal continues to pend until such time as it has been finally determined[89] which, in turn, does not occur while a further appeal may be brought.[90] So, in practice, this leave may continue until you have exhausted the appeals process. However, a person who has leave *only* as the result of the automatic extension during an appeal is still treated as being a person who is 'subject to immigration control' for benefit purposes (see p157).[91] It should be noted that it is only appeals against refusals to extend leave which allow leave to continue – no other immigration appeals have this effect.

Variation decisions made before 2 October 2000

In the case of variation decisions made before 2 October 2000, the Immigration (Variation of Leave Order) 1976 (known as VOLO) automatically extends leave that would otherwise run out before the Home Office makes a decision on your application for an extension.[92] As with decisions made on or after 2 October 2000 (see above), it is to be assumed (although the legislation is not express) that, because the leave is 'extended', the pre–existing other conditions remain the same. Before 1976, applicants who had made applications in time but were still awaiting a decision when their leave ran out became overstayers.[93] The effect of VOLO was to extend a period of limited leave from the day you make your application (provided the application is made in time) until 28 days after the date of the decision on the application.[94] The original purpose of the introduction of VOLO was not simply to prevent people from becoming overstayers if the Home Office delayed in making a decision, but also to ensure that they did not lose their right of appeal against the variation decision which is exercisable only if people had leave at the time they submitted their notice of appeal.[95]

However, in contrast to the situation where the appealable decision is made on or after 2 October, where an appeal is made in these cases, there is no automatic extension of leave during the appeals process.[96] After the 28-day extension therefore, a person becomes 'subject to immigration control' as an overstayer with the consequent implications for benefits simply because s/he has no leave.[97]

Also no stamps are placed in your passport or notice given that you have been granted an automatic extension of leave under the above rules while a decision is awaited while you appeal. It may therefore appear from the available stamps that a person's leave has expired when, in reality it has been extended. Benefit advisers need to be careful, therefore, to check whether a valid, in-time application has been made, what the original conditions were and whether the person is awaiting a decision or the outcome of an appeal. Evidence of an application may exist in the form of a copy of the application form, a covering letter of an immigration adviser enclosing the form, requests for further information from the Home Office after the application was made or indeed a Home Office receipt in respect of the application form. The Home Office always acknowledges receipt by tearing off and returning part of the prescribed form on which the application was made.

Example

Gloria, a national of Sierra Leone, had limited leave to remain until 1 July 2001 which was not subject to any conditions other than length of time. In May 2001, she married a British citizen and, on 28 June 2001, applied for leave to remain as the spouse of a British citizen. The couple were interviewed by the Home Office in November 2001 but a decision refusing the application was not made until 1 January 2002. A few days later, Gloria appealed against the Secretary of State's variation decision.

As a result of her in-time application for leave, Gloria's leave was automatically extended on the same conditions from the date of its natural expiry until 10 days after the decision. During the period of this extension, Gloria was not 'subject to immigration control' as she had an extended leave and that leave (like her original leave) was not subject to a condition that she would not have recourse to public funds, nor was it granted upon an undertaking of a third party to maintain and accommodate her. Gloria was not, therefore, during this period, excluded from non-contributory benefits by her immigration status. During the course of Gloria's appeal, she is subject to immigration control because, although she has extended leave as a result of her appeal, a person with such leave is defined as being 'subject to immigration control'. Note that if the decision refusing further leave had been made before 2 October 2000, Gloria's leave would have been extended until 28 days after that decision, at which point she would have become subject to immigration control as a person who had no leave.

Making the application for leave to remain

Prior to November 1996, there were no special rules on what counted as an application for an extension of leave. Any clear and unambiguous request to the Home Office, either in person or by letter accompanied by a passport or travel document, was acceptable.[98] Since 27 November 1996, however, all applications to the Home Office for leave to remain or to vary leave (other than asylum applications, applications for leave for which a work permit or a training/work experience permit is required – settlement applications are not included in this category – and European Economic Area (EEA) applications), must be made on the appropriate Home Office prescribed application form. The form must be properly completed and sent to the Home Office along with all the documents requested on the form, or an explanation for why those documents have not been supplied and when they will be sent. If these procedures are not followed your application will be treated as not valid. It may then be that your leave expires before you are able to re-submit a valid application (see pp79-81 for the consequences of failing to apply in time).

You can get the appropriate application form by telephoning the Application Forms Unit at the Home Office (see Appendix 2) or they can be downloaded from the Immigration and Nationality Directorate website: http://www.ind.homeoffice.gov.uk/

If you are sending your application by post you should send it by recorded delivery. There are currently eight prescribed application forms issued in April 2002 but they will only be valid for applications made before 15 November 2002 at which point new versions of the forms will become available. Using the correct application form for the purpose for which further leave is being requested is vital. You are, of course, always best advised to seek professional advice in making your application. The current forms are listed here.

1. **Form FLR(M)**. This form can be used to apply for further leave to remain in the UK as the spouse or unmarried partner of a person present and settled in the UK.
2. **Form SET(M)**. This form can be used by a person seeking indefinite leave to remain (settlement) as the spouse or unmarried partner of a person present and settled in the UK.
3. **Form FLR(S)**. This form can be used to apply for further leave to remain as a student or a student nurse.
4. **Form FLR(O)**. This form can be used to apply for further leave to remain as an au pair, doctor/dentist in postgraduate training, domestic worker, ship/aircraft crew, permit-free employment, visitor, private medical visitor, seasonal agricultural worker, person of UK ancestry, working holidaymaker, writer/artist/composer, or on any other basis.
5. **Form SET(O)**. This form can be used to apply for indefinite leave to remain as a person who has been in the UK for four years as a domestic worker, in any work permit-free category, as a person of UK ancestry, in work permit employment, as a writer/composer/artist or on any other basis.
6. **Form SET(F)**. This form can be used to apply for indefinite leave to remain in the UK as a family member (not husband, wife or unmarried partner) of a person present and settled in the UK.
7. **BUS**. This form can be used to apply for further leave or indefinite leave as a business person, sole representative, retired person of independent means, investor or innovator (it is available interactively on the Home Office website, see Appendix 2).
8. **Form ELR**. This form can be used to apply for further leave or indefinite leave as a person who was granted exceptional leave to remain after a refusal of asylum.

There have been very serious delays in dealing with applications by the Home Office over the past few years. Consideration times fluctuate: the Home Office has recently stated that it can deal with straightforward applications within three weeks of receipt and that about 65 per cent of such applications are dealt with within this period. Those which are not so straightforward and which are submitted to the case-working teams for consideration, are said to take approximately 12 weeks.[99]

Applications which do not need to be made on the prescribed forms

The following applications do not need to be made on the prescribed forms, described above, in order to be valid.

Asylum applications

In order to constitute an application for leave to enter or remain for asylum it is not necessary to complete an application form. The immigration authorities are instructed to accept any indication by a person who needs leave to be in the UK that they may be in some sort of danger in their own country, as a claim for asylum. This is also then treated as an application for leave to enter or remain as a refugee.

Work permit-related applications

Applications for further leave to remain for work permit employment (but not settlement applications in this category) are sent to Work Permits (UK), based in Sheffield, and its own forms are used – see Appendix 2. In practical terms, it is the employer who applies for an extension of the work permit by filling in form WP1X which can be obtained from Work Permits (UK) or downloaded from www.workpermits.gov.uk/

Applications can also be made by email using a similar form available on the same site. The passports and/or police registration certificates of the applicant and any dependants must always be included with the application (or if it is made by email, received within five working days of the application). Work Permits (UK) has now become part of the Home Office and has taken on additional staff so that it can both authorise an extension to the work permit and grant further leave. If it does do this, the passports are endorsed with the further leave and any conditions of leave and returned to the applicant.

European Economic Area applications

EEA nationals and their family members may make after-entry applications for residence permits (for EEA nationals) or for residence documents (for non-EEA family members of EEA nationals). Neither an EEA national with the right to live in the UK nor her/his family members (see p7) needs to have a residence permit/ document, their right to be in the UK exists independently of documentation. These can, however, be obtained as evidence of the person's status in the UK. Residence permits are normally valid for five years but they can be issued for less if the EEA national is working in the UK for a shorter period. If a residence document is given to a family member, it will be issued for the same period as the permit given to the EEA national. A non-EEA national family member who has a valid residence document does not need a new EEA family permit each time s/he returns to the UK after travelling abroad.

There is no charge for the issue of these permits/documents. Applications can be made on Form EEC1 which can also be downloaded from the Home Office website. When a person has been residing in the UK for four years in accordance with European rights of free movement, s/he is entitled to have her/his passport endorsed with indefinite leave to remain in the UK.

Returning passports when an application is outstanding

In order to make an application for leave to remain, the Home Office requires that you send in your passport. If you request the return of your passport in order to travel outside the CTA while your application is still outstanding, your application is treated as withdrawn when the passport is returned to you.[100] The Home Office will only speed up an application for leave so that you can travel if there is an emergency, such as a family illness. It is possible, however, to make arrangements with the Home Office for the return of your passport for other reasons without affecting your application, for example if you want to open a bank account or obtain a driving licence. If you do this you must make it clear that you are not requesting your passport in order to travel.

Decisions made by the Home Office where no application has been made

In certain circumstances, the Home Office can curtail limited leave to enter or remain (ie, bring your leave to an end before it is otherwise due to expire) without your making any application to the Home Office. An indefinite leave to enter or remain may not be curtailed[101] (although, in extreme circumstances, a person with indefinite leave can still be deported from the UK – see p79).

When your leave is curtailed, you become a person with no leave (an overstayer) which may have benefit implications as such a person is 'subject to immigration control' (see p157). However, if you appeal against the variation (see p83), then the variation will not take effect during the time that you are appealing which may preserve your position as a person not 'subject to control' if you were not one before, which means that you are not excluded from claiming benefit during this time.[102] Leave may be curtailed in the following circumstances:[103]

- false representations are made or there is a failure to disclose a material fact for the purpose of obtaining leave to enter or a previous variation of leave;
- failure to comply with any conditions attached to the grant of leave to enter or to remain;
- failure to maintain or accommodate yourself and any dependants without recourse to public funds;
- it is undesirable to allow you to remain in the UK in the light of your character, conduct, associations or the fact that you represent a threat to national security.

In addition, the Home Office may add, vary or revoke conditions attached to your leave without you making any application for this to be done.[104] There are no specific rules as to when this can be done. Both curtailment of leave and the addition of conditions are relatively rare occurrences.

Notice of decisions

If you apply to the Home Office for a variation of your leave and the application is successful, the Home Office will endorse the further leave/conditions in your passport or travel document and may also inform you in writing of the decision.[105] If you are unsuccessful in your application, or the Home Office has varied or curtailed your leave without your applying, then you will also be informed of this in writing,[106] and you will be informed of any right of appeal that you have against this decision.[107] See Appendix 9 in order to identify the stamps which may be endorsed on the passport in these circumstances.

Enforcement, registration and complying with conditions

Decisions to enforce a person's departure from the UK are also, of course, an important part of immigration control and involve both the immigration service and officials at the Home Office. There are other forms of immigration control which also operate after a person's arrival in the UK. S/he may be required to register with the police, or to comply with certain conditions upon which temporary admission or bail is granted. Enforcement and the other forms of control are dealt with separately in Chapter 7.

Notes

1. Immigration control before arrival

1 para 25 HC 395
2 para 24 HC 395
3 para 24 HC 395
4 para 1(a)-(d) Appendix 1 to HC 395
5 para 2 Appendix 1 to HC 395
6 Reg 12(1) I(EEA) Regs
7 Reg 12(2) I(EEA) Regs
8 Reg 13(1) I(EEA) Regs
9 para 24 HC 395
10 para 90 HC 395
11 Part II I(LER)O
12 Arts 2-3 I(LER)O, para 25A HC 395 as inserted by HC 704
13 Art 5 I(LER)O, s3 IA 1971
14 Art 6 I(LER)O
15 Art 4(2) I(LER)O
16 Art 4(1) I(LER)O
17 Art 4(3) I(LER)O
18 para 2 Appendix to HC 395
19 para 28 HC 395
20 The Foreign and Commonwealth Office publishes a list of such designated posts abroad.
21 para 28 HC 395
22 para 30 HC 395 and CF(A)O; fees were due to change again in early July 2002
23 The main form is Form IM2A.
24 This practice was condoned in *R v Hoque and Singh* [1988] Imm AR 216.
25 para 26 HC 395
26 para 27 HC 395
27 Regs 4(1) and 5 IAA(N) Regs
28 para 30A HC 395 inserted by para 2 HC 31
29 Arts 6(3) and 7(1) I(LER)O
30 s33(1) IA 1971
31 paras 128–135 HC 395
32 paras 116–121 HC 395
33 See guidance on Work Permits (UK) website under 'Making an initial application' and 'When should I apply'.
34 paras 116(i) and 128(i) HC 395
35 Art 7(1) I(LER)O; para 17A HC 395 as inserted by HC 704
36 Art 7(2)(3) I(LER)O
37 Art 7(4) I(LER)O
38 s4(1) IA 1971
39 s3A(2) IA 1971; art 8(2) I(LER)O
40 Arts 8(3)(4) and 9(1)(2) I(LER)O
41 See 'Background Information' to notes to changes of immigration rules, HC 704, previously contained on the Immigration and National Directorate website.

2. Immigration control on arrival

42 Sch 2 paras 2(1) and 2A, IA 1971
43 s3(8) and (9) and Sch 2 para 4 IA 1971; paras 11–13 HC 395
44 Sch 2 para 2A IA 1971
45 Art 11 I(LER)O
46 Art 4(2) and (3) I(LER)O; Sch 2 para 2A IA 1971
47 s3(4) IS 1971
48 Part IV I(LER)O, commencement provisions are contained in art 1(2)
49 s1(3) IA 1971; para 15 HC 395
50 Art 15(2) I(LER)O
51 Arts 13(1), (2) and (3) and 15(2) I(LER)O; paras 20 and 20A HC 395 as amended by HC 704
52 Art 13(4) I(LER)O; paras 20 and 20A HC 395
53 Art 13(4)(a) I(LER)O; paras 20 and 20A HC 395
54 Art 13(4)(b) I(LER)O
55 s3(4) IA 1971; art 13(10) I(LER)O
56 s3(3)(b) IA 1971 as amended by s10 and Sched para 1 IA 1988; para 20 HC 395
57 Sch 2 para 2A(7) and (10)IA 1971; para 10A HC 395 inserted by HC 704
58 Sch 2 para 2A(8) IA 1971; art 6(1) I(LER)O read also with art 13(5) I(LER)O, para 10B HC 395 inserted by HC 704
59 Sch 2 para 2A(2)-(4) IA 1971; para 321A HC 395 inserted by HC 704
60 Sch 2 para 2A(9) IA 1971 which treats such persons as having been refused leave to enter at a time at which they held a valid entry clearance for the purposes of the rights of appeal under Part IV IAA 1999
61 paras 17B and 321A HC 395 inserted by HC 704; arts 6(1) and 13(7) I(LER)O
62 s3(3)(a) IA 1971; art 13(8) ILEA; para 33A HC 395 as inserted by HC 704
63 paras 320–322 HC 395
64 ss60(3) and 69(1) IAA 1999
65 para 10 HC 395

66 s4(1) IA 1971 requires the grant/refusal of leave to enter to be notice in writing and see para 9 HC 395
67 Regs 4(1) and 5 INR 2000
68 Sch 2 para 8 IA 1971
69 Sch 2 paras 16 and 21 IA 1971
70 Sch 2 para 21(1) IA 1971
71 Sch 2 para 21(1) IA 1971
72 Sch 2 para 22 IA 1971
73 Sch 2 para 21(2) IA 1971

3. Immigration control after entry

74 See s33(1) IA 1971 for definiition of 'illlegal entry' and s11 IA 1971 for construction of 'entry' to the UK.
75 s4(1) IA 1971
76 s11 IA 1971
77 *Davoren* [1996] Imm AR 307 CA
78 s3(1)(c) IA 1971 which applies only to limited leave
79 para 32 HC 395
80 s115 IAA 1999
81 ss116–118 IAA 1999
82 See for example, paras 284(i) and 322(3) HC 395
83 s3(5)(a) IA 1971
84 s24 IA 1971
85 Sch 2 para 2(2) IAA 1999 (Commencement No. 6) (Transitional and Consequential Provisions) Order 2000
86 s3C IA 1971 as inserted by s3 IAA 1999
87 r.6(1) Immigration and Asylum (Procedure) Rules 2000
88 Sch 4 para 17(1)IAA 1999
89 s58(5) IAA 1999
90 s58(6) and (7) IAA 1999
91 s115(9)(c) IAA 1999
92 See art 2 of Immigration (Variation of Leave) (Amendment) Order 2000 disapplying VOLO to cases where the variation decision is made on or after 2 October 2000 but not to those made before that time.
93 *ex parte Subramaniam* [1977] QB 190 and *Suthendran v IAT* [1977] AC 359
94 para 3(1) VOLO
95 See pre-October 2000 variation appeal rights under s14(1) IA 1971, s8(2) AIAA 1993 and *ex parte Subramaniam* [1977] QB 190; *Suthendran v IAT* [1977] AC 35 and now ss61 and 69(2) and (3) IAA 1999

96 Art 3(1)(a), Sch 2 paras 1(5)(11)(b) and (c), 2(4) and 3(2)(b) IAA 1999 (Commencement No. 6) (Transitional and Consequential Provisions) Order 2000 maintaining in force the old variation appeals provisions under IA 1971 and AIAA 1993 in respect of decisions made before 2 October 2000 and lack of application of Sch 4 para 17(1) IAA 1999 (leave continuing pending appeal) to the old variation appeals as other provisions of IAA 1999 are applied to the old provisions by Sch 2 para 1(13) IAA 1999 (Commencement No. 6) (Transitional and Consequential Provisions) Order 2000
97 s115(9)(a) IAA 1999
98 *ex parte Oyele* [1994] Imm AR 265; *Adepoju* (12573) and commentary in *Immigration Nationality Law and Practice* Vol 10 No. 2 1996 p68
99 Immigration and Nationality Directorate website 'How to make an application', May 2001
100 para 34 HC 395
101 s3(3)(a) IA 1971
102 s14(1) IA 1971; Sch 2 para 7 AIAA 1993 (in respect of appeals under s8(2)) both as preserved by Sch 2 paras 2(5) and 3(4) IAA 1999 (Commencement No. 6) (Transitional and Consequential Provisions) Order 2000; Sch 4 para 16 IAA 1999
103 para 323 HC 395
104 s3(3)(a) IA 1971
105 s4(1) para 31 IA 1971
106 s4(1) para 31 IA 1971
107 Regs 4(1) and 5 IAA(N) 2000

Chapter 4

Leave and settlement

This chapter covers:
1. Leave to enter or remain (below)
2. Categories of leave and switching category (p51)
3. General reasons for refusing and curtailing leave (p55)

1. Leave to enter or remain

People who do not have the right of abode in the UK and who are therefore subject to immigration control require leave to enter (on arrival) and leave to remain (after entry).[1] (Special rules apply to certain special groups – see p6). Leave is of two kinds:[2]

- limited leave to enter or remain (see below);
- indefinite leave to enter or remain (see p49).

Leave is a specific permission to remain. It must be distinguished from, for example, a period of grace in order to allow time to make a voluntary departure from the UK.[3]

Limited leave

If you have limited leave, you can only remain in the UK for a certain period of time. In order lawfully to remain in the UK after the time permitted, you must obtain further leave to remain and the application must be made to the Home Office before the existing leave ends (see p38). Certain conditions can be attached to a limited leave to enter or remain which may:[4]

- restrict or prohibit the employment or occupation you can take in the UK;
- require you to maintain and accommodate yourself and any dependants without recourse to public funds;[5]
- in certain circumstances, require you to register with the police if you are not a citizen of a Commonwealth country or a European Economic Area national;
- require you to report to a medical officer at a specified time and date.

The immigration rules indicate the length of limited leave normally granted to a successful applicant in the different categories and, in some cases, the conditions that will be imposed upon that leave.

Employment conditions

The rules distinguish between:

- a prohibition upon employment (eg, visitors are usually prohibited from working);[6] *and*
- a restriction upon the freedom to take employment (given, for example, to students).[7]

While you can apply to the Home Office to get working restrictions lifted in order to work legally, if you have a prohibition on working you must apply to the Home Office for the terms of your leave to be varied. In the case of students, from 21 June 1999, the Home Office has operated a concession whereby students are automatically deemed to have been granted permission to work for not more than 20 hours a week during term time and full time during vacations.

Overstaying leave and breaching conditions of leave

The consequences of overstaying your leave or otherwise breaching the conditions of your leave are that:

- you may be 'removed' (see p78) from the UK;[8]
- you are liable to be prosecuted for a criminal offence (although prosecutions are rare);[9]
- your existing leave to enter or remain in the UK may be curtailed (if you are in breach of conditions of leave);[10]
- any future applications under the immigration rules for entry clearance, leave to enter and leave to remain are less likely to succeed.[11]

Indefinite leave

Indefinite leave to enter or remain in the UK is leave without a time restriction. No conditions relating to employment, public funds etc can be attached to an indefinite leave.[12] This is important for benefit purposes, as a person given a condition on her/his leave not to have recourse to public funds is 'subject to immigration control' and excluded from non-contributory benefit (see p157).[13] The only way in which a person who has indefinite leave can be subject to immigration control is where it was given on the basis of a maintenance undertaking of another person to provide for her/him.[14] Indefinite leave amounts to a right of permanent residence in the UK.

However, a person who has indefinite leave can still, in very limited circumstances, be required to leave the UK. Such people may be deported on grounds that their presence is not conducive to the public good or deported following a recommendation made by a criminal court.[15]

4

If you had indefinite leave when you left the UK you can seek to re-enter as a returning resident[16] provided you:
- wish to return to settle in the UK;
- have been away from the UK for no more than two years (unless there are special circumstances – eg, previous long residence);
- did not receive assistance from public funds towards the cost of leaving the UK (this refers to the special scheme which operates to enable people to ask for their costs of re-settling in their country of origin to be reimbursed; it does not refer to obtaining welfare benefits).

Settlement

A person who has indefinite leave is usually also 'settled' in the UK. To be settled, you have to be lawfully 'ordinarily resident' (see p132) in the UK without your stay being time-limited.[17] In practice, therefore, the terms 'indefinite leave to remain' and 'settlement' are often used interchangeably. A person who is settled may:
- come and go as a returning resident;
- have no conditions or limitations imposed on her/his leave; *but*
- be liable to deportation in the circumstances described above.

You must be settled in order:
- to naturalise or register as a British citizen;[18]
- for your children born in the UK to become British citizens by birth[19] (see Chapter 2);
- to bring members of your family to the UK under the immigration rules with a view to their living permanently in the UK with you (although people granted leave exceptionally following an asylum claim can do this after they have had that status for four years).[20]

The following are the most important routes to settlement.
- Certain categories of admission under the immigration rules lead to obtaining indefinite leave to remain and settled status (usually after a period of limited leave in that capacity). Other more temporary categories do not lead to settlement (see p53).
- Members of the family of a person (the 'sponsor') settled in the UK are also admitted with a view to settlement under the rules.
- Admission in other categories leads to settlement even though the immigration rules do not say so:
  - if you are a refugee you will normally be granted indefinite leave immediately on being granted refugee status;
  - if you are refused full refugee status but are nevertheless allowed to remain exceptionally because you are thought to be in need of some form of protection you may be granted indefinite leave after a period of four years'

leave (see p62). You are entitled to sponsor the admission for settlement of your spouse and children who are minors at this point as well;

– if you have lived in the UK for a long period of time, you may be eligible to be granted indefinite leave to remain outside the immigration rules. In order to qualify, you need to show that you have remained in the UK either lawfully for 10 years or otherwise for 14 years. Indefinite leave on the basis of long residence is wholly discretionary and all of your circumstances – in particular, the nature of your immigration history – will be taken into account;

– if you are liable for deportation or other forms of enforcement but the Secretary of State decides not to proceed against you or you are successful on appeal, then in order to regularise your position you would normally be granted indefinite leave even though you cannot fit into one of the categories under the immigration rules.

2. Categories of leave and switching category

Purpose for entering or staying in the UK

An application for leave is generally made for a particular purpose. If you do not state a purpose, the immigration authorities will ask you to say why you wish to enter the UK. For applications for leave to remain, the forms that must be used[21] mean that the nature of the application is taken from the form used. If, for example, when applying to enter:

● a Colombian man says that he wishes to enter 'in order to see his terminally ill mother in the UK before she dies';

● an Australian woman applies to come to the UK 'solely for a business meeting', both these applications would be treated as applications for a visit and, if the requirements of the rules are satisfied, the person will be admitted in the category of a visitor.

The immigration rules divide people into different categories according to the reason for seeking leave to enter or remain in the UK. In order to succeed in an application for entry clearance, leave to enter or an extension of leave you have to satisfy the appropriate requirements. It is not within the scope of this book to set out the requirements of the rules. Details are only given in this book as to the common 'maintenance and accommodation' requirements which are explained in Chapter 8. Owing to the importance of the category, the requirements to be satisfied for leave to enter or remain as a refugee are set out in Chapter 5. The following example sets out the requirements to be met for students.

Example

To obtain leave to enter the UK as a student, the rules state you must:[22]

– be accepted for a course of study at either a publicly-funded institution of further or higher education or a recognised private education institution or an independent fee-paying school outside the maintained sector; *and*

– be able and intend to follow either a recognised full-time degree course at a publicly-funded institution of further or higher education or a weekday full-time course at a further or higher education college including at least 15 hours' supervised study or a full-time course of study at an independent school; *and*

– if under the age of 16 years, be enrolled at an independent school for recognised full-time study; *and*

– intend to leave the UK at the end of your studies; *and*

– not intend to engage in business or take employment, except officially agreed part-time or vacation work; *and*

– be able to meet the cost of your course, accommodation and maintenance of yourself and any dependants without taking employment, engaging in business or having recourse to public funds (see p92).

To satisfy the immigration authorities, you will therefore need to provide details of your school/college/means/previous academic record. You may be admitted to the UK for a period appropriate to your course. You could still be refused leave even if you meet the above criteria if certain 'general grounds' of refusal (which apply to all cases except asylum applications) apply (see p55).[23] If you do not meet the rules for students you will not usually be given leave to enter.[24] In exceptional circumstances, the immigration authorities could waive the rules and admit you to the UK outside the rules (see Chapter 6).

As a student, you will probably have a condition attached to your leave that you maintain and accommodate yourself without recourse to public funds.[25]

Family members

Family members may apply to stay permanently with someone who is settled in the UK. You may, however, be admitted as a family member to join a person in the UK who is not here in a settled capacity. The conditions you must satisfy vary according to the status of the person you are joining. For example, a child joining a working holidaymaker must be under five, rather than under 18 (the usual criteria).[26] If the person you are joining is required not to have recourse to public funds, this will generally apply to you as well.

To count as a spouse under the immigration rules, you and your partner must be 16 or over. You cannot qualify as a spouse if your marriage is polygamous and there is another wife or husband alive who has *either*:[27]

• been in the UK since her/his marriage; *or*

- been recognised as having (by the issue of a certificate of entitlement) the right of abode, or has been granted entry clearance to enter the UK as the spouse of your wife or husband.

However, if another spouse was here as a visitor or entered illegally or did not disembark from the ship or aircraft this will not affect your rights as the spouse. You will also still qualify as the spouse if you:[28]

- were in the UK before 1 August 1988 having been admitted for settlement as the spouse of your present wife or husband; *or*
- have, since your marriage, been in the UK at any time since your wife or husband's other spouse died.

Temporary and permanent/settled purposes

Some people are only admitted for temporary purposes which do not lead to settlement. In these cases, the leave granted is always time-limited and applicants are expected to leave the UK when the purpose for which leave was granted has been fulfilled. Other people are admitted for longer term or permanent purposes which lead to indefinite leave and settlement in the UK. For some permanent/settled purposes, indefinite leave can be granted immediately, whereas for others, indefinite leave is usually only granted after a period of limited leave in the UK.

The **tables in Appendix 4 and Appendix 5** set out separately the temporary categories and the categories leading to settlement together with a reference to the appropriate paragraphs in the current immigration rules.[29] It is important to identify whether you are in a category leading to settlement and, if so, whether you have to wait one or more years with limited leave before applying for settlement or whether you may obtain settlement immediately. Settled status is advantageous as it gives you increased rights to benefits – see Part 2. The tables also list:

- maintenance and accommodation/public funds requirements relating to the applicant and any dependants in each category – this is important as it is more likely that you will have a condition imposed on your leave not to have recourse to public funds if you have been given leave in accordance with requirements of the immigration rules which require you to show that you can be maintained and accommodated without such recourse. It is the imposition of a condition which makes a person 'subject to immigration control' for benefit purposes (those given exceptional leave should not have a public funds condition attached to it); *and*
- employment conditions on limited leave granted in each category; *and*
- any requirements that relate to employment that you need to satisfy in order to obtain leave in that category; *and*
- whether an entry clearance is required for the *entry* of non-visa nationals – where this is the case, all applicants, whether they are visa nationals or not, require an entry clearance to come to the UK for this purpose; *and*

- at what point an applicant may apply for indefinite leave and become settled.

The employment requirements and conditions are relevant to the 'available for and actively seeking work' test which affects access to jobseeker's allowance (see pp240-242).

Switching categories

Switching between categories and acquiring more rights while in the UK has been made more difficult by changes in the immigration rules.

In general, it is not possible to switch from purely temporary categories to permanent categories, or between permanent categories. You can switch from temporary to temporary or from permanent to temporary, provided you satisfy the requirements of the rules – in particular, the intention to leave requirement relevant to most categories of temporary leave. However, even in these cases, the rules can be restrictive. The immigration rules prevent switching by imposing a requirement that the applicant entered the UK with a valid entry clearance in the same capacity as leave to remain is sought.

It is often possible to ask for further leave in the same capacity. However, some categories (eg, a visitor) have a maximum period it is permitted to spend in total before you are required to leave. In many permanent categories, the rules require you to remain in the UK with limited leave in the same capacity for a period of continuous years before applying for settlement.

The following are the exceptions to the general rules above:

- It is possible to switch into any of the following categories if you are in any permanent or temporary category:
  - a Commonwealth citizen with UK ancestry seeking to work in the UK (but not the spouse or child of such a person);[30]
  - a person intending to establish her/himself in business under the provisions of an European Community association agreement (but not the spouse or child of such a person);[31]
  - the spouse or unmarried partner of a person present and settled in the UK (note, however, that the requirements for obtaining leave as an unmarried partner can be very difficult to satisfy);[32]
  - the parent, grandparent or other dependent relative of a person present and settled in the UK;[33]
  - a refugee or accompanying spouse or child.[34]

The Government's 2002 White Paper (see p15) proposes to bring in rules to prevent people switching to stay as spouses when they have only been admitted for a period of six months or less – eg, as a visitor or student attending a short course.

- It is not possible, under the rules, to switch from a temporary or a permanent category into a temporary category for which an entry clearance or similar

documentation is generally required (unless such entry clearance was obtained prior to entry). In other words, it is not possible to switch to a:
- working holidaymaker;[35]
- seasonal worker at an agricultural camp;[36]
- teacher or language assistant under an approved scheme;[37]
- person undertaking approved training or work experience (unless you were admitted or allowed to remain as a student).[38]
- It is not possible for *visa nationals* to switch from a temporary or a permanent category into the following temporary categories even though an entry clearance is not mandatory for non-visa nationals:
  - student (including a student who is re-sitting, writing up a thesis or is a student union sabbatical officer);[39]
  - student nurse;[40]
  - prospective student.[41]
- It is not possible to switch to being an au pair. In order to obtain an extension in this capacity you need to have been granted leave to enter the UK as an au pair.[42]

Whatever your new category, you must show that you satisfy the requirements of the immigration rules for being here in that capacity. The Home Office can treat an application to switch as evidence that you did not genuinely enter for the purpose for which you were granted leave. Under these circumstances, you may be refused leave to remain, or even declared an illegal entrant (see pp83 and 81).

You should always seek professional advice before making your application to remain or to change status. Remember, even if you may not switch under the immigration rules, you may ask, exceptionally, for the 'no switching' requirement to be waived. The government is increasingly developing policies to allow more people to stay in the UK for economic reasons and, in practice, relaxes certain of the 'switching' rules for this reason.

3. **General reasons for refusing and curtailing leave**

Even if you satisfy the immigration rules which relate to the category in which you have applied, there is no guarantee that you will be granted leave. The rules say that where certain requirements are satisfied, leave (or entry clearance)[43] 'may' be granted for a particular period if particular conditions are satisfied.

There are general grounds on which you may be refused leave or have your leave curtailed. These general grounds do not apply to those applying for or granted leave as refugees.[44] It is not possible here to set out all of these rules. Most are self-explanatory and they are contained together in Part IX of the immigration rules.[45]

Some grounds for refusal are mandatory – ie, if such a reason applies to you, then your application must be refused under the immigration rules. For example, if you apply for leave to enter and you fail to produce a valid national passport or other satisfactory identity document you must be refused.[46] However, if you fail to observe the time limit or conditions on a previous leave or that leave was obtained by deception, then the entry clearance officer or immigration officer should normally refuse your application, although there is still a discretion to allow your application.[47] Again, discretion exists to allow your application for leave to remain where a sponsor refuses to give a written undertaking to be responsible for your maintenance and accommodation in the UK or fails to honour that undertaking.[48]

Notes

1. Leave to enter or remain

1 ss1 and 3 IA 1971
2 s3(1)(b) IA 1971
3 *R v SSHD ex parte Smith* [1996] Imm AR 337
4 s3(1)(c) IA 1971; para 8 HC 395 (the last complete statement of the immigration rules, 23 May 1994) as amended
5 Although this has been a requirement in the rules for a long time, it is only since 1 November 1996 that it has been elevated into a *condition* upon which leave may be granted – see para 8 HC 395 as amended by para 3 Command Paper 3365 (August 1996) and s3(1)(c) IA 1971.
6 paras 42 and 45 HC 395
7 paras 58 and 61 HC 395
8 s10 IAA 1999
9 s24(1)(b) IA 1971
10 para 323 HC 395
11 paras 320(11) and (17) and 322(3) HC 395
12 s3(3)(a) IA 1971
13 s115(9)(b) IAA 1999
14 s115(9)(c) IAA 1999
15 s3(5)(b) and (6) IA 1971
16 paras 18–19 HC 395
17 s33(2A) IA 1971 as amended; see also para 6 HC 395

18 ss4 and 6 and Sch 1 to BNA 1981
19 s1 BNA 1981
20 para 8 HC 395

2. Categories of leave and switching category

21 para 32 HC 395 as amended
22 paras 57 and 58 HC 395
23 paras 320–322 HC 395
24 para 59 HC 395
25 s3(1)(c) IA 1971
26 paras 101(ii), 102 and 103 HC 395
27 paras 277–280 HC 395
28 paras 277–280 HC 395
29 HC 395 as amended
30 paras 186–193 HC 395
31 paras 211–223 HC 395
32 paras 281–289 HC 395
33 paras 317–319 HC 395 and see also for certain children paras 297–303, 310–316 and 304–309
34 paras 327–352 HC 395
35 paras 95–103 HC 395
36 paras 103–109 HC 395
37 paras 110–115 HC 395
38 paras 116–121 HC 395
39 paras 57–62, 69A–69L and 87A–87F HC 395
40 paras 63–69 HC 395

41 paras 82–87 HC 395
42 para 92 HC 395

3. General reasons for refusing and curtailing leave

43 para 26 HC 395
44 paras 320–323 HC 395
45 paras 320–323 HC 395
46 para 320(3) HC 395
47 para 320(11) and (12) HC 395
48 para 322(6) HC 395 and see further para
     10 HC 31 from 1 November 1996

Chapter 5

....

Asylum seekers

This chapter covers:
1. Consideration of cases (p59)
2. Asylum decisions (p62)
3. Asylum support and the new procedures (p64)
4. The future of asylum (p68)

There were over 77,000 applications for asylum in 2000[1] and over 118,000 decisions were made in response to asylum claims in 2001. Asylum seekers and refugees are the largest single group of people who require leave to enter and remain in the UK who require advice about benefits and welfare provision. The following is a description of the immigration process as it relates specifically to asylum seekers and those who are granted exceptional leave having applied for, but been refused, refugee status in the UK. Exceptional leave is not defined anywhere and failed asylum seekers constitute only one group who may be granted leave exceptionally. For an explanation of the wider groups who may be granted leave exceptionally, see Chapter 6.

It is not possible, under the immigration rules, to apply for an entry clearance to come to the UK as a refugee[2] and therefore in all but a very few cases, asylum seekers apply for leave as refugees either at the port (known simply as '**port applications**') or from inside the country ('**in-country applications**'). There is no prospect of an immediate decision for those who apply for asylum. As a result, asylum seekers are either given 'temporary admission' (see p113) or they are detained. If the application is made at port, rather than in-country, then in order to decide whether or not the individual may be granted leave to enter as a refugee, the immigration officer has to refer the application to the Home Office for a decision.

Initially asylum seekers are put through a screening process intended to establish their identity and nationality. Their fingerprints will also be taken at this stage with the intention of preventing multiple applications for asylum by the same person among the different countries of the European Union (EU). In addition, the screening interview is intended to establish whether an asylum seeker may be returned to a 'safe' third country which has responsibility for determining the claim to asylum. This is usually, although not always, a country through which the asylum seeker has travelled to arrive in the UK. In particular the member states of the EU have set out criteria for themselves under the 'Dublin Convention'[3] for deciding which one of them has responsibility for determining asylum applications. These depend upon factors such as: where the applicant first entered the territory of the EU, whether any of the national states had issued a visa to the claimant, etc. If it is determined that another state has the responsibility for dealing with the asylum seeker, the Home Office may seek to return that person to that state without considering whether in fact the person qualifies for asylum as a refugee.[4]

There are procedures for treating certain applications more quickly than others. Applications for asylum from nationals of certain countries whose claims are said to be 'straightforward' have been referred to the Oakington Reception Centre, near Cambridge, where the applicants are kept in detention for approximately one week while their application is considered very swiftly and determined at the end of that week.

1. **Consideration of cases**

To determine whether a person is a refugee, the asylum application is considered by caseworkers at the Home Office who have access to information concerning the particular country from which the asylum seeker has come.[5] To assist in this process, the Home Office has prepared detailed 'country assessments' which describe the conditions in those countries which produce substantial numbers of asylum seekers. These are updated every six months and are available on the Home Office website. Generally, asylum seekers are given a statement of evidence form (SEF) to complete and return to the Home Office within 10 working days. It must be completed in English and if it is not completed and returned in time, the Home Office may make a decision on the existing evidence without considering the detailed claim that the asylum seeker wishes to put forward. This will almost always result in a refusal. Following the submission of the SEF, the asylum seeker may be interviewed and asked questions arising out of the SEF. The asylum seeker or her/his representative is also able to submit any further representations and documents in support of the application. Practice in the asylum process can change rapidly and does not need legislation in order to change. Some applicants are not given SEFs but proceed directly to interview. It is not always possible to predict how an asylum applicant will be treated, particularly those who claim at port.

In 2000/01 a problem arose in respect of the SEF procedure. Large numbers of asylum seekers had submitted their SEFs in time but, due to errors at the Home Office, the SEFs were not considered and, accordingly, the cases were refused on the basis that the asylum seekers had failed to put before the Home Office evidence of their claim regarding fear of persecution and had failed to comply with the Home Office procedure for the determination of cases.[6] When the problem became clear, the Home Office agreed to withdraw the letters giving reasons for refusal of asylum and to reconsider the cases but it did not agree to the actual decision recording the claim as determined being withdrawn. The result of this was that all those who had received an erroneous non-compliance refusal would continue to be unable to access social security benefits if, for example, they were entitled to benefit as a pre-April 2001 transitionally-protected 'on arrival' asylum seeker (see p275) and would become eligible for National Asylum Support Service or interim asylum support instead and might face dispersal. In addition, in line with the Secretary of State's policy of granting permission to work to asylum seekers who have not had an initial negative asylum decision within six months of their claim for asylum, the withdrawal of the reasons for refusal but not the refusal itself, would still prevent them from working.

Following a High Court challenge to this response to its own errors,[7] the Home Office agreed to change its practice. As a result, any asylum seeker whose claim for asylum was refused on the ground that an SEF form was not received within the prescribed time limit, where in fact the SEF form was received within that time limit, will have the decision withdrawn by the Home Office and her/his application will be reconsidered.[8] This is provided s/he has requested that the decision is withdrawn within three months of the receipt of the decision. Those affected by these withdrawals, therefore, maintain their social security benefit until such time as the Home Office makes a further decision in their case.[9]

Criteria applied under the immigration rules

To obtain leave to enter the UK as a refugee, you must:[10]
* be in the UK or have arrived at a port of entry in the UK; *and*
* be a **'refugee'**. A refugee is defined as a person who 'owing to a well–founded fear of being persecuted for reasons of race, religion, nationality, membership of a particular social group or political opinion, is outside his country of nationality and is unable or, owing to such fear, is unwilling to avail himself of the protection of that country; or who, not having a nationality and being outside the country of his former habitual residence ... is unable or, owing to such fear, is unwilling to return to it'.[11] This definition is taken from the UN Convention Relating to the Status of Refugees (1951).

You can still be refused asylum and leave to enter or remain in the UK as a refugee if you can be sent to another (known as a 'third') country[12] of which you are not a national or citizen, in which your life or liberty would not be threatened for a Convention reason and which will consider your claim to asylum. The third country must be one:
* in which the government of that country would not send you on to the country in which you have a well-founded fear of persecution; *and*
* through which you travelled in order to come to the UK and you had the opportunity there to make contact with the authorities of that country in

order to claim asylum *or* a country to which there is clear evidence that you would be admitted.

Where a person is sent to a third country under the Dublin Convention,[13] the law presumes that the country is safe and it can be very difficult to prevent removal on this basis unless there are separate human rights reasons (see below) why the person should not be returned to that third country.[14]

The onus is on applicants to show they satisfy the rules. Obtaining the necessary evidence and ensuring that there are no misunderstandings, errors or discrepancies in the application is of the utmost importance. The credibility of the case presented is particularly important in refugee cases.

Human rights and asylum

There is no specific criteria in the immigration rules for allowing people to remain in the UK on the basis of their human rights although the rules do require immigration officers, entry clearance officers and all of the officers of the Secretary of State at the Home Office to make their decisions in compliance with the rights guaranteed by the European Convention on Human Rights (ECHR) which is now, effectively, incorporated into UK law.[15] In the context of asylum, this is particularly strange since applications for asylum support under the new asylum support scheme are actually defined as applications to remain in the UK as refugees under the 1951 Convention *or* applications to stay in the UK under Article 3 ECHR (freedom from torture or inhuman and degrading treatment or punishment).

The group of people who fall within the protection of Article 3 ECHR is broader than those who fall within the Refugee Convention. For example, under Article 3 you do not need to show that you will be ill-treated for a particular reason. Article 3 is also an absolute right, which means that, even if a person is a danger to the country which they are in, they cannot be returned if they will face torture or inhuman or degrading treatment or punishment. The 1951 Refugee Convention contains exclusions for people who are a danger to the host country or who have committed very serious offences against humanity or the principles of the United Nations. Article 3 also provides greater protection than the 1951 Refugee Convention for those who are fleeing the effects of civil war.

Both groups are treated in the same way for the purposes of asylum support under the scheme for providing support for asylum seekers established by the Immigration and Asylum Act 1999. For strictly immigration purposes, however, they are treated differently. Only those who fit the criteria under the 1951 Refugee Convention (see above), are recognized as refugees and granted leave under the asylum part of the immigration rules. Those who are allowed to remain under Article 3 ECHR are granted 'exceptional leave' (see Chapter 6).

Article 3 is not the only provision of the ECHR by which people may be allowed to stay in the UK. People commonly seek to rely upon Article 2 (right to life);

Article 5 (right to liberty); Article 6 (right to a fair trial); Article 8 (right to respect for family life – ie, in circumstances where a person may be separated from family members if not able to stay in the UK); Article 9 (freedom of religion and belief); Article 10 (freedom of expression). There has been some argument about whether a person can rely on human rights (other than Article 3) in relation to being removed to another country. The European caselaw is clear that where people are to be removed from the UK, Articles 2, 3,[16] 8[17] and possibly 6[18] apply. Following a decision by the Court of Appeal, the impact of the other human rights in the context of immigration decisions was uncertain.[19] The Immigration Appeal Tribunal has now confirmed that all the Articles do have extra–territorial effect.[20]

2. Asylum decisions

If the Home Office decides that the person is a refugee, then the s/he must be granted leave to enter or remain in the UK as a refugee. The immigration rules state that the person is to be granted limited leave[21] but, in practice, since July 1998,[22] refugees have immediately been granted indefinite leave to remain (before that time it was the practice of the Home Office to grant refugees four years' limited leave and then, upon their application, to grant indefinite leave after that time). The leave granted to a refugee is never such as to make her/him 'subject to immigration control' (see p157) and s/he is therefore not excluded from non-contributory benefits. Once recognised as a refugee, s/he may seek to backdate entitlement to benefit (see Chapter 16).

Also since July 1998,[23] those granted exceptional leave to remain, are granted limited leave for a period of four years after which time they are eligible to apply for indefinite leave. Before July 1998, exceptional leave was first granted for 12 months followed by two consecutive periods of three years so that after a period of seven years, the person would be eligible to apply for indefinite leave.

Those who already had been recognised as refugees or had been granted exceptional leave to remain by the time the changes were introduced in July 1998, also benefited from those changes. A refugee within the four-year limited leave period could apply immediately for indefinite leave and a person with limited exceptional leave became entitled to indefinite leave as soon as s/he had been in the UK with limited leave for four years.[24] The leave which is granted to those given exceptional leave on this basis generally is not given with a condition that the holder will not have recourse to public funds, nor on the basis of a maintenance undertaking, and so those with exceptional leave generally find themselves not subject to immigration control and therefore not excluded from benefit entitlement by their immigration status.

The decision to recognise a person as a refugee and to grant her/him asylum or to refuse to recognise her/him is not the same as the immigration decision which is subsequently made. The asylum decision is one which is made in accordance with the criteria set out above and which must be made by the Home Office's Asylum Directorate. If asylum is refused, the question of whether exceptional leave on the basis of ECHR or other humanitarian/compassionate reasons is also automatically given consideration by the caseworker at the Home Office (see Chapter 6 for the criteria). Once it is decided whether to accept or reject the application for asylum and, if rejected, whether to grant or refuse exceptional leave, the immigration consequences of the decision depend upon where in the immigration system the asylum applicant is. If the case is a 'port' claim (see p58), the papers are normally returned to the port in question by the Home Office for the implementation of the decision. If the decision is positive, and the case is a port case, leave to enter is granted. Otherwise, leave to remain is granted. If the decision is negative, the immigration authorities may, depending on the case, make any of the following immigration decisions:

- refuse leave to enter and set directions for the removal of the individual (where the person claimed asylum at port);
- set directions for removal of the asylum seeker as an illegal entrant (where the person entered the UK unlawfully and subsequently claimed asylum);
- set directions for the removal of a person as an overstayer (or in breach of their other conditions of leave – where the person entered lawfully but then claimed asylum having overstayed or breached their conditions of leave or obtained leave to *remain* by deception);
- refuse to extend leave so as to grant leave to remain as a refugee and/or to curtail existing leave (where the person makes an in-country claim for asylum within the period of a separate leave, eg, as a visitor);
- issue a notice of intention to deport a person (where the person claiming asylum is liable to be deported because the Secretary of State has determined that her/his presence is not conducive to the public good); *or*
- issue a deportation order (where the person claims asylum after notice of intention to deport has been issued or a court has recommended deportation as part of her/his sentence; s/he having been convicted of a criminal offence); *or*
- refuse to revoke a deportation order (where a person claims asylum after a deportation order has already been made).

For an explanation of the different processes for enforcing immigration control as part of these negative immigration decisions following the rejection of an asylum claim, you need to refer to Chapter 7.

The asylum refusal itself will be set out in a 'reasons for refusal letter', which gives the substantive reasons why asylum has been refused. This will be sent to the applicant, together with one of the administrative immigration decisions referred to above. If the refusal is based on the fact that the person is the responsibility of a third country, this will also be clear from the letter.

In addition, if an asylum application is refused, the caseworker will also decide whether to **'certify'** the claim to asylum and the claim to remain on human rights grounds.[25] Claims may be certified if the evidence adduced in support of the claim does not establish a reasonable likelihood that the person has been tortured in the country to which they are to be sent *and* one of a variety of other factors is met. Examples of the other conditions for certification are:

- the person failed to produce a valid passport on arrival without reasonable explanation;
- the claim does not even begin to show a case under either the 1951 Refugee Convention or the ECHR;
- the claim was made after an immigration enforcement decision (see above) had been made; *or*
- the claim is manifestly false or fraudulent.

The effect of certifying a claim is that if, on an appeal against the asylum decision, the immigration adjudicator agrees with the certificate, the asylum seeker is denied the right of appealing further, namely to the Immigration Appeal Tribunal.[26] Notice that the claim has been certified will be contained in the reasons for refusal letter. In its 2002 White Paper (see p15), the Government indicated that it would abolish these certificates to simplify the asylum process – it is not clear whether the new legislation will finally put an end to them.

3. Asylum support and the new procedures

In December 1999, the Government introduced a new national system for the support of asylum seekers under the Immigration and Asylum Act 1999.[27] The intention of the new system was to enable asylum seekers to be supported outside of the system of means-tested benefits and without recourse to the resources of local authorities under the National Assistance Act 1948. From 1996, asylum seekers who had not claimed asylum on arrival or had been refused and were waiting for their appeals to be determined were no longer supported through the means-tested benefits system and were therefore destitute. Support under the National Assistance Act was therefore forced to step in.

The new system introduced in 1999 is split into two:

- **Asylum support provided by the National Asylum Support Service (NASS).** NASS is part of the Home Office and is able to arrange for asylum seekers to be supported through different consortia of providers in 'dispersed' accommodation in different areas throughout the country. One of the main aims of the new system was to ensure that the pressure on London and the South East was reduced in favour of using less expensive accommodation in other parts of the country. The NASS part of the system came into operation on 3 April 2000 and all new asylum seekers are referred to NASS rather than to local authorities under the 'interim asylum support scheme' (below).

- **Asylum support provided by local authorities under the 'interim asylum support scheme'.** This came into operation on 6 December 1999 and complicated rules have been implemented to determine who was entitled to asylum support under this scheme and who was entitled to asylum support from NASS for the period after 3 April 2000. The interim scheme was intended to end in April 2002 when all existing asylum seekers still under the interim scheme would be transferred over to NASS. This will now not happen until at least April 2004. Those currently receiving interim asylum support, therefore, will continue to obtain it from local authorities for as long as they continue to qualify as destitute asylum seekers. We do not cover asylum support in this book other than in the outline given in this chapter. For further details about asylum support, you should consult LAG's *Support for Asylum Seekers*.

What can be provided as asylum support

Asylum support is provided in the form of accommodation, which must be adequate for the asylum seekers and their dependants and support to meet their 'essential living needs'. Under the NASS scheme there are scale rates for support for essential living needs for couples, single persons and lone parents. The rates also depend on the age of the asylum seekers. The rates represent 70 per cent of income support applicable amounts. The Home Office justifies this on the basis that asylum seekers will have the costs of utility bills and certain other expenses met through the provision of accommodation. The rates were uprated, in line with income support, from 8 April 2002.

Support can also be provided to assist asylum seekers with their expenses in pursuing their asylum claims (including travel to hearings and bail hearings) and services in the form of education (including English language lessons). The Home Office has the power to make available any other, exceptional, form of support which appears to be necessary. Interim asylum support is less well defined but is broadly intended to meet the same needs.

When the Government introduced the scheme, an important aspect of it was the provision of support in the form of vouchers. Faced with heavy criticism this policy has now been withdrawn and, following an internal review, NASS is no longer required to provide the majority of support in this form.[28] NASS has begun issuing vouchers which are redeemable for cash and it intends to phase out vouchers altogether by the end of 2002.

A further change which is proposed by the Nationality, Immigration and Asylum Bill 2002 (see p14) is to prevent asylum seekers from being able to access support for essential living needs only. This will mean that asylum seekers may be forced to accept NASS accommodation, wherever it may be, if they are to obtain any support for their living needs.

How long does asylum support continue

A destitute asylum seeker continues to obtain asylum support for as long as s/he is an asylum seeker for asylum support purposes. A person continues to have the status of 'asylum seeker' after s/he has made a claim for asylum under the 1951 Refugee Convention *or* Article 3 of European Convention on Human Rights (ECHR) (see p61). S/he maintains the status of asylum seeker for as long as there is no decision on her/his claim and throughout the immigration appeals process.[29]

If the asylum seeker has a child dependant living as part of her/his household, s/he continues to be an asylum seeker even after her/his appeals have been dealt with for as long as s/he remains in the UK or until the child reaches 18 years of age or leaves the household.[30]

When the Home Office (or on appeal, an immigration adjudicator or the Immigration Appeal Tribunal) makes a positive decision on an asylum seeker's case, that person ceases to be an asylum seeker and ceases, also, to be entitled to asylum support. In these circumstances, it is anticipated that the person will become entitled to benefit either because s/he is given the status of 'refugee' or because a decision has been taken that s/he should be granted 'exceptional leave' under the ECHR or for other humanitarian reasons. Although people in this position lose their entitlement to asylum support, however, they remain 'subject to immigration control' for benefit purposes until they are actually given a notice granting them leave.

The administrative decision to grant leave can often lag behind the decision of the Home Office or the appeal authorities to recognise someone as a refugee. Accordingly, when a positive decision on an asylum seeker's case is made and the person's status as an asylum seeker for support purposes comes to an end, there is a grace period while the person remains entitled to asylum support. This period is 28 days[31] (before 8 April 2002, it was 14 days) following:

- notification of a decision to grant asylum; *or*
- notification of a decision to refuse asylum but to grant exceptional leave; *or*
- the decision of the adjudicator or the Immigration Appeal Tribunal to allow an appeal against a decision of the immigration authorities.

After this time, even if the asylum or exceptional leave decision has not been implemented so that a person can obtain benefit, asylum support will cease.

In cases where negative immigration decisions are made which terminate asylum support, the grace period is now 21 days.[32] When this period runs out an asylum seeker faces destitution. S/he may be able to obtain support from the local authority under the National Assistance Act if s/he is elderly, disabled or ill.[33] In very restricted circumstances s/he may be able to obtain support from the NASS hard cases fund (see p67).

Hard cases support

NASS operates a 'hard cases' fund for those who are destitute and have ceased to be asylum seekers for the purposes of asylum support.[34] Support is provided in the form of accommodation and board outside London. It is, however, under NASS policy available only to a person:

- who is genuinely unable to leave the UK as a result of a physical impediment on her/his travelling, for example, illness or pregnancy; *or*
- whose circumstances are 'exceptional' and who is taking all reasonable steps to leave and is fully co-operating with the efforts of the immigration authorities to remove her/him; *or*
- who has been granted permission to apply for judicial review in relation to any decision concerning her/his asylum application *and* the Home Office does not think that the application is unfounded.

New procedures

The Nationality, Immigration and Asylum Bill 2002 (see p14) makes way for a modified asylum process with further implications for the support of asylum seekers. In summary it provides for an 'end-to-end' system whereby asylum seekers can be processed through a number of centres resulting in either their recognition as refugees and integration into the UK or removal to their country of origin. At least in its initial stages, the newly proposed procedures will not be used for all asylum seekers. For example, the new 'accommodation centres' are to operate on a trial basis for a proportion of asylum seekers. The criteria for referral to an accommodation centre are likely to include the asylum seeker's language, family circumstances and their port of arrival. The proposals are as follows:

- Asylum seekers will initially be placed in an '**induction centre**' where the asylum process and system of asylum support are explained to them. Asylum seekers can be required to stay in an induction centre for up to 14 days, whether or not they have other accommodation and support available to them. Those who do not need any support are likely to remain in the centre for only one day. Those who are to be referred to an accommodation centre (see below) are likely to stay in the induction centre for about two days. Those who are likely to be provided with 'ordinary' NASS support in dispersed accommodation will probably remain in the induction centre for up to ten days. The first induction centre opened in Dover on 21 January 2002.
- Those who are referred to an '**accommodation centre**' will receive all the support which they need in the centre – ie, food, cash, transport, medical facilities. Children of asylum seekers will be housed with them in the accommodation centres and will receive education there rather than in local education authority schools. Asylum seekers will be required to reside at the accommodation centre throughout the entire asylum process and will be

required to report regularly within the centre. Asylum seekers will not be detained (ie, held under lock and key), in either the induction or the accommodation centres, but if they refuse the offer of receiving their support and accommodation within an accommodation centre they can be refused 'ordinary' NASS support.

- **'Removal centre'** is the new label attached to immigration detention centres. The Home Office intends to greatly expand its detention estate and has re-designated detention centres under the name removal centres to emphasise that they are primarily intended as places where people (generally asylum seekers) are detained pending their removal from the UK. Following the failure of her/his asylum claim, a person may, therefore, be detained when s/he reports within her/his accommodation centre and be transferred to a removal centre to await removal from the UK.

4. The future of asylum

In addition to the innovations relating to induction centres and accommodation centres, noted above, the Government's immediate plans in relation to developing the asylum system are to:

- increase the numbers returns of failed asylum seekers;
- encourage further voluntary (rather than enforced) returns;
- increase the detention estate so that more asylum seekers may be detained;
- implement technological advances in X-ray and automated fingerprinting systems to stem illegal entry into the UK;
- deliver faster decisions to both facilitate removal in 'undeserving' cases and the integration of refugees accepted for settlement; *and*
- reform the existing arrangements for the determination of the country with responsibility for the determination of refugee status among the member states of the European Union (EU).[35]

A further aim of the Government, developed in a number of speeches during 2000/01[36] is, by agreement with the other EU countries, to harmonize across the EU both the procedures for determining refugee status and the interpretation given to the 1951 Refugee Convention as to who qualifies for refugee status.

Notes

1 Home Office, 'Asylum Statistics: December 2000'
2 This is partly because one of the criteria for qualifying as a refugee is that the applicant is 'outside their country of nationality or former habitual residence' (art 1A(2) 1951 Refugee Convention) although the Immigration & Nationality Directorate does, in very rare cases, consider applications for asylum from abroad outside the immigration rules where the UK is the most appropriate country of refuge
3 Convention Determining the State Responsible for Examining Applications for Asylum Lodged in One of the Member States of the European Communities, 15 June 1990, the 'Dublin Convention' – it is likely to be updated
4 ss11–12 IAA 1999; para 345 HC 395 as substituted by Cmnd 3365 from 1 September 1996 and amended from 2 October 2000 by Cmnd 4851 (the last complete statement of the immigration rules, 23 May 1994)

1. Consideration of cases
5 para 328 HC 395 under the criteria of the 1951 UN Convention
6 para 340 HC 395 and *Ali Haddad* [2000] INLR 117
7 *R on the application of Karaoglan v SSHD* CO/409/01; *Hadavi* CO/4634/00; *Bashiri*
8 para 8 – statement of reasons for consent order in the above joined cases, 4 May 2001
9 Further details of this litigation are contained in a detailed briefing from Gill & Co Solicitors enclosed in an 'Exceptional Mailing' to members of the Immigration Law Practitioners Association, 8 May 2001.
10 paras 334 and 345 HC 395 as amended by Cmnd Paper 3365 August 1996
11 Art 1A(2) UN Convention on Refugees 1951
12 para 345 HC 395; ss11–12 IAA 1999
13 The 'Dublin Convention' – see note 3
14 s11 IAA 1999
15 HRA 1998; para 2 HC 395 as amended by Cmnd 4851 from 2 October 2000

16 *Soering v UK* [1989] 11 EHRR 439
17 *Abdulaziz* [1985] 7 EHRR 471
18 *Soering v UK* [1989] 11 EHRR 439
19 *Holub v SSHD* [2001] INLR 219 LA
20 *Kacaj* [2001] INLR, [2002] Imm Ar 281 IAT

2. Asylum decisions
21 paras 330 and 335 HC 395
22 Home Office White Paper, *Fairer, Faster, Firmer* July 1998 and SSHD letter of 27 July 1998 to the Immigration Law Practitioners Association.
23 See note 22
24 Table set out in SSHD letter of 27 July 1998 to the Immigration Law Practitioners Association.
25 Sch 4 para 9 IAA 1999
26 Sch 4 para 9(2) IAA 1999

3. Asylum support and the new procedures
27 Part VI and Schs 8–10 IAA 1999
28 Asylum Support (Repeal) Order 2002; reg 4 AS(Amdt) Regs
29 s94 IAA 1999
30 s94(5) IAA 1999
31 reg 3 AS(Amdt) Regs; reg 4 AS(IP)Amdt Regs
32 reg 3 AS(Amdt) Regs; reg 4 AS(IP)Amdt Regs
33 *R (Murua) v Croydon LBC* CO/2463/01, 25 October 2001 (unreported); *R (Mani & others) v Lambeth LBC* [2002] EWHC (Admin) 18 April 2002
34 The legislative basis is s4 IAA 1999

4. The future of asylum
35 Home Office paper, *Asylum Reforms: next phase*, 23 March 2001; *Secure Borders, Safe Havens* White Paper 2002
36 See Rt Hon Jack Straw MP, previously Secretary of State for the Home Department, speech to the Foreign Press Association on 25 April 2001

6

Chapter 6

Exceptional leave

This chapter covers:
1. Meaning of exceptional leave (below)
2. Importance of exceptional leave (p71)
3. Narrow meaning of exceptional leave (p71)
4. Other circumstances when exceptional leave may be granted (p73)

1. Meaning of exceptional leave

There is no definition of exceptional leave and the only real way to understand the concept is in relation to leave that is granted under the immigration rules which, by contrast, is ordinary leave. The immigration rules are rules of practice[1] forming the minimum level of treatment those applying for leave can expect to receive. The immigration authorities are, however, able to treat persons more favourably than the immigration rules allow.[2] Immigration advisers often talk of the Home Office's discretion to 'depart from' the immigration rules or to 'waive' the rules or 'act outside' the rules. Whenever applicants are treated more beneficially than the immigration rules allow, they can be said to be treated 'exceptionally' – ie, granted exceptional leave to enter if the person has not already entered the UK or exceptional leave to remain if they have already entered. 'Exceptional leave to remain' is the term most frequently loosely used to cover both. Immigration officers and entry clearance officers can also treat people more beneficially than the rules allow although they generally do so at the direction of the Home Office.[3]

Although everyone who is not held to the letter of the immigration rules may be said to be treated exceptionally, there is a narrower sense in which the term 'exceptional leave' (see p71) is used in immigration law. This is to describe leave granted to asylum seekers who are not found to be refugees but the Home Office, for humanitarian or compassionate reasons, determines it would not be right to require to return them to the country from which they have come.

It is impossible to define all the circumstances in which a person may be said to have been granted exceptional leave. This is the case, in particular, because a waiver of any one requirement of the rules which if applied would lead to a refusal under the immigration rules, will mean that leave has been granted exceptionally.

This may occur as an act of individual discretion in a particular case or it may result from a case forming part of a group of similar cases in which the Home Office has a declared a general policy or practice of treating more favourably than the rules allow. More and more of these groups are being incorporated as new categories of entry within the framework of the immigration rules.

A further difficulty of identifying people who have been granted leave exceptionally is that, aside from the narrowly defined exceptional leave, the actual grant of leave itself is unlikely to indicate that it has been granted exceptionally and advisers must look for clues in the correspondence between the applicant and her/his immigration advisers and the Home Office. The examples of exceptional leave set out in the remainder of this chapter, indicate the circumstances to look out for.

2. Importance of exceptional leave

The question of whether you have exceptional leave to enter or remain (ELR) in the UK is perhaps not as important as it was before 3 April 2000. Before that date, the benefit regulations specifically provided favourably for those with exceptional leave. However, the new test of being 'subject to immigration control' for benefit purposes under the Immigration and Asylum Act 1999 (see p14), does not treat those who have exceptional leave differently or specially from other groups. The definition of a 'person who is subject to immigration control' includes those who have leave to enter or remain in the UK given subject to a condition that they do not have recourse to public funds.[4] People who have ELR could in principle have that leave made subject to such a condition since the power to impose these conditions[5] and the immigration rules themselves[6] give no guidance as to when conditions should and should not be attached to leave.

It is, however, very unlikely that a person who has been granted exceptional leave will be given a condition that s/he is not to have recourse to public funds. A person who has been granted leave exceptionally but whose leave is subject to a condition that s/he should not have recourse to public funds, or it was granted on the basis of a maintenance undertaking so that s/he is 'subject to immigration control', should seek specialist advice about applying to the Home Office to remove the condition.

Whether you have exceptional leave is also relevant to the question of whether you are exempt from the habitual residence test which remains important for your benefit entitlement (see p135).

3. Narrow meaning of exceptional leave

There is a narrow and more common use of the term exceptional leave (ELR) which refers to the immigration status of a person who has applied for and been refused refugee status, but who the Home Office nonetheless believes is in need of some sort of protection. Whenever the Home Office refuses an application for asylum as a refugee, it will always consider whether to grant ELR instead.[7]

The circumstances in which exceptional leave may be granted following the failure of an asylum application are stated by the Home Office to be 'where the 1951 Refugee Convention requirements are not met but return to the country of origin would result in the applicant being subject to torture or other cruel or inhuman or degrading treatment or the unjustifiable break up of family life'.[8] The examples given by the Home Office are:[9]

- where there are grounds for believing that you will suffer a serious and disproportionate punishment for a criminal offence;
- your medical condition is such that your return to the country concerned would result in your being subjected to acute physical and mental suffering due to the standard of medical facilities in the country and where your life expectancy would be reduced. It must also be clear from the circumstances of the case, that the UK can be said to have assumed responsibility for your care;
- you do not satisfy the UN 1951 Refugee Convention but there are compassionate or humanitarian reasons why you should not return to your country of origin.

It also often the case that the Home Office will adopt a policy of granting exceptional leave to people who are nationals of particular countries undergoing severe upheavals or periods of instability. At different times this has applied to nationals of Afghanistan, Iran, Lebanon, Poland, Uganda, El Salvador, Bosnia, Sri Lanka and Somalia. The list of such countries changes from time to time and it is available on the Home Office website in the Asylum Policy Instructions at Annex A to Chapter 5. For example, there is a situation of civil war in the country from which you come, although you may be a target for serious physical harm or death by one of the opposing sides because of your clan, religion or ethnicity, because of a decision of the House of Lords[10] you are not a refugee within the 1951 Convention. However, it is very likely that you will qualify for exceptional leave in these circumstances even if the country from which you come is not actually on the list.

The above conditions for getting exceptional leave following an asylum application reflect certain rights derived from the European Convention on Human Rights (ECHR). Most of the rights which are protected by the ECHR are, from 2 October 2000, incorporated into UK law.[11] The most important rights as far as exceptional leave is concerned are Article 3 (no one shall be subject to inhuman or degrading treatment or punishment), Article 2 (right to life) and Article 8 (right to respect for private/family life). Although these rights are part of the law, it is surprising that they have not been specifically set out as a basis for being granted leave in the immigration rules.[12] Accordingly, people who are granted leave on a human rights basis, may still be said to be granted 'exceptional leave'.[13]

Before July 1998, exceptional leave was first granted for 12 months followed by two consecutive periods of three years so that, after a period of seven years, the person would be eligible to apply for indefinite leave. However, since July 1998, a person who is granted exceptional leave is given four years' limited leave in the first instance and is eligible for indefinite leave after that time.[14] The Home Office has indicated that it may, however, now revert to temporary forms of protection in certain cases. In countries where the position is expected to improve or where there is a present practical inability to return people, the Home Office is likely to begin granting periods of 12 months' exceptional leave and then review the position after that time. Nationals of Afghanistan and Kurds from the autonomous region of Northern Iraq may find themselves in this situation, as may Somalis.

The Secretary of State's policy is that the spouses and children of people granted this form of exceptional leave, who are abroad, may apply to join their sponsor in the UK after the sponsor has been in the UK for four years with exceptional leave. These dependants must still, however, satisfy the other provisions of the immigration rules, including the requirement that they can be maintained and accommodated without recourse to public funds. An application may be considered earlier than four years if there are 'exceptional compassionate circumstances'.

4. **Other circumstances when exceptional leave may be granted**

As well as individual cases where the Home Office may treat a person exceptionally, there are some common situations where the Home Office has a set policy of acting outside the confines of the immigration rules. Where you fall into one of these groups, the Home Office is generally bound to treat you exceptionally. This is because, as a matter of fairness, people in similar circumstances should be treated similarly. Therefore, when the Home Office acts outside the rules, it must have regard to its own established policies or practices. These may:

- relate to persons in particular circumstances or to nationals of particular countries;
- become known in the form of guidance or instructions, letters or statements (although most policies are now contained in the Home Office's publicly available instructions to its own staff, the *Immigration Directorate Instructions* and *Asylum Policy Instructions*).

It is open to the Home Office to simply incorporate well established policies into the immigration rules (for example, unmarried and same sex partners were previously contained in a policy but are now provided for under the immigration rules).[15] It remains unclear why the Home Office does not simply incorporate all of the policies into the immigration rules, particularly as the courts have made it clear that, when a person appeals to the immigration appellate authorities, they too may have regard to policies when deciding immigration appeals.[16] The Secretary of State is, of course, not under the same duty to announce policy changes in Parliament as must be done when a change is made to the immigration rules which may be disapproved by either House of Parliament.[17]

The following is a non-exhaustive list of circumstances where the Secretary of State commonly acts outside the immigration rules.

Family reunion with refugees for applicants other than spouse and minor children

Spouses and minor children may be admitted under the immigration rules themselves.[18] Adult dependent children, elderly parents or other close dependent family members, may also be admitted depending on their particular circumstances but they would be admitted outside the immigration rules.[19] In the case of Somali nationals, the family reunion provision was at one stage extended to other family members if they had been 'dependent members' of the sponsor's family unit before the sponsor came to the UK.[20]

Long residence concessions

In deciding whether to enforce departure from the UK, the Home Office will have regard to the length of continuous residence in the UK. If you have remained lawfully within the UK for a continuous period of 10 years (you are allowed sporadic short absences of up to six months abroad), you may expect your application for indefinite leave to remain in the UK to be considered sympathetically, even if you do not meet any of the requirements for settlement under the rules. If you can show that you have remained continuously in the UK lawfully or unlawfully for a period of 14 years or more, then, provided there are no very strong 'countervailing factors' (such as a blatant disregard for the immigration law), you may expect to be granted indefinite leave.[21]

Enforcement action involving family and children

Where the Home Office is considering enforcing a person's departure, there may be prevailing compassionate family reasons why people should be allowed to remain in the UK and granted exceptional leave accordingly. The immigration rules prohibit a person who is in the UK from being given leave to remain as a spouse if s/he does not have limited leave at the time that s/he applies, or if s/he has breached the immigration law.[22]

In March 1993, the Home Office issued internal guidance to its officers detailing the circumstances involving marriage or children where, even though a person does not have leave and her/his departure may be enforced under the immigration rules, it would not be correct to proceed to enforce departure.[23] The instructions were changed and became more restrictive with effect from March 1996.[24] Part of the purpose of these instructions is to ensure that immigration decisions are in line with the UK's obligations under Article 8 of the European Convention on Human Rights (ECHR), namely the right to respect for private and family life. The most important part of this policy states that a husband or wife will not usually be required to leave the UK (and will therefore be granted leave) 'where the subject has a genuine and subsisting marriage with someone settled here and the couple have lived together in this country continuously since their marriage for at least two years before the commencement of enforcement action *and* it is not reasonable to expect the settled spouse to accompany her/his spouse on removal.'

In addition, where a child has been resident in the UK for seven or more years, neither the child nor her/his parents will normally be required to return to their country of origin.[25] However, this will not automatically apply, the Home Office will always consider all of the relevant circumstances of the case.

Elderly dependent relatives

Dependent relatives in the UK, aged 65 or over, of sponsors with settled status in the UK, are generally granted indefinite leave to remain without detailed enquiries, provided a maintenance undertaking is provided by the sponsor.[26] Note that this does not help elderly people applying for leave to enter or entry clearance.

People who have HIV, AIDS or another serious illness

The only really beneficial part of Home Office policy relating to those who have HIV/AIDS applies to those who have already entered the UK and are applying to stay in the UK. They are not covered by the immigration rules in any application to stay in the UK to receive NHS treatment. Leave will be granted exceptionally if:[27]

- the UK can be regarded as having assumed responsibility for the person's care; *and*
- there is credible evidence that return to the country of origin, due to a complete absence of medical treatment in the country concerned, would significantly reduce the applicant's life expectancy; *and*
- the applicant would face acute physical and mental suffering if returned.

The policy does not really give any greater benefit to applicants than the UK's obligations under Article 3 ECHR. The policy also applies to those who have 'serious illnesses', which for these purposes is defined as any condition which is 'seriously debilitating, terminal or life threatening'.

Domestic violence concession

Spouses are initially admitted to the UK for a 'probationary period' of 12 months after which, if the marriage continues to subsist, the partner from abroad may apply for indefinite leave. Some husbands have been known to take advantage of the vulnerability of a woman's position during this period resulting in domestic abuse. In order to enable people trapped in such relationships to leave their spouse but still be permitted to remain in the UK, the Home Office introduced the domestic violence concession to enable leave to be granted exceptionally.[28]

In order to benefit from the concession, the applicant needs to show that the marriage has broken down *as a result of* domestic violence during the 12-month period. However, the policy is very restrictive because the violence itself needs to be proved by one of the following pieces of evidence:

- a court injunction, non-molestation order or other protection order (other than an *ex parte* or 'interim' order); *or*
- a criminal conviction against the abusive spouse; *or*
- a police caution issued to the abusive spouse.

It should also be noted that the 2002 White Paper (see p15) proposes to increase the probationary period for spouses from 12 months to 24 months.

Domestic servants and overseas domestic workers

Domestic servants/overseas domestic workers who are aged over 18 are able to accompany their employers to the UK in order to continue to work for their employer in this country without having to comply with the work permit scheme. The worker must have worked for the employer overseas for at least 12 months preceding the date of the application and must apply for entry clearance before coming to the UK.[29] The Home Office has introduced measures at the entry clearance stage so as to ensure that such workers are provided with proper maintenance and accommodation by their employers and are not otherwise exploited. Although, at present, this is a category of exceptional leave, it is likely to be incorporated into the immigration rules when the next main statement of immigration rules is issued.

Carers

Special concessions are made outside the rules for people present with leave in a temporary capacity who seek to remain in the UK to care for a friend or relative who is suffering from a terminal illness or is mentally ill or disabled.[30]

Other circumstances

Help outside the rules has also been given to certain adoptive children, children under 12 seeking to join a single parent settled in the UK and people who lose their appeals but are granted a discretionary 'recommendation' by the immigration adjudicator.

Not all Home Office policies and practices relate to the grant of leave itself. For example, dependants of students are generally prohibited from working if they are granted less than 12 months' leave.[31] However, where a student would have qualified for more than 12 months' leave at the date of the application but, because of delays in dealing with the application, less than 12 months was granted, the immigration minister has said that discretion can be exercised not to impose an employment prohibition on the leave given to the dependant.

Notes

1. **Meaning of exceptional leave**
   1 *Pearson v IAT* [1978] Imm AR 212
   2 This is either as a result of a statutory discretion (s4(1) IA 1971) or prerogative powers.
   3 Sch 4 para 21(4) IAA 1999; Sch 2 para 1(3) IA 1971; *R v SSHD ex parte Hosenball* [1977] WLR 766; *Pearson v IAT* [1978] Imm AR 212

2. **Importance of exceptional leave**
   4 s115(9)(b) IAA 1999
   5 s3(1)(c)(ii) IA 1971
   6 para 8 HC 395 (the last complete statement of the immigration rules, 23 May 1994)

3. **Narrow meaning of exceptional leave**
   7 Home Office evidence given in case *R v SSHD ex parte Alakesan*, unreported, 22 April 1996 QBD and see current API
   8 Chapter 5, s1 para 2 API; note that this is the policy as set out in the last revision of the published criteria. In early 2002, the API were being updated on this issue.
   9 See note 8
   10 *Adan* [1999] 1 AC 293
   11 Human Rights Act 1998
   12 A statement amending the immigration rules, Cmnd 4851, had effect from 2 October 2000, the same day that the rights guaranteed by the ECHR became part of UK law, but simply inserted a general statement into the rules that the immigration authorities must carry out their duties 'in compliance with the provisions of the Human Rights Act 1998'.

   13 See para 4.90 White Paper 2002; Chapter 5, s4 para 4.3 API where the Home Office states this explicitly.
   14 SSHD policy letter of 27 July 1998 to the Immigration Law Practitioners Association and 1998 White Paper *Fairer, Faster, Firmer*.

4. **Other circumstances when exceptional leave may be granted**
   15 paras 295A–295M HC 395 as inserted by para 32 HC 704
   16 *DS Abdi* [1996] Imm AR 148 LA
   17 s3(2) IA 1971
   18 para 352A–352F HC 395 as inserted by para 50 Cmnd 4851
   19 Chapter 6, s2 para 2 API and see *UNHCR Handbook*, para 185
   20 Letter from Home Office to Tower Hamlets Law Centre 17 May 1990; reported also at [1993] Imm AR 40
   21 Chapter 18 IDI. The concessions are based on the principles of the European Convention on Establishment ratified by the UK in October 1969.
   22 para 284 HC 395
   23 Home Office internal instructions, DP/2/93
   24 Home Office internal instructions, DP/3/96
   25 Home Office internal instructions, DP/069/99
   26 Chapter 8, s6 IDI
   27 Chapter 1, s8 IDI
   28 Chapter 8, s1 IDI
   29 Chapter 5, s12 IDI
   30 Chapter 17, s2 IDI
   31 para 77 HC 395

Chapter 7

· ·

Enforcement and appeals

This chapter provides a summary of the main problems people may face under immigration law if they wish to enter or remain in the UK but have had their application to do so refused by the immigration authorities, who then proceed to enforce their departure from the UK; and the rights of appeal which are available against negative immigration decisions. It covers:

1. Deportation, illegal entry and removal (below)
2. Refusals and appeals (p83)

---

1. **Deportation, illegal entry and removal**

If you are in the UK and you need leave to enter or remain here (see p29), but you cannot satisfy the immigration rules, then the immigration authorities have the power to enforce your departure. There are also possible criminal penalties if you are in breach of immigration control, although criminal court cases are not frequent. The immigration authorities also have wide powers of detention to assist with regulating control and enforcement. Detention powers may be used against individuals, whether or not they are charged with any offence, either immigration or otherwise. Much criticism has been directed at the widespread and apparently arbitrary use of these powers. There is a suspicion that powers of detention have been used for the wider purpose of punishment and deterrence rather than for the narrow purposes of enforcement for which they are strictly provided.

'**Deportation**' means sending people away from the UK under an order signed by the Secretary of State and forbidding their re-entry. Before 2 October 2000, deportation powers were used to enforce the departure from the UK of people who had been granted leave to enter or remain the UK but who then overstayed that leave or broke a condition which had been imposed on their leave; who obtained leave to *remain* by deception; or who were involved in other (often criminal) conduct which merited their being forced to leave. The circumstances in which deportation is used are now much fewer (see below).

Many people who would previously have been deported are now subjected to a much faster process of 'administrative removal'. The process of '**administrative removal**' is very similar to both the removal of persons who arrive in the UK and who are not granted leave to enter and to the removal of those who the Secretary of State decides have entered the UK illegally and are known as **'illegal entrants'**. The basic four methods of enforcing a person's departure from the UK can be described as:

- removal following refusal of entry (see below);
- deportation (see below);
- administrative removal (see p81); *and*
- removal of illegal entrants (see p81).

The form which this 'enforcement' takes for different people depends on their immigration status.

Removal following refusal of entry

If you arrive in the UK and you are refused leave to enter in whatever category you apply to come in (for example, as a visitor, student, refugee), the process by which you may be forced to leave the UK is known simply as **'removal'**. Removal does not have to take place immediately after you arrive in the UK. It may not be possible to make a decision on whether you should be granted leave to enter straight away and you may have a right of appeal before you can be removed. In refugee cases, the process can often take years before you may be removed. During the time you are waiting for, or appealing against, a decision to refuse to grant you leave to enter, you are not treated as having actually entered the UK.[1] During this period you may either be granted temporary admission to the UK (this is a licence to be in the UK which may be granted subject to conditions as to work, address etc – see p113) or detained.[2] This process, therefore, applies to people who present themselves to the immigration officer when they arrive but who are, either immediately or eventually, refused entry.

Deportation

People who are not British citizens or do not have the right of abode can, in principle, be deported. Other people exempt from deportation include:

- diplomats;[3]
- certain Commonwealth nationals and citizens of the Republic of Ireland who were ordinarily resident in the UK on 1 January 1973;[4] *and*
- people who become British citizens after the deportation process has commenced.[5]

The rules relating to deportation changed on 2 October 2000 subject to some transitional provisions.[6] If the immigration authorities decide to enforce your departure from the UK on or after this date, you can only be deported if you fall into one of the following groups:[7]

- the Secretary of State decides that your deportation is conducive to the public good;

- you have overstayed leave which was granted to you (see p49), *and, before 2 October 2000, you made a valid application to the Secretary of State to 'regularise' your stay in the UK* (the application must have been made setting out certain required information);[8]
- you have been convicted of an imprisonable offence and a criminal court makes a recommendation that you be deported; *or*
- you are the family member (spouse or child under 18) of a person in any of the above categories who is to be deported.

It is up to the Home Office to prove that there are grounds to deport you.[9] The immigration rules[10] state that when the Home Office considers whether to deport people, it must take into account all relevant factors known, including:

- age;
- length of residence in the UK;
- strength of connections with the UK;
- personal history, including character, conduct and employment record;
- domestic circumstances;
- the nature of any offence of which the person has been convicted;
- previous criminal record;
- compassionate circumstances;
- any representations received on the person's behalf.

If you are to be deported as a member of the family of someone who is to be deported, the Home Office must also consider whether you are able to maintain and accommodate yourself, and in the case of children, the effect on your education and the practical arrangements for your care in the UK if your parents are deported.[11] If you already have permission to stay indefinitely, or were living apart from the person who is to be deported, your deportation would not normally be considered.[12]

Normally, the first step in the deportation process is for the Home Office to make a decision in principle to deport you. When the Home Office makes this decision it must inform you in writing, normally on a standard letter (APP 104). There is a right of appeal (see p83). At present, however, where a person is being deported following a recommendation by a criminal court, the Home Office proceeds directly to making the deportation order if it decides to follow the recommendation. The two-stage process to even this form of deportation is likely to be introduced by the Nationality, Immigration and Asylum Bill 2002 (see p14).

If the appeal is lost, the Home Secretary can then sign a deportation order and force you to leave.[13] If you are deported, you cannot return unless the deportation order is revoked. Usually you have to be outside the UK for at least three years before the Home Office will consider this. After the order has been revoked, you would once again need to satisfy the ordinary requirements of the immigration rules in order to re-enter.[14]

Administrative removal

The new powers of administrative removal, in force from 2 October 2000, apply to many people who would previously have been liable to deportation (see above). You are liable to be administratively removed after 2 October 2000 if:[15]

- you were allowed to enter or remain in the UK for a certain length of time and have overstayed your leave to enter or remain *and you did not apply to the Secretary of State to regularise you stay in the UK before 2 October 2000*;
- you have broken a condition of your leave – eg, you have worked when prohibited from doing so, or you have claimed a public funds benefit when you had a condition stating that you must maintain and accommodate yourself without recourse to public funds. After your leave has expired, there can no longer be any question of any conditions applying because the conditions can only be attached to the leave itself (although after leave has expired, you will become an overstayer);
- you obtained leave to *remain* in the UK by deception. This ground was introduced on 1 October 1996;[16] *or*
- you are the spouse, or the child under 18, of a person who is to be deported.[17]

The Home Office may obtain evidence about breaching conditions from an employer (about working without permission) or from the DWP (about claiming benefits in breach of your conditions).

Unlike deportation, there are not two stages to administrative removal. You may be removed after the immigration officer sets directions for your removal. The rights of appeal before you can be removed are less comprehensive than for those who are being deported. You only have an in-country right of appeal on human rights or asylum grounds. Although your appeal rights are less extensive, it is important to note that, before you can be removed under these powers, the Home Office must consider the same general factors relating to you as in deportation cases (see p83).[18] Detailed representations referring to these factors should, therefore, be made.

Illegal entry

The Secretary of State can decide to treat you as an illegal entrant if you:[19]

- avoid the immigration officers altogether (this is sometimes known as 'clandestine' entry – ie, arriving in the back of a lorry or in a sealed container and passing through controls without being examined by the immigration officer);
- enter while a deportation order is in force against you; *or*
- obtain entry by deceiving an immigration officer about your identity or your reasons for coming to the UK.

The last is the most common ground for being considered an illegal entrant.[20] A person will often have stamps on her/his passport which state that s/he has been granted leave to enter and will not understand how s/he can be illegal. The Home Office or the immigration service may say that s/he told lies when applying for permission to enter. There is often no evidence to support the Home Office view, so it relies heavily on questioning people about their entry and using their answers against them. Those who use false passports or other identity documents (for example, European Economic Area (EEA) national travel documents) are also illegal entrants. You may also be an illegal entrant where, although you used no deception yourself, someone else told lies in order to secure your entry. This can happen in cases where family members or sponsors have made inaccurate statements to an immigration officer or an entry clearance officer.

If you are treated as an illegal entrant, you will be informed in writing on Form IS 151. The way the Home Office and the courts interpret illegal entry has been extended over recent years. Illegal entrants are also removed from the UK, although illegal entry has become less used since the introduction of administrative removal (see above). This is because those who are administratively removed can be required to leave just as quickly as illegal entrants and with just as few appeal rights. The immigration authorities do not gain any advantage, therefore, by declaring those who can be administratively removed, as 'illegal entrants'.

In cases of removal after being refused leave to enter, administrative removal and illegal entry, the Home Office may try to act very quickly. It is necessary for you or your advisers to act promptly in making representations. The Home Office may delay removing you while the case is being considered, particularly if your MP has agreed to take it up. You may also be able to apply for judicial review of the decision. While representations are being considered, or a judicial review is pending, arrangements for your removal will be delayed. If you are released on temporary admission while your case is considered, you will be told the terms and conditions of your release on Form IS 96.

When there are strong compassionate or family reasons why you should be allowed to stay in the UK, representations can be made to the Home Office to exercise discretion to treat you exceptionally and grant leave to enter or remain, even if there is no way of contesting the power to remove you.

Other enforcement procedures

There are various other procedures which may be invoked in order to enforce the departure of individuals in certain circumstances:

* European Union/EEA nationals may be removed from the UK if they cease to exercise free movement rights or if their removal is justified on grounds of public policy, public security or public health.[21]
* People who are members of the armed forces of various friendly states may be arrested, detained and removed from the UK if a request is made by the country concerned.[22]

- Certain people who are receiving in-patient treatment for mental illness may also be removed from the UK with the approval of a mental health review tribunal provided that proper arrangements have been made for their treatment and it is in the interests of the person to be removed.[23]
- People whose return is requested by foreign authorities in respect of criminal offences may be removed from the UK in a procedure known as 'extradition'. This is a large subject with rules of its own. It is not a common occurrence.[24]

Working unlawfully

From 27 January 1997, it has been an offence for an employer to employ someone who is not permitted to work in the UK.[25] It is unlawful for an employer to employ a person who:

- has not been granted leave to enter or remain in the UK; *or*
- has overstayed their leave; *or*
- has leave containing a condition prohibiting her/him from taking the particular job.

It is not unlawful, however, for an employer to employ an asylum seeker who has been given written permission to work by the immigration authorities.

Furthermore, employers will not be legally liable if, before the employment started, they saw and kept a copy of one of a number of specified documents relating to the employee. Such documents include an official document containing the person's national insurance number (eg, a P45), as well as passports and Home Office letters which indicate that the employee is lawfully able to work in the UK.[26] The offence only relates to people who started jobs from 27 January 1997.

2. **Refusals and appeals**

When you apply to come to, or remain in the UK, the immigration authorities may grant or refuse your application. If the Home Office considers that you satisfy the requirements of the immigration rules in the particular category in which you are applying, you should be granted permission to come or to stay here (see Chapter 3). If you do not fit into the rules but the Home Office believes there are good reasons, usually of a compassionate or family nature, to make an exception to the rules, you may be granted permission to enter or remain exceptionally (see Chapter 6). Otherwise, your application will be refused. Depending on the nature of the application and whether or not it was validly made while you had permission to be in the UK, there may be a formal right of appeal against a refusal. The immigration authorities can also make decisions without any application being made to them which affect people's immigration status and against which there may be a right of appeal.

When people can appeal

There are rights to appeal against many immigration decisions and against most asylum refusals. When such decisions are made, you should be given:[27]

- notice of the decision and the reasons for it; *and*
- essential information concerning your rights of appeal – eg, the time limit for appealing and the place to which the notice of appeal should be sent.

There are very strict time limits laid down in special procedure rules with regard to lodging appeals. These time limits are important because the right of appeal may be lost if the forms are not received in time. When you have been refused, therefore, and have a right of appeal, the first thing to check is the date of refusal. This is to ensure that any appeal is still in time. In order to ensure that there is proof that the forms have been sent back, they should be posted by recorded delivery to addresses in the UK and by registered post abroad.

It is not always necessary to give full details of the reasons for the appeal; the grounds of appeal may be a bald statement such as, 'the decision is not in accordance with the immigration law and rules applicable and discretion ought to have been exercised differently', or 'the appellant qualifies as a refugee under the terms of the UN Convention'. There are, however, exceptions to this. In some circumstances you will be given a **'one–stop'** appeal notice which invites you to set out any grounds upon which you wish to remain in the UK which have not been raised previously with the Home Office. One-stop notices are issued to people who make a human rights or asylum claim in the UK. They are also issued to anyone who has made any immigration application which has been refused and against which they have an in-country right of appeal. If there are further reasons why you wish to stay in the UK, you should set these out in full.

If you are given a notice of refusal or directions for removal or a notice relating to deportation and, in particular if you want to appeal, you should immediately seek further specialist advice. The Immigration Advisory Service and the Refugee Legal Centre are funded by the Home Office to provide free appeal representation; law centres and other specialist advice centres may be able to give free help as can solicitors who have a contract to do immigration work under the Community Legal Service (see Appendix 1).

Situations where people have appeal rights

The system of appeal rights was revised from 2 October 2000.[28] There are also rules of procedure to be followed during appeals.[29] The Nationality, Immigration and Asylum Bill 2002 (see p14) proposes further changes, although the basics of the system will remain the same. If you claim to be able to remain in the UK on grounds of asylum or under the European Convention on Human Rights (ECHR), then, in general, there is a right of appeal while you remain in the UK (see p86).

Outside the UK

When entry clearance is refused at a British embassy or high commission abroad, there may be a right of appeal from abroad against that decision. Visitors (except for those coming to visit a family member) may not appeal against refusals of entry clearance, nor can students coming to study a course of six months or less, or those who are intending to study but have not yet been accepted on a course. In addition, there is an appeal right exercisable from abroad against some refusals of leave to enter where you have no current entry clearance or work permit when you arrived in the UK.[30]

If you are removed from the UK as an illegal entrant or under the immigration officer's new powers of 'administrative removal', you may appeal against the directions to remove you (after you have already been removed!) on the very narrow basis that there was no legal power to remove you on the ground given by the immigration officer.[31]

You may also appeal from abroad (again after you have been removed) if you have claimed asylum but the Home Office has decided that it is safe to remove you to a European Union country under the Dublin Convention or to another specified *safe* third country (namely Canada, the USA, Norway or Switzerland).[32] There is an in-country right of appeal in these cases where the removal is not to any of these countries *or* where the applicant alleges that her/his removal to the third country would breach her/his human rights. But even where the applicant alleges a breach of human rights, the Home Office can still deny an in-country appeal by declaring the claim to be 'manifestly unfounded'.

At the port

When you are refused entry at a British port, there may be a right of appeal. If you obtained entry clearance or a work permit you may usually remain in the UK while the appeal is under consideration. If you did not have entry clearance or a work permit, you can only appeal after you have returned.[33] You may also appeal against a refusal to grant you refugee status or on human rights grounds[34] when you are denied entry at the port.

After entry to the UK

When the Home Office refuses you permission to stay longer in the UK after you make an in-time application (see p38), there is a right of appeal against the decision.[35]

When the Home Office makes a notice of intention to deport you for any reason, there is a right of appeal.[36] If you were last granted leave to enter the UK less than seven years before the date of the decision and the appeal is against a notice of intention to deport you on grounds of overstaying or breach of conditions, the appeal is only on the legal facts of the case. This will, of course, now only apply to notices of intention to deport issued before 2 October 2000 and notices of intention to deport issued after that time where a 'regularisation' application was made before 2 October 2000 (see p79).[37] For example, if you have been in the UK for less than seven years and you are being deported because you have overstayed, you can only argue at the appeal that you did not in fact overstay and the Home Office had granted you leave to be here. The appeal cannot consider any family or compassionate reasons why you should not be deported.

You may also appeal while you are in the UK against a decision to refuse to allow you to remain as a refugee under the 1951 Refugee Convention or against any decision to require you to leave the UK after you have claimed asylum. You can also appeal after you have entered the UK, against any immigration decision which you allege is in breach of your human rights.[38]

Human rights appeals and 'one-stop' appeals

There is a right of appeal for any person who alleges that a decision taken by the immigration authorities relating to her/his right to enter or remain in the UK is 'in breach of [her/his] human rights' or which racially discriminates against her/him.[39] The appeal may be brought on these grounds alone or, alternatively, human rights grounds may be argued in the course of any other appeal.[40] They may be brought against *any* immigration decision which concerns a person's right to be in the UK (except a decision relating to nationality) and may be brought before or after a person has entered the UK or after s/he has been removed. As with claims to be a refugee, all the provisions restricting and excluding appeal rights, need to be considered subject to a claim being made under the ECHR.

A decision which is in breach of an individual's 'human rights' means a decision which is in contravention of her/his rights under the ECHR, incorporated into UK law by the Human Rights Act 1998.[41] The most important rights affecting immigration decisions are the right to respect for private and family life (which may be interfered with by immigration decisions which cause separation between family members) (Article 8), and the prohibition on subjecting people to torture or inhuman or degrading treatment or punishment (Article 3). This will be contravened if the Home Office proposes to send a person to another country where s/he will be subjected to that treatment (see p61 for the differences between Article 3 and the 1951 Refugee Convention).

Whenever a person has a right of appeal against a decision which may be exercised in the UK after 2 October 2000, s/he is given a notice telling her/him that s/he must give notice of any further grounds upon which s/he wishes to stay in the UK, which the immigration authorities and, on the appeal, the appellate authorities may consider.[42] This is the opportunity for the appellant to raise any further grounds which may be human rights grounds or other compassionate grounds relating to the exercise of the immigration authorities' discretion outside the immigration rules (see Chapter 6) possibly on the basis of one of the Home Office's written concessions. This 'one-stop' notice is also issued to people who make an asylum or human rights claim.[43] The matter can then be dealt with together with the matters raised in the other appeal under a one-stop appeal. If you fail to raise your further grounds at this stage, you may be prevented from raising them later.[44]

Exclusions from appeals

Visitors, prospective students and short-term students

Visitors, prospective students and students coming for courses of six months or less have no right of appeal against being refused entry clearance abroad (unless they are a 'family visitor') or against being refused entry at a port if they have no entry clearance for these purposes.[45]

Mandatory refusals

When a refusal is mandatory under the immigration rules there is no right of appeal against a decision to refuse to grant leave to enter or to grant extensions of leave.[46] A mandatory refusal relates to people who:

- do not have a document specified as required under the immigration rules – ie, entry clearance, passport or other identity document, or work permit; *or*
- do not meet a requirement of the rules as to age, nationality or citizenship. For example, a working holidaymaker must be a Commonwealth national aged between 17 and 27. A 29-year-old Romanian who applied for entry as a working holidaymaker would have no right of appeal against refusal (the 2002 White Paper (see p15) proposes changes to the working holidaymaker scheme which *may* relax the age limitation and expand the number of countries whose nationals may apply); *or*
- apply to remain longer than permitted under the rules – eg, a visitor applying to stay longer than six months.

When the Home Office refuses your application, it will inform you in writing stating that the application has been refused, that there is no right of appeal, and that you should leave the country within 28 days. If you do not leave within that time, the Home Office may, if you have no other basis of stay, make a decision to administratively remove you.[47] Where similar decisions are made by entry clearance officers abroad or immigration officers at the port, they should also issue you with a notice explaining the basis of the decision and explaining that there is no right of appeal. It may be possible to contest these refusals by applying for judicial review in the courts.

Decisions based on national security grounds

You may not appeal in the ordinary way against an immigration decision where the Secretary of State has determined that your exclusion from the UK is justified on grounds of national security. If a decision is made, against which you would ordinarily have the right of appeal but for the fact that the decision was made on national security grounds, you will have a right of appeal instead to the Special

Immigration Appeals Commission (SIAC), which has a special and complicated procedure of its own.[48]

There are very few decisions and appeals under these procedures. The role of SIAC has recently been extended by the Anti-terrorism, Crime and Security Act 2001 under which suspected 'international terrorists' can be subject to immigration detention on an indefinite basis. SIAC is the body to which these people can appeal or apply for their detention to be reviewed.

The appeal process

When the Home Office receives the completed appeal forms, it sends an acknowledgement letter to you, as the person appealing. Whether you may appeal while in the UK depends on the rules set out above. The time limits for appealing are 10 days when the appeal is being made within the UK and 28 days if the appellant is overseas (although if the notice is being sent to you overseas, then you are not taken to have received it for 28 days and time begins at that point).[49]

The next stage is that the Home Office will send the appeal documents to the adjudicator.[50] This will be sent, together with any documentary evidence, to the immigration appellate authorities, who will fix a date for hearing the appeal. The main hearing centre is at Taylor House, Rosebery Avenue, Clerkenwell, London, but there are other hearing centres in London and throughout the country. Recently, because of the very great number of appeals, appeal hearings have been held using the spare capacity of other courts such as in magistrates' and county court rooms.

Appeals can be a very slow process – delays in the past led to people frequently waiting more than a year for a hearing date – but, at the time of writing, they can usually be listed within a matter of months.

Appeals are first heard by a single adjudicator. The losing side then has the right to apply for leave to appeal to the Immigration Appeal Tribunal to review the case. The Immigration Appeal Tribunal is a two- or three-person panel and will grant leave to appeal when it believes that there is a legal point at issue, or if there are other special circumstances which it believes justify a further appeal. You should apply to the Tribunal for leave to appeal when you are in the UK, within 10 days of the date of the adjudicator's decision and, when you are appealing from outside the UK, within 28 days after the written decision.[51]

If the Tribunal refuses leave to appeal, the only remedy, unless the Tribunal has committed an administrative or procedural error,[52] is to apply for a judicial review of its decision. Specialist advice is necessary for this process. If there is an administrative or procedural error, the Tribunal can be asked to set aside its own decision. The Nationality, Immigration and Asylum Bill 2002 (see p14) proposes to prevent judicial review of Tribunal decisions and to introduce, instead, a separate statutory review procedure outside of the ordinary procedures of the High Court.

If the Tribunal dismisses the appeal after hearing it in full, there may be grounds for applying to the Tribunal for leave to appeal to the Court of Appeal and then directly to the Court of Appeal if the Tribunal refuses leave.[53]

Protection from removal while an appeal is pending

Non-asylum cases

Although, in many cases while you have an appeal pending, you may no longer have any leave to stay in the UK, you are generally still protected from being removed from the UK as follows:[54]

- Where you have an in-country appeal pending against a refusal of leave to enter the UK, no directions for your removal from the UK may be given and any directions already given will have no effect.
- Where you have an appeal pending against any decision to refuse to extend existing leave, you cannot be required to leave the UK.
- Where you have an appeal pending against a decision to make a deportation order, no deportation order may be made.
- Where you appeal against removal directions on the basis of an objection to the destination, you may not be removed while the appeal is pending.

Asylum cases

In asylum cases, you may not be removed from, or required in any way to leave the UK during the period beginning when you make a claim for asylum till the time the Secretary of State gives you notice of the decision in your case.[55]

- If you bring an appeal under s69 of the Immigration and Asylum Act 1999 (ie, against any of the particular immigration decisions or actions named there upon asylum grounds) then you are protected against removal. You cannot be removed until there has been a final determination. This includes any further appeals to the Tribunal or Court of Appeal.[56]
- An exception to this protection for asylum seekers is where the Secretary of State issues a certificate after the asylum claim to the effect that you may be sent to a safe third country which is a member state of the European Union or has been designated for such purpose by the Secretary of State. In such a case, you may be removed to the safe third country without being able to bring an asylum appeal although you may be able to bring a human rights appeal.[57]

Human rights cases

Human rights appeals also generally operate to suspend a person's removal from the UK.[58] If the claim is particularly unmeritorious and has been made late in the day then the Home Office may try to prevent asylum and human rights appeals by issuing a certificate to that effect which can only be challenged by judicial review.

Disputes over whether you can appeal in-country

The common sense approach must also be that the powers given to protect your removal from the UK pending an appeal can only apply where there is a valid in-country right of appeal against a particular decision. But what happens if there is a dispute about whether the right of appeal is in-country or not? For example, what happens if there is a dispute between you and the Secretary of State as to whether you held a current entry clearance at the time you were refused leave to enter at the port, entitling you to an in-country right of appeal against the refusal of leave to enter and you give notice of appeal? There may then be a dispute as to whether you are entitled to protection from removal pending the appeal. It is probably the case that you may only be removed after the issue has been determined against you by the appellate authorities because it is they who must decide whether there is a right of appeal and, while that matter has not been determined, the appeal is, on the face of it, pending.[59]

Notes

1. Deportation, illegal entry and removal
1 s11 IA 1971
2 Sch 2 para 21 IA 1971
3 s8(3) IA 1971; I(EC)O
4 See s7 IA 1971 for details.
5 ss2(2) and 5(2) IA 1971
6 The main new provision is s10 IAA 1999.
7 s3(5) and (6) IA 1971 (as amended by Sch 14 para 4(2) IAA 1999)
8 ss9 and 10(2) IAA 1999; Immigration (Regularisation Period for Overstayers) Regulations 2000
9 *Offeh* (9662)
10 para 364 HC 395 (the last complete statement of the immigration rules, 23 May 1994)
11 para 367 HC 395 as substituted
12 paras 365-366 HC 395 as substituted
13 s5(1)(2) IA 1971
14 paras 390-392 HC 395
15 s10 IAA 1999
16 s3(5)(aa) IA 1971 as added by Sch 2 para 1(2) AIA 1996 but now contained in s10(1)(b) IAA 1999
17 s10(1)(c) IAA 1999
18 para 395C HC 395 as inserted by para 67 HC 704
19 s33 and Sch 2 para 9 IA 1971

20 s33(1) IA 1971 as amended by Sch 2 para 4(1) AIA 1996
21 See reg 21 Immigration (European Economic Area) Regulations 2000
22 Visiting Forces Act 1952
23 s86 Mental Health Act 1983
24 If you need to know more about extradition, you should consult *Jones on Extradition and Mutual Assistance* (2001) Alun Jones QC, Sweet & Maxwell
25 s8 AIA 1996
26 Immigration (Restrictions on Employment) Order 1996

2. Refusals and appeals
27 Regs 4-5 IAA(N) Regs
28 Part II of the IA 1971 which provided for appeals has been repealed and replaced with a revised scheme set out in Part IV and Schs 3 and 4 IAA 1999.
29 IAA(P) Rules replacing the Asylum Appeals (Procedure) Rules 1996 and the Immigration Appeals (Procedure) Rules 1984

30 ss59 and 60 IAA 1999 but there is no right of appeal, even from abroad, against refusal of leave to enter to visitors, students on short courses or prospective students who do not hold an entry clearance on arrival.
31 s66 IAA 1999
32 See ss11, 12 and 71 IA 1999
33 s60 IA 1999
34 ss65 and 69(1) IAA 1999
35 s61 IAA 1999
36 s63 IAA 1999
37 s15 IA 1971 and s5 IA 1988 (as continued for certain persons by paras 11 and 12 Sch 15 IAA 1999)
38 ss65 and 69 IAA 1999
39 s65 IAA 1999
40 s65(1) and (3) IAA 1999
41 s6 Human Rights Act 1998
42 s74 IAA 1999
43 s75 IAA 1999
44 ss73-76 IAA 1999
45 s60 IAA 1999. Note that 'family' visitor is fairly widely defined under reg2(2) of the Immigration Appeals (Family Visitor) (No.2) Regulations 2000
46 ss60 and 62 IAA 1999
47 s10 IAA 1999
48 Special Immigration Appeals Commission Act 1997; Special Immigration Appeals Commission (Procedure) Rules 1998
49 rules 6 and 48 IAA(P) Rules
50 rule 10 IAA(P) Rules
51 rules 6 and 18 IAA(P) Rules
52 rule 19 IAA(P) Rules
53 Sch 4 para 23 IAA 1999
54 Part II Sch 4 IAA 1999
55 s15 IAA 1999
56 Part II, Sch 4 IAA 1999
57 ss11, 12, 65 and 71 IAA 1999
58 Sch 4 para 20 IAA 1999
59 *Lokko* [1990] Imm AR 111

8

Chapter 8

Recourse to public funds under the immigration rules

This chapter covers:
1. The importance of the public funds requirements (below)
2. What are public funds (p94)
3. Recourse to public funds: the general tests (p94)
4. Applying the public funds tests (p100)
5. Sponsorship and undertakings (p104)

1. The importance of the public funds requirements

Requirements under the rules

In the majority of cases, in order to obtain entry clearance or leave under the immigration rules you will need to show that you and your dependants will be adequately maintained and accommodated without recourse to public funds (see p94). The Government's reason for the predominance of this requirement in the immigration rules is to protect the taxpayer from those who are believed to be here to take advantage of the social security system or who may become a burden on it. The categories of leave to which these requirements are applied are set out in the tables in Appendices 4 and 5. The only categories to which these requirements do not apply are:

- visitors in transit;[1]
- holders of special vouchers (the Government stopped issuing special vouchers on 5 March 2002);[2]
- non-British citizen children born in the UK to parents given leave to enter or remain;[3]
- refugees and their dependants;[4]
- a bereaved spouse of a person who was present and settled in the UK, but who died during the 12-month initial period of leave;[5]
- a bereaved unmarried partner of a person who was present and settled in the UK, but who died during the initial period of leave.[6]

Chapter 8: Recourse to public funds under the immigration rules
1. The importance of the public funds requirements

8

Returning residents (who will have had indefinite leave)[7] also do not have to satisfy these requirements, but they have to show that they did not receive assistance from public funds towards the cost of their previous departure from the UK. Changes in the rules from 1 November 1996 added postgraduate doctors and dentists, au pairs and seasonal workers at agricultural camps to the list of categories to which the public funds requirements are applied.[8]

If leave is granted 'exceptionally', it is usually not necessary to satisfy the maintenance and accommodation requirements. Whether the requirements need to be satisfied depends on the basis on which exceptional leave is granted. If it is granted on a humanitarian basis instead of granting refugee status or if it is granted on human rights grounds under the European Convention on Human Rights, the maintenance and accommodation requirements will not be applied. Where, however, the dependants of a person granted exceptional leave are seeking family reunion, they are expected to meet the maintenance and accommodation requirements.

If you are not in any of the above groups, in order to obtain entry clearance, leave to enter or leave to remain, you will have to show that you can satisfy the public funds requirements.

The immigration rules about public funds do not entirely match the social security rules relating to entitlement to public funds benefits. You could, therefore, be entitled under the social security rules but damage your immigration position by claiming. If you are in doubt, you should seek further advice.

The Home Office has indicated that it will not normally treat a person as having had recourse to public funds if s/he claims benefit and has evidence from the DWP that s/he was eligible under exemptions relating to the European Convention on Social and Medical Assistance or the Social Chapter (see pp416–417).[9]

Conditions of leave

From 1 November 1996, being able to maintain and accommodate yourself and your dependants without recourse to public funds may also be a condition attached to your limited leave.[10] If you do subsequently have recourse to public funds, this will be in breach of your conditions of leave. The possible consequences of this are severe (see Chapter 7), since you:

- are liable to administrative removal (see p78);[11]
- are liable to be prosecuted for committing a criminal offence;[12]
- may be refused entry clearance, leave to enter or leave to remain in the UK on any future application (see p49);[13]
- may have your leave curtailed (see p49).[14] This is an exceptional course only to be used where a person is likely to be a continuing and significant burden on public funds.[15]

People who need to satisfy the public funds requirements under the rules are likely to have a public funds condition attached to any leave which they obtain.

8

Chapter 8: Recourse to public funds under the immigration rules
1. The importance of the public funds requirements

Even if no public funds condition was *actually* imposed on your leave but, nevertheless, you had to satisfy the public funds requirements under the rules to get leave, your application for further leave to remain could still be affected.[16]

A public funds condition can also be added to your existing leave by the Home Office.[17] There is no right of appeal, at present, against a decision to add a condition to a person's leave.

2. What are public funds

Not all benefits and services count as public funds. The NHS and education services are not public funds.[18] Public funds are presently defined as:[19]

- housing provided by local authorities – either under homelessness legislation or from the housing register;[20]
- attendance allowance (AA);[21]
- severe disablement allowance (SDA);[22]
- invalid care allowance (ICA);[23]
- disability living allowance (DLA);[24]
- income support;[25]
- working families' tax credit (WFTC);[26]
- council tax benefit;[27]
- disabled person's tax credit (DPTC);[28]
- housing benefit;[29]
- income-based jobseeker's allowance (JSA);[30]
- child benefit.[31]

AA, SDA, ICA, DLA and DPTC were added to the list of public funds from 4 April 1996.[32] Housing provided by local authorities (in addition to provision for the homeless), child benefit and income-based JSA were added to the list of public funds from 1 November 1996.[33] The immigration rules lag behind the changes in legislation. For example, they still refer to 'family credit' rather than WFTC and to old housing legislation. However, because they are loose rules of *practice* rather than legislation which is to be strictly interpreted, they are probably still effective in defining all the above benefits/housing rights as they are sufficiently identified in the rules even if slightly out of date.

3. Recourse to public funds: the general tests

The specific requirements for each category are set out in the immigration rules (see tables in Appendices 4 and 5). In interpreting the rules it is also useful to consider Home Office policy as stated in the Immigration Directorate Instructions and as contained in comments made by Home Office ministers.

Adequate maintenance without recourse to public funds

There is no specific guidance on how much income will be sufficient to adequately maintain an applicant and her/his dependants. Determining adequate maintenance in any one case is, therefore, not a simple question of calculation. You should, however, try to work out your outgoings and income and regular commitments such as rent, bills, travel and tax, so that an approximate figure for disposable income is available. The increasing complexity of the public funds requirements, together with the broadening definition of what constitutes public funds, means that decision makers and the appellate authorities must establish precisely:[34]

- what assets/resources are available for maintenance;
- what accommodation can be provided; *and*
- the level of resources that will be required.

For example, the Immigration Appeal Tribunal has taken the view that it is not sufficient to demonstrate that an amount equal to the personal amount of income support (IS) or income-based jobseeker's allowance (JSA) would be available.[35] The reasoning is that that amount would not be sufficient to meet outgoings such as rent and other housing costs which a person entitled to means-tested public funds would be able to meet with the assistance of further benefit (housing benefit (HB) and council tax benefit in particular). A figure higher than IS (or income-based JSA) is, therefore, required.

An applicant can be indirectly reliant upon the public funds claimed by a third party (eg, a settled spouse who can get working families' tax credit (WFTC) or HB) if no extra benefit is claimed (see p96). Where this happens, there may still be a question of whether there are 'adequate' means of maintaining the applicant. It is not possible for an applicant to rely upon the proceeds of illegal (eg, working when not permitted by immigration law to work) or fraudulent activities for maintenance because then her/his income would be very insecure that s/he would not satisfy the test.[36]

If the leave which is sought by an applicant would entitle her/him to work, then reliance for maintenance might be placed on the income to be obtained from employment in the UK. Evidence of job offers and formal skills will be important, but a person's general resourcefulness and good character are also relevant.[37] The expression of a mere hope of obtaining employment is unlikely to be sufficient unless, of course, as happened in one case before the appellate authorities, the grounds for the hope are not challenged by the Home Office.[38]

Adequate accommodation without recourse to public funds

In order to be adequate for the needs of the applicant, the appellate authorities have adopted tests used in housing legislation – ie, the accommodation available must:[39]

- comply with the environmental health provisions so that it must not be 'statutorily unfit';
- be capable of accommodating the sponsor and the applicant(s) without overcrowding.

Overcrowding is decided in accordance with housing legislation.[40] Accommodation will be overcrowded if two people, aged 10 or over, of opposite sexes (other than partners) have to sleep in the same room. This is known as the 'room standard'. The accommodation will also be overcrowded if the number of people sleeping in the house is greater than that permitted by the housing legislation, having regard to the size of the accommodation. This is known as the 'space standard'. The housing legislation sets out two tests for measuring the space standard but, in practice, it is the following test that is used by the Home Office.[41] The number of people who are allowed to stay in the accommodation depends on the number of rooms available as set out in the table below. A room for this purpose must be 50 square feet or more. Living rooms count, but bathrooms, kitchens etc do not. Children between one and 10 years old only count as half a person; children under one year do not count at all. The number of permitted persons to each room is as follows:[42]

Rooms	Permitted number of persons
1 room	2 persons
2 rooms	3 persons
3 rooms	5 persons
4 rooms	7 and a half persons
5 rooms	10 persons, with an additional 2 persons for each room in excess of 5

The provider of the accommodation, whether it is the sponsor (see p104), friend, relative or applicant, must have some form of interest in the property. They do not need to own the freehold or leasehold as long as they have a tenancy or a licence to occupy. As far as the common requirements of the rules are concerned, there is no objection to sharing communal facilities.[43] The immigration rules relating to family members frequently state that the accommodation must be owned or occupied 'exclusively' by the sponsor for the use of the family. The Home Office has confirmed that this does not mean that accommodation cannot be shared, provided that part of it is for the exclusive use of the sponsor and their dependants – this may be as much as a separate bedroom.[44]

Additional recourse to public funds

In some cases, an applicant may wish to rely on public funds claimed by another person. Whether this is acceptable has been considered twice in the High Court[45] and in both instances the rules were construed strictly against the applicant. In one case,[46] the sponsor proposed to support two applicant sons seeking entry as dependent children out of savings of £3,000 accrued from supplementary benefit (which was then a public fund). The Court said that if such a sponsor did manage to save a little money out of supplementary benefit, what 'he has saved should be available for use by him and his wife in a future time of their need and can hardly be regarded within the confines of the supplementary benefit legislation and the Immigration Act as being available to supply the means of others who arrive in this country'.

In some cases, the immigration appellate authorities have followed this strict interpretation of the law.[47] In other cases, the opposite view has been expressed, requiring there to be additional recourse to public funds *caused* by the applicant's admission to or remaining in the UK before the rules are contravened.[48] The strict approach was adopted particularly in the context of foreign spouses/fiancé(e)s applying for leave to join partners in the UK where the immigration rules require both parties to maintain and accommodate *themselves* without recourse to public funds. In other categories (eg, visitors) the 'no additional dependence' interpretation was more readily adopted.[49]

In some cases, the appellate authorities applied an extremely strict interpretation and effectively found that the maintenance and accommodation requirements were not satisfied in any case where, on the applicant's admission, either the applicant or the sponsor would be in *receipt* of public funds.[50] But this reasoning seems at odds with common sense as it would require an applicant, as was observed in one case,[51] not only to show that s/he would not become a burden on public funds, but also that s/he would remove her/his sponsor from such reliance.

Despite the view taken by some courts, the Home Office view has always been that the proper application of the maintenance and accommodation requirements is that indirect reliance upon funds claimed by others is perfectly permissible provided that there is no *additional* recourse to public funds. This view was expressed regularly in correspondence from ministers responsible for immigration.[52] For example, in October 1994, Nicholas Baker MP (the responsible minister) wrote to Sir Giles Shaw MP stating:[53]

> The question is whether additional recourse to public funds would be necessary on the applicant's arrival here. The sponsor's means, including any public funds to which they are entitled in their own right, must therefore be sufficient to provide adequate maintenance and accommodation for the applicant and their dependants.

The Home Office's own internal instructions then confirmed this approach.[54] The Home Office consciously followed this policy contrary to the High Court decisions and later tribunal decisions on the issue were in the applicant's favour.[55] The Home Office policy has since been endorsed in the High Court[56] in a case where the judge stated that, if the rule was given an interpretation which excluded people even where there was not going to be an overall increase on the demand on public funds, the maintenance and accommodation requirements would be contrary to Article 8 of the European Convention on Human Rights (right to respect for private and family life).[57] The judge was of the view that, if immigration law was interpreted this way, it would require families seeking to be united in the UK to be kept apart even when there was no public interest justifying such a course. Tribunals then determined that they must apply the Home Office's stated interpretation/application of the rules or, put more bluntly, 'ignore the rules, and apply the less stringent dictate of government policy'.[58]

The debate, however, is now over as the immigration rules themselves have been amended, from 2 October 2000,[59] to provide:

> For the purposes of these Rules, a person is not to be regarded as having (or potentially having recourse to public funds merely because he is (or will be) reliant in whole or in part on public funds provided to his sponsor, unless, as a result of his presence in the United Kingdom, the sponsor is (or would be) entitled to increased additional public funds.

The key question then is: will the admission of the applicant or extension of leave to remain granted to the applicant cause an extra demand upon public funds? The answer may not always be straightforward.

Example

In one case,[60] the sponsor's father, after giving a capital asset (a house) to his daughter became entitled to IS as a result. The house was to be the matrimonial home of his daughter (the sponsor) and son-in-law (the applicant) on the son-in-law's arrival in the UK. However, the reason for the gift existed independently of the applicant's admission. It was also to reward the sponsor for her efforts on behalf of the family over the years, and the sponsor's father did not foresee any increase in his benefit at the time the gift was made.

The tribunal held that there would be no 'recourse' caused by the admission of the applicant. The link between the extra benefit obtained by the father and the admission of the applicant to the UK was not sufficiently direct. It could not be said that simply because a third party gives away capital and is then awarded IS, the receiver of the gift (in this case, the house) has recourse to public funds. The tribunal stated 'there is a need for a direct link between the grant of support and the beneficiary'. In the same case, the tribunal determined that the dependence of the sponsor on her father for meals at a time when the father was in receipt of public funds was also insufficient to demonstrate any sufficient 'recourse' to public funds as, given the size of the sponsor's family and the relatively small proportion of IS (public funds) in relation to the overall income being drawn upon (£31.28 of £261.43 weekly), it could not be sensibly said that the meals were being provided through the small part attributable to IS.

If an applicant seeks to live in accommodation without making a contribution to the costs of the accommodation or paying rent and the owner or occupier receives benefit which includes an element of housing costs, tribunals have held that there will be an indirect recourse to public funds.[61] In one case, the reasoning was that, if the sponsor's father charged rent or board and lodging and declared this income to the (then) DSS, his own weekly benefit would be reduced. By allowing the couple to live rent free, the sponsor's father was securing a higher weekly benefit and was, in turn, subsidising the couple.[62]

Note: that where this is the situation, advisers should be ready to point out the likely reduction in the amount paid in housing benefit due to non-dependant deductions (see CPAG's *Welfare Benefits Handbook*) and to question whether there is, in fact, any additional demand on public funds created in these circumstances. Applicants should also be advised of the likelihood of a non-dependant deduction being made. Another problem may occur where the effect of a partner joining a sponsor is to increase the council tax benefit claimed because the 25 per cent single person deduction is lost.[63]

The Home Office's policy instructions state that there is no objection to a settled family member claiming WFTC and child benefit to which s/he is entitled – there is no intention to prevent those who are not 'subject to immigration control' from accessing their benefit entitlement.[64] The Home Office has also stated that where a partner who is subject to control, claims WFTC on behalf of her husband who is present and settled in the UK, this will not be considered as having recourse to public funds.[65] Immigration applications will also not be refused on public funds grounds in marriage cases where one partner is settled and the only benefit being claimed is child benefit.[66]

The ability to rely on public funds provided to the sponsor was successful in a case before the tribunal involving a disabled sponsor who was receiving £120 a week, including his disability living allowance. If entitled to IS or income-based jobseeker's allowance, the couple would receive approximately £80 a week. The tribunal accepted that the additional amount was sufficient to satisfy the rules.[67]

When the test has to be satisfied

Maintenance and accommodation can become an issue overseas when applications for entry clearances are made. The means to maintain and accommodate do not have to exist at the time the decision on the application is made, but only when the applicant expects to arrive in the UK.[68] However, only resources that are reasonably foreseeable at the date of the decision can count. If financial arrangements to support the applicant are put in place at a later date, the applicant will not be able to argue that means are available at the time when the decision is made.[69] Where a sponsor is in receipt of public funds at the date of the decision, this will not, therefore, necessarily defeat the application.[70] In practice, the 'rule of thumb' test which has been applied has been whether the means will be usually available six months after the decision on the application as:[71]

- entry clearances have, until recently, been valid for six months; *and*
- there is unlikely to be an actual date for when the applicant will arrive in the UK so it is assumed s/he will arrive at any date within six months of the decision.

The operation of entry clearances has now changed so that the period of validity of the entry clearance is (other than in visitor cases) the same as the length of leave that will be given. Entry clearance officers and the appellate authorities are more likely, therefore, to focus on the date of the applicant's proposed arrival rather than apply the 'six-months' test. At present, it is possible for the appellate authorities to take account of evidence that comes to light after the decision itself in order to determine whether the rules are satisfied. This includes evidence to show that there are arrangements – which were already in place at the time of the entry clearance officer's decision – to ensure that support will be available when the applicant arrives.[72] The Nationality, Immigration and Asylum Bill 2002 (see p14), however, proposes to prevent adjudicators and the Immigration Appeal Tribunal from taking into account any evidence which was not available to the entry clearance officer.

If the rules are satisfied, but only from a later date, this could form the basis of a request to an adjudicator to make a recommendation that entry clearance or leave be granted, or alternatively, could be put forward in a fresh application.

In one case,[73] a Tribunal took into account an offer of accommodation made after a refusal of entry clearance, because:

- the offer was made contingent on any difficulties arising over the couple's accommodation; *and*
- the house was made available as soon as the difficulties were made known.

In the same case, which involved a wife seeking to join her student husband (the sponsor), the Tribunal took account of the husband's industrious nature and the fact that his family also had the means to assist when assessing the ability of the couple to maintain themselves once the wife had arrived in the UK.[74]

Where the partner in the UK is living in her/his own accommodation and is in employment, the maintenance and accommodation test is likely to be satisfied unless there is evidence that the circumstances are likely to change.[75]

4. **Applying the public funds tests**

Are the requirements the same?

Where maintenance and accommodation without recourse to public funds is a requirement of the rules, there are a number of ways in which the rules vary in relation to the different categories of applicant. There are three main ways in which the requirements appear to differ.

Resources that are not included

In many categories, the maintenance and accommodation requirements must be met not only without recourse to public funds but also without income from working or business activities in the UK or without working *except* in certain employments. This stipulation is added where the rules for leave in a particular category require that the person does not intend to engage in any economic activity, or does not intend to engage in any economic activity other than that for which s/he has been granted leave (see below). Indeed, a condition is likely to be imposed upon the leave preventing the person from doing any other economic activity. In this way the maintenance and accommodation requirements closely reflect the rules for granting leave in each category. The following are examples of these rules.

Writers, composers and artists

A writer, composer or artist[76] must show that s/he will be able adequately to maintain and accommodate her/himself and any dependants without recourse to public funds from her/his own resources without working except as a writer, composer or as an artist. This stipulation reflects the fact that:[77]

- it is a requirement of getting leave in these capacities that the applicant does not intend to do work except in the occupation for which s/he is admitted; *and*
- a condition will normally be attached to her/his leave to the same effect.

Work permit holders/working holidaymakers

The same pattern is not followed for each category. Work permit holders, for example, can apparently rely on income from work other than that specified in the work permit.[78] However, in practice if it is clear you will be relying on funds from economic activities from which you are prohibited (or must show that you will not undertake), then you are likely to be refused leave. Even if you were not refused on maintenance and accommodation grounds, you could legitimately be refused because you are likely to enter such economic activity in order to maintain and accommodate yourself.

The maintenance and accommodation requirements for a working holidaymaker[79] are not expressly qualified by the words 'without taking any employment other than that which is incidental to a holiday' – ie, the requirement in the working holidaymaker rules. However, if it is clear that, in order to maintain and accommodate her/himself and any dependants, an applicant would have to spend more than 50 per cent of her/his time in the UK in full-time employment (which is the Home Office's rule of thumb as to whether the work is only 'incidental' to the holiday), then s/he would be likely to be refused admission. The ground for refusal, if s/he was not refused under the maintenance and accommodation rules, is the rule requiring applicants not to intend to take such employment. This would also apply to a teacher or language assistant under an approved scheme[80] or a person undertaking approved training or work experience.[81]

Students and visitors

Another example is the difference between the maintenance and accommodation requirements for students and visitors. Students must be able to meet the requirements without having to take account of any earnings from employment or business in the UK.[82] However, after entry to the UK students may get permission to do part-time or vacation work,[83] (and in fact, from 21 June 1999, students on courses longer than six months have automatically been treated as having permission to work – although for not more than 20 hours a week during term time). A common sense interpretation of the rules suggests that reliance on this income from limited work would not mean students should be counted as failing the maintenance and accommodation requirements.

Some visitors to the UK transact business while here, although they are not allowed to produce goods or services or take employment. The activities which 'business' visitors can engage in are limited but the immigration rules make no attempt to exclude any income derived in part from business transactions conducted while in the UK when considering whether a visitor can maintain and accommodate her/himself.[84]

Reliance on third-party support for maintenance and accommodation

The rules across the different categories also suggest that there may be differences about when it is permissable to rely on resources provided by a third party (see pp103–104). In some categories, the rules state that a person must be 'able to meet' the costs of her/his maintenance and accommodation; in others it is necessary to show that you 'can and will' be maintained and accommodated; in others you must be 'able and willing' or have 'sufficient funds available' or 'resources available [to you]' to be so maintained and accommodated without recourse to public funds. (For the rules for the different categories of leave see the tables in Appendices 4 and 5.)

Again, the differences reflect the different purposes and nature of the leave being sought (see following examples) and we suggest that third-party support is generally acceptable. The difference in the wording of the rules can be interpreted as simply describing the different scenarios for different applicants. An interpretation which denied entry, even where there was, in fact, likely to be no demand on public funds may, in family cases, be in breach of Article 8 of the European Convention on Human Rights (ECHR). The most restrictive formulation of the rules, as far as preventing third-party support is concerned, is the way they are written for 'retired persons of independent means' and 'persons intending to establish themselves in business' (see p104).

Visitors

Visitors should maintain and accommodate themselves:[85]

- out of resources available to them; *or*
- through the support of relatives or friends.

Clearly, it is reasonable to expect that a short-term visitor to the country may be maintained or accommodated over a limited period by a sponsoring relative or a friend.

Children

The dependent characteristic of children means that the maintenance and accommodation requirements in relation to children are usually to the effect that the child 'can and will' be maintained and accommodated without recourse to public funds. Certain amendments to the immigration rules for children seeking settlement in the UK, require the child to be supported by the parent or relative who is sponsoring them.[86] This appears to be an amendment to try to prevent the children from being supported by third parties other than their parent or relative, or at least to prevent the parent or relative from using third-party funds to help support the children.[87] A restrictive interpretation would be likely to breach Article 8 of the ECHR.

Fiancé(e)s and spouses

There has been a difference of view in the Immigration Appeal Tribunal as to how the rules about fiancé(e)s and spouses should be interpreted – in particular, whether the wording of the fiancé and marriage rules require a couple to be self-supporting. One leading commentator has referred to the fact that the rules are expressed in terms of the parties being able to 'maintain themselves and their dependants' but not necessarily be maintained 'by themselves'.[88] This view is supported by several Tribunal cases[89] and has now also been upheld in the High Court.[90] The other interpretation, also expressed in the Tribunal, which places emphasis on self-support,[91] or stresses the view that third-party support may only be sufficient in the short term,[92] must now be regarded as incorrect. The correct approach is that third-party support is sufficient, although the caselaw which states that it may more difficult to *demonstrate* that there will be *lasting* third-party support still probably applies. So, in cases where the applicant is seeking indefinite leave to remain, the evidence of the lasting nature of third-party support needs to be particularly clear and cogent compared with when an applicant proposes to maintain and accommodate her/himself out of her/his own resources or those generated by her/his own work.[93]

Retired people of independent means, people intending to establish themselves in business

In order to obtain leave, retired people of independent means must have an income of £25,000 a year which is under their control and is disposable in the UK. They must also be able and willing to maintain and accommodate themselves and any dependants indefinitely in the UK:[94]

- from their own resources with no assistance from any other person; *and*
- without taking employment; *or*
- without having recourse to public funds.

People who wish to establish themselves in business (under the EC association agreements or otherwise) have to show that their share of the profits from the business will be 'sufficient to maintain and accommodate' themselves and any dependants without recourse to public funds.[95]

Accommodation 'owned or occupied exclusively'

For certain permanent categories of leave – in particular, spouses and fiancé(e)s – the maintenance and accommodation requirements specify that the accommodation must be owned or occupied exclusively by the parties (to a marriage), the sponsor, parent or relative.[96] Exclusive occupation does not mean occupation of the entire premises in which you reside. Provided the relevant person occupies a bedroom within those premises for themselves only, the remainder of the facilities on the premises (eg, kitchen, living room, toilet, bathroom, halls etc) can be shared with other people.[97]

5. **Sponsorship and undertakings**

The sponsor (usually a relative or friend) of any person seeking leave to enter or to remain in the UK may be asked to give a written undertaking to be responsible for that person's maintenance and accommodation for the period of leave granted and any further period of leave to remain that s/he may be granted while in the UK.[98] The rules are drafted very widely, so it is possible that such an undertaking could be required of a sponsor even if the requirements of the rules under which leave is sought do not specify that the applicant is maintained and accommodated without public funds. However, in practice, it is very unlikely that an undertaking would be required in such a case. Examples of cases where undertakings are often requested are:

- dependent relatives (although not for children under 12 years coming for settlement);
- students relying upon a private individual in the UK.

The Home Office has stated that it rarely asks for undertakings from spouses/ fiancé(e)s or unmarried partners.[99] One reason for this is that people entering in these categories will normally be granted limited leave with a public funds condition attached, meaning that initially they will not generally be able to access public funds. Those admitted as dependent relatives are given indefinite leave immediately and so, unless an undertaking is entered into, they would not be 'subject to immigration control' for benefits purposes.

If you are asked to give an undertaking you must be aware that, depending on the circumstances of the case, this commitment could last a lifetime. If the person sponsored subsequently claims benefit while in the UK, you may be asked to pay back any benefit which is claimed (see p207).[100] Court action may be initiated to enforce payment if it is not forthcoming. However, it is government policy to do this only where the sponsor, although financially able, refuses to honour the undertaking without good reasons.[101]

The rules regarding entitlement to means-tested benefits for people granted leave on the basis of a maintenance undertaking were changed on 5 February 1996 so that they are not entitled to benefit even if their sponsor does not maintain them.

A person who has leave to enter or remain given as a result of a maintenance undertaking is, from 3 April 2000, within the definition of a 'person who is subject to immigration control' and is excluded on this basis.[102] There are, however, exceptions for those whose sponsor has died and those who have been in the UK for five years since the date of the undertaking or the date of entry (whichever is later (see p160).

Often sponsors voluntarily make declarations as to maintenance and accommodation without being asked to provide an undertaking. Because of the possible consequences, it is advisable not to make such declarations of sponsorship unless specifically asked to make such a promise. However, where a person makes an informal sponsorship declaration, we suggest that this will not be enough to turn the person they are sponsoring into a person who is 'subject to immigration control'. This is because a 'maintenance undertaking' for these purposes is defined as one given 'in pursuance of the immigration rules'.[103] The immigration rules prescribe a form for certain applications (SET(F))[104] which has a supplementary form attached which can be used for maintenance undertakings. We suggest that a formal form similar to the one supplied with SET(F) must be used for the undertaking to be effective.

Note that where the sponsor of a person refuses to give an undertaking to be responsible for an applicant's maintenance and accommodation in the UK after being requested to do so, the applicant is likely to be refused entry clearance or leave to enter or remain.[105]

Notes

1. The importance of the public funds requirements

1 paras 47-50 HC 395 (the last complete statement of the immigration rules, 23 May 1994)
2 paras 249-254 HC 395
3 paras 304-309 HC 395
4 paras 327-352 HC 395
5 para 287(b) HC 395 as inserted by para 31 HC 704
6 para 295M HC 395 as inserted by para 32 HC 704
7 paras 18-20 HC 395
8 paras 3, 6, 7, 8 and 9 HC 31
9 Letter to UKCOSA, 5 December 2000
10 s3(1) IA 1971 as amended by Sch 2 para 1(1) AIA 1996 and para 8(ii) HC 395 as substituted by para 3 Comnd 3365 August 1996
11 s10 IAA 1999
12 s24(1)(b) IA 1971
13 paras 320(11) and 322(3)(4) HC 395
14 para 323 HC 395
15 'Policy and Practice', *Immigration and Nationality Law and Practice,* January 1988, p102
16 paras 322(4) and 323 HC395
17 s3(3)(a) IA 1971

2. What are public funds

18 See *Dumerville* (9395); *Stein* (7978)
19 para 6 HC 395
20 Under Housing Act 1985, Parts I or II Housing (Scotland) Act 1987 or Part II Housing (Northern Ireland) Order 1988
21 Under Part III SSCBA 1992 or Part III SSCBA (Northern Ireland) 1992
22 See note 21
23 See note 21
24 See note 21
25 Under Part VII SSCBA 1992 or Part VII SSCBA (Northern Ireland) 1992
26 See note 25
27 See note 25
28 See note 25
29 See note 25
30 Under JSA 1995
31 Under Part IX SSCBA 1992 and Part IX SSCBA (Northern Ireland) 1992 and s10 AIA 1996
32 para 1 HC 329
33 para 1 HC 31

3. Recourse to public funds: the general tests

34 See comments in *R v IAT ex parte Shaim Begum* [1995] *Times,* 15 February 1995 QBD per Schiemann J; also noted in *Legal Action* (1995) July, p21; and see *Zia v SSHD* [1993] Imm AR 404; *ex parte Aslam* 12 May 1997 (unreported); *Begum (Fiaz)* (13212); *Osman* (162497; *Begum (Sufia)* (20498); *Hashm* (20719)
35 *Azem* (7863), *Uvovo* (00/TH/01450) and see *Begum* (Momotaz) (18699)
36 *Tedeku* (6024)
37 *Dumerville* (9395)
38 *Egal*
39 See *Begum* (3811) and see *Mushtaq* (9343)
40 ss324-325 Housing Act 1985
41 See Home Office instructions set out in *Immigration and Nationality Law and Practice,* July 1987, vol 2 p26; IDI Chapter 8, annex H para 6.3
42 s326 Housing Act 1985
43 *Kasuji* [1988] Imm AR 587; *Musrat Jabeen* (14925) *Ahmed* (8260); *Zia v SSHD* [1993] Imm AR 404 *(obiter)* cf *Kausar* (8025)
44 IDI, Chapter 8, annex H para 6; *Kasuji* [1988] Imm AR 587
45 *R v IAT ex parte Chhinderpal Singh and Gurdip Singh* [1989] Imm AR 69 and *R v SSHD ex parte Islam Bibi and Dilshad Begum* [1995] Imm AR 157
46 *Chhinderpal Singh*
47 *Azem* (7863); *Buchaya* (9025); *Quiambo* (12416); *Uddin* (12429); *Shah* (12444)
48 *Bashir Ahmed* [1991] Imm AR 30; *Ahmed* (9028), *Pervez Hussain* (7509); *Ishaque* (6752)
49 *Buchanan* (11280); *Uddin* (9170); *Singh* (7387)
50 *Agub* (9547); *Begum* (8582); *Mohd Ramzan* (11185); *Patel* (11278)
51 *Muktar Ahmed* (9028)

52 *Legal Action* (1995) July, p21 and *IAS Law Digest,* 26 October 1995 for text of letters from Nicholas Baker MP (Minister) to Max Madden MP, 26 April 1995 and 2 October 1995 respectively. See also letter of 12 March 1997 to BM Birnberg and Co in relation to child benefit.

53 The letter is set out in more detail in *Legal Action* (1995) March, p20.

54 IDI Chapter 1, s7 para 2.2

55 See for further detail of Home Office stated interpretation 'Recourse to public funds and indirect reliance', *Immigration and Nationality Law and Practice* Vol 10, No.2 1996, pp50-53; *Immigration Law Digest* Vol 1 26 September 1996, pp22-24; and in earlier articles in *Immigration and Nationality Law and Practice* Vol 9:1 1995 p29, and Vol 6:3 1992 p99.

56 *ex parte Arman Ali per Collins J* [2000] Imm AR 134; [2000] INLR 89

57 Art 8 is one of the rights incorporated into domestic UK law by the Human Rights Act 1998.

58 *Reem Louis Shekouri* (13711); *Clevon Marcus Scott* (13389); *Neharun Begum* (13489) although see the contrary view in *Javaid Iqbal* (12528) but this latter case was decided prior to a key decision in relation to appellate authority jurisdiction; *SSHD v DS Abdi* [1996] Imm AR 148; and see *Begum* (15409); *Farkhanda* (14633); *Rahman* (14527) and agreed by the Home Office by consent in *ex parte Georgeson* (CO/2403/96)

59 para 6A HC 395 inserted by para 4 HC 704

60 *Mohammed Yousaf* (9190)

61 *Azem* (7863), *Buchiya* (9025), *Ahmed* (9028), *Yousaf* (9190), *Isaque* (6752) and *Muhmood* (12833)

62 *Azem* (7863)

63 *Din* (18884)

64 IDI, Chapter 8, annex H para 2

65 IDI, Chapter 1, annex W para 2.4

66 IDI, Chapter 1, annex W para 2.5

67 *Iqbal* (00/TH/277) but see the decision in *Akhtar* (L18942) where the disabled sponsor was receiving only £14 a week additional benefit

68 See *Munir Jan* (1517); *Sultan Begum* (3155)

69 *Kazmi* (5866)

70 *Bakiserver* (1151)

71 *Bahir Ahmed* [1991] Imm AR 130; *Sabir Hussain* (5990)

72 *Afzal* (11853)

73 *Akhtar* (7837)

74 See also *Keyani* (5662) for anticipated earnings

75 *Sabir Hussain* (5990)

4. **Applying the public funds tests**

76 paras 232-239 HC 395

77 See note 76

78 paras 128-135 HC 395

79 paras 95-100 HC 395

80 paras 110-115 HC 395

81 paras 116-121 HC 395

82 paras 57-62 HC 395

83 paras 57(v) and 58 HC 395

84 paras 40-46 HC 395

85 paras 40-46, 51-56 HC 395

86 paras 297(iv)-(v) and 298(iv)-(v) HC 395

87 *Arman Ali* [2001] INLR 89, [2000] Imm AR

88 See Jackson, *Immigration Law and Practice,* Sweet and Maxwell

89 *Hussain* (5990); *Azad* (5993); *Sadiq* (6017); *Saleem* (6017); *Akhtar* (7837); *Kaur* (12838); *Akhtar* (9903); *Khan* (6283); *Yousaf* (9190); *Njoku* (18520)

90 *ex parte Arman Ali per Collins J*

91 For example, see *Azra Tubeen* [1991] Imm AR 178; *Ansar Mahmood* (8402); *Ishaque Ahmed* (12992); *Nanjo* (9730); *Neesa* (11545). Some Tribunal decisions applying a very restrictive narrow approach were quashed by consent: *Ahmed (Ishaque)* (12292); *Begum (Zabeda)* (16677)

92 *Kauser* (8025); *Mahmood* (8402); *Wray* (9022); *Rafaqat* (9445); *Mistry* (12160); *Akhtar* (11658); *Nguyen* (18738)

93 See *Jabeen* [1991] Imm AR 178 where the sponsor was detained and there was no actual evidence of third-party support; *Ildaphonse* (8464); *Begum* (8582); *Wray* (9022); *Mohammed Hussain* [1991] Imm AR 476; *Hussain* (11372); *Azad* (5993); in *Bibi (Sonor)* (19199), IAS 1999, Vol.2, No.17 the Tribunal held that a dependent child's earnings could be taken into account.

94 paras 263-270 HC 395

95 paras 201(ix), 206(ix), 212(iv) and 217(ii) HC 395

96 Introduced in 1994 (see note 1)

97 Letter from Nicholas Baker MP (Minister) to Sir Giles Shaw MP, October 1994 (the time when the rules came into force); *Legal Action* (1995) March p20; IDI Chapter 8, annex H para 6.3.

● ●

5. Sponsorship and undertakings

98 para 35 HC 395
99 IDI Chapter 8, annex H para 5.1
100 para 35 HC 395; ss78, 105 and 106
    SSAA 1992; SSAA (Northern Ireland) Act
    1992
101 Parliamentary answer 29 January 1986
    of Secretary of State for Social Services
    and letter 4 January 1991 from DSS to
    JCWI.
102 s115(9)(c) IAA
103 s115(10)
104 para 32 HC395
105 paras 320(14) and 322(6) HC 395

Chapter 9

··

Determining immigration status

This chapter covers:
1. British citizens and those with the right of abode in the UK (below)
2. Leave to enter (p110)
3. Leave to remain (p112)
4. Refugees, asylum seekers and those with exceptional leave (p112)
5. Those whose departure is being enforced (p114)
6. Other endorsements on passports (p115)

··

The stamps referred to in this chapter can be found in Appendix 9 to this book. See also *JCWI Immigration, Nationality and Refugee Law Handbook* for more examples of stamps and endorsements in passports.

··

---

1. British citizens and those with the right of abode in the UK

Passports give evidence of national status at the time they were issued. They are not necessarily conclusive evidence of your current status and they cannot account for any change of circumstance or status.

British citizens

People with passports issued before 1 January 1983, which describe them as a citizen of the United Kingdom and Colonies (CUKC) (on page one) with the right of abode (on page five) are almost certainly British citizens. If you have a passport issued after 1 January 1983, it should simply describe you as a British citizen. Although you have the right of abode, a statement to that effect is not endorsed on the passport. Passports issued now are the uniform European Union passports which are maroon in colour.

Other British nationals and Commonwealth citizens

If your passport was issued:
- before 1 January 1983 and you are a British overseas citizen (BOC), a British subject, etc (see p20), it should describe you as a CUKC (on page one) but the statement of right of abode (on page five) will be crossed out or there may be no such statement;
- after 1 January 1983, it should describe you as a BOC, British subject, etc on the same page as your personal details are set out.

If you are a Commonwealth citizen with the right of abode in the UK, any passport issued should have a stamp of 'certificate of patriality' if it was issued before 1 January 1983. Passports issued after this date should be endorsed with a 'certificate of entitlement to the right of abode' to demonstrate that the person has the right of abode in the UK. Certificates of entitlement to the right of abode are endorsed in the passport in the form of a sticker together with the stamp of the issuing post or the Home Office (Appendix 9, Figure 1).

For the grant of British citizenship to British overseas territories citizens and, under the Nationality, Immigration and Asylum Bill 2002, to some British overseas citizens, see Chapter 2.

Citizenship by registration/naturalisation

If you have been granted citizenship after having applied to register or naturalise, the Home Office will issue a certificate of naturalisation or registration as evidence of citizenship. You can apply to the Passport Agency for a British passport.

2. Leave to enter

As described on pp29-35, entry clearances (visas) now operate as leave to enter. The conditions which the leave is subject to are stated on the entry clearance sticker itself. If the entry clearance is to have effect as indefinite leave this will also be stated on the entry clearance sticker. The new style entry clearances have been in use since 2 October 2000. Old style entry clearances may be used if they are still valid but will not have effect as leave when a person arrives.

New style visit entry clearances are issued in the form of a green 'uniform format visa' (Appendix 9, Figure 2). All other new style entry clearances are red (Appendix 9, Figure 3). When a person arrives with a new style entry clearance and the immigration officer admits her/him (for circumstances in which an immigration officer can still refuse to admit a person with an entry clearance or other person who has leave when s/he arrives, see p35), the officer will probably simply place a rectangular date stamp, with the name of the port of entry, over the entry clearance (Appendix 9, Figure 4). This is known simply as a 'date stamp'.

Entry clearances state the purpose for which they are granted. However, where a person arrives without an entry clearance and is granted leave to enter (because they are non-visa nationals entering in a category for which an entry clearance is not needed or because they are admitted as refugees or exceptionally) the endorsement which the immigration officer places in the passport does not state the purpose for which leave is granted. If limited leave is granted, the endorsement is a rectangular stamp which states the period for which leave is granted and what, if any, conditions are attached to the leave. The example shown (Appendix 9, Figure 5) is the kind of stamp usually issued to a student on a short course (of six months or less). The student is prohibited from working and there is a condition prohibiting recourse to public funds. This means that s/he is a 'person subject to immigration control' (PSIC) for benefit purposes. If the person had been admitted as a spouse or unmarried partner for the probationary initial period, the endorsement would look the same but the third box would read simply 'no recourse to public funds' indicating that, while s/he may work, s/he is also a PSIC.

If a person is granted indefinite leave to enter, then this will be indicated in the endorsement shown (Appendix 9, Figure 6). A person recognised as a refugee and granted indefinite leave to enter will not be able to use her/his own national passports (even if s/he has one) and, therefore, this stamp will be endorsed on the letter informing her/him that s/he has refugee status (see p112). Those returning to the UK who already have indefinite leave to enter, will simply be given a date stamp if re-admitted with indefinite leave. Each of the stamps issued by an immigration officer to grant leave to a person who does not have an entry clearance will be accompanied by the immigration officer's rectangular date stamp (see above).

Refusal of leave to enter

If a person arrives in the UK with leave (either granted by an entry clearance, or because s/he is returning to the UK with leave which did not lapse (see p35), or if s/he has otherwise been granted leave before her/his actual arrival in the UK), and the immigration officer refuses to admit her/him, her/his leave is 'cancelled'. The immigration officer will endorse a large 'CANCELLED' stamp across the previous endorsement granting leave *or* will write the same endorsement across the stamp in either red or black ink.

Where a person who arrives without leave is refused leave to enter, a date stamp with an ink cross through it is placed in the passport as shown (Appendix 9, Figure 7). A person will also be given a written notice of refusal of leave to enter which will notify them of any appeal rights which they have.

3. **Leave to remain**

Leave to remain (ie, after a person has already entered the UK), is granted by officials at the Home Office. Where limited leave is granted, the endorsement will show the length of the leave granted and the condition attached to it. The example shown in Appendix 9 indicates that the person is subject to immigration control because a public funds conditions is included (Appendix 9, Figure 8). When the Home Office grants leave to remain, the endorsement signed by the official who has granted the leave is accompanied by a pentagonal date stamp (Appendix 9, Figure 9).

When the Home Office grants indefinite leave, the passport is endorsed with a green vignette (sticker) as shown (Appendix 9, Figure 10). Before 1992, the Home Office used a stamp which stated 'given leave to remain in the UK for an indefinite period'.

Refusal of leave to remain

Where the Home Office refuses to grant leave to remain, it will underline the most recent grant of leave, or the date stamp accompanying it, to show the refusal. Where the person does not have a grant of leave in her/his current passport to enable this to be done, the Home Office may write the person's Home Office reference number on the inside back cover of the passport and underline it. A **'Home Office reference number'** is the reference number given to anyone who has dealings with the Home Office (as opposed to the officials at the ports of entry), for example, by applying to extend her/his leave after s/he has entered the UK. It is normally the first letter of the her/his surname followed by six or seven numbers. S/he will also be given a written notice of the refusal of leave to remain with details of any rights of appeal.

4. **Refugees, asylum seekers and those with exceptional leave**

Until early 2002, asylum seekers were issued with a 'standard acknowledgement letter' (SAL). 'SAL1' was issued to those claiming asylum at the port and 'SAL2' was issued to those who claimed asylum once they were already in the UK. The Home Office has been phasing in the **'application registration card'** for asylum applicants (Appendix 9, Figure 11). These contain details about the applicant – eg, whether s/he has any dependants, and whether s/he has permission to work.

When a person is granted refugee status, s/he is issued with a letter informing her/him that s/he has been recognised as a refugee and explaining certain of her/his rights in the UK. This letter should be endorsed with indefinite leave which, since July 1998, is immediately given to those recognised as refugees (Appendix 9, Figure 12).

Those who are granted exceptional leave following a refusal of refugee status are also given a letter explaining that they have been refused asylum but granted exceptional leave instead. The letter explains the various rights and entitlements the person has as a result of her/his exceptional leave (Appendix 9, Figure 13). Many of those who are granted exceptional leave under the European Convention on Human Rights are granted this status following a refusal of asylum under the 1951 Refugee Convention. Where leave is granted exceptionally other than after an asylum claim (see Chapter 6), this may be difficult to identify. The person should have an endorsement granting leave in her/his passport or, if s/he does not have a passport, on a letter. Normally where leave is granted exceptionally it will be given without a public funds condition (see p92), which is the most important consideration for benefit purposes. It will certainly be granted without a public funds condition when it is granted on a humanitarian basis following a refusal of asylum under the 1951 Refugee Convention.

Refugees may also be issued, on application to the Home Office, with a blue UN Refugee Convention travel document. The indefinite leave endorsement will be placed inside it.

Those with exceptional leave may obtain from the Home Office a 'certificate of identity', otherwise referred to as an 'exceptional leave travel document'. These are brown in colour and a person's leave will be endorsed inside. Some countries, however, refuse to accept them as valid for travel.

Policy on obtaining travel documents for those with exceptional leave has changed over time. Broadly speaking, people who were first granted exceptional leave after July 1993, should be able to obtain documentation without difficulty. Those first granted exceptional leave prior to that time will usually have to show that it would be unreasonable to expect them to approach their own national authorities to ask for documentation or that they had been unreasonably refused such documentation by their national authorities. People in this last category, however, should now all be in a position to naturalise as British citizens and obtain British passports in order to travel.

Temporary admission

Claims for asylum take time to be determined and most asylum seekers do not have any leave when they claim. While the claim, and appeal, are being determined the person is either detained or granted a licence to be in the UK. This licence is known as 'temporary admission'. Temporary admission is not 'leave' and it can be taken away at any time. Notice of temporary admission is usually given on Form IS96 as shown (Appendix 9, Figure 14). There are variants on temporary admission, for example, 'temporary release' for a person who has been detained and later released by the immigration authorities and 'restriction orders' for a person who would otherwise be detained on the basis that s/he is liable to deportation. Temporary admission is normally granted with conditions, which are stated on the form itself – eg, a restriction to reside at a particular address. Asylum seekers who have been waiting for a decision from the Home Office on their asylum application for six months or more can apply for their working restriction to be lifted.

Temporary admission is not only given to asylum seekers, it can also be granted to anyone who needs leave to be in the UK but does not have it and is awaiting a decision on their application for leave or, in some cases, pending immigration enforcement action being taken against them.

Where someone who is liable to be detained is released on bail by the immigration appellate authorities (ie, the adjudicator or the Immigration Appeal Tribunal), they will have forms issued by the appellate authority stating the terms and conditions of their bail.

Because temporary admission is not leave, but is given to a person who needs leave, those granted temporary admission are 'persons subject to immigration control' for benefit purposes (see p157).

5. **Those whose departure is being enforced**

Illegal entry and administrative removal

When the immigration authorities decide that a person is liable to removal (and detention – although this power may not be exercised) as an illegal entrant or someone who may be 'administratively removed' from the UK, they give that person a form explaining this (Appendix 9, Figure 15). Those who can be administratively removed from the UK are overstayers (who are 'subject to immigration control'), those who have breached their conditions of leave and those who have obtained leave by deception (both these categories are likely to be, but are not always, 'subject to immigration control'). The vast majority of those who are subject to administrative removal are overstayers.

Deportation

Those who are being subject to deportation are first issued with a notice of intention to deport against which there is a right of appeal. Following any appeal, they can then be issued with a deportation order which states that the 'Secretary of State by this order requires the said [...*NAME*...] to leave and prohibits him/her from entering the United Kingdom so long as this order is in force'. Those who are being deported following the recommendation of a criminal court are not, at present, first given a notice of intention to deport. If it chooses to follow the recommendation of the court, the Home Office will proceed directly to the making of the deportation order. This practice may, however, change under the Nationality, Immigration and Asylum Bill 2002 (see p14).

Removal

The final stage for enforcing a person's departure from the UK is the setting of removal directions (see p78). This is the case whether a person is being forced to leave after having been refused leave to enter at port; declared to be an illegal entrant; notified of her/his liability to be 'administratively removed'; *or* if s/he has had a deportation order made against her/him. The form which is given stating when and where a person is to be removed by the carrier varies depending on the procedure which led to their being removed. The form shown in Appendix 9 is the one given to notify a person refused asylum who has also been classed as an illegal entrant or as a person liable to be administratively removed, of the directions made for her/his removal (Appendix 9, Figure 16).

6. **Other endorsements on passports**

Embarkation from the UK

You may see a triangular stamp on a passport (Appendix 9, Figure 17). This stamp has not been issued since March 1998. It used to be issued to mark a person's departure from the UK, but passports are no longer routinely marked to show the date of embarkation from the UK.

New passports and endorsements

Where a person has limited leave and obtains a new passport, s/he may obtain a stamp from the Home Office in the new passport which states that 'the holder has leave to enter/remain' and states the date it was granted and the date on which it expires. The endorsement will also contain a reference to a 'code' which indicates the conditions to which the leave is subject. When a person who has indefinite leave obtains a new passport, the indefinite leave will be endorsed into the new passport by the Home Office with a stamp which states 'there is at present no time limit on the holder's stay in the UK'. When a person enters at port with existing indefinite leave in an old passport but bearing a new one, the immigration officer will generally issue the ordinary 'given indefinite leave to enter the United Kingdom' stamp into the new passport.

Illegible passport stamps

If the stamp in your passport is either unclear or illegible, you will be deemed to have been granted leave to enter for six months with a condition prohibiting you from taking employment.[1]

If you arrived in the UK before 10 July 1998 and were given an unclear or illegible stamp in your passport, you are deemed to have been given indefinite leave to enter the UK.[2]

If you are a person who requires leave to enter the UK and no stamp is placed in your passport (because, for example, you were simply waved through by the immigration officer), through no fault of your own you may, nevertheless, be considered an 'illegal entrant'.[3]

Notes

6. Other endorsements on passports
1   Sch 2 para 6(1) IA 1971 as amended
2   Sch 2 para 6(1) IA 1971 prior to
    amendment and as interpreted by the
    courts
3   *Rehal v SSHD* [1989] Imm AR 576

Part 2

Immigration and benefits

Chapter 10

· ·

Immigration and benefits

This chapter covers:
1. Social security and immigration control (below)
2. Home Office links with benefits authorities (p120)
3. National insurance number requirement (p122)
4. National insurance contributions (p123)
5. Proving immigration status, age and relationships (p126)

As well as special benefit rules for migrants, the interaction of social security and immigration control may cause problems. Migrants may have special difficulties proving identity, age or relationships. Migrants whose first language is not English may have practical difficulties in claiming benefits and be more likely to make mistakes when claiming.

For more information, see CPAG's *Welfare Benefits Handbook*.

1. **Social security and immigration control**

Social security rules and administration are a key part of government immigration policies. From 3 April 2000, entitlement of non–European Economic Area (EEA) nationals to all non-contributory social security benefits is governed by the Immigration and Asylum Act 1999.[1] This is the latest and most extreme legal instrument intended to exclude non-British citizens from access to social security and consequently to deter migrants from coming to the UK.[2]

The exclusion of some of the most vulnerable people from the social security system is of considerable concern. Furthermore, the linking of entitlement to benefit to immigration status has meant that the benefit authorities have had to take on the role of immigration officers, but they are not trained to do so. This inevitably leads to errors and confusion with people who are eligible for benefit being wrongly refused.

This policing role by benefit authorities has led to a fundamental clash of cultures. The basic purpose of benefits authorities and their staff is to ensure payment of benefits to members of the community who cannot support themselves or who require special support. Increasingly, immigration legislation seeks to exclude people from access to the welfare state even where the individual is severely disabled or where the family includes children or other vulnerable people.

2. **Home Office links with benefits authorities**

Benefits are administered by several different government bodies, some of which are divided into different agencies (see below). All of these have links with the Home Office which administers immigration control in the UK.

The benefits authorities

The main benefits authority responsible for overall administration and policy work concerning social security benefits is the Department for Work and Pensions (DWP). Tax credits are dealt with by the Tax Credit Office of the Inland Revenue.

The Inland Revenue administers working families' tax credit, disabled person's tax credit (from offices in Preston and Belfast) and national insurance (NI) contributions (from Newcastle).

The administration of housing benefit (HB) and council tax benefit (CTB) is carried out by local authorities.

Benefits authorities staff are expected to understand immigration law as well as the complicated benefits rules. In practice, their understanding is very limited because they have virtually no training or support in this area.

Even though the benefits rules which apply to migrants may be different from those for other people, benefits decisions are made in the same way and by the same authorities and staff, regardless of the immigration status of the claimant. All claimants have the same rights of review and appeal. For details of how decisions are taken and how to appeal, see CPAG's *Welfare Benefits Handbook*.

Immigration checks by benefits authorities

All benefits authorities have links to the Home Office. The main purpose of the links is for benefits authorities to check whether your immigration status affects your rights to benefits.

Immigration checks are usually triggered if a benefits authority believes you may not be British. In the case of income support (IS) and income-based jobseeker's allowance (JSA) claimants, the claim form asks, 'Have you, your partner, or any of the children you are claiming for, come to live or returned to live in the UK in the last five years?' If you answer 'yes' you are asked for the nationality of any person who has come in the last five years, the date you last came, whether you came to work or live in the UK and details of any limits on your stay in the UK. Claim forms for other benefits have similar questions. Immigration checks may also be triggered if:

- the Home Office gives the DWP information about a claimant as part of a Home Office query about benefit claims or simply 'information-sharing';
- you do not have an NI number or your IS reference number is not an NI number (see p122);
- you have a foreign sounding name;
- you speak to a benefits officer but are not fluent in English;
- an allegation that you are not British is made to a benefits authority, either by another benefits authority or government agency, or by an individual.

If you are being paid IS/income-based JSA, a local authority dealing with a claim by you for HB/CTB should not make immigration checks.[3]

If you give your nationality as other than British, you will normally be asked to show the DWP a passport or, for European Union /European Economic Area nationals, an identity card. The benefits authority may take your immigration status from your passport or from any letter sent to you by the Home Office. Otherwise, the benefits authority is likely to contact the Home Office to establish your immigration status. This may still be done even if your passport shows your status. If you have a British passport but are not a British citizen (eg, you are a British overseas citizen) the benefits authority may check or may treat you as a British citizen (see Chapter 2).

The Home Office Immigration Status Enquiry Unit is responsible for dealing with immigration status enquiries from benefits authorities. Enquiries are usually made by faxing an enquiry form[4] to the Unit which is then returned with the information completed. Sometimes enquiries are made by telephone. There are sometimes long delays in receiving information. For advice on proving your immigration status, see p126.

Links with entry clearance officers abroad

There are also links between the DWP Overseas Benefits Directorate (see Appendix 2) and entry clearance officers (sometimes called visa officers – see p12) abroad. If you are a non-British citizen living abroad and you claim a retirement pension or bereavement benefit on the basis of your spouse's contributions, the Overseas Directorate may contact an entry clearance officer in your country to see whether you have ever been refused a UK visa. Extracts from the entry clearance officer's file may be sent to the DWP. If there was an appeal against the visa refusal, the entry clearance officer's explanatory statement for that appeal will usually be passed to the DWP but other documents, including those which were sent in to support your visa request, may not be passed on. The entry clearance officer's papers are most important if the visa was refused because the entry clearance officer did not accept that you were married as claimed. The DWP may agree with the entry clearance officer and refuse benefit on the ground that, for example, you are not a widow. If this happens, you should appeal and get advice. The vast

majority of visa refusals made in disputed relationship cases in the 1970s and
early 1980s were wrong, as was proved by later DNA tests.[5]

Home Office use of benefits information

The Home Office uses its links with benefits authorities to check on immigrants
and to locate those not here legally with whom it is has lost contact:

- If you are not here legally and the Home Office has lost contact with you,
  information from a benefits authority query may allow the Home Office to
  start or continue removal action against you (see Chapter 7).
- If you apply for further leave to remain in the UK, the Home Office application
  form asks whether you are receiving benefits, which count as public funds. If
  you are applying for leave as the spouse of a settled person, you are also asked
  whether your spouse is receiving public funds. The Home Office will normally
  not refuse further leave just because your partner has claimed benefits to which
  s/he is entitled. However, a claim could lead the Home Office to decide that
  you cannot *adequately* support yourself without recourse to public funds (see
  p92).
- If you apply for a visa to come to the UK, the entry clearance officer may
  contact the benefits authorities in the UK to see whether your sponsor is
  claiming benefits, or even whether you have claimed benefits on a previous
  visit. However, we have never heard of this happening in practice.

3. National insurance number requirement

In order to claim most benefits it is now necessary to satisfy the national insurance
(NI) number requirement, known as the NINO requirement. You satisfy this
requirement if you:

- provide an NI number together with evidence to show that the number is
  yours;
- provide evidence or information to enable your NI number to be traced; *or*
- apply for an NI number and provide sufficient information or evidence for one
  to be allocated.

If you do not satisfy the NINO requirement you are not eligible for benefit. This
requirement applies both to the claimant and any person for whom s/he is
claiming benefit, but it does not apply to any child or young person that you may
be claiming for. An application for a NINO can be made at a local social security
office on Form CA5400 and it must be accompanied by sufficient documentary
evidence of identity. For example, this might include a birth certificate, a passport
or an identity card.

The NINO requirement is particularly controversial. Despite apparently
neutral criteria, the requirement appears to have had a disproportionate effect on

black and minority ethnic claimants. This appears to be because, in practice, benefit authority staff work to a set list of documents that may be produced as evidence of identity. However, many non-British claimants do not have these documents and therefore fall foul of the rule.

A further problem arises where couples have different immigration status. A person who is not a 'person subject to immigration control' (see p157) will find that s/he is refused benefit because her/his partner does not have and is unable to obtain a NINO. However, such an application of the law may well be incompatible with Article 8 of the European Convention on Human Rights (ECHR) (right to respect for family life) because the only way in which the settled person can obtain benefit is to separate from her/his partner. A number of legal challenges have been started on this point, but before any case has reached the courts the DWP has so far resolved the matter favourably towards the claimant. If you are refused benefit on this basis, contact CPAG.

National insurance numbers

Your NI record is kept under an NI number which looks like this: MN 42 56 93 D. This number is also used as a reference for tax and for contribution-based benefits. If you do not have or know your number, benefits authorities, employers and the Inland Revenue are likely to want to check your immigration status.

National insurance numbers are now allocated automatically to children shortly before their 16th birthday, but only if child benefit is being claimed for them. If child benefit was being claimed for you at that time, you should have an NI number. The number you are given is based on the child benefit reference number.

Some income support (IS)/income-based jobseeker's allowance (JSA) claimants who do not have an NI number when they claim benefit are given a temporary IS/income-based JSA reference number which looks like an NI number. This is not an NI number.

If you do not have an NI number, you can apply for one. Having an NI number is important because:
- an employer should accept it as showing that there is no bar under immigration law on you taking work;
- it means any contributions you or your employer make should be correctly allocated to your name;
- it means any contributions for which you are credited should be correctly allocated to your name;
- you can deal more easily with other official bodies, such as the Inland Revenue.

4. National insurance contributions

Many benefits are paid out of the national insurance (NI) fund, which is funded by social security contributions of employees, employers, the self-employed and other people who choose to make them. In this book we only cover the rules that particularly affect migrants.

There are five types or *classes* of contribution payable by employed earners:[6]
- Class 1 – payable by employed earners and their employers;
- Class 1A – payable by employers of employed earners;
- Class 2 – payable by self-employed earners;
- Class 3 – payable by voluntary contributors;
- Class 4 – payable by self-employed earners.

Contributions are collected and recorded by the Inland Revenue. Contact with the Inland Revenue may lead to information about you being passed to the Home Office (see p120).

For full details of the NI scheme and contribution conditions for benefits, see CPAG's *Welfare Benefits Handbook*.

Residence and presence

If your earnings are high enough for you/your employer to have to pay contributions, those contributions only have to be paid if the residence and presence rules apply (see Chapter 23). If contributions are not compulsory, you can pay voluntary Class 2 or 3 contributions to help you meet the contribution conditions for benefits. If you wish to pay contributions while abroad, the application form is in DWP leaflet NI38.

Contributions paid in Northern Ireland or the Isle of Man count towards British benefits. You may also be able to use special rules if you have lived in another European Union/European Economic Area member state (see Part 4) or a country with which the UK has a reciprocal agreement (see Part 5) even if you are not a national of that country.

Class 1 contributions

You are liable for Class 1 contributions in any week in which you are:
- employed in Great Britain (GB):[7] *and*
  – either resident or present in GB; *or*
  – ordinarily resident in GB;[8]
There is an exception to this rule if you are not ordinary resident in the UK, are employed by an overseas employer and normally work abroad.[9] You are only liable once you have been resident in the UK for one year. This also applies to some overseas students and apprentices;[10] *or*
- employed abroad, but only for the first year of that employment (after that you can voluntarily pay Class 3 contributions – see p125)[11] if:[12]
  – your employer has a place of business in GB; *and*
  – you were resident in GB before your employment started; *and*
  – you are ordinarily resident in GB.

Class 2 contributions

You are liable for Class 2 contributions in any week in which you are self-employed in GB and either:[13]
- you are ordinarily resident in GB; *or*
- you have been resident in GB for at least 26 weeks in the last year.

You can voluntarily pay Class 2 contributions for any other week in which you are either employed or self-employed and present in GB.[14]

If you are self-employed abroad, you can voluntarily pay Class 2 contributions if you were employed or self-employed immediately before you left GB and:[15]
- you have been resident in GB for a continuous period of at least three years at some time before that; *and*
- you have paid sufficient GB contributions to give you a full contribution record for three past contribution years (for details see CPAG's *Welfare Benefits Handbook*).

If you are a volunteer development worker employed abroad but ordinarily resident in GB, you can voluntarily pay Class 2 contributions.[16] These are paid at a special rate and (unlike normal Class 2 contributions) count for contribution-based jobseeker's allowance. They are only payable if the Inland Revenue certifies that it would be consistent with the proper administration of the law to allow you to do so.

Class 3 contributions

Class 3 contributions are always voluntary. You can pay them:
- for any year during all of which you were resident in GB; other conditions apply where you have recently arrived in GB;[17] *or*
- for any year, part of which you were outside the UK, if you meet the conditions for voluntary payment of Class 2 contributions (see above), except that you do not need to have been employed or self-employed before you left GB;[18] *or*
- if you have previously been paying Class 1 contributions from abroad.

Class 4 contributions

You are liable for Class 4 contributions in any week in which you are resident in GB for income tax purposes.[19]

Credits and home responsibilities protection

You may be credited for Class 1 or 2 contributions in certain weeks, normally where you would satisfy the qualifying conditions for a benefit, including if you are incapable of work, or unemployed and actively seeking and available for work. Credits help meet the contribution conditions for benefits. The various types of credit each have their own residence conditions, usually linked to those for the equivalent benefit. For details of credits, see CPAG's *Welfare Benefits Handbook*.

Making the most of your contribution record

Your benefits entitlement may depend upon your contribution record. In particular, your right to a state retirement pension and the amount of that pension is set by the number of contributions you have made. A small shortfall in your record may make a big difference to your benefits. A shortfall may, in some cases, be made up by voluntary contributions or by allocating to your name contributions already made.

If you have returned from abroad you should ask the Inland Revenue Contributions Office for a copy of your contribution record. You can then check that contributions have been made while you were abroad. You may also be able to make up any shortfall in your record by voluntary contributions.

You may have used another person's number or a false number while in GB because you did not wish to come to the attention of the Home Office. If you have since been given leave to remain in the UK, you should apply for an NI number in your own name. You may wish to ask the Contributions Office to transfer contributions allocated to the number you used in the past to the number issued in your name. This would mean that the contributions paid for your work would be allocated to you. You may need to provide evidence that the contributions were paid because of your work. However, you may have committed a criminal offence by using a number which was not allocated to you – eg, if you used that number to get work you may have committed the offence of obtaining property (your wages) by deception (pretending that the number was allocated to you). Because of this, you should take independent advice before asking the Contributions Office to transfer contributions to your name.

5. **Proving immigration status, age and relationships**

For most people, proving immigration status, identity, age and their relationships to others (eg, marriage or parentage) is straightforward. However, some people may have problems and migrants are most likely to be affected.

Immigration status

It is often difficult for people who have come from abroad to prove their immigration status. Often documents will have been sent to the Home Office and the claimant may not have any documentation to show to the benefit authority. Equally, although the benefit authority may contact the Home Office for details of the individual, it often does not bother to do so and even when it does Home Office staff often say that they cannot locate a file. Even where documents are available – eg, a passport – these may not clearly indicate a person's immigration status. The absence of clear documentation means that benefit authority staff have to make decisions on an individual's immigration status. However, with virtually no training in this area they are not equipped to do so.

Age

Your age, or the age of members of your family, may affect your rights to benefit, or the amount of that benefit. This most commonly arises in claims for retirement pension, but the amount of other benefits (eg, income support) can also be affected.

The most common situation in which the benefits authorities dispute age is where you were born abroad in a place where dates of birth were not accurately recorded at that time.

Benefits authority officials are generally more willing than the Home Office to accept foreign records as accurate. If you have a birth certificate, that will usually be accepted as proof of your birth date. Other evidence which can show your birth date includes:

- passport or identity card;
- school or health records;
- army records;
- statements from people who know you or your family;
- astrological charts made for a baby at the time of the birth.

You may be able to show your birth date by referring to the accepted birth dates of other relatives. For example, if you are recorded as the eldest child and your sister has been accepted as born on a date in 1937, you must have been born before that date.

Medical assessments are sometimes used as evidence of age. This involves a doctor examining you and guessing how old you are. Some doctors use X–rays as part of this assessment. In adults this method is only accurate to within a few years at best.

A common problem is conflicting evidence. Your birth date may have been wrongly recorded in your passport when it was issued – eg, because you gave the wrong date or because of an administrative error. Passports are commonly recorded as '1 January' where the exact date is unclear. The date in the passport may then have been used in many other official documents. It may be difficult to persuade the benefits authorities that all these dates are wrong. You should explain that all these dates come from one document, so the only real evidence for the date is the passport. If there is other evidence showing that date is not right, the passport is not conclusive evidence.

While each piece of evidence has to be considered, the oldest documents may be more reliable, since they were made nearer to the time of the events to which they refer.

If there is no documentary evidence, the benefits authorities should accept your own statements unless they are contradictory or improbable.

Your birth date may be given in the document(s) as a year or a month rather than an actual date. If this applies, the DWP will assume your birth date is the date least favourable to you. If you claim retirement pension, this will be the last day of the year/month. However, this date should then be used for all other benefit decisions, even if that is more favourable to you.

If a benefits authority refuses to accept your evidence about your age and so refuses benefit or pays it at a lower rate, you should appeal and take independent advice.

Marriages and divorces

You may need to show that you are/were married to your partner. This is most likely to apply to claims for bereavement benefits. It may also apply where there is a question of the validity of the marriage (see p151).

A marriage certificate is the best evidence that you are or were married. However, if one is not available, other evidence can count. Your own statement that you were married should be enough. This is because, unlike date of birth, you can be expected to remember that you were married and to whom. If there is contradictory evidence, or if you are claiming benefit as an appointee for a person whose mental state prevents them from making such a statement or for a person who has died, you may need to show by other ways that there was a marriage.

The most important of these is the cohabitation presumption. If a couple live together as if they were husband and wife, it is presumed that they are married to each other, unless there is clear contradictory evidence to which the benefits authority can point.[20] Evidence of living together will usually be easier to get than evidence of the wedding, which may have happened a long time ago. This presumption is even stronger where there are children of the couple, because the effect of a decision that there was no wedding would be that the children were illegitimate. This presumption is different from benefit rules which treat unmarried couples as if they were married. You must still show that you were/are married, but showing that you were/are living together as husband and wife is enough, unless there is contradictory evidence.

Parentage

In rare cases you may need to show that you are (or your late spouse was) the parent of a child. This could apply where child benefit is claimed for a child by you and one or more other people, none of whom is living with the child. In this situation, a parent has priority over other claimants.[21] It may also arise if you are refused widowed parent's allowance (or awarded it at a reduced rate) because it is disputed that your child or children are children of your late spouse.[22]

DNA testing may be able accurately to establish whether the person is/was the parent of the child concerned. If this is not possible, the parent may be able to use the presumption of legitimacy. If the child was conceived by or born to a married woman, there is a legal presumption that her husband is the father.[23] If you were married to the mother, you are presumed to be the father. In the case of widowed parent's allowance, your late husband is therefore presumed to be the father of any child conceived or born during the marriage. The presumption applies even if the child was born after the wedding but obviously conceived before.[24] The presumption can be overridden by evidence that the husband was not the father.[25] For the benefits authorities to do this, there must be evidence that shows the child was probably not legitimate.[26] If you are the claimed father but the mother was married to another man, he, rather than you, is presumed to be the father.

If the mother was not married at the time of conception or birth, there is no presumption.

Notes

1. **Social security and immigration control**
   1 In particular, s115 IAA 1999. For the rules before that date, see the 2nd edition of this *Handbook*.
   2 For an overview of the development of these rules and those applying to local authority assistance see Hale LJ's judgment in *O v LB Wandsworth, Bhika v Leicester City Council*, unreported, 21 June 2000, CA.

2. **Home Office links with benefits authorities**
   3 HB/CTB Circular A1/96 para 4
   4 The DWP uses a DCI 100 form.
   5 See Dummett and Nicol, *Subjects, Citizens, Aliens and Others*, Weidenfeld & Nicholson, 1990, p233

4. **National insurance contributions**
   6 s1(2) SSCBA 1992
   7 s2(1)(a) SSCBA 1992
   8 Reg 119(1)(a) SS(Con) Regs
   9 Reg 145(2) SS(Con) Regs
   10 Reg 145(3) SS(Con) Regs
   11 Reg 146(2)(b) SS(Con) Regs

12 Reg 146 SS(Con) Regs
13 s2(1)(b) SSCBA 1992; reg 145(1)(d) SS(Con) Regs
14 Reg 145(1)(c) SS(Con) Regs
15 Reg 147 SS(Con) Regs
16 Regs 149-154 SS(Con) Regs
17 Reg 145(1)(e) SS(Con) Regs
18 Reg 147 SS(Con) Regs
19 Reg 91 SS(Con) Regs

5. **Proving immigration status, age and relationships**
   20 *Re Taylor* [1961] WLR 9, CA. For more cases see Keane, *The Modern Law of Evidence*, Butterworths
   21 Sch 10 SSCBA 1992
   22 s39A(3) SSCBA 1992
   23 See Keane (note 20)
   24 *The Poulet Peerage Case* [1903] AC 395. In Scotland, s5(1)(a) Law Reform (Parent and Child) (Scotland) Act 1986
   25 For possible sources of evidence, see Keane (note 20).
   26 s26 FLRA 1969; *S v S* [1972] AC 24 at 41. In Scotland, s5(4) Law Reform (Parent and Child) (Scotland) Act 1986

Chapter 11

Presence and residence

This chapter covers:
1. Presence and absence (p131)
2. Ordinary residence (p132)
3. Habitual residence (p135)

Presence and absence are quite straightforward, but 'ordinary' and 'habitual' residence can cause problems.[1]

Problems most often arise with the habitual residence test for income support, income-based jobseeker's allowance, housing benefit and council tax benefit, but they can arise with ordinary residence. Benefit rules are usually precise, even if they are complicated. However, the residence conditions are simple but very vague. They need judgement and weighing up of many different factors. Two different decision makers can legally reach different opinions about the residence of a particular person. The vagueness of the residence conditions also allows for extremely restrictive interpretation, deliberate or accidental use of personal bias and assumptions about how people do or should lead their lives. This is most obvious when the decision maker lacks knowledge of, or ignores, the claimant's own culture.

Guidance to benefits staff states that a decision must be made on all the facts, but sets out certain factors which may be relevant. Because staff are used to applying precise rules, they tend to change these factors into checklists. This often leads to far too much weight being given to certain factors and to decisions which are obviously wrong from a common sense point of view.

Example

One tribunal decision[2] concerned a British citizen born abroad who lived and worked in the UK for two years and who then made an overseas visit of one month to her estranged husband who was very ill. The tribunal decided that on her return she was not habitually resident in the UK because her husband and children lived abroad and she was unlikely to be able to afford ever to bring them to the UK, even if they were permitted to enter and she may have owned property abroad. That decision was clearly wrong on any understanding of habitual residence. The length of time the claimant had lived here, renting her own flat with her own permanent job (from which she had been made redundant), meant she became habitually resident, regardless of the whereabouts of her family and property or her prospects of finding work. Her visit abroad did not break that residence. The tribunal went wrong because it focused on her family ties and prospects of employment.

Caselaw gives examples of how residence conditions have been considered and the factors which were important in those cases. However, it is important that these factors do not become *conditions* which the claimant has to meet. Each case is different: a factor which is crucial in one case may not be crucial in another.

Ordinary residence has only one meaning,[3] so a case on ordinary residence in one area of law applies to ordinary residence in a different area of law. Likewise, habitual residence only has one meaning, so a case on one area of law also applies in another. The only exception to this is where a court decides that, because of the legal context, ordinary (or habitual) residence has a special meaning in that area of law. Cases from that area of law will then not apply outside that area.

Sometimes you can use the facts of another case on residence (ordinary or habitual) to support your argument that you are resident. There are two sorts of residence case. First, where the court or tribunal is making a decision on residence itself – eg, family court cases. Here the facts of the case being considered may be a useful example. The second sort is where the court or tribunal is considering whether another body (eg, Inland Revenue) was legally justified in deciding that, on the evidence before it, a person was (or was not) ordinarily resident. The facts of the second sort must be used more carefully because the court has only considered whether a person in that situation can be considered as resident, not whether the person is resident.

1. **Presence and absence**

Presence means physical presence. Great Britain (GB) is Wales, Scotland, England and adjacent islands (but not the Isle of Man or Channel Islands).[4] The UK is GB and Northern Ireland.[5]

The UK includes UK territorial waters and GB includes UK territorial waters adjacent to GB.[6] Territorial waters are those within 12 miles of the shore,[7] except off Dover and near the Isle of Man where they stop mid-point to France/Isle of Man.[8] This means that if you travel to GB by boat, you become present when the boat enters these adjacent territorial waters. If you travel to GB by plane, you become present when the plane lands.

If you have to be **present** in GB to be entitled to a benefit, you must show that you were in GB from midnight to midnight.[9] If a benefits authority wants to disqualify you from benefit because you were absent from GB, it must show you were absent throughout that day. This means that on the day you leave GB and the day you arrive in GB you count as neither present nor absent.

The rules for child benefit are different. When working out whether a person was present or absent in the UK on a particular day, it is the situation at midnight at the beginning of the day that counts.[10] When working out whether a person is in a particular situation in any week, it is the situation at midnight at the beginning of that Monday that counts for the whole of the following week.[11] This means that, if you arrive in GB at 11.50 pm on Sunday, you count as present for the whole of the following week, but if you arrive at 12.10 am on Monday, you count as absent for that week.

2. Ordinary residence

You must be ordinarily resident in Great Britain (GB) to be entitled to:
- working families' tax credit;[12]
- disabled person's tax credit;[13]
- disability living allowance;[14]
- attendance allowance;[15]
- invalid care allowance;[16]
- severe disablement allowance;[17]
- Category D retirement pension.[18]

If a person stops being ordinarily resident in GB, the amount of her/his retirement pension (of any category) is frozen (see p185).

There is no definition in the benefits regulations of ordinary residence. This means that 'ordinary residence' is given its ordinary and natural meaning.[19] The most important case on ordinary residence is *Shah*.[20] In that case the House of Lords decided that ordinary residence means:[21]

> a person's 'abode in a particular place or country which he has adopted voluntarily and for settled purposes as part of the regular order of his life for the time being, whether of short or long duration.'

It should usually be clear whether residence is voluntary or for a settled purpose.[22]
The caselaw on ordinary residence shows that:
- ordinary residence can start on arrival in GB, or it can start before (see p133);
- a person in GB for a temporary purpose can be ordinarily resident in GB (see p133);
- a person who lives in GB but has no fixed abode can be ordinarily resident;[23]
- ordinary residence can continue during absences from GB, but leaving to settle abroad will normally end ordinary residence (see p133);
- a person who spends most of the time (or even almost all of the time) outside GB can be ordinarily resident;[24]
- a person can be ordinarily resident in more than one place or country;[25]
- ordinary residence is different from the concept of 'domicile'.[26]

Special rules apply to children (see p134) and other people whose place of residence is beyond their control (see p134).

Ordinary residence on arrival

Ordinary residence can begin immediately on arrival in GB.[27] In a family law case, a man who separated from his wife in one country (where he had lived and worked for three years) and went to live at his parent's house in another, was found to become immediately ordinarily resident there.[28] The Court of Appeal said that, where there is evidence that the person intends to make a place his home for an indefinite period, he is ordinarily resident when he arrives there. In another case, a court decided that a woman returning from Australia after some months there had never lost her ordinary residence in England, but, if she had, she became ordinarily resident again when the boat embarked from Australia.[29] The students in *Shah* had to show that they were ordinarily resident within a few weeks of first arriving in the UK, but it was not argued that they could not be ordinarily resident because they had only just come to GB.[30]

Temporary purpose

To be ordinarily resident in GB you do not have to intend or be able to live here permanently. The purpose can be for a limited period and Lord Scarman said that 'education, business or profession, employment, health, family, or merely love of the place spring to mind as common reasons for a choice of regular abode'.[31] You may have several different reasons for a single stay – eg, to visit relatives, get medical advice, attend religious ceremonies and sort out personal affairs.[32]

The reason must be a settled one. This does not mean that the reason has to be long-standing,[33] but there must be evidence of it. In most of the cases on ordinary residence, the court was looking back to see whether a person had been ordinarily resident months or years before.[34] This is much easier than deciding whether a person has recently become ordinarily resident. There is no minimum period of residence before you are ordinarily resident. If, for example, you have arrived in the UK and started work, the benefits authorities should consider how long you are likely to reside in the UK. If you intend to live here for the time being, the benefits authorities should accept your intention as sufficient, unless it is clearly unlikely that you are going to be able to stay. The benefits authorities should not make a deep examination of your long-term intentions.[35] The type of accommodation you occupy may be relevant.[36]

Absence from the UK

If you are ordinarily resident in GB, you can lose that status if you go abroad. This depends upon:
- why you go abroad;

- how long you stay abroad;
- what connections you keep with GB – eg, accommodation, furniture and other possessions.[37]

If you decide to move abroad for the foreseeable future, then you will normally stop being ordinarily resident in GB on the day you leave.[38] A possible exception to this is where your plans are clearly impractical and you return to GB very quickly.

If your absence abroad is part of your normal pattern of life, your ordinary residence in GB will not be affected.[39] This applies even if you are out of GB for most of the year.[40] For example, if you spend each summer in GB but all winter abroad, you may be ordinarily resident in GB.

If your absence abroad is extraordinary or temporary, and you intend to return to GB, your ordinary residence will not be affected.[41] A British woman who spent 15 months in Germany with her husband over a period of three years kept her ordinary residence in England. She had always intended to return here.[42]

However, if you are away from GB for a long time and do not keep strong connections with GB you may lose your ordinary residence, even if you intend to return. A citizen of the United Kingdom and colonies (see Chapter 2) lived in the UK for over four years, and then returned to Kenya for two years and five months because her business here failed, and there was a business opportunity in Kenya. She intended to make enough money to support herself on her return to the UK. Her parents and parents-in-law remained in the UK. She was found to have lost her ordinary residence during her absence.[43]

Involuntary residence

A person who is held in a place against her/his will may not become ordinarily resident. These cases are very rare. Examples given by the courts are kidnap victims and being stranded on a desert island.[44] The courts have recognised that circumstances which limit or remove a person's choice, may not stop them from being ordinarily resident where they reside.[45] A woman who became mentally ill on a visit to England and remained in an asylum until she died over 50 years later, was ordinarily resident in GB by the time she died, even though she never decided to stay here.[46] Deportation to GB does not prevent you becoming ordinarily resident here.[47] We consider that the issue is whether the person's residence is part of their settled purpose. If you have decided to live in GB, it does not matter that you have made that decision because you have been deported here.

Children

If you are aged 16 or 17, ordinary residence is decided using the same rules as for adults.[48]

The only benefit for children under 16 with an ordinary residence test is disability living allowance. The residence of a child aged under 16 is usually decided by her/his parent(s) or person(s) with parental responsibility (or in Scotland, parental rights and responsibilities). Therefore, if the child lives with that person, the child will usually have the same ordinary residence as that person.[49] So, a child joining a parent or other person with parental responsibility may become ordinarily resident almost immediately.[50] If there is only one person with parental responsibility, the child has the same ordinary residence as that person.[51]

Where there are two such people who live apart, one of them should get the consent of the other to a change of residence of the child, otherwise the child may be treated as abducted. A child who is abducted is considered still to have the same ordinary residence as the person(s) with parental responsibility.[52] Agreement to a change of residence may be assumed if the other person takes no action.[53]

3. **Habitual residence**

If you are not habitually resident in the UK, Ireland, Channel Islands or Isle of Man, you are not entitled to income support (IS), income-based jobseeker's allowance (JSA), housing benefit or council tax benefit.[54] For exceptions, see the chapter relevant to your immigration status.

Habitual residence test and international law

If you are a national of a European Economic Area (EEA) state, refusal of benefit because of the habitual residence test may breach European Community (EC) law (see p137).

If you are a national of Cyprus, Czech Republic, Hungary, Malta, Poland, Slovakia or Turkey, refusal of benefit because of the habitual residence test may break the UK's international obligations. Under the 1961 European Social Chapter[55] the UK must not discriminate on nationality grounds in providing these benefits to nationals of those countries.[56] The habitual residence test is discriminatory on national grounds. This charter is not part of British law (unlike the European Convention on Human Rights) so breaches of the UK's obligations do not make the benefit refusal unlawful.[57] UK compliance with these treaties is supervised by the Council of Europe Committee of Experts and a complaint may lead the UK government to change the law. If this applies to you, contact a specialist advice agency.

The meaning of habitual residence

A person is habitually resident if s/he is **ordinarily resident** in the UK, Ireland, Channel Islands or Isle of Man (see p132) and has been **resident for an**

appreciable period of time.[58] The length of the appreciable period depends on your case but may be short, for example, a month.[59] However, there is no fixed minimum period.[60] Therefore, it might be a matter of days. It can include visits to prepare for settled residence made before that residence is actually taken up.[61] There are some situations when no appreciable period may be necessary:

- where you have been habitually resident in the UK in the past, even though the length of your absence means that the previous habitual residence has come to an end. This exception originates from a comment made in a House of Lords' case that 'there may indeed be special cases where a person concerned is not coming here for the first time but is resuming an habitual residence previously had'.[62] The DWP often uses this exception in favour of UK citizens returning after a long period living in one of the former colonies;
- where you can take advantage of EC law (see p137).

The factors that are relevant to deciding whether you are habitually resident include:[63]

- bringing possessions;
- doing everything necessary to establish residence before coming;
- having a right of abode (see p22);
- bringing or seeking to bring family;
- ties with the UK.

To be habitually resident you must be seen to be making a home here, but it does not have to be your only home or a permanent one.[64] So a long-standing intention to move abroad (for example, when debts are paid) does not prevent a person from being habitually resident.[65]

You can be seen to be making a home here even though you have very few or no resources. For example, approaching housing associations and trying to find work help to show that you are making a home here.

The practicality or 'viability' of your arrangements for residence might be relevant to deciding whether you are resident and the length of the appreciable period.[66] We consider that a person who has no money to support her/himself in Great Britain but who intends to stay is likely to be resident here for the foreseeable future because s/he cannot afford to go anywhere else. So a person with no income will have a short appreciable period. Lack of viability can only make it more difficult to show habitual residence if it means that you are likely to leave the UK soon.

Events after the benefit claim or decision may show that your intention was always to reside in the UK.[67] For example, if you are refused income-based JSA because the DWP does not accept you have a settled intention to stay in the UK, the fact that you are still here by the time of the appeal hearing may help to show that you always intended to stay.

The decision about whether or not you are habitually resident has to be made on the 'balance of probabilities'. If the probabilities in favour of each answer are exactly equal, the decision should be that you *are* habitually resident. This is because the benefits authority has to show that you are *not* habitually resident.[68]

Dealing with the habitual residence test

You will normally be interviewed. You should explain the steps you have taken to make the UK your home. You should provide any documents which will help your case – eg, registration with local doctor; school/college enrolment; evidence of looking for work; letters from relatives and friends settled in the UK.

The DWP and local authorities do not apply the habitual residence test properly or even consistently. In practice, the test usually means that you are denied benefits at first, but not indefinitely. Local offices may have a rule of thumb, such as one month, after which a person will pass the test. However, practice varies between and within offices, so even if you fail the test at one office, you could pass it at another. However, once you are accepted as habitually resident, you are very unlikely to fail the test at a later date, even if your benefit claim stops or you change benefit offices.

Because establishing an appreciable period of residence is only a matter of time, if you fail the test, you should make further claims at regular intervals. You should appeal against every refusal, but the tribunal which hears that appeal will only be able to consider whether you were habitually resident on or before the DWP decision. Some DWP offices tell claimants the appreciable period for them to be accepted as habitually resident. If this applies, you should reclaim when you have been resident for that period but still appeal the earlier refusal.

Habitual residence under European Community law

Under the EC co-ordination rules (see p345), you are entitled to receive any 'special non-contributory benefits', which include IS, in the EU member state in which you reside, so long as you qualify for it under that country's social security scheme.[69] For this purpose, 'residence' means 'habitual residence'.[70] This phrase has a different meaning in EC law than UK law. There, if you come under the co-ordination rules, you are entitled to have the question of your habitual residence for IS purposes dealt with under EC law rather than UK law.

Habitual residence in EC law is not defined. The caselaw of the European Court of Justice (ECJ)[71] explains what habitual residence means, but (except for *Swaddling*) only in the situation where a person wishes to claim an unemployment benefit in a country other than the one where s/he last worked.[72] The ECJ decided that, because this is a special situation, there must be a very restrictive approach to who can qualify. For that reason we consider that the caselaw on this special provision is not useful guidance on habitual residence in other situations under British or EC law.

Unlike UK law, EC law does *not* always require an 'appreciable period' for habitual residence.[73] This only applies to you if you can rely on the EC co-ordination rule (see p346). This is most likely to apply if you are returning to the UK, but it might apply in other cases. In the case of *Swaddling* the ECJ said 'the length of residence cannot be regarded as an intrinsic element of the concept of [habitual] residence'.[74] This has been explained in a commissioners' decision[75] as meaning that it is not essential under EC law that the residence should have lasted for any particular length of time, but the length of residence remains a factor to be considered. So, in some cases where other factors point in favour of you being considered habitually resident, this can be so from the date of your arrival in the UK.

EC law may allow your residence in another EEA country to count towards any appreciable period of residence under UK law.[76]

Notes

1 See *Failing the Test*, NACAB, February 1996, for a detailed account of the habitual residence test in practice.
2 R(IS) 6/96
3 *R v Barnet LBC ex parte Shah aka Akbarali v Brent LBC* [1983] 2 AC 309; [1983] 2 WLR 16; [1983] 1 All ER 226 [1983] 127 SJ 36; [1983] 81 LGR 305; [1983] 133 New LJ; HL, Lord Scarman at p343H

1. Presence and absence
4 Union With Scotland Act 1706; Sch 2 para 5(a) IntA 1978
5 Sch1 IntA 1978, definition of 'UK'; R(S) 5/85
6 s172 SSCBA 1992; s35(1) JSA 1995, definition of 'GB'
7 s1 Territorial Sea Act 1987
8 Territorial Sea (Limits) Order 1989 SI No.482
9 R(S) 1/66
10 Reg 1(3) CB(RPA) Regs
11 s147(1) SSCBA 1992, definition of 'week'

2. Ordinary residence
12 Reg 3(1)(a) FC Regs
13 Reg 5(1)(a) DWA Regs
14 Reg 2(1)(a)(i) DLA Regs
15 Reg 2(1)(a)(i) AA Regs

16 Reg 9(1)(a) SS(ICA) Regs
17 Reg 3(1)(a)(i) SS(SDA) Regs
18 Reg 10(b) SS(WB&RP) Regs
19 R(M) 1/85
20 *Shah* (see note 3)
21 *Shah* p343H
22 *Shah* p344G
23 *Levene v Inland Revenue Commissioners* [1928] AC 217, HL
24 *Levene; Inland Revenue Commissioners v Lysaght* [1928] AC 234, HL
25 eg, Lysaght was found to be ordinarily resident in England even though he was clearly also ordinarily resident in the Irish Free State.
26 *Shah* p345E-H (see note 3)
27 R(F) 1/62
28 *Macrae v Macrae* [1949] P 397; [1949] 2 All ER 34; 93 SJ 449; 47 LGR 437, CA (the countries were Scotland and England which are separate for family law purposes). In R(IS) 6/96 para 27 the commissioner doubts the correctness of *Macrae* because he considers it used a test very close to the 'real home' test rejected in *Shah*. He does not seem to have heard any argument about this: *Macrae* was cited in *Shah* and was not one of the cases mentioned there as wrong: pp342-43.

29 *Lewis v Lewis* [1956] 1 WLR 200; [1956] 1 All ER 375; 100 SJ 134, High Court

30 The facts are in the Court of Appeal's judgment: *R v Barnet LBC ex parte Shah* [1982] QB 688 at p717E; [1982] 2 WLR 474; [1982] 1 All ER 698; [1982] 80 LGR 571

31 *Shah* p344C-D (see note 3). In R(F) 1/62 education was the purpose

32 *Levene*

33 For example, Macrae's decision to move to Scotland was made shortly before he went.

34 For example, *Shah*

35 *Shah* p344G (see note 3)

36 R(F) 1/82; R(F) 1/62; R(P) 1/62; R(P) 4/54

37 R(F) 1/62; R(M) 1/85

38 *Hopkins v Hopkins* [1951] P 116; *R v Hussain* (1971) 56 Crim App R 165, CA; *R v IAT ex parte Ng* [1986] Imm AR 23, QBD

39 *Shah*; CG/204/1949; *R v IAT ex parte Siggins* [1985] Imm AR 14, QBD

40 *Levene; Lysaght*

41 *Shah* p342D (see note 3)

42 *Stransky v Stransky* [1954] 3 WLR 123; [1954] 2 All ER 536

43 *Haria* [1986] Imm AR 165, IAT

44 *Shah*

45 *Lysaght*

46 In *Re Mackenzie* [1941] 1 Chancery Reports 69

47 *Gout v Cimitian* [1922] 1 AC 105, PC: deportation of an Ottoman subject from Egypt did not stop him becoming ordinarily resident in Cyprus.

48 *Re A (A Minor: Abduction: Child's Objections)* [1994] 2 FLR 126: on habitual residence, but also applies to ordinary residence.

49 *Re M (Minors) (Residence Order: Jurisdiction)* [1993] 1 FLR 495, CA: on habitual residence, but also applies to ordinary residence.

50 *Re M (Minors) (Residence Order: Jurisdiction)* [1993] 1 FLR 495, per Hoffman LJ: on habitual residence, but also applies to ordinary residence.

51 *Re J (A Minor) (Abduction: Custody Rights)* [1990] 2 AC 562 at 578

52 *Re M (Minors: Residence Order: Jurisdiction)* [1993] 1 FLR 495

53 *Re A (A Minor) (Abduction: Acquiescence)* [1992] 2 FLR 14: on habitual residence, but also applies to ordinary residence.

3. Habitual residence

54 Reg 21(3) IS Regs 'person from abroad'; reg 85(4) JSA Regs 'person from abroad'; reg 7A(4)(e) HB Regs; reg 4A(4)(e) CTB Regs

55 Text available at http://conventions.coe.int/treaty/en/Treaties/Word/035.doc The European Convention on Social and Medical Assistance has the same effect but only for Cyprus, Malta and Turkey.

56 The UK has ratified Art 13(4) of the Charter which prohibits discrimination on national grounds in the field of social assistance against nationals of other states which have ratified it. At the time of writing the Charter had been ratified by the states listed in the text and by the EEA states.

57 *R v SSHD ex parte Brind*, HL [1991] 1 AC 696; [1991] 1 All ER 720; [1991] 2 WLR 58

58 *Nessa v Chief Adjudication Officer* [1999] 1 WLR 1937; [1999] 4 All ER 677; [1999] 2 FLR 1116, HL

59 *Re F (A Minor) (Child Abduction)* [1994] FLR 548, CA, cited in *Nessa v Chief Adjudication Officer* [1999] 1 WLR 1937, HL; R(IS) 2/00

60 R(IS) 2/00 para 24; *Cameron v Cameron* [1996] SLT 306

61 R(IS) 2/00 para 26

62 R(IS) 2/00 (House of Lords decision)

63 R(IS) 2/00

64 CR(IS) 6/96 para 19

65 *M v M (Abduction: England & Scotland)* [1997] 2 FLR 263, CA

66 R(IS) 6/96 paras 28-30; R(IS) 2/00 para 28

67 R(IS) 2/00 para 30

68 R(IS) 6/96 para 15

69 Art 10A(1) EC Reg 1408/71

70 Art 1(h) EC Reg 1408/71

71 R(U) 7/85; R(U) 8/88 and the cases listed in that case

72 Under Art 71(1)(b)(ii) EC Reg 1408/71

73 Case C-90/97 *Swaddling* [1999] 2 CMLR 2679; [1999] 2 FLR 185

74 para 30

75 R(IS) 3/00 para 16

76 Under Art 10a(2) EC Reg 1408/71. This argument was mentioned but not resolved in R(IS) 3/00.

Chapter 12

Special rules for family members

This chapter covers the special rules which apply to:
1. Families with different immigration statuses (below)
2. Couples where one partner is abroad (p141)
3. Families where a dependent adult is abroad (p148)
4. Families where a child is abroad (p149)
5. Polygamous marriages (p151)
6. Children born in the UK without the right of abode (p158)

For the rules where the whole family is abroad, see Part 3.

There are special rules to stop you losing benefit if you move between Great Britain and Northern Ireland.[1] You may also be able to use special rules if you have lived in another European Economic Area member state (see Part 4) or a country with which the UK has a reciprocal agreement (see Part 5) even if you are not a national of that country.

1. Families with different immigration statuses

Sometimes members of the same family may have different immigration statuses. For example, a husband may be a British citizen or have indefinite leave to remain while his wife has limited leave to remain as a spouse. Couples with different statuses often have difficulties with benefit claims. One of the couple may be eligible for benefit but they may have difficulty convincing the benefit authorities that they are eligible and in particular that they satisfy the national insurance number requirement (see p122). A major consideration is often whether or not a claim will jeopardise the immigration position of the partner who wishes to settle in the UK. Where a couple are asylum seekers one of the couple may have been granted exceptional leave to remain or full refugee status while their partner awaits a decision on their asylum claim and therefore remains an asylum seeker. Some benefits have rules which deal with this type of situation. For example, the income support and income-based jobseeker's allowance rules allow a couple with 'mixed' immigration statuses to claim benefit at the single person's rate. In order to establish the benefit position for couples and families in this situation you should check the individual chapter for that immigration status in this book.

2. **Couples where one partner is abroad**

If you are in Great Britain (GB) but your partner (see below) is abroad, your benefit entitlement may be affected. For example, if your partner is working full time while abroad, you may be refused income support (IS)/income-based jobseeker's allowance (JSA).

If you are entitled to maternity allowance, incapacity benefit, a retirement pension, or invalid care allowance, you may get an increase for your spouse, even though s/he is abroad. For the rules on increases for adult dependants other than spouses, see p148.

Household

Under the rules for:
- IS;
- Income-based JSA;
- housing benefit (HB);
- council tax benefit (CTB);
- working families' tax credit (WFTC);
- disabled person's tax credit (DPTC);

a person can only count as your partner if you share the same household.

This applies if you are a married couple[2] or an unmarried couple.[3] A **'household'** is something abstract, not something physical like a home. It is made up of either a single person or a group of people held together by social ties.[4] A person cannot be a member of two households at the same time.[5] A person can be temporarily absent from the home but still be a member of the household.[6] If it is not obvious whether people share a household, the important factors are:
- whether they share the same physical space – eg, a house, flat or room(s) in a hostel;
- whether they carry out chores for the benefit of all of them – eg, cooking, shopping, cleaning.

Each benefit has special rules allowing certain temporary absences of one partner from other members of the family to be ignored when considering whether there is a common household. These special rules do not override *all* the normal rules above about what is a household.[7] This means that, even if the temporary absence is ignored, your general situation may have changed enough for your partner to no longer be in your household. This is most likely to apply if your partner is now a member of a different household abroad.

Income support/income-based jobseeker's allowance

If a person abroad counts as your partner for IS/income–based JSA (see below) then:

- if your partner is in full-time employment (see CPAG's *Welfare Benefits Handbook*) you are *not* entitled to IS/income-based JSA.[8] This applies even if your partner is employed abroad and her/his earnings are very low in British terms or cannot be exchanged for pounds sterling;
- your partner's income and capital is taken into account as if they were your income or capital.[9] There are special rules about calculating capital abroad (see CPAG's *Welfare Benefits Handbook*);
- your applicable amount (see glossary of terms at the beginning of this book) includes an amount for your partner, but only in certain cases and then only for up to eight weeks (see p148);
- you lose any entitlement to family premium at the lone parent rate (which applies to some pre-6 April 1998 claimants, see CPAG's *Welfare Benefits Handbook*).[10]

If a person abroad counts as your partner, these rules mean that you may be paid less IS/income-based JSA than if s/he were living with you, or none at all. If this applies you can use the following rules to argue that the person should not count as your partner. If you receive income from that person while s/he does not count as your partner, that counts as maintenance and so might be disregarded as your income (see CPAG's *Welfare Benefits Handbook*). If these rules would mean that you do not have enough to live on, then that may breach the European Convention on Human Rights.[11] However, the Human Rights Act 1998 requires tribunals and courts, if possible, to interpret the law to avoid such a breach.[12] By interpreting 'partner' (see below) to apply to a couple who cannot practically live together at the moment, such a breach can usually be avoided.

When does a person count as your partner

A person of the opposite sex can count as your partner even though you are not married to her/him. This only applies if you are living with that person as if they were your spouse. In practice, if your unmarried partner is abroad, the DWP will usually not treat you as a couple for benefit purposes (but see p144 for when you may want to argue against this decision).

A person only counts as your partner if you are members of the same household (see p141). Some absences of your partner from you are ignored when considering whether you remain members of the same household. These rules do not apply if you have never actually shared a household with your partner.[13]

Example

Rifat marries Amjad in Pakistan. They have a week-long honeymoon. Rifat then returns to her home in the UK. Amjad intends to apply for a visa to join her in the UK. He works full time but earns the equivalent of £10 a week. Rifat loses her job and has to claim income-based JSA. The honeymoon was too short to count as sharing a household. Because they have never shared a household, the rules about ignoring temporary absences do not apply and Amjad does not count as Rifat's partner.

Temporary absences from other family members

If you are the claimant and your partner is temporarily living away from you (for the meaning of temporary, see p293), that absence is ignored when considering whether you share a household with your partner *unless*:[14]

- your partner and/or you do not intend to resume living with each other.[15] You may intend to resume living with each other, but your intentions may depend upon something beyond your control, such as getting a visa (see p144) or a job. If this applies, you may be able to argue that your intention does not count because it depends on these things;[16]
- your absence from each other is likely to exceed 52 weeks, but not if:
  – there are exceptional circumstances. The rules give an example of your partner having no control over the length of the absence, which would include delays caused by immigration controls; *and*
  – the absence is unlikely to be substantially more than 52 weeks;
- your partner is detained in custody serving a sentence imposed by a court pending trial or sentence.

These rules can apply where your partner is abroad.

Your partner's absence is from *you*, not from the family home, so these rules can apply even if your partner has never lived in your current home.[17] The length of the absence is worked out from when it started to when it is likely to finish. If circumstances change so that the likely total absence gets longer (or shorter) – eg, a family member falls ill – then the absence may become too long (or short enough) to count as temporary under these rules.

Example

Rifat joins Amjad in Pakistan for three months. She then returns home to the UK but, because of sickness, claims IS. Amjad applies for a visa to come to the UK. Because his absence from Rifat is likely substantially to exceed 52 weeks, she is treated as a single person and is entitled to IS. Three months later, Amjad is refused a visa on maintenance and accommodation grounds (see Chapter 5) and he appeals. One year later he wins his appeal and a visa is issued. Before he can travel to the UK his mother falls ill and he stays in Pakistan to care for her. Her illness is only expected to last a short time so Amjad expects to travel to the UK within a month. However, because his total absence from Rifat is now substantially more than 52 weeks, he is not treated as her partner even though the absence is expected to end soon.

If a couple is separated because one partner has to apply for a visa to come to the UK, there may be delay:

- to meet the immigration rules before applying for a visa, for example:
  - trying to get a job (or a job offer for the partner) so that the maintenance and accommodation rules are met;
  - waiting for recognition as a refugee, or for four years' exceptional leave to remain, or for indefinite leave to remain;
- waiting for a decision on a visa application – this often takes months;
- waiting for an appeal against a visa refusal – this usually takes at least six months from bringing the appeal until a visa is issued, if successful, and would often take at least a year.

The likely length of your separation depends upon how likely you are to be refused a visa. Refusal rates are high in African and Asian countries. If the absence is likely substantially to exceed 52 weeks, your absence from each other will not count as temporary (see above).

Getting income support/income-based jobseeker's allowance for a partner abroad

If your partner is temporarily absent (see p143) from GB but you are in GB, then for the first four weeks (or eight weeks if your partner is taking a child or young person abroad for treatment under the rules described on p298):

- your applicable amount continues to include any amounts for your partner;[18] *and*
- your partner counts as a member of your household, so her/his income and capital is taken into account in the usual way.[19]

This does not apply if your partner counts as a 'person subject to immigration control' (see p157).

If your partner stops meeting the temporary absence rules, or is absent for more than four/eight weeks, your applicable amount is reduced to that for a single person, even though any income or capital of your partner still counts as your income.[20] You may then want to argue that s/he no longer counts as your partner (see p142).

Housing benefit and council tax benefit

Claimant on income support/income-based jobseeker's allowance

If you are being paid IS/income-based JSA your partner's absence does not affect the amount of your HB, and will only affect CTB in exceptional circumstances (see p146). This is because you are treated as having no income or capital, so you are entitled to maximum HB/CTB regardless of whether your applicable amount is for a single person or a couple.[21] The local authority dealing with your HB/CTB claim should not make enquiries about your partner's absence.

Claimant not on income support/income-based jobseeker's allowance

If you are *not* being paid IS/income-based JSA the HB/CTB rules about who counts as your partner and temporary absences are the same as for IS (see pp142–143), except:[22]

- there are no special rules for partners;
- for CTB, there are no rules setting out the exceptions to the general rule that a temporary absence is ignored. However, absences which are likely to be more than 52 weeks may not count as temporary anyway. In practice, local authorities deal with CTB in the same way as HB.

If a person abroad counts as your partner under these rules then:

- your partner's income and capital is taken into account as if they were your income and capital.[23] There are special rules about calculating capital abroad (see CPAG's *Welfare Benefits Handbook*);
- your applicable amount includes an amount for your partner;[24]
- you lose any entitlement to family premium at the lone parent rate (which applies to some pre-6 April 1998 claimants, see CPAG's *Welfare Benefits Handbook*);[25] and
- for HB, your partner's absence does not affect the fact that you normally occupy your accommodation as your home.[26]

These rules mean that your HB/CTB will usually be the same as if your partner were living with you. This is different from the IS/income-based JSA rules, under which you may be often worse off.

If a person abroad does *not* count as your partner, your applicable amount will be for a single person, not a couple, so your HB/CTB may be paid at a lower rate.

In very unusual cases the person abroad may still be liable for current council tax, even though s/he no longer counts as your partner under CTB rules.[27] This is because the rules about council tax liability are different from those for CTB entitlement. If this happens, your CTB is calculated on the basis of your 'share' (ie, half the council tax) even though you are legally liable to pay all the council tax.[28] If this applies, the local authority can top up your CTB to the amount of your liability. You should ask it to do this and also try to get your partner's name removed from the list of liable people. For more details, see CPAG's *Council Tax Handbook*.

For more information about HB/CTB temporary absences, see p301.

Working families' tax credit and disabled person's tax credit

If your partner is in another European Economic Area member state, different rules may apply (see p381).

If a person abroad counts as your partner for WFTC/DPTC then:
* if s/he is working full time abroad and has no earnings from the UK, you are not entitled to WFTC/DPTC, even if you are employed full time in GB (but see below);[29]
* if s/he is not ordinarily resident (see p132) in GB, you are not entitled to WFTC/DPTC;[30]
* your partner's income and capital are taken into account as if they were your income and capital.[31] There are special rules about calculating capital abroad (see CPAG's *Welfare Benefits Handbook*);
* your WFTC applicable amount and maximum WFTC are still the same as for a single person or lone parent;[32]
* your DPTC applicable amount and maximum DPTC are higher for a couple than for a single person, although they are the same as for a lone parent so the amount of any benefit to which you are entitled may be higher.[33]

These rules mean that you may not be entitled to WFTC/DPTC, even though you would be if no one counted as your partner. If this applies you can use the following rules to argue that the person should not count as your partner. If you receive any income from that person while s/he does not count as your partner, that will count as maintenance and so might be disregarded as your income (see CPAG's *Welfare Benefits Handbook*).

If you are lawfully working in the UK and a national of a country which is a party to the Fifth ACP (Africa, Caribbean, Pacific) – European Community Convention (see p419), some of the above rules may breach European Community (EC) law. EC law may override the rules that your partner must be ordinarily resident in GB and must not receive all her/his earnings from full-time employment abroad.[34] If this may apply to you, ask an advice agency to contact CPAG.

When does a person count as your partner

A person only counts as your partner if you are members of the same household (see p141).[35] If you are living apart, but both of you intend to live together again, you are treated as being members of the same household.[36] This does not apply if you have never actually shared a household with your partner (see example on p143).[37] You may be able to argue that your intention only counts if it is unqualified and does not depend upon something beyond your (or your partner's) control, such as getting a visa (see p144) or a job.[38]

A person abroad is treated as if s/he were not in your household (and so does not count as your partner) if s/he is detained in custody serving a court sentence of 52 weeks or more.[39]

Child benefit

If a person abroad counts as your partner, you lose any entitlement to the lone parent rate (which applies to some pre-6 July 1998 claimants, – see CPAG's *Welfare Benefits Handbook*).[40] If the person who counts as your partner is also entitled to child benefit for a different child, then higher rate child benefit is only paid for the oldest of the children for whom both you and your partner are paid child benefit.[41]

Married couple

If you have a spouse abroad you lose any entitlement to the higher lone parent rate if you are residing together.[42] You count as residing together even while you are apart unless:[43]
* you have been separated from each other:
  – by court order or deed of separation; *or*
  – for 91 consecutive days; *and*
* this separation is likely to be permanent.

This rule will usually mean that you are not entitled to the higher rate if you and your spouse want to reside together, but are separated by immigration laws, war, persecution or simply lack of money. However, because you only need to show that the separation is likely to be permanent, if your spouse will probably never be able to join you, you are entitled to the higher rate.[44]

Any separation only because one (or both) spouses is an in-patient in a hospital or similar institution does not count as separation under this rule, even if it may be permanent.[45]

Unmarried couple

If you live with a person of the opposite sex as if you were married to each other, you lose any entitlement to the higher lone parent rate.[46] You can still count as living together during a temporary separation, but all the other circumstances of your relationship must be taken into account.[47] For living together as husband and wife, see CPAG's *Welfare Benefits Handbook*.

Spouse increase for contributory benefits and disability benefits

You may be entitled to an increase for your spouse (see CPAG's *Welfare Benefits Handbook*) if you are entitled to:

- incapacity benefit;
- invalid care allowance;
- maternity allowance;
- Category A or C retirement pension.

This increase is still payable while your spouse is abroad, if you are residing together.[48] You are treated as residing together during any temporary period (see p143) apart from each other.[49] Even if you both intend to be permanently absent from GB, as long as your absence from each other is only temporary, the increase for your spouse is not affected.[50]

Any separation only because one (or both) spouses is an in-patient in a hospital or similar institution does not count as separation under this rule, even if it may be permanent.[51]

There are special rules if your spouse is in another European Economic Area member state (see Part 4) or you are a national of Algeria, Morocco, Slovenia, Tunisia or Turkey (see p418).[52]

3. Families where a dependent adult is abroad

You may be entitled to an increase for a dependent adult who is looking after a child for whom you are responsible (for spouses see p141). This most commonly applies where you and the dependent adult are living together as husband and wife. You can get an increase (see CPAG's *Welfare Benefits Handbook*) if you are entitled to:

- incapacity benefit;
- invalid care allowance;
- maternity allowance;
- Category A or C retirement pension.

This increase is still payable while the adult is abroad, but only if you are residing together outside GB and you are not disqualified from receiving the benefit because of any absence from GB.[53] You are treated as residing together during any temporary absence (see p143) from each other.[54] Even if you both intend to be permanently absent from GB, as long as your absence from each other is only temporary, the increase is not affected.[55]

There are special rules if the adult is in another European Economic Area member state (see Part 4) or you are a national of Algeria, Morocco, Slovenia, Tunisia or Turkey (see p418).[56]

4. **Families where a child is abroad**

Some benefits are paid at a higher rate if you are responsible for a child. If that child goes abroad, your benefit entitlement may be affected.

Income support/income-based jobseeker's allowance

Your income support (IS)/income-based jobseeker's allowance (JSA) applicable amount includes an amount for each child for whom you are responsible.[57] This only applies to a child who is in your household (see p141).[58] You also get a family premium which may be paid at the lone parent rate (for certain pre-6 April 1998 claimants) and, in some cases, a disabled child premium (see CPAG's *Welfare Benefits Handbook*).

When considering whether the child remains a member of the household, only the following temporary absences (see p143) of a child from your household are ignored:

- up to eight weeks' absence from the UK if you and/or your partner meet the temporary absence rules for IS/income-based JSA due to treatment of a child abroad for a medical condition (see p298);[59] *otherwise*
- up to four weeks' absence from the UK.[60]

If you claimed either IS or income-based JSA after the child went abroad and you were not entitled to the other benefit immediately before claiming, these periods run from the date of claim.[61] If the child is abroad for longer than these periods, your IS/income-based JSA is worked out ignoring the child.

Housing benefit and council tax benefit

If you are being paid IS/income-based JSA a child's absence from the UK does not affect the amount of your housing benefit (HB)/council tax benefit (CTB). If you are not being paid IS/income-based JSA, then you may lose money if a child is treated as not being in your household. The following rules apply.

Your HB/CTB applicable amount includes an amount for each child for whom you are responsible.[62] This only applies to a child who is in your household (see p141).[63]

For HB/CTB, temporary absences (see p143) from your household of a child are ignored when considering whether the child remains a member of the household. For HB, the exceptions to this rule are if:[64]

- the child and/or you do not intend to resume living with each other;
- your absence from each other is likely to exceed 52 weeks, unless:
  - there are exceptional circumstances. The rules give an example of you having no control over the length of the absence; *and*
  - the absence is unlikely to be substantially more than 52 weeks.

For CTB, there are no rules setting out the exceptions to the general rule that a temporary absence is ignored. However, absences which are likely to be more than 52 weeks may not count as temporary anyway. In practice, local authorities are likely to deal with CTB in the same way as HB.

Child benefit and guardian's allowance

For the rules which apply when a child is abroad, see p178.

Working families' tax credit and disabled person's tax credit

You are only entitled to working families' tax credit (WFTC) if you or your partner is responsible for a child.[65] The child does not have to be present or ordinarily resident in the UK. For disabled person's tax credit (DPTC), the applicable amount (see glossary of terms at the beginning of this book) is higher for a lone parent than for a single person.

A person is responsible for a child under the WFTC/DPTC rules if the child normally lives with her/him.[66] This applies if the child spends more time with that person than anyone else.[67] If the child spends equal time with one or more person, or there is no established pattern, then the person responsible for the child under WFTC/DPTC rules is:[68]

- the person receiving child benefit for that child;
- if no one receives child benefit and only one person has claimed child benefit, that person; *otherwise*
- the person with 'primary responsibility' for the child. Primary responsibility is not defined in the rules.

If a person counts as responsible for a child at the beginning of a WFTC/DPTC award, that person counts as responsible for the rest of the 26-week period of that award.[69]

Child increase for contributory benefits and disability benefits

You may be entitled to an increase for a child (see CPAG's *Welfare Benefits Handbook*) if you are entitled to:

- incapacity benefit;
- invalid care allowance;
- widowed parent's allowance;
- Category A, B or C retirement pension

The increase is payable while the child is abroad, as long as you are entitled to child benefit.[70] If you are not entitled to child benefit, that does not affect payability of the increase if:[71]

- the only reason you are not entitled to child benefit is that the child benefit residence conditions (see p178) are not met;
- no one else is entitled to child benefit for the child; *and*
- the absence from GB was (throughout) intended to be temporary.

If you are absent on the annual up-rating day for child benefit, your increase will continue to be paid at the same rate, even if the rules about overlapping benefits mean that it should be reduced. There are special rules if the child is in another European Economic Area member state (see Part 4).

5. **Polygamous marriages**

A polygamous marriage is a marriage which took place under a law which allows polygamy – ie, for one person to be married to two or more people.[72] Usually it is the husband who has more than one wife, but the rules work in the same way if a wife has more than one husband (but such a marriage would need to be legal in the country where it was contracted and this will rarely be so). These rules only apply to people who are married and not to people who live with more than one person as if they were married.

Under British law a man and a woman do not usually count as legally married unless their marriage is monogamous. However, there are special rules for benefits.

For means-tested benefits, a polygamous marriage is treated very much like a monogamous marriage (see below). For non-means-tested benefits, parties to polygamous marriages are often not entitled to benefits to which they would have been entitled if the marriage was monogamous (see p152).

Means-tested benefits

For income support (IS), income-based jobseeker's allowance (JSA), housing benefit (HB), council tax benefit (CTB), working families' tax credit (WFTC) and disabled person's tax credit (DPTC) all your spouses under polygamous marriages count as your partners, but only if you share a household (see p141). If you are not legally married or do not share a household, they may claim benefit in their own right. The special rules for polygamous marriages are as follows.

For IS, income-based JSA, HB and CTB the applicable amount is worked out differently.[73] If you qualify for more than one premium based on different partners, you are entitled to the highest of those premiums. Instead of the couple personal allowance, you are entitled to a personal allowance of:

- the couple allowance based upon your oldest partner; *plus*
- an allowance for each extra partner equal to the allowance for a couple aged over 18 minus the allowance of a single person aged over 25.

For IS/income-based JSA, you only get this extra allowance for a partner who is:[74]
- aged 18 or over;
- responsible for a child; *or*
- would be entitled to IS/income-based JSA in her/his own right.

For WFTC/DPTC, the maximum WFTC/DPTC includes an extra amount for each extra partner equivalent to the amount allowed for a child aged 16-18.

Income and capital of all your partners counts as your income/capital.[75]

If any of your partners is working full time you are not entitled to IS/income-based JSA.

Non-means-tested benefits

For non-means-tested benefits a person does not count as a spouse on any day on which a marriage is actually polygamous.[76] A polygamous marriage is treated as monogamous on any day on which it is only potentially polygamous (ie, neither husband nor wife has ever had more than one spouse) or when it is formerly polygamous (ie, the husband and/or wife has had other spouses in the past but now they have all died or been divorced).

You are not entitled to a bereavement benefit if your marriage was actually polygamous on the day your spouse died.[77] You are not entitled to an increase for a spouse for any day on which your marriage is actually polygamous.

If you have been refused benefits because your marriage is or was polygamous you should take advice. The rules about British recognition of foreign marriages and divorces are very complicated and are not dealt with here. A marriage or divorce you think is legal may not be recognised in British law even if it was recognised in the country where it was carried out.

6. **Children born in the UK without the right of abode**

Since 1 January 1983 not all children born in the UK are British citizens by birth (see p25). The child may have the nationality of her/his parents but have no immigration status in the UK. S/he is not an overstayer nor an illegal entrant, even if her/his parents were at the time of the birth. A deportation order can be made against the child if the parent(s) are to be deported or removed. The child may have a right to register as a British citizen (see p26).

The benefit rules which apply where a child does not have leave are covered below. A child may reach the age of 16 without an application for citizenship having been made and wish to apply for benefits in her/his own right. This is very unlikely, so we do not deal with it. Such a person should seek expert immigration advice.

Benefit rules for children with no right of abode

For almost all benefits the status of a child is irrelevant. The only effects are as follows.

Income support/income-based jobseeker's allowance

The child's status only affects entitlement where the claimant's partner is a 'person subject to immigration control' (PSIC) (see p157) and it does not matter where:

- both members of the couple are PSICs; *or*
- neither member of the couple is a PSIC.

In particular, if both the couple are PSICs any entitlement to urgent cases payments of income support is not affected.

Where the claimant is not a PSIC but the partner is, the claimant's applicable amount does not include an amount for a child who is a PSIC.

A child born in the UK without the right of abode who has not been given leave to remain is a PSIC. That is because the child's immigration status is clear: s/he is a person who requires leave to enter or remain in the UK but does not have that leave.

Housing benefit/council tax benefit

The status of the child is irrelevant.

Notes

1 Reg 2 and Sch 1 SS(NIRA) Regs

2. **Couples where one partner is abroad**
2 s137(1) SSCBA 1992 'married couple'
3 s137 SSCBA 1992 'unmarried couple';
R(SB) 17/81
4 *Santos v Santos* [1972] 2 WLR 889;
[1972] 2 All ER 246, CA
5 R(SB) 8/85
6 R(SB) 4/83
7 CIS/671/1992
8 s124(1)(c) SSCBA 1992; s3(1)(e) JSA
1995
9 s136(1) SSCBA 1992; s13(2) JSA 1995
10 Sch 2 para 3 IS Regs; Sch 1 para 4 JSA
Regs
11 Denial of benefits of last resort to a
person in GB on the ground of income
or work abroad which cannot provide
support for them here may breach
Article 8 ECHR (private & family life &
home). Article 14 (discrimination) may
also be relevant.
12 s3 Human Rights Act 1998
13 The rules say 'resume living with': reg
16(2) IS Regs; reg 78(1) JSA Regs
14 Reg 16(1)-(3) IS Regs; reg 78(1)-(3) JSA
Regs. Only the rules relevant to partners
abroad are dealt with here.
15 Reg 16(2)(a) IS Regs; reg 78(2)(a) JSA
Regs. Either person's lack of intention
counts because the rules refer to the
'person who is living away from the
other members of his family' and each
partner is living away from the other.
16 See CIS/508/1992 and CIS/484/1993
on a similarly worded IS housing costs
rule: now Sch 3 para 3(10) IS Regs
17 Reg 16(1) IS Regs; reg 78(1) JSA Regs.
Compare with the pre-4 October 1993
version of reg 16(1) which refers to
absence from the home.
18 Reg 21(1) and Sch 7 paras 11 and 11A IS
Regs; reg 85(1) and Sch 5 paras 10 and
11 JSA Regs
19 Reg 16(1) IS Regs; reg 78(1) JSA Regs
20 Reg 21(1) and Sch 7 paras 11 and 11A IS
Regs; reg 85(1) and Sch 5 paras 10 and
11 JSA Regs
21 Sch 4 para 4 and Sch 5 para 5 HB Regs;
Sch 4 para 4 and Sch 5 para 5 CTB Regs

22 Reg 15(1) and (2) HB Regs; reg 7(1) CTB
Regs
23 s136(1) SSCBA 1992
24 Reg 16(a) and Sch 2 para 1 HB Regs; reg
8(a) and Sch 1 para 1 CTB Regs. These
apply because you still count as a
couple.
25 Sch 2 para 3 HB Regs; Sch 1 para 3 CTB
Regs
26 para A3.16 GM
27 These comments do not apply to
arrears.
28 Reg 51(3) CTB Regs: reg 51(4) will no
longer apply. Every resident of a
dwelling is jointly and severally (ie,
collectively and individually) liable to
pay all the council tax. If there are two or
more people liable for council tax on
your accommodation, your CTB will be
worked out on the basis that the total
liability is divided equally between
them.
29 Reg 3(1)(d) FC Regs; reg 5(1)(d) DWA
Regs
30 Reg 3(1)(b) FC Regs; reg 5(1)(b) DWA
Regs
31 s136(1) SSCBA 1992
32 Regs 46(1)(a) and 47(1) FC Regs
33 Regs 51(1) and 52(1) DWA Regs
34 This is because you may be entitled
under EC law to social security benefits
linked to employment on the same basis
as UK nationals: para 2 Annex VI Council
& Commission Decision 91/400/ECSC,
EEC: OJ No. L 229, 17 August 1991,
p249. These rules about your partner
may be indirectly discriminatory
because they are more likely to apply to
people from African, Caribbean and
Pacific countries than UK nationals.
35 s137(1) SSCBA 1992 'married couple'
and 'unmarried couple'
36 Reg 9(1) FC Regs; reg 11(1) DWA Regs
37 Because the rules refer to '*resume* living
together': reg 9(1) FC Regs; reg 11(1)
DWA Regs
38 See CIS/508/1992 and CIS/484/1993
on a similarly worded IS housing costs
rule: now Sch 3 para 3(10) IS Regs
39 Reg 9(2) FC Regs; reg 11(2) DWA Regs
40 Reg 4 CB&SS(FAR) Amdt Regs

41 Reg 2(2ZA) CB&SS(FAR) Regs
42 Reg 2(2)(b) CB&SS(FAR) Regs as
continued in force by reg 4 CB&SS(FAR)
Amdt Regs
43 Reg 11(1) CB Regs made under s147(4)
SSCBA 1992
44 CF/1/1981. The commissioner decided
that the political situation in Vietnam
meant the claimant's wife would
probably never join him in the UK. See
also *Welfare Rights Bulletins* 75 and 79.
45 Reg 11(2) CB Regs
46 Reg 2(2)(c) CB&SS(FAR) Regs
47 Reg 11(3) CB Regs treats unmarried
parents as residing together during any
temporary absence, but the higher rate
rules refer to *living*, not residing,
together, so reg 11(3) does not seem to
make a difference to higher rate.
48 Reg 13 SSB(PA) Regs disapplying s113
SSCBA 1992
49 Reg 2(4) SSB(PRT) Regs made under
s122(3) SSCBA 1992
50 CSS/18/1988
51 Reg 2(2) SSB(PRT) Regs
52 CS/15000/1996

3. Families where a dependent adult is abroad
53 Regs 10(2)(c) and (3) and 12 and Sch 2
para 7(b)(iv) SSB(Dep) Regs; reg 14
SS(IB-ID) Regs. The general
disqualification in s113 SSCBA 1992
does not apply to adult dependant
increases.
54 Reg 2(4) SSB(PRT) Regs made under
s122(3) SSCBA 1992
55 CSS/18/1988
56 CS/15000/1996

4. Families where a child is abroad
57 Reg 17(b) IS Regs; reg 83(b) JSA Regs
58 s137(1) SSCBA 1992 'family' (b) and (c);
s35(1) JSA 1995 'family' (b) and (c)
59 Reg 16(5)(aa) IS Regs; reg 78(5)(b) JSA
Regs
60 Reg 16(5)(a) IS Regs; reg 78(5)(a) JSA
Regs
61 Reg 16(5)(a)(i) and (aa)(i) and (5A) IS
Regs; reg 78(5)(a)(i) and (b)(i) and (6)
JSA Regs
62 Reg 16(b) HB Regs; reg 8(b) CTB Regs
63 s137(1) (b) and (c) SSCBA 1992 'family'
64 Reg 15(1)-(3) HB Regs. Only the rules
relevant to partners abroad are dealt
with here.

65 s128(1)(d) SSCBA 1992. If you are
responsible for a child, s/he is treated as
a member of your household: reg 8(1)
FC Regs
66 Reg 7(1) FC Regs; reg 9(1) DWA Regs
67 CFC 1537/1995
68 Reg 7(2) FC Regs; reg 9(2) DWA Regs;
CFC/1537/1995
69 Reg 7(3) FC Regs; reg 9(3) DWA Regs
70 ss80(1) and (5) and 90 SSCBA 1992; reg
12 and Sch 2 para 2 SSB(Dep) Regs. The
general disqualification in s113(1)
SSCBA 1992 does not apply to child
increases.
71 Reg 13A(3) SSB(PA) Regs

5. Polygamous marriages
72 ss121(1)(b) and 133(1) SSCBA 1992;
reg 2(1) IS Regs 'polygamous marriage';
reg 1(3) JSA Regs 'polygamous
marriage'; reg 2(1) HB Regs
'polygamous marriage'; reg 2(1) CTB
Regs 'polygamous marriage'; for child
benefit: reg 12(2)(a) CB Regs; for other
non-means-tested benefits: reg 1(2)
SSFA(PM) Regs
73 Reg 18 IS Regs; reg 84 JSA Regs; reg 17
HB Regs; reg 9 CTB Regs
74 Reg 18(2) IS Regs; reg 84(2) JSA Regs
75 s136(1) SSCBA 1992; s13(2) JSA 1995
76 Reg 2 SSFA(PM) Regs
77 R(G) 1/93

Chapter 13

••

Immigration status and benefit entitlement

This chapter provides an overview of how your immigration status affects your entitlement to benefit. It covers:
1. Immigration status and benefit entitlement (below)
2. Non-means-tested benefits (p158)
3. Means-tested benefits (p159)
4. Urgent cases payments (p162)

1. Immigration status and benefit entitlement

It is important, before making a claim for benefit, to know your immigration status. This is not only because this can determine your right to social security benefits but also because a claim for benefit can affect your right to remain in the UK. If you are unsure about your immigration status you should seek specialist advice.

Most people, apart from British citizens, are subject to immigration control. This means that you cannot freely enter the UK, but will be subject to scrutiny by the immigration authorities. The degree of control varies according to your nationality, for example, European Economic Area (EEA) nationals do not need leave to enter or remain and therefore enjoy much greater freedom to enter by virtue of European Community law. If you are subject to immigration control you require leave, or permission, to enter or remain. Such leave can be:
• limited leave to enter or remain;
• indefinite leave to enter or remain;
• exceptional leave to enter or remain.

If you have limited leave you are only permitted to remain in the UK for a limited period of time. Certain conditions are frequently attached to a grant of limited leave. For example, a restriction may be made on your working or claiming benefits. If you breach these conditions you may put your right to remain in the UK at risk. For more information, see Chapter 4.

The interrelationship between immigration and social security law is extremely complex and your immigration status may not always be clear. There are close links between the benefit authorities and the Home Office (see Chapter 10). Making a claim for benefit could alert the immigration authorities to the fact that you are here unlawfully, or that you have broken your conditions of entry by claiming 'public funds'. It is vitally important, therefore, to get specialist advice before claiming if you are unsure about your position. You can get advice from your local law centre, citizens advice bureau or other advice agency which deals with immigration problems. If you are a community legal services contract holder (in any branch of law) you can also get specialist advice from the Joint Council for the Welfare of Immigrants (JCWI) or the Immigration Advisory Service. If you are a refugee or asylum seeker, you can contact the Refugee Council (see Appendix 1).

Person subject to immigration control

You are not eligible for most benefits if you are a 'person subject to immigration control' (PSIC). This phrase has a special meaning for benefit purposes.

You are a **'person subject to immigration control'** if you are not an EEA national and:
- you require leave to enter or remain but do not have it;
- you have leave to enter or remain with a public funds restriction (see p92);
- you have leave to enter or remain and are the subject of a formal undertaking (see p104);
- you are appealing a decision about your immigration status.

Even if you fall within the above definition, regulations nevertheless treat certain people from abroad as not being PSICs. The exemptions vary according to the benefit involved (see below), and there remain some transitional regulations that provide entitlement to some claimants.

Benefits which are affected by immigration status[1]

Attendance allowance

Child benefit

Council tax benefit

Disability living allowance

Disabled person's tax credit

Housing benefit

Incapacity benefit (non-contributory)[2]

Income-based jobseeker's allowance

Income support

Invalid care allowance

Severe disablement allowance

Social fund payments

Working families' tax credit

Who is entitled to all benefits

You are *not* a PSIC and therefore cannot be excluded on grounds of immigration status if you are:

- a British citizen;
- a person with right of abode/certificate of patriality;
- a British national with right of re-admission;
- an EEA national;
- a refugee;
- a person with exceptional leave to remain;
- from Northern Ireland, the Channel Islands or the Isle of Man;
- a person with indefinite leave to enter/remain (but not if you are the subject of a formal undertaking (see p104);
- a person who left Montserrat after 1 November 1995 because of a volcanic eruption there.

There are some people who come within the general definition of a PSIC who are nevertheless eligible for some benefits. For details about who can qualify, see below for non-contributory non-means-tested benefits, p159 for tax credits, p159 for means-tested benefits and p162 for urgent cases payments of income support and income-based jobseeker's allowance.

Public funds

Most people admitted to the UK with limited leave, such as spouses or visitors, are given limited leave to stay here on condition that they do not have recourse to 'public funds'. If you have recourse to public funds in breach of your permission to stay (your 'leave conditions') you could be liable to deportation, refusal of further leave and prosecution. See Chapter 8 for more information.

2. **Non-means-tested benefits**

Contributory benefits

Your immigration status does not, by itself, prevent you from getting contributory benefits, but in practice you may have paid insufficient national insurance contributions to be entitled. Moreover, to qualify for contributory benefits you will normally have had to have worked in the UK.

Non-contributory benefits

You should be aware of your immigration status before claiming non-contributory benefits (ie, attendance allowance (AA), child benefit, disability living allowance (DLA) and invalid care allowance) because these are public funds (see p92). A claim could have serious consequences on your immigration status. Non-contributory incapacity benefit is not listed as a public funds benefit but some people subject to immigration control are excluded from access to it.

Attendance allowance, child benefit, disability living allowance, invalid care allowance and non-contributory incapacity benefit

You are not excluded from getting these benefits by your immigration status if:[3]
- you come within one of the groups on p158;
- you are a person with indefinite leave to remain and you are subject to a formal undertaking (see p104);
- you are a family member of a European Economic Area national regardless of your nationality or whether or not your partner is a 'worker' (see p7);
- you, or if you are living with them a member of your family, are *lawfully working* in Great Britain and are a citizen of a state with which the European Community has an agreement concerning equal treatment in social security. This applies to citizens of Algeria, Morocco, Slovenia, Tunisia and Turkey (see p418). The DWP often argues that an asylum seeker cannot be *lawfully working*. However, a commissioner recently considered the position of an asylum seeker who had been excluded from family credit by UK social security rules. The asylum seeker had worked in the UK and the commissioner found that this was sufficient to enable him to fulfil the condition of 'lawfully working' and therefore held that he was eligible for family credit despite the then exclusion from benefit;[4]
- in the case of AA/DLA and child benefit you are covered by a reciprocal arrangement;
- you are a person who is protected by the 1996 transitional rules relating to asylum seekers (see p276) and others with limited leave.

3. Means-tested benefits

You should be aware of your immigration status before claiming means-tested benefits. These are 'public funds' and claiming could affect your right to stay or chance of getting indefinite leave to stay (see p92).

Income support, income-based jobseeker's allowance, housing benefit, council tax benefit, working families' tax credit, disabled person's tax credit and the social fund

You are not excluded from getting these benefits by your immigration status if:[5]

- you are a person who comes within one of the groups listed on p158;
- you are a national of a country that has ratified the European Convention on Social and Medical Assistance or the Council of Europe Social Chapter (1961) (Cyprus, Czech Republic, Hungary, Latvia, Malta, Poland, Slovakia, or Turkey) and you are lawfully present. These rights do not stem from European Community (EC) law and consequently do not override any 'public funds' restriction attached to your stay. Therefore, any claim for benefit could affect your right to remain in the UK. However, it is current Home Office policy normally not to consider that a person has had recourse to public funds if s/he has evidence from the DWP to show that s/he was eligible for benefit under these agreements.[6] This provision clearly protects those with limited leave, such as students or visitors, but the position is less clear when it concerns asylum seekers. The Court of Appeal[7] has recently ruled that an asylum seeker with temporary admission could not be 'lawfully present' and therefore could not benefit from these agreements. The case concerned access to housing rather than social security benefits and consequently there are a number of challenges pending. Furthermore, the decision does not exclude asylum seekers who entered the UK in some lawful capacity but have limited leave (such as a visitor or student) from relying on the agreements (Note: this does not apply to tax credits);
- you are a family member of a European Economic Area national who is a 'worker' or a person covered by EC Regulation 1408/71 (see p7);
- you are a person with indefinite leave and are the subject of a formal undertaking that was given five or more years ago and you have been in the UK for five years or more (see p104);
- you are the subject of a formal undertaking given within the past five years but the person who gave the undertaking has died;
- you have limited leave and there is a 'public funds' restriction attached to your stay and your funds from abroad are disrupted (Note: this does not apply to tax credits);
- you are an asylum seeker who has transitional protection (see p275). In some cases this can include the separated partner or grown-up children of the asylum seeker (Note: this does not apply to tax credits).

If you qualify for benefit it is usually paid at the normal rate. However, if you qualify for income support (IS) or income-based jobseeker's allowance (JSA) on the basis that funds from abroad are disrupted, your sponsor has died or because you are an asylum seeker with transitional protection, you receive benefit at the urgent cases rate (see p162).

For the social fund, working families' tax credit and disabled person's tax credit, you are also exempt from the restriction if you are *lawfully working* in Great Britain and are a national of Algeria, Morocco, Slovenia, Tunisia or Turkey.

Couples and families

The following rules apply where one or more members of your family are 'persons subject to immigration control' (PSIC).

- If you claim IS/JSA as a PSIC, you are not entitled to any benefit for yourself or for any members of your family, unless you come under one of the exemptions on p160.
- If your partner is not a PSIC but you are, s/he can claim IS/JSA under the normal rules but does not receive any benefit for you or any other family member who is a PSIC. Full housing costs are payable.[8] You are still treated as a couple, so your joint resources are taken into account.
- Couples where both partners are not PSICs and lone parents who are not PSICs, can claim IS for children who are.[9] But claimants who are 'subject to immigration control' cannot claim benefit for children even if the children are *not* 'subject to immigration control'.
- Foreign fiancé(e)s and spouses who are admitted for settlement on the condition that they can maintain and accommodate themselves, count as PSIC, and are not entitled to IS/JSA until they are granted indefinite leave to remain in the UK.
- Prior to April 2000 people on urgent cases payments could get benefit for their partner and for any children. However, some very poor drafting of the 2000 amendment regulations has resulted in confusion and the DWP also appears to be unclear as to whether the current rules allow urgent cases payments to include an amount for your partner. The DWP interpretation of the regulations is that if you are eligible for an urgent cases payment as an asylum seeker and you are joined by a partner, or if you break your current claim, you will not be eligible for benefit for your partner. No new guidance has been issued which reflects this interpretation. Existing internal guidance, however, suggests that you can claim urgent cases payments for your partner. CPAG believes that the DWP's latest interpretation of the law is wrong and a refusal to pay the couple rate of urgent cases should be challenged. The DWP interpretation of the law may be in breach of Article 8 of the Human Rights Act in that it may interfere with your right to family life under the Act.[10] If you are refused benefit for your partner you should challenge the decision on the basis that the applicable amount for asylum seekers is calculated only in accordance with the rules covering urgent cases payments and this does not include the regulation defining a 'partner of a person subject to immigration control' on which the DWP bases its argument. When a child joins a parent s/he usually is given the same status as the parent. Sometimes however a child is given a different

immigration status to that of the parent. If the child has limited leave this does not affect the parent's entitlement to benefit, it is the parent's immigration status that is important. However, where there are parents of different statuses and the child is here with limited leave and subject to a public funds condition a claim for benefit could be recourse to public funds. It would probably be unwise to claim unless the child comes within one of the above groups who satisfy the immigration status test despite the public funds condition.

- A person can qualify for JSA without having to satisfy the joint-claims rules if her/his partner is a PSIC.

4. Urgent cases payments

For more information about urgent cases payments of income support (IS), see CPAG's *Welfare Benefits Handbook.*

Urgent cases payments are payments of IS and income-based jobseeker's allowance (JSA) at a reduced rate. Certain people who are excluded from ordinary rate benefit because of their immigration status may be eligible for an urgent cases payment.

If you are not entitled to normal rate IS or income-based JSA because you are classed as a 'person subject to immigration control' (see p157) you may be entitled to urgent cases payments if:

- you have 'limited leave' to remain in the UK on the condition that you do not have recourse to 'public funds' (see p92) but you are temporarily without money; *and*
  - you have supported yourself without recourse to public funds during your limited leave; *and*
  - you are temporarily without funds because remittances from abroad have been disrupted; *and*
  - there is a reasonable expectation that your supply of funds will be resumed; *or*[11]
- you have been in the UK subject to a sponsorship undertaking for less than five years and your sponsor has died (see p104); *or*
- you are an asylum seeker entitled to benefit under transitional protection rules (see p275).

How to claim

There is no special procedure for claiming urgent cases payments. You claim IS or income-based JSA in the normal way. You do not have to make a separate claim for an urgent cases payment. In practice, you may need to request the urgent cases payment and should not rely on the DWP to decide automatically whether you are entitled.

Amount of the payment

Urgent cases payments of IS and income-based JSA are paid at a reduced rate. Your applicable amount (see glossary of terms at the beginning of this book) is:

- a personal allowance for you and possibly your partner. This is paid at 90 per cent of the personal allowance that would have been paid had you qualified for benefit in the normal way; *plus*
- full personal allowances for your children; *plus*
- premiums and housing costs (see CPAG's *Welfare Benefits Handbook* for more details).

Income

All of your income counts, but the following is ignored:[12]

- any tariff income from capital. However, as all capital is taken into account this concession is of very little assistance;
- any arrears of urgent cases payments of IS or income-based JSA;
- concessionary urgent cases payments of IS or income-based JSA;
- any housing benefit (HB) and/or council tax benefit;
- any payment made to compensate you for the loss of entitlement to HB;
- social fund payments;
- any payment from any of the Macfarlane Trusts, the Eileen Trust, the Fund, or the Independent Living Funds;
- payments made by people with haemophilia to their partners or children out of money originally provided by one of the Macfarlane Trusts. If the person with haemophilia has no partner or children, payments made to a parent, step-parent or guardian are also disregarded, but only for two years. These payments are also disregarded if the person with haemophilia dies and the money is paid out of the estate;
- payments arising from the Macfarlane Trusts which are paid by a person to a partner who has haemophilia, or to their child(ren).

Certain income is treated as capital if you get IS under the normal rules. However, if you apply for an urgent cases payment the following capital is treated as income:[13]

- any lump sum paid to you not more than once a year for your work as a part-time firefighter, part-time member of a lifeboat crew, auxiliary coastguard or member of the Territorial Army;
- any refund of income tax;
- holiday pay which is not payable until more than four weeks after your job ended;
- any irregular charitable or voluntary payment.

Capital

Your capital is calculated in the usual way, but the usual disregards do not apply to urgent cases payments. Any capital taken into account affects your urgent cases payment, not just that over the capital limit. However, arrears of urgent cases payments are disregarded.

Notes

1. Immigration status and benefit entitlement
1 s115 IAA 1999
2 Reg 16 SS(IB) Regs

2. Non-means-tested benefits
3 s115(9) IAA 1999; regs 2, 12 and the Schedule Part II to the SS(IA)CA Regs; reg 16(1)(b) Social Security (Incapacity Benefit) Miscellaneous Amendments Regulations 2000, SI No.3120
4 CFC/2613/1997 (*25/00)

3. Means-tested benefits
5 s115(9) IAA 1999; regs 2 and 12 and the Schedule Part I SS(IA)CA Regs
6 This statement was made in a letter to UKOSA on 5 December 2000
7 *Kaya v LB Haringey*
8 Sch 7 para 16A IS Regs
9 Regs 21(3), 70, 71 and Sch 7 para 16A IS Regs
10 Art 8 Human Rights Act 1998 gives the right to family life.

4. Urgent cases payments
11 Reg 2 SS(IA)CA Regs
12 Reg 72(1) IS Regs; reg 149(1) JSA Regs
13 Reg 72(1)(c) IS Regs; regs 149(1)(c) and 110(1)-(3) and (9) JSA Regs

Chapter 14

··

British citizens and others with the right of abode

This chapter contains the benefit rules that affect British citizens and those with the right of abode in the UK. It covers:
1. Income support (p166)
2. Income-based jobseeker's allowance (p172)
3. Housing benefit and council tax benefit (p173)
4. Working families' tax credit and disabled person's tax credit (p175)
5. Child benefit and guardian's allowance (p177)
6. Contribution-based benefits (p181)
7. Retirement pensions and bereavement benefits (p184)
8. Maternity allowance (p188)
9. Industrial injuries benefits (p188)
10. Disability benefits (p191)
11. Statutory sick pay and statutory maternity pay (p194)
12. The social fund (p195)

Who has the right of abode?

Nearly everyone who has the right of abode in the UK is a British citizen. All British citizens have the right of abode, but most of those who hold some other form of British nationality do not. Some Commonwealth citizens, including people who hold another British nationality, also have the right of abode, but it has not been possible to gain the right of abode since 1983 without also being a British citizen. Commonwealth citizens who had the right of abode then will still have it, but since the beginning of 1983 the only way to obtain the right of abode is by becoming a British citizen. For full details of British citizenship and the right of abode, see Chapter 2.

If you are a British citizen or have the right of abode for other reasons:
- you are not a 'person subject to immigration control' (see p157);
- you do not need leave to enter or remain in the UK;
- you are exempt from deportation; *and*
- any leave you were given, and any conditions attached to it, has no effect once you become a British citizen.

The right of abode is a 'stronger' status than indefinite leave to remain. The only real limitation as far as benefit entitlement is concerned is that as a British citizen you may still have to satisfy certain residence and presence tests for some benefits (see p130).

British citizens and European Community rights

British citizens may also be able to claim using European Community (EC) law. If you are a British citizen who is able to use EC law you should also check Part 4. You can also check whether you are a 'qualified person' under UK law (see p71). These rights are not available to Commonwealth citizens or people who hold another form of British nationality with the right of abode.[1]

1. Income support

General rules

You are only entitled to income support (IS) if you are:
* in Great Britain (GB)[2] (see p131), or temporarily absent from GB[3] (see p293); *and*
* *either* actually habitually resident (see p135) in the UK, Ireland, the Channel Islands or the Isle of Man *or* exempt from the habitual residence test (see below).

For the rules about the amount of IS if one or more members of your family are 'persons subject to immigration control', see p162.

Habitual residence test

For fuller details of the habitual residence test, see p135. Briefly, the test is of habitual residence in the 'Common Travel Area', which is made up of the UK, the Republic of Ireland, the Channel Islands and the Isle of Man. The test applies to the claimant, and not to any other member of the family. If you have a partner who would be more likely to qualify you should consider swapping the claimant so that your partner claims, but be careful, because in some cases you may lose out, for instance because of transitional rules (see CPAG's *Welfare Benefits Handbook*).

You are habitually resident if:
* you have a settled intention to be here, and this can be for a temporary period or indefinitely;
* you have been actually resident for an 'appreciable period of time'. This may be as little as a month, but could be more, depending on your circumstances. There are some exceptions to this requirement (see p167);

- you are exempt from the test, in which case you are automatically treated as habitually resident (see below);
- you have been away temporarily and have not lost your habitual residence.

The term 'habitual residence' is not defined in the rules. For interpretations given to it by social security commissioners and the courts, see p136. A different meaning is given to the term for European Economic Area (EEA) nationals who have to satisfy the test (see p137).

European Economic Area citizens

You may satisfy the test more quickly and easily if you are an EEA national who has worked in another EEA state before returning to the UK. This rule applies to British citizens who have worked in another EEA country and are returning to the UK just as much as to nationals of other EEA states. Anyone who is treated under European Community (EC) law as having 'exercised Treaty rights', as an employed person in an EEA state other than their own may qualify more quickly, because the rule about having been here for 'an appreciable period' may not apply.

Commonwealth citizens with the right of abode

You must still satisfy the general rules on habitual residence unless you are exempt (see below). You cannot use the rule that can apply to British citizens and other EEA nationals returning to the UK in order to get around the 'appreciable period of time' requirement unless you are a dual national who has both Commonwealth citizenship and either British or some other EEA citizenship.

If you are a national of Cyprus or Malta (the two Commonwealth countries that have also ratified the Council of Europe Social Chapter of 1961) you may be able to argue that the habitual residence test may break international legal obligations. But there is very little you can do in practice to challenge a decision by the DWP to refuse you benefit because of the habitual residence test. Turkey and Latvia have also ratified the Social Chapter but nationals of Turkey and Latvia are not Commonwealth citizens.

It is likely that only those people from Cyprus who can produce passports from the main (Greek) administration in the south of the island would qualify, since the northern part of the island has not been recognised internationally. There do not seem to have been any cases on this in social security law, but an immigration case has looked closely at the law and decided that the northern administration is not capable of giving citizenship.[4]

Exemptions from the habitual residence test

You are exempt from the habitual residence test if you:
- are an EEA national who has worked (been 'economically active') since your arrival in GB (see Part 4 for more details);

- are a British citizen who has worked in another EEA state, and have worked since your return to GB, even though you may now be unemployed;
- have been deported, expelled or compulsorily removed from another country to the UK and you are a British citizen, an EEA national, or a Commonwealth citizen with the right of abode. You are most likely to be sent to the country of your nationality, so may be sent to the UK if you are British, even if you have not lived here before.

If you were previously a refugee and have since become a British citizen, you may be able to argue that the exemption from the habitual residence test that applies to refugees (see p215) still applies to you. In practice the question may arise only rarely, because the law imposes residence tests in order to qualify for citizenship. It may also be difficult because a person cannot be a refugee, in international law, in the country of her/his nationality, and British citizens cannot have leave to remain. But if you were a refugee or had exceptional leave to remain before you became a British citizen and you have failed the habitual residence test, you should consider seeking specialist advice on this argument.

If you fail the habitual residence test

If you are not exempt and you fail the habitual residence test you are referred to under the rules as a 'person from abroad'. You are not entitled to benefit, even at the urgent cases rate, but you may be able to get help from a local authority under the National Assistance Act 1948 or under legislation for the support of children. You should claim benefit again within a few weeks, and be prepared to appeal against a refusal of benefit.

Disputed nationality or right of abode

Even if you have a passport showing that you are a British citizen, the Home Office may refuse to accept it. This is unusual, but it is a problem that may also occur if your claim to the right of abode is denied. If this happens:
- **at a port**, an immigration officer may:
  - either detain you;
  - or give you temporary admission to the UK (see p113); *or*
- **when you are already in the UK**, an immigration officer may:
  - either decide that you are an illegal entrant (see p81) and detain you or give you temporary admission to the UK;
  - or simply tell you that your case will be investigated.

If you are given temporary admission, you are likely to be treated as a 'person subject to immigration control' (PSIC), and not entitled to IS.[5]

If the Home Office later accepts that you are a British citizen or have the right of abode and you have lost benefit, seek expert advice, whether you have claimed benefit and been refused or have not lodged a claim, for instance, on advice that you would not be able to succeed while your right of abode remained in dispute.

A household or family abroad

If your spouse is living abroad and you once lived with her/him abroad this could affect your entitlement here (see p141). If you are treated as being part of a household abroad even though you are living here, you may not be entitled to benefit. This will depend on whether your partner is working or has income that would affect any claim for benefit you might make. If your partner is not likely to join you within 52 weeks you do not count as a couple anyway, so any earnings your partner has, or whether s/he is in full-time work will not be relevant. If your partner is away for slightly longer than 52 weeks and the reason for the extended absence was outside her/his control then you will continue to be treated as a couple. For more details see pp141-144. If your partner is temporarily away from this country, see p143.

The amount of benefit you get may be affected even if you are not counted as part of a household abroad. You may also get less benefit if your child is abroad (see p149). If you are not treated as responsible for your child because the child is abroad this may mean you need to qualify for IS on different grounds if you originally qualified as a lone parent. If you do not qualify for IS you may need to claim income-based jobseeker's allowance instead as a person who has to be available for and actively seeking work. See CPAG's *Welfare Benefits Handbook* for the rules on who can receive IS.

If a member of your family is a 'person subject to immigration control'

General rules

You may be entitled to a benefit because you are a British citizen or have the right of abode but if you are claiming a means-tested benefit which includes an applicable amount for other people in your family then problems may arise in relation to public funds. See Chapter 8 for more details of the treatment of public funds in immigration law. The calculation of how much benefit is payable, and whether a PSIC's needs are included, vary according to the means-tested benefit concerned. It may therefore not be enough to know whether *you* are entitled. You will need to know whether a claim for benefit by you will mean that your spouse or dependent children are having 'recourse to public funds' through you. A person who is admitted to the UK subject to a condition that s/he should have no recourse to public funds may find her/his status in jeopardy or s/he may be refused indefinite leave when s/he applies for it if s/he has failed to keep to her/his conditions in this way. Breaching a condition of stay is also a criminal offence, although the Home Office does not seem to prosecute anyone for receiving benefits.

Even if there is no recourse to public funds there is a second question to answer. *Is it desirable that you claim a public funds benefit?* A list of the benefits included in the public funds conditions can be found on p94. If a person is admitted to the UK on condition that s/he will have no recourse to public funds then it will be because another person has said that s/he can be accommodated and maintained without recourse to public funds. A claim for benefit is an indication that you are not able to maintain yourself, let alone your partner or children, and therefore calls into question any previous commitment you may have given that you would do so. In the case of a spouse joining a partner here, no formal 'undertaking' (see p104) will have been given, but there is an assumption in the immigration rules that the couple will maintain each other. A claim for benefit which calls into question your ability to maintain the other person could mean that the other person's application for indefinite leave to remain is initially refused. This does not mean that you should never claim if you have a partner who is still on a time limit. There may be circumstances such as unexpected illness or accident where it is necessary, but you should consider carefully, and take advice if possible.

How your income support is affected

You will not get benefit for a spouse who is a PSIC, unless s/he is in one of the exempt categories (see p158). See p157 for the rules on who is counted as a PSIC for IS. You will also not get any benefit for a child who counts as a PSIC if your partner is a PSIC. If you are a British citizen, an EEA national or a Commonwealth citizen with the right of abode and your partner is not a PSIC you can get benefit for the children regardless of their status.

For Home Office purposes it may not be desirable to claim unless you are financially desperate and cannot get financial support from another source because getting benefit indicates that you cannot maintain yourself let alone your spouse or children (see above, and Chapter 8). You should seek further advice.

If you have worked in the EEA and therefore exercised Treaty rights of free movement, your spouse may have a right to join you in the UK, regardless of her/his nationality or country of origin. This applies if you are a 'worker' for the purposes of EC Regulation 1612/68 (see p390), or a 'qualified person' under British law.[6] If this is the case you can claim benefit for your partner and children immediately and the question of recourse to public funds does not arise. In this situation the person who has come from abroad has a right to reside in GB and does not count as a PSIC.[7] This also applies to any children you have.

If your spouse or child is an overstayer or does not have permission to be here you should get immigration advice first before claiming IS even for yourself.

If your spouse is an asylum seeker s/he may be receiving support from the National Asylum Support Service (see p64). This will not affect your benefit claim for yourself. If s/he came to GB before 2 April 2000 and claimed asylum before that date s/he may be exempt from the PSIC rules (see p275).

'Qualified persons' under European Economic Area rules

EEA nationals are given rights by EC law, most of which need to be set out in UK Regulations.[8] They are not excluded from claiming benefits under domestic (UK) law, and in certain circumstances they may have additional rights under EC law, including Regulation 1408/71 and Regulation 1612/68 (see pp346 and 391). Some of these rights are set out in UK rules, though if there is any doubt, the European Directives can be looked at since the UK regulations are intended to make the principles of the Directives effective in the UK. The Regulations describe:

- who has a right to enter and remain in the UK;
- which EEA nationals can confer rights on other members of their family, even if they are not themselves EEA nationals. In these cases, so long as the EEA national is a 'qualified person', the non-EEA family members may have an entitlement to benefit even if they would otherwise count as PSICs. For example, Latif, as asylum seeker from Algeria joins his wife Malika, who is French, and is a 'qualified person'. Both will have entitlement to benefit in their own right. Latif is not a PSIC;
- who counts as family members. The definition is wider than the definition of 'family' for the purpose of means-tested benefits. Family is not defined for the purpose of non-means-tested benefits.

Under the Regulations the list of those who count as qualified persons is as follows:[9]

- a worker (including a person who is temporarily incapable of work as a result of illness or accident, and a person involuntarily unemployed, if s/he has been registered by the employment office as such);
- a self-employed person (including a person temporarily incapable of work as a result of illness or accident);
- a provider of services;
- a recipient of services;
- a self-sufficient person;
- a retired person;
- a student; *or*
- a self-employed person who has ceased activity;
- the family member of a self-employed person who has died, if the family member was residing with her/him in the UK immediately before the death;
- the family member of a self-employed person who has ceased activity and has died, if the family member was residing with her/him immediately before the death, as long as the family member had lived in the UK for at least two years by the date of death (absences of up to three months in any year are ignored),

or if the self-employed person died as the result of accident at work or an occupational disease, *or* if the surviving spouse is a UK national.

The main categories in this list come directly from the EC Treaty, so the definitions are the ones that apply there. See Chapter 25 for more details.

If you do not come within the list of qualified persons under the EEA Regulations you should check Part 4 to see whether you have additional rights under Regulation 1612/68 (see p391). For example a person who is voluntarily unemployed under the Regulations may not be a qualified person but may count as a worker under Regulation 1612/68 and thus confer rights on family members.

Under the EC Regulation the list of family members who have a right to enter and remain in the territory of a member state with an EEA worker, or a self-employed person, is as follows:[10]

- the worker's spouse;
- children, step-children, adopted children or grandchildren who are under the age of 21 *or* over that age but still dependent on the worker;
- parents and grandparents of the worker and of the worker's spouse, of whatever age.

In addition to the people mentioned, member states have to give special consideration (shall 'favour' [11] or 'facilitate the admission' [12]) of any other member of the family, of the worker or the worker's spouse, who is dependent, or who was living under the same roof in their country of origin.

Other 'qualified persons' have the same family rights as workers, except in the case of students who can only be joined by a spouse and any dependent children.

2. Income-based jobseeker's allowance

For contribution-based jobseeker's allowance (JSA), see p182.

The income-based JSA rules about who is a 'person subject to immigration control' (PSIC) are the same as for income support (IS) (see p166).[13] For the rules about the amount of income-based JSA if one or more members of your family are PSIC, see Chapter 13.

Some couples are required to make a joint claim for income-based JSA (see CPAG's *Welfare Benefits Handbook*). Certain couples are not required to make a joint claim, for example if they have children. If your partner is a PSIC you will still qualify for income-based JSA paid at the single rate even if your partner does not make the claim with you, provided you satisfy the means test, are not entitled to IS and meet the conditions for getting JSA apart from making the joint claim. If you have a child, even if that child is a PSIC, you are exempt from satisfying the conditions for joint-claim JSA.

Remember that you have to be able to take employment as a condition of getting JSA. European Economic Area nationals and Commonwealth citizens with the right of abode have a right to take employment.

Disputed nationality or right of abode

The circumstances are generally the same as for IS (see p168), but if there is a doubt about whether or not you are available for work, you may be able to qualify for a hardship payment (see CPAG's *Welfare Benefits Handbook* for details) of income-based JSA, which is payable at a lower rate than the usual amount. You will need to show that you will suffer hardship as a result of being without benefit while the question is being decided.

If the dispute is all sorted out, and you subsequently claim and are paid full rate income-based JSA, your claim will be backdated to cover the period of the hardship payment, but the amount you have received will be deducted from the backdated payment.

---

3. Housing benefit and council tax benefit

You are entitled to housing benefit (HB) or council tax benefit (CTB) if:
- you are in Great Britain (GB) (see p131), or only absent temporarily; *and*
- either you satisfy the habitual residence test (see p135) or you are exempt, or you are being paid income support (IS) or income-based jobseeker's allowance (JSA);[14] *and*
  - for HB, you have accommodation in GB which you normally occupy as your home (which may apply during a temporary absence – see p302);[15] *or*
  - for CTB, you are liable to pay council tax for accommodation in which you reside (see p303);[16] *and*
- you are not part of a household abroad (see below).

Habitual residence

The habitual residence test applies to the claimant only. If you are not entitled you are a 'person from abroad'. The groups that are exempt are the same as for IS. For details see p166.

You are treated as habitually resident if you are receiving IS or income-based JSA.[17] The local authority should make no enquiries about your residence.[18]

Disputed nationality or right of abode

See under IS for details, on p168.

This issue should not arise if you are already receiving IS or income-based JSA as you are entitled to HB and CTB automatically because of payment of those benefits.

Household or family members abroad

This may affect your entitlement or reduce the amount of benefit you get. Broadly, the rules are the same as for IS except that if you are receiving IS or income-based JSA you are entitled to the *maximum* HB and CTB anyway.

If your spouse is living abroad this could affect your entitlement here (see under IS on p169).

If your spouse is abroad but you do not count as part of her/his household (see p141) then your HB or CTB is calculated on the basis of the members of the family who are living here. If the spouse abroad is temporarily absent s/he may be treated as being here for the purposes of calculating benefit (see p145). If you are getting IS or income-based JSA the absence of your spouse abroad will not affect your HB and will only affect your CTB in exceptional circumstances (see p145).

The amount of benefit you get may be affected if you have a child abroad (see p149), but only if you are *not* already receiving IS or income-based JSA, because these benefits give you maximum HB or CTB.

If a member of your family is a 'person subject to immigration control'

For the general position see under IS, on p169. However, the rules for claiming HB and CTB where a member of the family is a 'person subject to immigration control' are different to those that apply to IS and income-based JSA. The fact that a member of the family is a PSIC will make no difference to your HB if you are getting IS or income-based JSA, but see below for special considerations.

Your HB or CTB is calculated taking into account all the members of the family, regardless of their immigration status. If one or more of your family members is a PSIC and is here with a condition that s/he has no recourse to public funds, your claim for HB or CTB could affect her/his right to stay. This is because her/his presence in the household will increase the amount of HB and CTB payable (see p169, under IS). This problem does not arise, however, if you are already getting IS or income-based JSA as you will already be getting maximum HB and CTB and there is therefore no question of additional public funds being paid out because the PSIC members of the family are now included in your claim.

The second question (see p170) about the desirability of making a claim is still an issue.

If your spouse is an overstayer or does not have permission to be here you should get immigration advice before making a claim for benefit.

Chapter 14: British citizens and others with the right of abode
4. Working families' tax credit and disabled person's tax credit

14

4. Working families' tax credit and disabled person's tax credit

Working families' tax credit (WFTC) and disabled person's tax credit (DPTC) are administered by the Inland Revenue. They replaced the former benefits of family credit and disability working allowance in 1999. The change of name reflects the way they are administered,[19] but the conditions of eligibility are largely the same as for the former benefits, although the rates of payment are more generous. WFTC is paid to top up the low earnings of people with children and DPTC is paid to top up the low earnings of some disabled people. For details of entitlement and amounts payable see CPAG's *Welfare Benefits Handbook*. A new tax credit system will be introduced in 2003. For details of the changes see future editions of CPAG's *Welfare Rights Bulletin* or the *Welfare Benefits Handbook*.

General rules

To be entitled to WFTC or DPTC you must:
- satisfy the residence test (see below); *and*
- not be treated as part of a household abroad (see p176).

WFTC can be claimed by either member of the couple, as long as you (or your partner) are responsible for at least one child, even though that child does not need to be present or ordinarily resident in Great Britain (GB) when you claim.[20] DPTC can only be claimed by the person who has the disability and is working.[21] If both partners are disabled workers, the couple can decide who makes the claim.[22] If one partner is responsible for a child and the disabled partner fails (or would fail) the immigration test (see p169) the other partner may be able to claim WFTC, but see below for possible effects on immigration status.

Both tax credits include disability credits. These are only payable if the person concerned qualifies for disability living allowance (DLA), a benefit which is not payable to or for a person who is a 'person subject to immigration control' (PSIC). Even where immigration status is not an issue, DLA has a residence test (see p192). However, this will not affect a person who is a European Economic Area (EEA) national who has worked in another EEA country and has moved to GB, including a British citizen who has been working elsewhere in the EEA. For details see p356, which explains how a period of residence in another EEA state counts towards the residence requirement for DLA here.

Residence

There is a unique presence test for these tax credits, which involves tests of residence, presence and source of earnings. To qualify you must be treated as present in GB.[23] You are only present in GB if:[24]
- you are present in GB; *and*

- you and any partner (see glossary of terms at the beginning of this book) are ordinarily resident (see p132) in GB; *and*
- at least part of your earnings (or those of a partner) come from full-time work in GB (for the definition of full-time work, see CPAG's *Welfare Benefits Handbook*); *and*
- neither you nor your partner receives all your earnings from full-time work done outside GB (see below); *and*
- for WFTC, you have a child who normally lives with you or is treated as living with you (see below).

If your spouse is counted as your partner for the purposes of a claim, then s/he must be ordinarily resident as well. See p141 for the meaning of a 'household', and when a spouse counts as a partner under social security rules.

If you do not meet these rules because you (or your partner or child) have been present, resident or working in another European Union or EEA member state you may be entitled because of European Community law (see Part 4). This will also apply to a British citizen who has worked in another EEA state, is now in GB and wants to claim one of these credits.

If you or your partner are entitled to WFTC or DPTC in Northern Ireland you are treated as not being present in GB.

Spouse abroad

If you shared a household with your partner abroad and you intend to live together again (it does not matter whether it is in this country or abroad) you are likely to be treated as part of your partner's household now and not entitled to benefit (see p141 for details).

If a member of your family is a 'person subject to immigration control'

As a British citizen or Commonwealth citizen with the right of abode you are entitled, and the nationality and immigration status of your partner and children make no difference to eligibility for WFTC or DPTC because the rules only apply to the WFTC or DPTC claimant.[25] A claim for WFTC can be made by either partner, so if one of you is not a PSIC then that partner should make the claim.

Although WFTC and DPTC are not listed in the immigration rules as 'public funds', they will be treated by the Home Office as 'recourse to public funds' for immigration purposes.[26] For information on public funds and the immigration rules, see Chapter 8. The Home Office generally accept that if a person here qualifies for a tax credit no public funds issue should arise. But there will be cases where an adult here is joined by a spouse *and* child, when additional funds will be payable. The rate for a couple is the same as the rate for a single person claiming WFTC, but the presence of children will alter the amount payable.[27] The Tax Credit Office may pass information about you to the Home Office (see Chapter

10), so if your partner or any child is covered by Chapters 18 or 19 of this book or is a national of a country outside the EEA and is abroad, you should seek specialist advice before claiming or renewing a claim.

EEA nationals can claim for partners and dependent children who are third country nationals (ie, who are not nationals of EEA countries) and who would normally be classed as PSIC. This is because an EEA national who is a 'qualified person' (see p171) or who is a worker (see p390) confers a right of residence on the family members and this changes their status for benefit purposes.

5. **Child benefit and guardian's allowance**

Child benefit

Residence

You are only entitled to child benefit for a child if:[28]

- you are in Great Britain (GB) (claimant presence rule); *and*
- the child is in GB (child presence rule); *and*
- you have, and either the child or one of the parents of that child has, been in GB for more than 182 days in the last 52 weeks (182-day rule); *and*
- none of your earnings or those of your spouse are exempt from UK income tax (see p180).

There are exceptions to these rules and there are special rules for people working overseas, including civil servants and serving members of the armed forces (see p179).

There are special rules to stop you losing benefit if you move between GB and Northern Ireland.[29] You may also be able to use special rules if you have lived in another European Union (EU) or European Economic Area (EEA) member state (see Part 4) or a country with which the UK has a reciprocal agreement (see Chapter 28), even if you are not a national of that country.

Disputed nationality or right of abode

The nationality of the child for whom you claim is irrelevant. British citizens and others with the right of abode do not require leave to be in the UK so cannot be denied child benefit as 'persons subject to immigration control'. If you are responsible for a child and another person has been refused child benefit for that child because of that person's immigration status, you should claim child benefit instead. For details see CPAG's *Welfare Benefits Handbook*. For the position if you are a British citizen or have the right of abode but this is disputed by the Home Office, see under income support on p169.

A member of the household abroad

If you often go abroad and may lose entitlement to child benefit under these rules, you should consider whether there is another person who could make a claim instead. If your partner, for example, does not often go abroad, s/he could claim. For the rules on who can claim, see CPAG's *Welfare Benefits Handbook*.

For presence and absence, see p131. You are exempt from the claimant presence rule while you are absent from GB for up to eight weeks, if the absence was throughout intended to be temporary and *either:*[30]

- you were entitled to child benefit for the week before the week in which you left; *or*
- you are the mother of the child the claim is for and *either:*[31]
  - you left GB after your child was born but in the week of the birth; *or*
  - the child was born outside the UK in the first eight weeks of your absence and you could have been entitled to child benefit for that child if s/he had been born on the Monday before you left GB.

If the claimant dies while entitled to the benefit of this exemption from the presence rule as a person entitled to child benefit for the week before the absence began, any person who then claims child benefit for that child is entitled to take advantage of that exemption for the remainder of the eight-week period.[32]

You are exempt from the child presence rule while the child is absent from GB if:[33]

- someone was entitled to child benefit for the week before the week in which the child left; *and*
- the absence has always been intended to be temporary; *and either*
  - the absence is eight weeks or less; *or*
  - the absence is in an EEA member state or because the child is on an educational exchange or visit approved by the educational establishment the child normally attends;[34] *or*
  - the absence is for the child to receive treatment for an illness or disability which began before the absence and the Secretary of State has agreed to the absence.[35]

You are also exempt from this rule for any week in which you are exempt from the claimant presence rule as the mother of a child born abroad or taken abroad in the week of birth.[36]

There are exceptions also for the 182-day rule, so that:

- you are treated as present in GB on any day you are exempt from the claimant presence rule (see p179);[37] *and*
- a child is treated as present in GB on any day s/he is exempt from the child presence rule (see p179).[38]

There are three ways a claimant present in GB can be exempt from the 182-day rule.

The first claimant exception applies if your stay in GB (including the days you have already stayed) is likely to be at least 183 consecutive days (ignoring up to 28 days of absence) and one of the following applies:
- you have been employed or self-employed in the UK during that stay;[39] *or*
- you have been entitled to child benefit for any child in the last three years;[40] *or*
- you have a spouse who was entitled to child benefit for any child in the last three years and who either was living with you at that time or is now living with you.[41]

The second claimant exception applies if you live with your spouse and s/he meets (or is exempt from) the 182-day rule.[42]

The third claimant exception applies if:
- the child meets (or is exempt from) the child presence rule; *and*
- the child meets (or is exempt from) the 182-day rule (unless that exemption is because the parents satisfy or are exempt from the rule – see below); *and*
- either of the following applies:
  - the child is living with you (or is treated as living with you – see CPAG's *Welfare Benefits Handbook*); *or*
  - you are contributing at least the weekly rate of child benefit to the cost of providing for the child (see CPAG's *Welfare Benefits Handbook*).[43]

A child is exempt from the 182-day rule if s/he is in GB and *either*:
- one of the parents satisfies or is exempt from the 182-day rule;[44] *or*
- the child lives with someone other than her/his parents, is likely to continue to live with that person permanently and unlikely again to live with either parent, and the person with whom the child lives meets or is exempt from the 182-day rule;[45] *or*
- guardian's allowance would be payable if the child were exempt from the 182-day rule.[46]

Special rules for people working abroad

You are also exempt from the claimant presence rule and the 182-day rule if you are:[47]
- a UK civil servant, unless you became a civil servant or were recruited outside the UK (except if that was when you were a serving member of the UK's armed forces); *or*
- a serving member of the UK's armed forces overseas; *or*
- employed outside GB and half or more of your income from that job will be liable to UK income tax in the current tax year[48] and you are only temporarily absent from GB because of that job; *or*
- the spouse of a person in one of the above situations; *or*

- the unmarried partner (see glossary of terms at the beginning of this book) of a person in one of the above situations and you were the partner of that person when both of you were last in GB.

Any child living with you is also exempt from the child presence rule and the 182-day rule if s/he is *either*:[49]
- your son or daughter; *or*
- you have been entitled to child benefit for that child before.

You may also be exempt from the 'living with' rule, which is not covered here.[50] For details, see CPAG's *Welfare Benefits Handbook*.

If you cannot use these rules remember that you may be able to use European Community rules (see Part 4) or a reciprocal agreement (see Part 5).

People exempt from UK income tax

If any of your earnings, or – so long as you are living with your spouse or partner – your spouse's/partner's earnings, is exempt from UK income tax because of a double taxation treaty or an exemption for foreign officials, you are not entitled to child benefit. [51]This applies even if the majority of your earnings are not exempt. This is most likely to affect you if you are (or your spouse is) a member of a foreign armed service or a diplomat.

If a member of your family is a 'person subject to immigration control'

The immigration status of the child for whom you claim is irrelevant. British citizens and others with the right of abode do not require leave to be in the UK so cannot be denied child benefit as 'persons subject to immigration control' (PSIC). If you are responsible for a child and another person has been refused child benefit for that child because of that person's immigration status, you should claim child benefit instead. For details see CPAG's *Welfare Benefits Handbook*.

Guardian's allowance
General rules

Guardian's allowance is paid to a person entitled to child benefit for a child who is not her/his child where both of the child's parents are dead, or, in some situations, where only one parent is dead (for details of these situations, see CPAG's *Welfare Benefits Handbook*).[52] The nationality and immigration status of the child is irrelevant. This means the rules that apply where nationality or the right of abode is disputed (where a member of the family is abroad, or a member of the family is a PSIC) are the same as for child benefit.

Residence rules

You may also be able to use special rules if the parent(s) lived in another EU or EEA member state (see Part 4) or a country with which the UK has a reciprocal agreement (see Part 5), even if those parents were not nationals of that country. There are special rules to stop you losing benefit if the parent(s) moved between GB and Northern Ireland.[53]

The 182-day rule for child benefit is waived for a child where that would lead to guardian's allowance.[54]

You are only entitled to guardian's allowance if:[55]

* one or both of the child's parents was born in the UK; *or*
* at the date of the parent's death which led to the claim, one or both of the child's parents had been in GB for at least 52 weeks out of any period of two years since that parent's 16th birthday. The 52-week period does not have to be continuous.

For the 52-week exception, an absence from GB is ignored if that parent was absent only because s/he was:[56]

* an offshore worker under GB national insurance contributions rules;[57]
* a serving member of the armed forces; *or*
* a mariner or airman or airwoman under contributions rules.[58]

If you are not ordinarily resident (see p132) in GB, or you cease to be ordinarily resident in GB, then the amount of guardian's allowance paid for any day you are absent is frozen. The allowance will be paid at the rate paid when you stopped being ordinarily resident, or the rate at which it was first paid, if that was later.[59]

If one parent is dead, guardian's allowance can be paid while the other parent is in prison.[60] Only serving prisoners (and those detained in hospital by order of a court because of mental illness) are treated as being 'in prison' under the guardian's allowance rules.[61] A person serving a sentence of two years or more in a prison abroad should count as a person 'in prison'. Anyone detained under Immigration Act powers of administrative detention, however, is not counted as being 'in prison' for this purpose.

When a child is adopted, the adoptive parents usually take on the full legal status of parents, and are treated as such under guardian's allowance rules. This rule applies only to adoptions carried out in the UK, or to foreign adoptions recognised under British law.[62] This means that a person can only get guardian's allowance if the adoptive parents are both dead or, in certain situations, if one is dead.[63] An overseas adoption that is not recognised under British law does not have this effect. An unrecognised adoption will not confer full legal parentage, and if both (or, in certain situations, one) of the child's natural parents are dead, the unofficial adoptive parents may be entitled to guardian's allowance.

6. **Contribution-based benefits**

Until 6 April 2001 it was also possible to claim severe disablement benefit, but it has now been abolished and no more claims can be made. People who were already entitled to receive it may continue to qualify on the same terms as before (for details see the previous edition of this *Handbook*).

Contribution-based jobseeker's allowance

General rules

Entitlement to contribution-based jobseeker's allowance (JSA) depends on having worked and paid national insurance contributions, or had contributions credited, in the two complete tax years before the calendar year in which you make your claim (see CPAG's *Welfare Benefits Handbook* for details). There are no conditions about residence in Great Britain (GB), but the need to have paid contributions means you must have been present for long enough to qualify. You must be 'capable of work',[64] and show that you are 'available for work'[65] and 'actively seeking work'[66] by signing on. In certain circumstances you may be treated as available for work even though in fact you are not (see CPAG's *Welfare Benefits Handbook*).[67]

Residence rules

Because you must also meet the contribution conditions (see CPAG's *Welfare Benefits Handbook*), you are unlikely to qualify unless you have lived and worked in the UK for several years or unless you can use a reciprocal agreement (see p411).

There are special rules to stop you losing benefit if you move between GB and Northern Ireland.[68] You may also be able to use special rules if you have lived in another European Union or European Economic Area (EEA) member state (see Part 4) or a country with which the UK has a reciprocal agreement (see Part 5), even if you are not a national of that country.

It is also possible to receive contribution-based JSA during a temporary absence from this country if the reason is that:

- you are taking a child or young person who is a member of your family for medical treatment – benefit is payable for up to eight weeks;
- you are attending a job interview – you will need to tell the employment officer in advance; benefit is payable for one week;
- you receive a pensioner or disability premium for your partner, and you are both away from GB – benefit is payable for up to four weeks.

Disputed nationality or right of abode

It is not a condition of entitlement to contribution-based JSA that you hold a particular immigration status. You simply need to qualify according to the normal contribution rules. This means that a dispute about your citizenship or whether you have the right of abode in the UK will not, on its own, affect a claim to this benefit. But if, as a result of a dispute, you are detained, or are unable to make or pursue your claim to contribution-based JSA for a while, it is possible that you no longer satisfy the contribution conditions by the time you have sorted out your status. This could happen if you claim when you return to the UK after a period away, so that the extra delay in making your claim means you now claim in the next calendar year. In this case it may be possible to 'link' your new claim to the previous period, and still qualify (see CPAG's *Welfare Benefits Handbook* for more details).

If you qualify for a top-up allowance of income-based JSA because of your financial circumstances, this will not be covered by the contribution rules, so that unlike contribution-based JSA it will be affected by a dispute about your immigration status.

If a member of your family is a 'person subject to immigration control'

Contribution-based JSA is paid only to the applicant. There are no additions for dependants. This means it will make no difference to your entitlement to contribution-based JSA if you have family members who are 'persons subject to immigration control' (PSIC). This rule does not apply, of course, to any income-based JSA you may expect to receive as a top-up allowance.

Incapacity benefit

General rules

Incapacity benefit (IB) can be paid whether or not you are still employed, and your entitlement is not affected by any savings you may have. If you are working and become sick you will usually claim statutory sick pay (see p194) for up to 28 weeks, and may become eligible for IB after that. You can make a claim before the 28-week period is complete if it seems likely that you will not be able to return to work at the end of that time. Some young people may qualify for IB without needing to have worked (see CPAG's *Welfare Benefits Handbook* for details of entitlement).

You are only entitled to IB if you are:[69]
- present in GB (see p131); *or*
- treated as present in GB (see below).

Residence rules

You may also be entitled for a maximum of 26 weeks while you are temporarily absent from GB (see Part 3).[70] There is no definition of when an absence is 'temporary', except that a permanent absence, or staying away for an indefinite period, will not count.[71] All the circumstances of the absence must be taken into account, but an absence of over 12 months will usually not be treated as temporary unless you can show that there are exceptional reasons.[72]

If your absence is not 'temporary' you will not be able to receive IB during the absence. You will also need to satisfy the contribution conditions on your return, which you may not be able to do if you have been away from GB for a long period (see CPAG's *Welfare Benefits Handbook* for details).

You are treated as in GB while you are absent if the reason for the absence is that you are a mariner or an offshore worker.[73]

If a member of your family is a 'person subject to immigration control'

Additional amounts can be paid with IB for a spouse or other dependant. The rules vary depending on whether you receive IB paid at the higher or lower rate of short-term IB, and there are different rules also for long-term IB (for details see CPAG's *Welfare Benefits Handbook*). IB does not count as 'public funds' for the purposes of the immigration rules.[74] If you are paid IB and receive an additional allowance for a person who is a PSIC, this will not count as 'additional recourse to public funds', and should not be taken into account by the Home Office. Receipt of these payments does not need to be declared on the standard Home Office form when making an application for indefinite leave to remain, and cannot be taken into account, under the immigration rules, when deciding on an application for entry from a family member who is overseas.

Contributory benefits (including dependant additions) do not count as public funds for immigration purposes.[75] But, because of DWP/Home Office links (see Chapter 10), information about a dependant may be passed to the Home Office. If it is, and if the Home Office then takes the claim into account in a way that might harm your dependant's immigration status, you should take advice, because the decision should be challenged.

7. Retirement pensions and bereavement benefits

These benefits are Category A, B, C and D retirement pensions, bereavement payment, widowed parent's allowance, and bereavement allowance. These three bereavement benefits replaced the previous benefits of widow's allowance, widowed mother's allowance and widow's pension for people whose spouse died on or after 6 April 2001. The new benefits are equally available to either surviving spouse, where the previous benefits were available only to a wife on the death of her husband.

Retirement pensions

Residence rules

If you are present in Great Britain (GB) these benefits are calculated in the normal way, even if you are not ordinarily resident (see p132) in GB.[76]

There are no residence conditions imposed on the first claim for these benefits except Category D pension.

Because you (or your late spouse in the case of bereavement benefits) must meet the contribution conditions (see CPAG's *Welfare Benefits Handbook*), you are unlikely to qualify unless you have (or your late husband had) lived in the UK for several years or you are able to make use of a reciprocal agreement (see Part 5).

You may wish to 'de-retire' to increase the amount of your pension (see CPAG's *Welfare Benefits Handbook*). You can only do this if you are ordinarily resident (see p132) in GB.[77]

There are special rules to stop you losing benefit if you move between GB and Northern Ireland. [78]You may also be able to use special rules if you have lived in another European Union/European Economic Area member state (see Part 4) or a country with which the UK has a reciprocal agreement (see Part 5), even if you are not a national of that country.

Household or family abroad

If you are not ordinarily resident (see p132) in GB, then the amount of benefit (except a lump-sum bereavement payment) paid for any day you are absent from GB is normally frozen, unless you are residing in some countries with which there is a reciprocal agreement (see Part 5). It is frozen at the rate paid when you stopped being ordinarily resident, or at the rate it was first paid, if that was later (except Category A and B pension for certain claimants – see below).[79] Freezing also applies to additional state pension and any graduated retirement benefit.[80]

Your frozen benefit may be paid at a higher rate than it would be under current rules if it was frozen before 7 August 1991.[81] Those old rules are not covered in this book.

There are special rules (see below) for certain benefits.

Category A and B pensions

If your entitlement to part or all of a Category A or B pension depends on your husband or former spouse's national insurance (NI) contributions, your annual up-rating of that pension is not frozen if your husband/former spouse whose contributions are used is ordinarily resident (see p132) in GB on the day before the date of that up-rating.[82]

You are still entitled to annual up-rating of your Category B pension even while you are not ordinarily resident in GB if:[83]

- the spouse on whose contributions the Category B pension is based has died or you are divorced from her/him; *and*
- you have married again; *and*
- your new spouse was not entitled to a Category A pension before the up-rating date; *and*
  - either you were still married to your new spouse on the day before the up-rating date; *or*
  - you married her/him on or after that date.

Category C pension

Category C pension is a non-contributory pension payable to some men born before 1884 (and/or their wives or ex-wives) and women born before 1889. For details, see *Ethnic Minorities Benefits Handbook* 1st edition, p206.

Category D pension

You are only entitled to a Category D pension if:[84]

- you were resident in GB for at least 10 years in any continuous period of 20 years ending on or after your 80th birthday; *and*
- you were ordinarily resident (see p132) in GB on:
  - *either* your 80th birthday;
  - *or* the later date on which you claimed Category D pension.

Age addition

You are only entitled to an age addition for any day you are absent from GB, if either:[85]

- you are ordinarily resident (see p132) in GB; *or*
- you were entitled to an age addition before you stopped being ordinarily resident in GB; *or*
- you are entitled to an increased rate of any category of retirement pension under a reciprocal agreement (see Part 5).

If a member of your family is a 'person subject to immigration control'

For adult and child dependant increases, see Chapter 12.

Retirement pensions are not within the list of benefits restricted by immigration status (see p157), so it should make no difference to your eligibility for an addition if any dependant is a 'person subject to immigration control' (PSIC). Similarly, receipt of a retirement pension can be treated as income under the immigration rules, in the same way as earnings, and will not count as recourse to public funds.

Bereavement benefits

General rules

Payment of the three bereavement benefits depends on whether your late spouse satisfied the contribution conditions (see CPAG's *Welfare Benefits Handbook* for details), although you may qualify if s/he died as the result of an industrial disease or an accident at work, even if the contribution conditions are not met. They can be paid whether or not you are working, and any savings you have will not be taken into account. Some people who claim bereavement allowance or widowed parent's allowance may have to attend a work-focused interview (see CPAG's *Welfare Benefits Handbook*).

Bereavement payment

You are only entitled to this lump-sum payment if either:[86]
- you were in GB at the time of your spouse's death; *or*
- your spouse was in GB at the time of her/his death; *or*
- you returned to GB within four weeks of your spouse's death.

The payment is made at a single, once only rate, with no additions for any dependants, so if you have family members who are PSICs this will not affect your entitlement.

Bereavement allowance

This can be paid for up to 52 weeks. You must have been aged at least 45 but still under pension age by the date of death of your spouse. Your entitlement will end if you re-marry during the year.

No additions are paid for any dependants. If you have dependent children you should claim widowed parent's allowance instead.

Widowed parent's allowance

As the name suggests, this benefit is paid only to people who have the care of children, or to women who are pregnant at the time of their husband's death. It will be paid instead of bereavement allowance, and the two allowances cannot be paid together. Payment is not limited to a 52-week period. In order to qualify you must be responsible for a 'qualifying child', who must be:[87]
- living with you; *or*
- maintained by you, at least to the value of the child addition to widowed parent's allowance plus the amount of child benefit; *and either*
- the child of you and your late spouse; *or*
- a child for whom you or your late spouse were receiving child benefit at the time of death; *or*
- a child for whom you were receiving child benefit at the time of death and you were residing with your late spouse at that time.

This means that the only dependants taken into account for the purposes of widowed parent's allowance are qualifying children, and the conditions of qualification are the same as for child benefit (see p177). Immigration status will not be taken into account in any other circumstance, and receipt of widowed parent's allowance cannot count as recourse to public funds for immigration purposes.

8. **Maternity allowance**

General rules

Eligibility for maternity allowance (MA) does not depend on your national insurance (NI) contribution record, but you must have been working, either as an employee or a self-employed person, for a period before the expected birth, and earning at least a minimum, threshold amount. Maternity allowance can be paid as a flat-rate allowance, with additions, or it can be paid at a variable rate, if your earnings have been too low to pay NI contributions. For details of the general conditions of entitlement and of dependants' additions that can be paid with MA, see CPAG's *Welfare Benefits Handbook*.

Residence rules

There are no residence conditions for entitlement to MA, but the requirement to have been working and earning in the UK for a period of time means you are unlikely to qualify if you have not been resident.

If a member of your family is a 'person subject to immigration control'

Maternity allowance is not a benefit included in the list of benefits restricted because of a person's immigration status, and an addition can be paid for a dependant whether or not s/he counts as a 'person subject to immigration control'. Receiving MA does not count as recourse to public funds for the purposes of the immigration rules, so can be relied on, if necessary, in order to show an adequate income for a family reunion claim, either before entry or on an application to the Home Office.

9. **Industrial injuries benefits**

The benefits covered are disablement benefit, reduced earnings allowance, retirement allowance, constant attendance allowance and exceptionally severe disablement allowance. It used to be possible also to claim an industrial death benefit if your spouse died in work, but this ended in 1988, and does not apply for anyone who dies after that.

General rules

You are entitled to an industrial injuries benefit *for an accident* only if that accident 'arises out of and in the course of' employed earner's employment (see CPAG's *Welfare Benefits Handbook* for these rules).

You are entitled to an industrial injuries benefit *for a disease* only if that disease is 'prescribed in relation to' an employed earner's employment (see CPAG's *Welfare Benefits Handbook* for these rules).

Residence rules

To qualify for benefit as the result of an accident at work you must have been in Great Britain (GB) (which includes adjacent UK territorial waters – see p131)[88] when the accident happened.[89] And to qualify for benefit because of a disease you must have been engaged in GB in the employment which caused that disease (even if you have also been engaged outside GB in that employment).[90]

There are exceptions to these rules[91] for various categories of worker, as follows. You can qualify for benefit in respect of an accident which happens or a disease which is contracted outside GB while you are:

- employed as a mariner or airman or airwoman;[92]
- employed as an apprentice pilot on board a ship or vessel;[93]
- on board an aircraft on a test flight starting in GB in the course of your employment.[94]

In these cases there are also more generous rules for defining when accidents arise out of and in the course of a person's employment, and for complying with time limits under benefit rules.[95]

You can qualify for benefit if, since 1986, an accident happens or you contract a disease outside GB[96] while you are paying GB national insurance contributions, either a Class 1 rate or at Class 2 rate as a volunteer development worker.

Benefit is not payable until your return to GB after the accident or contracting the disease.

You can qualify for benefit if you count as an offshore worker when an accident happens or you contract a disease. This applies in two situations. The first is where the accident happens or the disease is contracted while you are in an area where the UK exercises sovereign rights over the exploitation of the natural resources of the seabed or travelling between that area and GB. [97]The seabed is where you:

- are employed on a rig or boat at sea in connection with exploring or exploiting the seabed, subsoil or natural oil or gas in an area over which a European Union (EU) state or Norway exercises sovereign rights over the exploitation of the natural resources of the seabed but which was outside any country's territorial seas; *and*
- sustained the accident or contracted the disease in an area over which the sovereign rights are exercised or travelling between that area and an EU state (including the UK) or Norway.[98]

In the second case, your employment also counts as employed earner's employment only if:[99]

- had it been in GB, it would have been employed earner's employment; *and*

- you are ordinarily resident (see p132) in GB; *and*
- you were resident (see p131) in GB immediately before the employment began; *and*
- your employer has a place of business in GB.

If you sustain an accident or contract a disease while in the territory of an EU member state, the accident or disease is treated as if it happened (or arose) in GB.[100]

You will *not* qualify for an industrial injuries benefit if you are:[101]

- a member of visiting armed forces; *or*
- a civilian employed by visiting armed forces, except if you are ordinarily resident (see p132) in the UK; *or*
- employed as a member of certain international organisations, *unless*:
  - there is liability for Class 1 national insurance contributions (see CPAG's *Welfare Benefits Handbook*); *and*
  - you are ordinarily resident (see p132) in the UK.

If the ordinary residence exceptions do not apply to you, you are treated as not being in 'employed earner's employment'.

If you qualify under the rules above you do not have to be present or resident in GB to be entitled to disablement benefit or retirement allowance.[102] They are up-rated annually regardless of where you live.

You are not entitled to reduced earnings allowance, constant attendance allowance or exceptionally severe disablement allowance unless you are *either*:[103]

- present in GB; *or*
- temporarily absent from GB (see p133).

For reduced earnings allowance, you count as present in GB while you are employed as a mariner or airman or airwoman.[104] This benefit was ended, for new claims, in 1990, but it is still possible to make a claim for reduced earnings allowance now if you suffered an accident at work or the onset of an industrial disease before then (see CPAG's *Welfare Benefits Handbook* for details).

For decisions on entitlement to constant attendance allowance and exceptionally severe disablement allowance there is no right of appeal to a tribunal, and any challenge must be in the High Court.[105]

There are special rules to stop you losing benefit if you move between GB and Northern Ireland.[106] You may also be able to use special rules if you have lived in another EU or European Economic Area member state (see Part 4) or a country with which the UK has a reciprocal agreement (see Part 5), even if you are not a national of that country. There are also rules enabling you to retain benefits while working as an offshore worker.[107]

If a member of your family is a 'person subject to immigration control'

None of the industrial injuries benefits is included in the list of benefits restricted because of a person's immigration status. It is not a condition of entitlement to these benefits that you should not be a 'person subject to immigration control'. None of them have any additional allowances for dependants, except that some people who have been receiving disablement benefit since before 1987 may receive a supplement (see CPAG's *Welfare Benefits Handbook*).

Receipt of one of these benefits does not count as recourse to public funds for the purpose of the immigration rules.

10. **Disability benefits**

These are disability living allowance (DLA), attendance allowance (AA), and invalid care allowance (ICA). Severe disablement allowance, which was previously grouped together with these benefits, ended for new claims from 6 April 2001, and is now only paid to people who were entitled to it before that date (for details see CPAG's *Welfare Benefits Handbook*).

There are special rules to stop you losing benefit if you move between Great Britain (GB) and Northern Ireland.[108] You may also be able to use special rules if you have lived in another European Union or European Economic Area (EEA) member state (see Part 4) or a country with which the UK has a reciprocal agreement (see Part 5), even if you are not a national of that country.

Disability living allowance and attendance allowance

General rules

Disability living allowance is payable to people who are under the age of 65 when they claim, and who satisfy the tests for residence and disability. It is in two parts, a care component and a mobility component. The care component is intended for people whose disability means that they need supervision or attention in their daily life, and is paid at one of three rates, higher, middle or lower, depending on the needs. The mobility component has a separate test, intended for people who cannot walk out of doors, or cannot do so without help. It is paid either at a higher or lower rate. DLA is a non-contributory benefit, and eligibility does not depend on a record of contributions or of employment, but a claimant must show that s/he has satisfied the disability condition for at least three months before the date of the claim.[109] For details of the conditions of entitlement, and rates of payment, see CPAG's *Welfare Benefits Handbook*.

Attendance allowance can be paid to claimants who are over the age of 65. The disability conditions are similar to those for DLA, but there is no mobility component with AA. It is payable either at a higher or lower rate, and claimants must have satisfied the disability conditions for at least six months before the date of claim. For details of the conditions of entitlement, and rates of payment, see CPAG's *Welfare Benefits Handbook*.

Residence rules

You are not entitled to DLA or AA for a day, unless on that day:[110]
- you are ordinarily resident (see p132) in Great Britain (GB); *and*
- you are present in GB (but see also below); *and*
- you have been present in GB for a total of at least 26 weeks in the last 52 weeks.

You are treated as present in GB for these rules, including the 26-week rule, if you are abroad only because:[111]
- you are a serving member of the armed forces; *or*
- you live with a serving member of the armed forces and are the spouse, son, daughter, step-son, step-daughter, father, father-in-law, step-father, mother, mother-in-law or step-mother of that person; *or*
- you a mariner or airman or airwoman;[112] *or*
- you are an offshore worker.[113]

You may also be treated as present in GB during a temporary absence (see p133). This may help you meet the 26-week presence rule.

If you are terminally ill, the 26-week presence rule is waived.[114]

For children aged less than six months, the 26-week period is reduced to 13 weeks.[115] Because presence does not start until birth,[116] a child born in GB must be 13 weeks old before being entitled to DLA, unless s/he is terminally ill, in which case the 13-week period is waived. If DLA entitlement begins before a child is six months old, the period of 26 weeks continues to be reduced to 13 weeks until the child's first birthday.[117]

There is an extra residence condition if any of your earnings or your spouse's earnings are exempt from UK income tax because of a double taxation treaty or exemption for foreign officials. This is most likely to affect you if you are (or your spouse is) a member of a foreign armed service or in exempt employment as a diplomat or a member of a foreign mission. This also applies to a child aged under 16 who is the daughter, step-daughter, son or step-son of a person receiving UK tax-free earnings. If this applies, the person receiving the tax-free earnings must have been actually present in GB for a total of 156 weeks in the four years before starting to receive tax-free earnings.[118] For this rule, you are not treated as present during any absence, but you may be able to use the special European Community rules (see Part 4). This rule is not waived if you are terminally ill.

Invalid care allowance

General rules

Invalid care allowance can be claimed by people who are engaged in 'regular and substantial' care for someone who receives higher or middle rate DLA, AA or a constant attendance allowance in respect of industrial or war disablement. As a non-contributory benefit there is no test of contributions or employment record, but there is an immigration condition (see below).

Residence rules

The rules for ICA are the same as those for DLA and AA (see p191) except that:[119]
- the 26-week rule is not waived if the disabled person is terminally ill;
- people who receive (or whose spouse or parents receive) UK tax exempt earnings are not treated differently;
- the detailed rules about temporary absence are different.

For adult and child dependant increases see Chapter 12. If your dependant is covered by Chapters 18 or 19 of this book or is a national of a country outside the EEA, and is abroad, you should seek specialist advice before claiming or renewing a claim.

If a member of your family is a 'person subject to immigration control'

There are no dependant additions payable with DLA or AA, but where the person with the disability is a child, benefit will be claimed on her/his behalf by a parent or guardian. An addition can be paid with ICA for the claimant's spouse or partner, or for children, although the partner's income will be taken into account.

Disability living allowance, AA and ICA all count as public funds for the purposes of the immigration rules.[120] It is a condition of entitlement that the claimant is not a 'person subject to immigration control' (PSIC), so if you are a British or Commonwealth citizen with the right of abode you will not be able to make a claim for DLA on behalf of a child who joins you in the UK from abroad, nor will you be entitled to an addition of ICA for a dependant, until that person has ceased to be a PSIC (see p157 for details). If you do so, it is likely to affect the immigration status of your partner and any children. The DWP may pass information about you to the Home Office (see Chapter 10). Similarly, if you are in need of care from a member of your family who is a PSIC it will not be possible for that person to make a claim for ICA until after the immigration restrictions have ended. On the other hand it should not matter if you qualify for a care component of either DLA or AA because of assistance given to you by a PSIC. That will be benefit money to which you are personally entitled, and could be claimed by you whether or not that person was in the UK. The Home Office cannot take it into account when it considers an application to stay on behalf of that member of your family under the immigration rules.[121]

If your partner or any child is covered by Chapters 18 or 19 of this book or is a national of a country outside the EEA and is abroad you should seek specialist advice before claiming or renewing a claim.

14

Chapter 14: British citizens and others with the right of abode
11. Statutory sick pay and statutory maternity pay

11. **Statutory sick pay and statutory maternity pay**

General rules

Both statutory sick pay (SSP) and statutory maternity pay (SMP) are benefits administered by employers and paid to their employees. Statutory sick pay is payable for up to 28 weeks if you are unable to work through sickness, and guarantees a minimum amount, whether or not you are also entitled to any sick pay under the terms of your contract of employment. There are no contribution conditions, and any savings you may have are not taken into account.

Statutory maternity pay is a minimum payment to employees who stop work because of pregnancy, and must be paid whether or not your employment continues. Your entitlement depends on conditions concerning your level of pay and on your having been employed for a continuous period of 26 weeks. See CPAG's *Welfare Benefits Handbook* for details of entitlement and payment of both these benefits.

Residence rules

The rules on entitlement are concerned with whether you count as an employee in this country rather than whether you are physically present here. You only count as an employee if you are:
* an employed earner for Great Britain (GB) national insurance purposes (even if you work outside GB);[122] *or*
* you are employed in a European Union (EU) country other than the UK and if that employment were in GB you would be an employee under SSP/SMP rules and the UK is the appropriate country under European Community rules (see p353);[123] *or*
* an offshore worker;[124] *or*
* a mariner (but see below);[125] *or*
* for SSP only, an airman or airwoman (but see below).[126]

Only mariners or airmen and airwomen who meet certain rules count as employees.[127] These are not dealt with here.

You can satisfy the test of continuous employment for SMP purposes if:[128]
* you were employed in another EU country in any week in the 26 weeks before the 15th week before your expected week of childbirth (see CPAG's *Welfare Benefits Handbook*); *and*
* you were employed in GB by the same employer in that 15th week.

Your entitlement to SSP or SMP is not affected by any absence from GB, but you can only receive SSP while you remain an employee.[129]

Your employer is not required to pay you SSP or SMP if:[130]
- your employer is not required by law to pay employer's Class 1 national insurance contributions (even if those contributions are in fact made) because at the time they become payable your employer is:[131]
  - not resident or present in GB; *nor*
  - has a place of business in GB; *or*
- because of an international treaty or convention your employer is exempt from the Social Security Acts or those Acts are not enforceable against your employer (for SMP, this appears to apply only if your employer is a woman).

In some cases the rules require notice to be given about SSP or SMP, either by you to your employer, or by your employer to you. If you are in one of the circumstances where notice is required but it cannot be given because you are outside the UK, you (or your employer) will be treated as having complied with the rules if the notice is given as soon as reasonably practicable.[132] For details of when notices must be given see CPAG's *Welfare Benefits Handbook*.

If a member of your family is a 'person subject to immigration control'

There are no additions payable with SSP or SMP for dependants. Neither of these benefits is included in the list of payments restricted because of immigration status.[133] This means that they cannot be taken into account by the immigration authorities when they are dealing with applications to enter or stay in the UK.

12. The social fund

The social fund is run by the DWP and is in two parts: regulated and discretionary. Decisions concerning the regulated social fund can be appealed to a tribunal in the same way as decisions about income support (IS), but there is a separate review and appeal system for discretionary social fund decisions. For a full description of the fund, see CPAG's *Welfare Benefits Handbook*.

Regulated social fund

General rules

There are four types of payments within the regulated social fund: maternity expenses, funeral expenses, cold weather payments and winter fuel payments.[134]

You are only entitled to a **maternity expenses payment** if, at the date you claim, you or your partner is entitled to IS or income-based jobseeker's allowance (JSA) (including urgent cases rate), working families' tax credit (WFTC) or disabled person's tax credit (DPTC).[135]

You are only entitled to a **funeral expenses payment** if, at the date you claim, you or your partner is entitled to IS or income-based JSA (including urgent cases rate), housing benefit, council tax benefit, WFTC or DPTC.[136]

The funeral (ie, the burial or cremation) must take place in the UK or (if you can claim rights under European Community (EC) law) another European Economic Area state.[137] This rule is not unlawful under British rules against racial discrimination.[138] However, it may contravene the Human Rights Act 1998. If you are refused a payment because the funeral took place outside the UK, you should appeal and seek advice.

The deceased must have been ordinarily resident (see p132) in the UK at the time of death.[139] This only applies to claims made after 6 April 1997. This rule may breach EC law.

You are not entitled to a **cold weather payment** unless, on a day within the cold weather period, you are entitled to IS or income-based JSA (including urgent cases rate) and this includes one of the pensioner or disability premiums.[140] Cold weather payments are normally paid without the need for a separate claim.[141]

To qualify for a **winter fuel payment** you must be aged over 60, but you do not have to be entitled to, or receiving, any other benefits.[142] For conditions of entitlement, and rules for people in certain kinds of accommodation see CPAG's *Welfare Benefits Handbook*. A 'person subject to immigration control' (PSIC) is not entitled to winter fuel payments.

Discretionary social fund

General rules

There are three types of payment: community care grants, budgeting loans and crisis loans.

You cannot be given a **community care grant** unless, when you apply, you are in receipt of IS or income-based JSA (including urgent cases rate), with one exception.[143] This means that, while there are no residence or presence conditions in the community care grant rules, you must meet the residence or presence rules for IS or income-based JSA (see pp166 or 172).

The exception is when:[144]

- the grant is to help you establish yourself in the community following a stay in institutional or residential care; *and*
- your discharge from that care is planned to be within six weeks; *and*
- you are likely to receive IS or income-based JSA upon that discharge.

If you are within this exception you do not need to show you are entitled to IS or income-based JSA in order to qualify, so you do not need to meet the residence or presence rules for either of those benefits when you apply. However, you must show that you are likely to meet those rules (and the other IS or income-based JSA rules) after you are discharged. The place providing your care does not have to be in the UK. This means that if you are being cared for abroad but intend to return to Great Britain (GB) on your discharge, you may be considered for a grant.

This type of grant can only be paid to 'establish' a person in the community. For these purposes it has been decided that 'the community' refers to GB, so to be eligible a person must intend to live in GB.[145]

You cannot be given a **budgeting loan** unless, when you apply, you are being paid IS or income-based JSA (including urgent cases rate).[146] This means that, while there are no residence or presence conditions in the budgeting loan rules, you must meet the residence or presence rules for IS or income-based JSA (see pp166 and 172).

You do not need to be receiving any benefits to be given a **crisis loan.**

If you are not entitled to IS or income-based JSA because you are a 'person from abroad' (see p135) (or would not be entitled if you claimed) you can only be given a crisis loan if you meet certain rules. You count as a 'person from abroad' if you are not habitually resident in the UK, Ireland, the Channel Islands or the Isle of Man and are not exempt (see p135).

The loan must be:[147]

- to meet expenses to alleviate the consequences of a disaster; *and*
- the only way to prevent serious damage or serious risk to your health or safety or to that of a member of your family.

A crisis loan will only be made if the DWP considers that you are likely to be able to repay it.[148] The overall maximum loan is £1,000.[149] The maximum loan for living expenses is 75 per cent of the IS personal allowance for you and your partner plus the full allowance for each child.

There is no definition of 'disaster'. If you have been refused IS because the DWP has decided that you are not habitually resident, you could argue that this refusal is a 'disaster' in the ordinary meaning of that word. You should explain why the refusal is disastrous for you and your family, and the serious damage/risk that the refusal causes.

You will also need to explain how you would repay the loan. Since it is only a matter of time before you are treated as habitually resident and awarded benefit, you will then be able to repay the loan.

It is not clear whether the DWP official dealing with your claim has to agree with the decision on your IS or income-based JSA claim that you are a 'person from abroad'.[150] The social fund directions do not refer to the IS or income-based JSA decision. We consider that the social fund decision maker has to reach her/his own opinion on this. When applying for the loan always explain why you consider yourself to be habitually resident.

If you are refused a loan, you should apply for a review of that refusal and seek specialist advice.

Residence rules

There are no residence or presence conditions for the claimant in the rules covering these payments, but because you must be in receipt of certain qualifying benefits to get a payment you must meet the residence or presence rules for one of those benefits.

Payments from the discretionary social fund can only be paid to meet needs that occur in the UK.[151] That should not exclude a need that occurs in the UK because of expenditure abroad – eg, a need for a budgeting loan because the claimant has spent money helping relatives abroad. It is the place of the need that matters, not the ultimate reason for that need. This rule may breach EC law (see p355).

If a member of your family is a 'person subject to immigration control'

The social fund rules do not generally provide for allowances in the same way as other benefits, so there are no specific rules concerning amounts for dependants, except for crisis loans. There may be difficulties in an application for a crisis loan for any partner or children who are PSICs, but as it is the claimant's needs as a whole that are considered you should argue that your own needs are greater because of your responsibilities for your family. If you need to receive a crisis loan it should not be taken into account by the Home Office when it deals with an application for your family members because it will only have been a loan, to be repaid, so there will have been no extra payment of any benefit because of their presence.[152]

In assessing other social fund payments it is likely that the only needs taken into account will be those of the person or family member for whom benefit is being paid. However, if the need is for a funeral expense, it should not matter if the deceased person was a PSIC, and no benefit was being paid for her/him, so long as the DWP accepts that it is reasonable for you to have to meet the expense rather than someone else.

Notes

1 See *Manjit Kaur* C-192/99 [2001] All ER (EC) 250

1. IS
2 s124(1) SSCBA 1992
3 s137(2)(b) SSCBA 1992; reg 4 IS Regs
4 *Veysi Dag* [2001] Imm AR 587
5 s115(9)(a) IAA 1999
6 Reg 5 I(EEA) Regs
7 Regs 11 and 14 I(EEA) Regs
8 I(EEA) Regs. These are required in order to give effect to the various EU Directives dealing with free movement. They do not cover the effect of EU Regulations, which have direct effect anyway, without needing national legislation.
9 Reg 5 I(EEA) Regs
10 Art 10 Reg 1612/68; and see Art 1 Directive 73/148
11 Art 1 Directive 73/148, for self-employed persons
12 Art 10.2 Reg 1612/68, for workers

2. Income-based JSA
13 s115(9) IAA 1999; reg 2 SS(IA)CA Regs; reg 85(4) JSA Regs

3. HB and CTB
14 Reg 7A(4) and (5) HB Regs; reg 4A(4) and (5) CTB Regs
15 s130(1)(a) SSCBA 1992; reg 5 HB Regs
16 s131(3)(a) SSCBA 1992
17 Reg 7A(5)(d) and (e) HB Regs; reg 4A(5)(d) and (e) CTB Regs
18 HB/CTB Circular A1/96 para 4

4. WFTC and DPTC
19 The rules governing the two credits are set out in the regulations for the previous benefits, which still apply, with suitable amendments. References in these notes for WFTC and DPTC are therefore to the Family Credit and Disability Working Allowance Regs respectively.
20 s128(1)(d) SSCBA 1992
21 s129(1) SSCBA 1992
22 Reg 4(3A) SS(C&P) Regs
23 **FC** ss128(1) and 137(2)(a) SSCBA 1992
DWA ss129(1) and 137(2)(a) SSCBA 1992

24 Reg 3(1) FC Regs; reg 5(1) DWA Regs. CFC/16/1991 decided that proving actual presence in the UK is not enough to qualify as 'present' for FC purposes but that these conditions must also be satisfied.
25 **FC** s128(1) SSCBA 1992; reg 3(1)(aa) FC Regs
DWA s129(1) SSCBA 1992; reg 5(1)(aa) DWA Regs
26 Although the definition of 'public funds' in para 6(b) HC 395 had not been amended to include the tax credits by Spring 2002, they are listed as public funds in s115(1) IAA 1999.
27 Reg 46(1)(b) and Sch 4 paras 2 and 3 FC Regs

5. Child benefit and guardian's allowance
28 s146(2) and (3) SSCBA 1992
29 Reg 2 and Sch 1 SS(NIRA) Regs
30 Reg 4(2) CB(RPA) Regs
31 Regs 4(3) and 1(3) CB(RPA) Regs; s147(1) SSCBA 1992 'week'
32 Reg 4(2A) CB(RPA) Regs
33 Reg 2(2) CB(RPA) Regs
34 Reg 2(2)(c)(ii) CB(RPA) Regs
35 Reg 2(2)(c)(iii) CB(RPA) Regs
36 Reg 2(3) CB(RPA) Regs
37 Reg 5(4) CB(RPA) Regs
38 Reg 3(4) CB(RPA) Regs
39 Reg 5(2)(b) CB(RPA) Regs
40 Reg 5(2)(d)(i) CB(RPA) Regs
41 Reg 5(2)(d)(ii) CB(RPA) Regs
42 Reg 5(2)(c) CB(RPA) Regs
43 Reg 5(2)(a) CB(RPA) Regs
44 Reg 3(2)(a) CB(RPA) Regs
45 Reg 3(2)(c) and (3) CB(RPA) Regs
46 Reg 3(2)(b) CB(RPA) Regs
47 Regs 6(1) and 7(1) CB(RPA) Regs
48 Reg 6(2) CB(RPA) Regs
49 Reg 7(2) CB(RPA) Regs
50 Reg 7(3) CB(RPA) Regs
51 s144(2) and Sch 9 para 4 SSCBA 1992; reg 9(1) CB Regs
52 s77 SSCBA 1992
53 Reg 2 and Sch1 SS(NIRA)Regs
54 Reg 3(2)(b) CB(RPA) Regs

55 Reg 6(1) SS(GA) Regs. The normal rule that benefits are not payable to a person absent from the UK; s113(1) SSCBA 1992 does not apply: reg 4(1) SSB(PA) Regs.
56 Reg 6(2) SS(GA) Regs
57 s120 SSCBA 1992; reg 114 SS(Con) Regs
58 Regs 112 and 118 SS(Con) Regs
59 Reg 5(3)(f) SSB(PA) Regs. See also s113(1) SSCBA 1992; reg 4(1) SSB(PA) Regs
60 s77(2)(c) and (8)(b) SSCBA 1992; reg 5 SS(GA) Regs
61 Reg 5 SS(GA) Regs
62 s77(8)(a) SSCBA 1992; reg 2 SS(GA) Regs. The reference in reg 2 to s4(3) Adoption Act 1968 is (because of s17(2)(a) IntA 1978), a reference to ss38(1)(d) and (e) and 72(1) and (2) Adoption Act 1976. The Adoption (Scotland) Act 1978 uses the same definition as under English law: ss38(1)(d) and 65(1) and (2).
63 Except where the adoptive parents were entitled to guardian's allowance immediately before adoption: s77(11) SSCBA 1992.

6. Contribution-based benefits
64 s1(2)(f) JSA 1995
65 ss1(2)(a) and 6(1) JSA 1995
66 ss1(2)(c) and 7 JSA 1995
67 Reg 14 JSA Regs
68 Reg 2 and Sch 1 SS(NIRA) Regs
69 s113(1) SSCBA 1992; s1(2)(i) JSA 1995
70 Regs 2 and 11 SSB(PA) Regs
71 R(S) 1/85
72 See generally *CAO v Ahmed* 16 March 1994, CA
73 SS(MB) Regs
74 para 6(b) HC (395); s115(1) IAA 1999
75 s115(1) IAA 1999 and para 6 HC 395 'public funds'

7. Retirement pensions and bereavement benefits
76 The disqualification under s113(1) SSCBA 1992 only applies on a day of absence from GB.
77 Reg 6 SSB(PA) Regs
78 Reg 2 and Sch 1 SS(NIRA) Regs
79 Regs 4(3) and (4) and 5(3)-(6) SSB(PA) Regs
80 Regs 4(4) and 5(3)(c) SSB(PA) Regs
81 Reg 5(8) and Sch to SSB(PA) Regs

82 Reg 5(3)(a) and (aa), (5) and (6) SSB(PA) Regs. These only disqualify where the husband/former partner is not ordinarily resident in GB.
83 Reg 5(7) SSB(PA) Regs
84 Reg 10 SS(WB&RP) Regs
85 Reg 8(1) SSB(PA) Regs
86 Reg 4(2B) SSB(PA) Regs
87 ss39A(3), 81(2) and (3) SSCBA 1992

9. Industrial injuries benefits
88 s172(a) SSCBA 1992
89 s94(5) SSCBA 1992
90 s109(1) SSCBA 1992; reg 14 SS(IIPD) Regs
91 ss109(2)(a), 117, 119 and 120 SSCBA 1992
92 Reg 2(1) SS(IIMB) Regs; reg 2(1) SS(IIAB) Regs. For 'mariner' and 'airman' see regs 4-7 and Sch 2 SS(EEEIIP) Regs
93 Reg 2(2) SS(IIMB) Regs
94 Reg 2(2) SS(IIAB) Regs
95 Regs 3, 4, 6 and 8 SS(IIMB) Regs; regs 3 and 6 SS(IIAB) Regs
96 Reg 10C(5) and (6) SSB(PA) Regs
97 Regs 11(3) SSB(PA) Regs
98 Reg 10C(2)(a) SSB(PA) Regs
99 Reg 10C(2A) SSB(PA) Regs
100 Reg 10C(2)(b) SSB(PA) Regs
101 Reg 3 and Sch 1 Part II paras 3 and 4 SS(EEEIIP) Regs
102 Reg 9(3) and (7) SSB(PA) Regs
103 s113(1) SSCBA 1992; reg 9(4) and (5) SSB(PA) Regs
104 Reg 5(b) SS(IIMB) Regs; reg 4(b) SS(IIAB) Regs. For 'mariner' and 'airman' see regs 4-7 and Sch 2 SS(EEEIIP) Regs
105 Sch 2 para 14 SS(SDA) Regs
106 Reg 2 and Sch 1 SS(NIRA) Regs
107 Reg 11(2) and (2A) SSB(PA) Regs

10. Disability benefits
108 Reg 2 and Sch 1 SS(NIRA) Regs
109 ss72 and 73 SSCBA 1992
110 Reg 2(1)(b) SS(AA) Regs; reg 2(1)(b) SS(DLA) Regs
111 Reg 2(2) SS(AA) Regs; reg 2(2) SS(DLA) Regs
112 Regs 112 and 118 SS(Con) Regs
113 s120 SSCBA 1992; reg 114 SS(Con) Regs
114 Reg 2(3) SS(AA) Regs; reg 2(4) SS(DLA) Regs
115 Reg 2(5) SS(DLA) Regs
116 R(A) 1/94
117 Reg 2(6) SS(DLA) Regs
118 Reg 2(1)(b) SS(AA) Regs; reg 2(1)(b) SS(DLA) Regs

119 Reg 9 SS(ICA) Regs
120 s115(1) IAA 1999
121 para 6 HC 395 as amended in October 2001, definition of 'public funds'

11. SSP and SMP

122 **SSP** ss151(1) and 163(1) SSCBA 1992 'employee', see reg 16(1) SSP Regs; reg 5A SSP(MAPA) Regs
SMP ss164(1) and 171(1) SSCBA 1992 'employee', see reg 17(1) SMP Regs; reg 2A SMP(PAM) Regs
123 Reg 5 SSP(MAPA) Regs; reg 2 SMP(PAM) Regs
124 Regs 4 and 8 SSP(MAPA) Regs; reg 8 SMP(PAM) Regs; s120 SSCBA 1992; reg 76 SS(Con) Regs
125 Reg 6 SSP(MAPA) Regs; reg 7 SMP(PAM) Regs; reg 81 SS(Con) Regs
126 Reg 7 SSP(MAPA) Regs
127 Regs 6 and 7 SSP(MAPA) Regs; reg 7 SMP(PAM) Regs
128 Reg 5 SMP(PAM) Regs
129 These rules changed on 6 April 1996 (SSP) and 18 August 1996 (SMP). Before that, entitlement normally ended when you were absent from the EU: reg 10(1) SSP(MAPA) Regs, reg 9(1) SMP(PAM) Regs before amendment.
130 Reg 16(2) SSP Regs; reg 17(3) SMP Regs
131 Reg 145(1)(b) SS(Con) Regs
132 Reg 14 SSP(MAPA) Regs; reg 6 SMP(PAM) Regs
133 s115(1) IAA 1999

12. The social fund

134 s138(1)(a) and (2) SSCBA 1992
135 Reg 5(1)(a) SFM&FE Regs
136 Reg 7(1)(a) SFM&FE Regs. See CPAG's *Welfare Benefits Handbook* for possible limits on CTB route.
137 Reg 7(1)(b) SFM&FE Regs
138 *Nessa v CAO* [1999] 4 All ER 677
139 Reg 7(1)(c) SFM&FE Regs as amended by reg 5 Social Fund and Claims and Payments (Miscellaneous Amendments) Regulations 1997 SI No.792
140 Reg 1A SFCWP Regs
141 SS(C&P) Regs still apply to cold weather payments (regs 4 and 2(2)(b)), but the particular rules and time limit have been revoked (reg 15A and Sch 4 para 9A).
142 Reg 2 SFWFP Regs
143 SF Dir 25(a)
144 SF Dirs 4(a)(i) and 25(b)
145 *R v SFI, ex parte Amina Mohammed, Times*, 25 November 1992
146 SF Dir 8(1)(a)

147 SF Dirs 3(1)(a) and 16(b)
148 SF Dir 22
149 SF Dir 18
150 SF Dir 16(b)
151 SF Dirs 2, 23(1)(a) and 29
152 para 6 HC 395

Chapter 15

....

Indefinite leave to remain

This chapter covers the benefit rules that affect people with indefinite leave to remain in the UK. The benefits covered are:
1. Income support (p205)
2. Income-based jobseeker's allowance (p208)
3. Housing benefit and council tax benefit (p209)
4. Child benefit and guardian's allowance (p209)
5. Working families' tax credit and disabled person's tax credit (p210)
6. Contribution-based jobseeker's allowance and incapacity benefit (p210)
7. Retirement pensions and bereavement benefits (p211)
8. Industrial injuries benefits (p211)
9. Attendance allowance, disability living allowance, invalid care allowance and non-contributory incapacity benefit (p211)
10. Statutory sick pay, statutory maternity pay and maternity allowance (p212)
11. The social fund (p212)

Generally people with indefinite leave to remain are not excluded from entitlement to social security benefits. The only two exceptions to this are:
• where the person with indefinite leave is subject to a formal sponsorship undertaking (see p203); *or*
• where s/he fails the habitual residence test (see p135).

What is indefinite leave to remain?

You have indefinite leave to remain if you have been given permission ('leave') to be in the UK with no time limit on your right to stay. This is also referred to in immigration law as 'settled' status.[1] It is sometimes known unofficially as 'permanent residence'. Once you acquire this status you will only lose it if a deportation order is made against you on criminal or security grounds, or if you remain outside the UK for a continuous period of more than two years. For full details see p49.

Acquiring British citizenship

If you become a British citizen you no longer have leave to remain because you are no longer subject to immigration control. Remember, however, that British nationals who are not British citizens can have indefinite leave to remain. If you become a British citizen, the most important changes in your rights to benefits are:

- the sponsored immigrant rule cannot apply (see p202); *and*
- you can use European Community (EC) rules on benefits (see Part 4).

European Economic Area nationals and indefinite leave

The immigration rules allow a European Economic Area (EEA) national to obtain indefinite leave to remain, although there is no requirement to do so, and most do not. This does not apply, of course, if you are a British citizen because British citizens are not subject to immigration control. If you are an EEA national with indefinite leave, you can use either the rules for people with indefinite leave or the rules for EEA nationals (see Part 4), whichever one is more favourable.

Indefinite leave with a sponsorship undertaking

Some people have indefinite leave to remain but only as a result of an undertaking having been made by another person (usually a relative) to maintain and accommodate them (see p104). A sponsorship undertaking can affect entitlement to certain benefits although this is only the case where the sponsorship undertaking is made in pursuance of the immigration rules; a voluntary commitment to maintain another person does not count as a sponsorship undertaking.

A written undertaking

Only an undertaking on an official form in response to a request should count, because otherwise it is not 'given in pursuance of the immigration rules' as the benefit rules require. Any other type of undertaking or promise, even one in writing, does not count.

When an application for leave to remain or for entry clearance is made for an elderly parent, a child aged between 16 and 18, or another, more distant relative, the Home Office or entry clearance officer dealing with the application may request a written undertaking. An undertaking will not usually be required for a spouse or for younger children. Applications on behalf of people who are already in the UK will be made on one of the Home Office's standard forms, usually the SET(F) form, although children may be included with the other parent on Form FLR(M). The SET(F) contains a section with a written undertaking, and though the use of this part of the form is strictly voluntary, the Home Office will usually expect it to be completed. If it has not been, or if children have been included on another form, there will be no written undertaking for the purpose of the rules unless the Home Office specifically requests that an undertaking is made. That may be done by sending a separate form, currently a RON 112. The forms in use for entry clearance (the visa application forms) do not include an undertaking, and unless the entry clearance officer requests a formal undertaking on a RON 112 form there will be no undertaking for the purpose of the benefit rules. An undertaking will usually be expected to be given by the relative whom the applicant is to join.

The benefits authorities are sometimes unclear as to who is a sponsored immigrant under benefit rules. Even where the Home Office has told the DWP that an undertaking has not been signed, claimants have sometimes been treated as sponsored immigrants. The main confusion lies with a failure to recognise the difference between sponsorship arrangements with formal undertakings and those with an informal sponsorship. For benefit purposes you can only be treated as a sponsored immigrant if the DWP can show that a formal undertaking has been given. If it cannot obtain the written undertaking on a SET(F) or RON 112 from the Home Office, or the RON 112 from the entry clearance officer, you should not be treated as a sponsored immigrant, and should not be refused benefit.

Leave to enter or remain in the UK

The benefit rules dealing with sponsored immigrants refer to people who have been given leave to enter or remain in the UK by the Secretary of State subject to an undertaking.[2] The effect of this is not entirely clear. There are two ways in which people are able to stay here because of a sponsorship undertaking. They can be granted a visa overseas to come to the UK for settlement, after an undertaking has been given to an entry clearance officer, or they can come in as visitors, or in some other way, and apply to the Home Office to stay on. Until 2000 it was clear, according to immigration law, that only the second group are given their permission by the Secretary of State. Only the officers who work in the Immigration and Nationality Directorate take decisions in the name of the Secretary of State. Their decisions agreeing or refusing to vary a person's stay in the UK are 'leave to remain'. Immigration officers, at the ports, give leave to enter.[3] This phrase in the rules therefore appeared to mean that, if an immigration officer gave you leave you were not a sponsored immigrant for benefits purposes.

Since 2000, people who are issued visas (entry clearance) overseas do not need to apply again to an immigration officer when they land in this country. The entry clearance sticker placed in the passport by the entry clearance officer shows the conditions of entry, and the immigration officer no longer needs to stamp these when you get here. This seems to mean that in these cases it is the entry clearance officer who gives you your leave to enter or remain, not the Secretary of State. But these changes are made by an Order, which is issued by the Secretary of State.[4] A tribunal might decide that this was enough to make sure your 'leave to enter or remain' had been given 'by the Secretary of State'. Remember that you are not a 'sponsored immigrant' if your sponsor has not given a written undertaking on a form which says that it may be given to the DWP for the purpose of recovering any benefit paid. You may also be able to say that the restriction does not apply to you if an exception has been made. In some cases, the Home Office agrees to waive one of the immigration rules when granting leave. If this happens you can argue that your leave has not been given under the immigration rules, but is exceptional leave to remain (see Chapter 6). In this case your leave to remain falls outside the immigration rules, so the undertaking will not have been given in pursuance of the immigration rules.

You should not use this argument unless you have a written record proving that the Home Office knew that you did not meet the requirements of the immigration rules. You must have this record because otherwise the Home Office may try to take your leave away on the ground that your leave was obtained by deception. Proof includes a letter from the Home Office agreeing to waive one of the immigration rules, or a letter from you or your adviser, which you know the Home Office received, stating that you do not meet one of the rules. If this argument applies, you should be able to claim any benefits to which you would otherwise be entitled, on the same terms as anyone else who is resident in Great Britain. You should also be exempt from the habitual residence test as a person with exceptional leave to remain. If you think this argument might apply to you, you should seek expert advice.

Only a person with leave to enter or remain in the UK can be a sponsored immigrant under the benefit rules. This does not seem to apply if you also have an EC law right to remain in the UK (see p390).[5]

When you stop being a sponsored immigrant for benefit purposes
You cease to be a sponsored immigrant when:
- you have been resident in the UK for five years;
- you become a British citizen;
- you acquire an EC right to reside in the UK because you become a family member of an EEA national.

Once you stop being a sponsored immigrant under the benefit rules, the ordinary rules on entitlement apply. Special rules apply if your sponsor dies within the first five years.

1. **Income support**

You are entitled to income support (IS) if:
- you are in Great Britain (GB)[6] (see p131) or temporarily absent from GB[7] (see p133); *and*

- you are habitually resident in the UK, Ireland, the Channel Islands or the Isle of Man, or you are exempt from the habitual residence test (see p135; *and*
- you are not a 'sponsored immigrant'; *or*
- you are a 'sponsored immigrant' but your sponsor has died.

Your entitlement might also be affected if you are a member of a household that includes a person living abroad.

In practice, if everyone for whom you are claiming has been present in the UK for the five years before you sign the IS claim form, the DWP will normally assume that you meet those rules. This is because the claim form asks if the claimant, partner or children being claimed for have come to live or returned to live in the UK in the last five years. However, even if you answer no to this question, the DWP might ask you extra questions about your immigration history, particularly if you have recently been paid IS or income-based jobseeker's allowance (JSA) at the urgent cases rate (see p162).

Sponsored immigrants and income support

You are only a sponsored immigrant for IS if you have been admitted to the UK or allowed to stay here because another person (known as your 'sponsor') gave a written undertaking under the immigration rules[8] to be responsible for your maintenance and accommodation in the UK.[9]

If this does not apply, you are not a sponsored immigrant and you are entitled to IS in the same way as any other person with indefinite leave to remain. If you are treated as a sponsored immigrant you should appeal and take independent advice.

If you are a sponsored immigrant you are not entitled to IS (or income-based JSA, housing benefit or council tax benefit), unless one of the exceptions below applies:[10]

- you have been resident in the UK for five years or more since the date you entered the UK or the date of the undertaking whichever is later; *or*
- you have been resident in the UK for less than five years but your sponsor has died.

If you are a sponsored immigrant under the benefit rules and the sponsor who gave the undertaking has died, you are entitled to IS at the urgent cases rate.[11] If more than one sponsor gave an undertaking (this would be exceptional, but is provided for), each of them must have died for this to apply to you. To work out the urgent cases rate, see Chapter 13.

If the sponsored immigrant rule stops applying to you (eg, you have been resident for five years) you get ordinary rate IS or income-based JSA.

If you are a sponsored immigrant, you should consider whether your partner, if you have one, should claim instead. For details of the rules dealing with the situation when a member of your family is a sponsored immigrant, see Chapter 12.

Five years' residence

Residence does not have to be continuous. Once you have been allowed to enter or stay on an undertaking, you remain a 'person subject to immigration control' (see p157), but you stop being a sponsored immigrant for benefit purposes when you have been resident (see p132) in the UK for five years.[12] This does not have to be continuous residence. The DWP is instructed to work out the length of your residence starting with the date you first entered the UK or if it was later, the date of the undertaking.[13] The rule is that you must be resident not present, so time abroad may count for your period of residence in the UK (see p133). If the DWP decides that, because your absences abroad do not count as periods of residency, you are still a sponsored immigrant even though five years have passed since you first entered, you should seek independent advice.

If you are given indefinite leave on an undertaking and you later travel abroad you continue to be subject to the undertaking. The Court of Appeal has held that on re-entry the original commitment of the sponsor continues to apply.[14]

Sponsor's liability to maintain and recovery of income support

Since 1980, the DWP has had the power to recover any IS paid to a sponsored immigrant from the person who gave the sponsorship.[15] Recovery is through the magistrates' court (in Scotland, sheriff's court). There is also a power to prosecute for failure to maintain the claimant.[16] The DWP has used the threat of court action to persuade sponsors to provide some financial support to the claimant concerned. If the sponsor could not support the claimant, the DWP usually took no further steps. Court action has apparently been rare, and is not likely to be considered where the sponsor is in receipt of benefits.

The definition of sponsored immigrant for the purpose of the rules on liability to maintain (see p104) is different from that for the claimant's benefit entitlement. Under the liability to maintain rules, a sponsored immigrant is a person for whom a sponsorship undertaking has been given after 22 May 1980.[17] There is no five-year rule, so there is no cut-off point, and a sponsor would, in theory at least, remain liable indefinitely.

These powers (or the threat of them) may still be used against sponsors of claimants on IS, especially where the claimant has transitional protection. If the DWP approaches you about an undertaking you have made, you should consider seeking advice. A liability to maintain should not delay an award of IS to which the claimant is entitled. Nor can any IS which is paid be recovered from the claimant.

The habitual residence test

The second way in which people who are settled or have indefinite leave to remain can be refused IS is by the habitual residence test (HRT). This usually happens because the person with indefinite leave to remain has been abroad for a period of time. The rules for the HRT and people with indefinite leave to remain are broadly the same as for British citizens (see p166). However a person with indefinite leave to remain may be more likely to be affected by the test – eg, because they have family or friends living abroad and may, therefore, travel abroad more frequently than a British citizen. In some cases people with indefinite leave to remain have been taken abroad as children and only return to the UK when they are adults. In such cases they will have great difficulty in establishing habitual residence immediately on arrival, but they may be able to show that they are habitually resident after a very short period.

Whether or not a person is habitually resident or indeed exempt from the test is a complex issue. This is primarily because there is no statutory definition of the term and consequently this has led to a considerable amount of caselaw on the point. What follows is a brief summary of the HRT. For more details of the test, see Chapter 11.

The area in which you must be habitually resident is wider than just the UK. It also includes Ireland, the Channel Islands and the Isle of Man (the Common Travel Area). Therefore any time spent living in the Republic of Ireland can be used towards establishing habitual residence. Some people are specifically exempt from the test – eg, European Economic Area workers and refugees. However, if you are not habitually resident and you are not exempt, you are a **'person from abroad'** for benefit purposes.[18] The consequence of which is that you are not eligible for IS even at the urgent cases rate.[19] The test only applies to the IS claimant, it does not apply to any partner or child for whom IS is being claimed. Therefore, if you might fail the test but have a partner who is more likely to pass, s/he can claim instead, though there may be disadvantages to such a decision. Even though you are excluded from social security benefit you may be able to get help from a local authority under the National Assistance Act 1948 or under the Children Act 1989. You are not excluded from this type of support even though you are a 'person from abroad' according to social security rules. A 'person from abroad' is not the same as a 'person subject to immigration control' and this term applies only to those failing the habitual residence test.

2. Income-based jobseeker's allowance

For contribution-based jobseeker's allowance (JSA), see p210.

The rules for income-based JSA in respect of people with indefinite leave to remain are the same as for income support (IS) (see p205).

The rules about liability to maintain (see p207) apply to income-based JSA as they do to IS, except that the DWP cannot recover from the sponsor any JSA paid to the claimant.[20]

3. Housing benefit and council tax benefit

Generally the housing benefit (HB) and council tax benefit (CTB) rules for people with indefinite leave to remain are the same as those for income support (IS) but there are some differences.

If you are being paid IS (including urgent cases rate) or income-based jobseeker's allowance (JSA) you are not a 'person subject to immigration control' (see p157) for HB or CTB.[21] The local authority that deals with your HB or CTB claim should not make enquiries about your immigration status or habitual residence.[22] If you are not being paid IS or income-based JSA the following rules apply.

You are only entitled to HB or CTB if:
- for HB, you have accommodation in Great Britain which you normally occupy as your home (which may apply during a temporary absence – see p302)[23] or, for CTB, you are liable to pay council tax for accommodation in which you reside (see p303);[24] *and*
- you are not a sponsored immigrant (see below); *and*
- you are either habitually resident in the UK, Ireland, the Channel Islands or the Isle of Man, or exempt from the habitual residence test (see p135).

If you do not meet these rules, you are not entitled to HB or CTB.[25]

The rules for sponsored immigrants are the same as those for IS (see p206), except that there is no urgent cases rate of payment, so if your sponsor has died you are entitled to HB or CTB at the normal rate.

The liability to maintain and recovery rules (see p207) do not apply to HB or CTB.

If you claim HB or CTB soon after you are given leave under an immigration rule requiring there to be no recourse to public funds, there is a theoretical risk to your immigration status (see p92).

If your partner or children have immigration leave on condition that they will be maintained without recourse to public funds, your HB or CTB claim may affect their immigration status (see p92).

4. Child benefit and guardian's allowance

The rules for child benefit and guardian's allowance are the same as those for British citizens (see p177). Sponsorship agreements do not affect entitlement to these benefits.

5. **Working families' tax credit and disabled person's tax credit**

The rules for working families' tax credit (WFTC) and disabled person's tax credit (DPTC) are the same as those for British citizens (see p175) apart from where you are the subject of a formal undertaking (see p104). Even if you are subject to an undertaking you will be eligible for WFTC or DPTC if:

- your sponsor has died; *or*
- the sponsorship was given more than five years ago.

WFTC and DPTC are counted as public funds for the purposes of the immigration rules.[26] Although those rules have not been amended to include the tax credits in the list of benefits taken into account, they are listed on the standard Home Office application forms, such as the SET(F) form, and they are included in the list of benefits excluded under the Immigration and Asylum Act 1999.[27] However, because no conditions can be attached to indefinite leave, claiming WFTC or DPTC after you have become settled does not break any immigration condition or put you at risk of prosecution. In theory, if your current indefinite leave was given under an immigration rule which requires no recourse to public funds (see p92), claiming WFTC or DPTC soon after that leave was granted might allow the Home Office to say that your leave was obtained by deception. The Home Office would have to show that it had been given false information about your finances or those of any sponsor or that you lied when you said you did not intend to claim public funds. It would be for the Home Office to prove this, and it would need some evidence. It would not be enough just to say that it was 'not satisfied', and leave you to prove your case. In any case this could probably not be done where your leave was as a returning resident (see p50), because the immigration rules allow returning residents to claim public funds. In practice, the Home Office has never been known to have done this and it is very unlikely to do so.

6. **Contribution-based jobseeker's allowance and incapacity benefit**

The rules for contribution-based jobseeker's allowance and incapacity benefit are the same as those for British citizens (see p181). People with indefinite leave, even if they are sponsored immigrants, are not excluded from access.

7. Retirement pensions and bereavement benefits

The rules for Category A, B, C and D retirement pensions, bereavement payment, widowed parent's allowance and bereavement allowance are the same as those for British citizens (see p184). If you are not entitled to a full pension because part of your working life (or your spouse's working life) was spent abroad you may be able to use European Community rules (see Part 4) or a reciprocal agreement (Part 5) to increase your pension. The bereavement benefits can be claimed by people whose spouse died on or after 9 April 2001, instead of the previous benefits of widow's allowance, widowed mother's allowance and widow's pension, which were payable only to bereaved women. Sponsorship agreements do not affect entitlement to these benefits.

These benefits are not 'public funds' for the purposes of the immigration rules.

8. Industrial injuries benefits

The rules for disablement benefit, reduced earnings allowance, retirement allowance, constant attendance allowance and exceptionally severe disablement allowance are the same as those for British citizens (see p188). Sponsorship agreements do not affect entitlement to these benefits. These benefits are not 'public funds' for the purposes of the immigration rules.

9. Attendance allowance, disability living allowance, invalid care allowance and non-contributory incapacity benefit

The rules for attendance allowance (AA), disability living allowance (DLA), invalid care allowance (ICA) and non-contributory incapacity benefit are the same as those for British citizens (see p191).

DLA, AA and ICA are counted as public funds for the purposes of the immigration rules.[28] However, because with indefinite leave there are no conditions to be broken, claiming these benefits should not affect your right to stay in the UK.

Sponsored immigrants remain 'persons subject to immigration control',[29] but they are exempted[30] from the usual ban on claiming these benefits.

10. **Statutory sick pay, statutory maternity pay and maternity allowance**

The rules for statutory sick pay, statutory maternity pay and maternity allowance are the same as for British citizens (see p194). Sponsorship agreements do not affect entitlement to these benefits.

11. **The social fund**

The social fund rules are the same as those for British citizens (see p195).

If a crisis loan is made to you and you are a sponsored immigrant under the liability to maintain rules (see p104) the DWP can recover the amount of that crisis loan from your sponsor.[31] Social fund guidance states that this will only be done if you are not entitled to income support (IS): if you are entitled to IS the loan will be recovered from you in the usual way.[32] This might arise after you have been here five years because there is no time limit on the effect of an undertaking for the purposes of liability to maintain, although there is for the benefit entitlement rules. For recovery of crisis loans, see CPAG's *Welfare Benefits Handbook*.

Notes

1   s33(2A) IA 1971
2   Schedule to the SS(IA)CA Regs
3   s4(1) IA 1971
4   I(LER)O
5   s7(1) IA 1988

1. **IS**
6   s124(1) SSCBA 1992
7   s137(2)(b) SSCBA 1992; reg 4 IS Regs
8   para 35 HC 395
9   s119(9) and (10) IAA
10   s115 IAA and reg 2 and Part 1 of the Schedule to the Immigration and Asylum (Consequential Amendment) Regulations
11   Sch Part 1 para 2 SS(IA)CA Regs; reg 70(2A) IS Regs
12   Sch Part I para 3 SS(IA)CA Regs
13   para 071896 DMG
14   *Mohammed Aziz Shah v Secretary of State for Social Security* [2002] EWCA CIV 285

15   s106 SSAA 1992
16   s105 SSAA 1992
17   ss78(6)(c) and 105(3) SSAA 1992
18   Reg 21(3) IS Regs 'person from abroad'
19   Sch 7 para 17 IS Regs

2. **Income-based JSA**
20   ss78(6)(c) and 105 SSAA 1992 as amended by s41(4) and Sch 2 paras 51 and 53 JSA 1995. s106 SSAA 1992 which gives the power to recover IS from a sponsor, was not amended to cover income-based JSA. **NB** This does not mean the benefit can be recovered from the claimant instead.

3. **HB and CTB**
21   Reg 7A(5)(d) and (e) HB Regs; reg 4A(5)(d) and (e) CTB Regs
22   HB/CTB Circular A1/96 para 4
23   s130(1)(a) SSCBA 1992; reg 5 HB Regs

24 s131(3)(a) SSCBA 1992
25 Reg 7A HB Regs; reg 4A CTB Regs

5. **WFTC and DPTC**
26 para 6(c) HC 395 'public funds'
27 s115(1) IAA 1999

9. **AA, DLA, ICA and non-contributory IB**
28 para 6(b) HC 395 'public funds'
29 s115(9) IAA 1999
30 Sch Part II para 4 SS(IA)CA Regs

11. **The social fund**
31 s78(3)(c) and (6)(c) SSAA 1992
32 para 4054 *Social Fund Decision and Review Guide* – publicly available

Chapter 16

Refugees

The benefits covered in this chapter are:
1. Income support (p215)
2. Income-based jobseeker's allowance (p218)
3. Housing benefit and council tax benefit (p219)
4. Child benefit and guardian's allowance (p219)
5. Working families' tax credit and disabled person's tax credit (p219)
6. Contribution-based jobseeker's allowance and incapacity benefit (p220)
7. Retirement pensions and bereavement benefits (p220)
8. Industrial injuries benefits (p220)
9. Disability benefits (p221)
10. Statutory sick pay and maternity benefits (p221)
11. The social fund (p221)

This chapter deals with refugees. Benefit rules often give equal treatment to refugees, and this is in line with the 1951 Refugee Convention, which obliges the UK authorities to provide refugees who are here lawfully 'the same treatment with respect to public relief and assistance as is accorded to their nationals'.[1]

For the rules applying to the dependants of refugees who do not themselves have asylum, see the chapter relevant to their status. Dependants of a person who has been recognised in the UK as a refugee should be given indefinite leave to remain on the same terms as that person, and are exempt from the 'no recourse to public funds' requirements set out in the immigration rules (see p15).

Who is a refugee?

A refugee is a person who is outside the country of her/his nationality because of a well-founded fear of persecution for reasons of race, religion, nationality, membership of a particular social group or political opinion.[2] Caselaw has established that you are a refugee from the moment that you meet this definition, not from the date that the Home Office recognised that status.[3] However, social security law and the DWP make a clear distinction between asylum seekers and refugees.

If you have been recognised by the Home Office as a refugee and given indefinite leave to remain in the UK as a refugee, you will have been sent a letter confirming that status. The DWP will accept this letter as proof that you are a refugee. Until July 1997, when a person was recognised as a refugee s/he would be granted asylum for a four-year period, and could apply for indefinite leave at the end of that time. From then on the Home Office practice has been to grant indefinite leave at once, as soon as the decision has been made to approve a person's asylum claim. Refugees accepted before July 1997 were able to apply for indefinite leave at any time, but there may be some people who have not done so. If you have been granted asylum in the UK as a refugee, your status as a refugee is the same, for benefits purposes, whether you have a time limit on that period or not. In either case you remain exempt from the habitual residence test (see p135).

If you have been recognised by another country as a refugee, the DWP should accept that you are a refugee.

1. Income support

If you are a recognised refugee the rules for income support (IS) are generally the same as those for British citizens. Recognised refugees do not fall within the definition of 'persons subject to immigration control',[4] and are exempt from the habitual residence test. You are entitled to ordinary rate IS but only if you satisfy the general conditions of entitlement[5]. You are entitled to IS if:

- you come within one of the groups of people eligible for IS (see CPAG's *Welfare Benefits Handbook* for full details of the groups that can qualify for IS);
- you are in Great Britain (GB)[6] (see p131) or temporarily absent from GB[7] (see p133);
- you satisfy the means test for IS.

Your entitlement might be affected if you are considered to be part of the same household as a person living abroad.

There is a special rule for IS entitlement,[8] allowing a refugee to receive benefit for up to nine months if:

- you are on a course of study for more than 15 hours a week in order to learn English;
- you are studying in order to improve your chances of finding work later;
- you begin the course within 12 months of arriving in the UK.

Backdating income support after recognition as a refugee

If you have been recognised by the Home Office as a refugee, you may be entitled to backdated IS for the period before you were recognised. The rules differ according to when you made your claim for asylum and whether or not you were receiving any urgent cases payments. There is also the possibility that some refugees can rely on European Community (EC) law. You may be able to make use of more than one of them. The possibilities depend on whether you:

- applied for asylum on or after 3 April 2000 (see below);
- applied at any time before 3 April 2000 and were not entitled to IS (see below);
- applied for asylum before 3 April 2000 and received urgent cases IS as an asylum seeker (see p217);
- you are an asylum seeker who can rely on EC law (see p217).

The important date here is the date of the application for asylum, not the date of the Home Office decision to recognise you as a refugee.

Applications made after 3 April 2000

If you applied for asylum after 3 April 2000 and you are subsequently granted refugee status you will be entitled to the full, ordinary rate of IS backdated to the date on which the Secretary of State recorded your application as having been made[9] whether to an immigration officer or in person at the Home Office. The normal rules on backdating do not apply and there is no three-month limit on arrears.[10] There is, therefore, scope for substantial backdating.

There will be no difference, in these cases, between people who applied on arrival at a port or after entry to the UK. Nor will there be any difference between those who are recognised straightaway, and those who are first refused and only succeed after making an appeal against the Home Office decision. If you are one of a couple, and both of you have been recognised as refugees, you can choose which of you should make the claim.[11]

You will be entitled to be paid the difference between the amount you would have been entitled to receive if you had been assessed as eligible for IS throughout, less any income and the value of any support you have received under the asylum support scheme.[12] For this purpose it will make no difference whether all or part of that support was provided under the interim arrangements[13] (see p275) or under the National Asylum Support Service (see Chapter 5).

You must make your claim for IS within 28 days of receiving the notice granting you indefinite leave to remain. There is no scope to extend this period so it is crucial to act quickly. If you do not receive the notice for some time, because of problems with the postal service, or because it has been sent to your legal representative rather than directly to you, you should make sure you keep some evidence of the delay, such as the envelope with the dated postmark, because you will need to show the actual date you received it.

Applied for asylum prior to 3 April 2000 and not entitled to income support

If you applied for asylum before 3 April 2000 but have been recognised as a refugee since that date you will be entitled to use the transitional arrangements.[14] These entitle you to a backdated payment of IS at the urgent cases rate,[15] rather than the ordinary rate.

If you were refused IS (or did not claim) for a period between your asylum claim and the date you were recognised as a refugee by the Home Office, you can claim a backdated payment within 28 days of receiving the Home Office written notification that you have been recognised as a refugee.[16] This time limit cannot generally be extended. Your claim is treated as made on the date you applied for asylum or on the date you ceased to be entitled to benefit. Any IS already paid to you or your partner for that period is offset against any extra IS to which you are entitled.

You may have been paid contribution-based jobseeker's allowance (JSA), but still lost out because this was less than urgent cases IS. If this applies, you cannot claim urgent cases IS for any period when you received contribution-based JSA.[17] This only applies to the JSA claimant so, if your partner has been recognised as a refugee and did not receive contribution-based JSA, s/he should make the claim for backdated IS instead. Your contribution-based JSA will be treated as income, so your partner will get the difference between that and urgent cases rate. If this is not possible you should ask the DWP to make an extra-statutory payment of the difference between contribution-based JSA and urgent cases IS and ask an adviser to contact CPAG about your case.

Applied for asylum prior to 3 April 2000 and in receipt of income support

If you fall within this category the backdating provisions are unlikely to help. This is because if you claimed asylum prior to 3 April 2000 the backdating provisions only allow backdating at the urgent cases rate. If you have received IS at the urgent cases rate the DWP will argue that you have not lost out and there are no arrears to be paid. It may be possible to argue that the DWP should award an *ex gratia* payment to cover the difference between the urgent cases rate and the full rate of benefit. The argument is that caselaw has established that a refugee is a refugee from the point that s/he claims asylum not from the date that s/he is recognised as a refugee by the Home Secretary.[18] Refugees are entitled to full benefit under UK social security rules and a claimant should not be penalised because of the delay by the Home Office in processing her/his asylum application. The difficulty with this argument is that the DWP is likely to say that there is a distinction in social security law between asylum seekers and refugees and it was correctly applying the law. There is also the difficulty in that, arguably, the claimant should have appealed the original decision and it would be for a tribunal to decide the point. The argument is much stronger for asylum seekers able to rely on EC law (see below).

Asylum seekers who are able to rely on European Community law

European Community law provides for equal treatment with British citizens for some refugees in respect of certain social security benefits.[19] A refugee is a refugee from the point that s/he claims asylum rather than the date when the Home

Secretary accepts her/him to be so. Where there is a conflict between EC and UK law, EC law prevails.[20] European Community law is therefore highly significant as it has the power to allow certain asylum seekers who are excluded from benefit entitlement to all those benefits falling within the scope of the regulation at the full rate. There have now been a number of legal challenges on this point culminating in a decision by the European Court of Justice (ECJ).[21] The ECJ has held that in order to rely on the relevant EC legislation (EC Regulation 1408/71) it is necessary for an asylum seeker or refugee to have crossed a European Economic Area (EEA) border. These judgments severely limit the scope of asylum seekers and refugees to rely on EC Regulation 1408/71 because asylum seekers and refugees do not have freedom of movement. Furthermore the Dublin Convention (see p61) seeks to prevent asylum seekers from claiming asylum in more than one EEA country. You are only likely to be able to use this EC rule if:

- you are an asylum seeker or a refugee; *and*
- you are an 'employed or self-employed person' for the purposes of EC Regulation 1408/71 (see p346) in the UK or elsewhere in the European Union or EEA. You need only have worked for a short period for this to apply; *and*
- you have crossed an EEA border; *and*
- you are 'habitually resident' in the UK in accordance with EC Regulation 1408/71 (see p137).

If you were paid urgent cases IS then the money you will gain by using this rule is the difference between urgent cases IS and ordinary IS, which is normally 10 per cent of the claimant's personal allowance.[22]

If you can use this rule, you may also be entitled to backdated disability living allowance, attendance allowance or invalid care allowance (see p00).

---

2. Income-based jobseeker's allowance

For contribution-based jobseeker's allowance (JSA), see p220.

Refugees are not 'persons subject to immigration control' and are exempt from the habitual residence test and, therefore, eligible for income-based JSA if they meet the general conditions of entitlement.[23] The rules are largely the same as those for British citizens (see p172). Before April 2000 the rules applying to income-based JSA were also the same as for income support (IS), in distinguishing between asylum seekers who were eligible for benefit and those who were excluded.

If you were not entitled to IS or income-based JSA before you were recognised as a refugee:

- you may be entitled to backdated urgent cases IS under British regulations (see p215). There is no equivalent regulation for income-based JSA;
- if you are one of the limited categories of refugee that can rely on European Community (EC) law (see p217) you may also be entitled under EC law to

backdated income-based JSA or IS at the ordinary rate. Income-based JSA is an 'unemployment benefit' under EC Regulation 1408/71.[24] The only advantage of asking for income-based JSA instead of IS is that you will be credited national insurance contributions for that period. As well as meeting the EC rules, you must show that you were actively seeking and available for work, and this may have required Home Office permission.

3. Housing benefit and council tax benefit

The rules of entitlement for housing benefit (HB) and council tax benefit (CTB) are largely the same as those for British citizens. If you are a recognised refugee you are not a 'person subject to immigration control' and you are exempt from the habitual residence test (see p157).[25]

Consequently you will be eligible for both HB and CTB if you meet the general rules for those benefits.

Backdating housing benefit and council tax benefit after recognition as a refugee

If you have been recognised by the Home Office as a refugee, you may be entitled to backdated HB or CTB for the period before you were recognised. This is under British law, and as neither of these benefits falls within the scope of EC Regulation 1408/71 it is not possible to rely on European Community law. The claim for backdated benefit should be made to the local authority where you are now living. That local authority then has to determine HB/CTB throughout the period in question even if you were living in a different authority's area. However, you will only be eligible for a backdated payment if you were liable for rent and or council tax.[26]

4. Child benefit and guardian's allowance

If you are a recognised refugee, the rules for child benefit and guardian's allowance are the same as those for British citizens (see p177).

5. Working families' tax credit and disabled person's tax credit

If you are a recognised refugee, the rules for working families' tax credit (WFTC) and disabled person's tax credit (DPTC) are the same as those for British citizens (see p175).

Backdating tax credits after recognition as a refugee

There is no WFTC or DPTC equivalent of the British regulations for backdating income support for recognised refugees (see p215). If you have been recognised as a refugee and were previously refused benefit because of your immigration status, you may, under European Community (EC) law, be entitled to backdated WFTC or DPTC for the period before recognition by the Home Office. This is because EC social security law specifies that refugees should enjoy equal treatment in respect of social security with British citizens.[27] However, there have been a number of challenges on this point and it has been decided by the European Court of Justice that in order for an asylum seeker or refugee to rely on this particular EC provision the person must have crossed a European Economic Area border.[28]

6. Contribution-based jobseeker's allowance and incapacity benefit

If you are a recognised refugee, the rules for contribution-based jobseeker's allowance and incapacity benefit are the same as for British citizens (see p181).

7. Retirement pensions and bereavement benefits

If you are a recognised refugee, the rules for Category A, B, C and D retirement pensions, bereavement payment, widowed parent's allowance and bereavement allowance are the same as those for British citizens (see p184). If you are not entitled to a full pension because part of your working life (or your spouse's working life) was spent abroad you may be able to use European Community rules (see Part 4) or a reciprocal agreement (Part 5) to increase your pension. The bereavement benefits can be claimed by people whose spouse died on or after 9 April 2001 instead of the previous benefits of widow's allowance, widowed mother's allowance and widow's pension, which were payable only to bereaved women.

8. Industrial injuries benefits

If you are a recognised refugee, the rules for disablement benefit, reduced earnings allowance, retirement allowance, constant attendance allowance and exceptionally severe disablement allowance are the same as those for British citizens (see p188).

9. **Disability benefits**

If you are a recognised refugee, the rules for disability living allowance, attendance allowance and invalid care allowance are the same as those for British citizens (see p191). You may be able to use European Community (EC) law to backdate a disability benefit for the period before you were recognised. There is no disability benefit equivalent of the British regulations for backdating urgent cases income support for recognised refugees (see p215).

If you have been recognised as a refugee, but before that you were not entitled to one of these benefits only because of your immigration status, you may be entitled under EC law to backdated benefit for the period before recognition by the Home Office.[29] However, the European Court of Justice has ruled that in order to rely on EC Regulation 1408/71 a refugee must have crossed a European Economic Area border. Therefore this provision is unlikely to be of wide application.

10. **Statutory sick pay and maternity benefits**

If you are a recognised refugee, the rules for statutory sick pay, statutory maternity pay and maternity allowance are the same as those for British citizens (see p194).

11. **The social fund**

There is no special treatment for recognised refugees in the social fund rules. The rules are the same as those for British citizens (see p195).

Notes

1 Art 23 Convention Relating to the Status of Refugees 1951 (Geneva)
2 Art 1A(2) 1951 Refugee Convention. Similar rules apply to refugees who are stateless.
3 CIS/564/1994 paras 19-24 and 39; *Khaboka v SSHD* [1993] Imm AR 484

1. IS
4 s115(9) IAA 1999
5 s124(1) SSCBA 1992

6 s124(1) SSCBA 1992
7 s137(2)(b) SSCBA 1992; reg 4 IS Regs
8 Sch 1B para 18 IS Regs
9 Reg 21ZB(3) IS Regs
10 Reg 6(4D) SS(C&P) Regs
11 Reg 4(3C) SS(C&P) Regs
12 Reg 21ZB(3) IS Regs
13 Sch 9 IAA 1999
14 Reg 12(1) SS(IA)CA Regs
15 Reg 21ZA(2) IS Regs
16 Reg 21ZA(2) and (3) IS Regs

Chapter 16 : Refugees

Notes

17 s124(1)(f) SSCBA 1992
18 *Khaboka v Home Secretary* [1993] Imm AR 484 at 489
19 Arts 2(1) and 3(1) EEC Reg 1408/71
20 s2 European Community Act 1971
21 In CIS/564/1994 it was argued that asylum seekers could rely on the Regulation even if they had never worked. The commissioner rejected this argument but confirmed the decision of the Court of Appeal in *Khaboka* that a refugee was a refugee from the point that s/he claimed asylum not the date s/he was granted refugee status. In *Krasniqi v CAO and Secretary of State for Social Security* Court of Appeal reported as R(IS) 1/99, the Court of Appeal considered whether a Turkish asylum seeker who had worked in the UK was eligible for IS under EC Reg 1408/71. By the time the case reached the Court Mr Krasniqi had been granted refugee status and the DWP subsequently backdated his IS to the date of asylum. The case therefore rested largely on whether Mr Krasniqi was eligible for the 10 per cent difference between urgent cases provisions and the normal rate of IS. The Court of Appeal rejected the argument on the basis that in order to rely on EC Reg 1408/71 it was necessary for the asylum seeker or refugee in question to have crossed an EC border. In R(FC) 1/01 the argument was resurrected on the basis of a number of cases having been referred by the German courts on much the same basis as *Krasniqi*. In that case the commissioner did not decide on the 1408/1971 point but held that the claimant who was a Turkish asylum seeker who had worked in the UK was eligible under the EC Turkish Association Agreement. The claimant had not moved between the EC but had obviously moved from Turkey to the UK. In the most recent case, CF/3662/1999, an asylum seeker had been refused child benefit. It was argued that the claimant had worked in the UK and child benefit was a family benefit under EC Reg 1408/71, therefore, the claimant was entitled to equal treatment with UK nationals. In this case, the first in which legal aid was awarded for a hearing before the commissioner, the claimant sought a reference to the ECJ finally to decide the

point. The commissioner refused the reference on the basis that five cases had already been referred by the German courts and there was no need for another reference. The ECJ has now held in *Khalil v Bundesanstalt für Arbeit* (C-95/99) that in order for a refugee/asylum seeker to rely on EC Reg 1408/71 it is necessary for her/him to have first crossed an EEA border. This judgment is likely to severely restrict the use of this Regulation.

22 It may be more if your urgent cases IS was reduced because of income or capital.

2. Income-based JSA

23 s115 IAA 1999; reg 85(4) JSA Regs
24 In *Hockenjos* the Court of Appeal held that income-based JSA was an unemployment benefit for the purposes of EC Directive 79/7.

3. HB and CTB

25 Reg 7B, Sch A1 and reg 7A(7) HB Regs 'refugee'; reg 4D, Sch A1 and reg 4A(7) CTB Regs
26 Reg 7B HB Regs and reg 4D CTB Regs

5. WFTC and DPTC

27 Arts 2(1) and 3(1) EC Reg 1408/71 prohibit discrimination against refugees residing in a member state if they have moved within the EEA.
28 *Khalil v Bundesanstalt für Arbeit* ECJ C-95/99

9. Disability benefits

29 Arts 2(1) and 3(1) EC Reg 1408/71 prohibit discrimination against refugees residing in a member state.

Chapter 17

••

Exceptional leave to enter or remain

The benefits covered in this chapter are:
1. Income support (p226)
2. Income-based jobseeker's allowance (p226)
3. Housing benefit and council tax benefit (p226)
4. Child benefit and guardian's allowance (p227)
5. Working families' tax credit and disabled person's tax credit (p227)
6. Contribution-based jobseeker's allowance and incapacity benefit (p227)
7. Retirement pensions and bereavement benefits (p228)
8. Industrial injuries benefits (p228)
9. Disability benefits (p228)
10. Statutory sick pay, statutory maternity pay and maternity allowance (p229)
11. The social fund (p229)

This chapter deals with benefits for people who have 'exceptional leave to remain' (ELR) – see Chapter 6. Exceptional leave to remain is not defined in either the benefit rules or the immigration rules but, as the name suggests, is leave to remain outside the normal immigration rules, which is granted where the Home Office considers that there are exceptional circumstances. If you have ELR you are generally put in the same position as a British citizen claiming benefit. You are not a 'person subject to immigration control' (PSIC) if you have ELR unless you have a public funds restriction attached to your stay.

The main group of people that have ELR are those who have applied for asylum. The Home Office will have considered that they do not meet the strict criteria of the 1951 Refugee Convention but nevertheless believes that the person may be in danger if s/he is returned home or there may be other compassionate grounds upon which the Home Office grants permission to stay. However, ELR is not limited to people who were refused refugee status, although they are the largest group of people covered by this provision.

People who have been granted ELR are treated, under UK benefit rules, in much the same way as British citizens and generally are not excluded from benefits. They are not, however, given the same rights as those granted refugee status. Firstly, they are not able to rely on European Community law in the way that refugees may.[1] Another advantage that refugees have is that they may claim income support while studying but those with ELR cannot.[2] Another major difference is that if you are granted refugee status you may put in a backdated claim for certain benefits to the date that you claimed asylum. This can amount to several years' worth of benefit. However, this backdating provision only applies to refugees not to people granted ELR.[3]

Immigration law generally makes a distinction between exceptional leave to remain and exceptional leave to enter, but in the benefits rules people with either exceptional leave to remain or enter are treated in the same way.[4] If you apply for further leave (of any kind) before your ELR runs out, your ELR is automatically extended until a decision is made on that application, by a process of statutory leave, under section 3C of the Immigration Act 1971.[5] If the application is refused, your ELR continues for as long as you have a right to appeal against that decision, which is a period of 10 days. For details see p83. Once an appeal is lodged, however, you become a PSIC and are excluded from entitlement to benefit.[6]

Normally, ELR is given on the understanding that you can have recourse to public funds but occasionally a person with ELR will have a public funds restriction attached to their stay. If your leave was given on the understanding that you would not have recourse to public funds you can be treated as a PSIC for certain benefits and a claim for any public funds benefit could affect your immigration position.

For example, you are given leave to remain as an artist even though you entered on a student visa. Because the Home Office waived the rule that you should have an artist visa, you may be able to argue that you have exceptional leave. However, even though your leave is exceptional, it has been given on the understanding that you would maintain and accommodate yourself without recourse to public funds (unless that condition has also been waived). A benefit claim could lead to a refusal to extend leave, or your current leave could be taken away, on the ground that your leave was obtained by deception.

Similarly, you may have been given leave to enter or remain as the dependant of a person with ELR. The normal policy would be only to permit family reunion after four years with ELR, after which time the person should be given indefinite leave to remain. The family reunion would then go ahead under the usual condition in the immigration rules, prohibiting recourse to public funds. In compassionate cases reunion will be permitted earlier, and if the 'no recourse' condition is applied an application for indefinite leave could be jeopardised by a benefit claim.

If this might apply to you, take expert advice before claiming any public funds benefit.

Showing that you have exceptional leave to remain

If you have limited ELR as a failed asylum seeker, the Home Office will have written to you stating that the Secretary of State has decided 'exceptionally to give you leave' or 'to give exceptional leave to remain'. This letter (see Chapter 9) should be good enough evidence of your immigration status to satisfy the benefits authorities. If you still need to show, once you have been given indefinite leave to remain after completing four years, that you were given ELR, you may need to show this letter as well as the letter granting you settlement.

If you have ELR as the dependant of a failed asylum seeker you may not have such a letter. The benefits authorities should accept your claim if you can show your relative's letter and show that your leave was granted in line with that of your relative.

If you have other sorts of ELR it may be difficult to persuade the benefits authorities. If the Home Office stated in writing when giving leave that it is exceptional, this should be enough. It will normally do so if you have been given leave after making an application for asylum, or for leave to remain under the European Convention on Human Rights (see p61), including cases where leave has been given for compassionate medical reasons. It may also be possible to argue that you have exceptional leave if you have been accepted within one of the categories of the immigration rules, but the Home Office has agreed to waive one or more of the requirements.

If the Home Office did not clearly state in writing that your leave was exceptional, you should try to produce any correspondence with it before leave was granted showing that it knew that you did not meet the requirements of the rules, so that your leave must be exceptional. If need be, the Home Office could be asked to state whether your leave was exceptional and, if not, under which part of the immigration rules it was granted.

If the Home Office has not already accepted in writing that your leave is exceptional, seek expert advice before approaching it or claiming to have ELR because your immigration status may be affected.

Problems can arise when you have applied to renew or vary your immigration leave, and then need to make or renew a claim to benefits. While your papers are under consideration by the Home Office you will not have proof of your current status, but you will be protected by the arrangements for statutory leave, which means that the conditions of your permission to stay continue, until the Home Office makes a new decision. You should be able to satisfy the benefits authorities of this by producing evidence of your most recent grant of ELR and of the date you applied for further leave.

The benefits authorities are often unclear about ELR. They can confuse it with 'indefinite leave to remain'. This is sometimes made worse by taking advice from Home Office staff who are rarely aware of all the different Home Office policies and practices about giving leave. Some DWP guidance may suggest that only exceptional leave for failed asylum seekers counts under the benefit rules.[7] This conclusion would be wrong, because the benefit rules do not limit ELR in this way.

1. Income support

Generally people with exceptional leave to remain (ELR) are not excluded from income support (IS)[8] and the rules of entitlement are broadly the same as for British citizens (see p166). You are not a 'person subject to immigration control' unless you have a public funds restriction attached to your stay.[9] In order to be eligible for IS you must meet the general conditions for IS. This means that you must come within one of the categories that are able to claim IS, such as a lone parent, and you must meet the income and capital rules.

If you are an asylum seeker who is eligible for urgent cases rate of IS (see p162) and you are subsequently granted ELR you are no longer eligible for urgent cases payments and must meet the general conditions for entitlement to benefit. Unless you are able to fit within one of the groups eligible for IS you must sign on and claim income-based jobseeker's allowance rather than IS.

People with ELR are exempt from the habitual residence test.[10]

2. Income-based jobseeker's allowance

For contribution-based jobseeker's allowance (JSA), see p227.

Income-based JSA rules about who is a 'person subject to immigration control' are the same as those for income support (IS) (see above).[11] People with exceptional leave to remain are not excluded from benefit as long as they meet the general conditions of entitlement, unless they have a public funds restriction attached to their stay. The test for habitual residence[12] is also applied in the same way as for IS.

3. Housing benefit and council tax benefit

If you have exceptional leave to remain or exceptional leave to enter you are generally not excluded from benefit as long as you meet the general conditions of entitlement. You are not a 'person subject to immigration control' for housing benefit (HB) or council tax benefit (CTB) unless you have a public funds restriction attached to your stay, and people with exceptional leave are specifically exempt from the habitual residence test.

Chapter 17 : Exceptional leave to enter or remain
6. Contribution-based jobseeker's allowance and incapacity benefit

17

If you are already in receipt of income support or income-based jobseeker's allowance the local authority that deals with your HB or CTB claim should not make enquiries about your immigration status or habitual residence.[13]

4. Child benefit and guardian's allowance

The rules for child benefit and guardian's allowance are broadly the same as those for British citizens (see p177). You are not a 'person subject to immigration control' unless you have a public funds restriction attached to your stay. Even if you have a public funds restriction you may still be exempt from the immigration condition if you are a national of a country with which the UK has a reciprocal agreement.[14]

Child benefit is a public funds benefit under the immigration rules. Guardian's allowance is not a public funds benefit but in order to qualify you must be receiving child benefit.

5. Working families' tax credit and disabled person's tax credit

The rules for working families' tax credit (WFTC) and disabled person's tax credit (DPTC) are similar to those for British citizens (see p175).

If your exceptional leave to enter or remain was given on the understanding that you would not have recourse to public funds, you will be a 'person subject to immigration control', and will not be entitled to WFTC or DPTC.[15] Neither of these benefits are covered by the definition of 'public funds' set out in the immigration rules but they are listed on the Home Office application forms and are considered to be public funds (see p92).[16]

6. Contribution-based jobseeker's allowance and incapacity benefit

The rules for contribution-based jobseekers' allowance (JSA) and incapacity benefit are the same as those for British citizens (see p181). There are no immigration conditions for these benefits. The habitual residence rules only apply to income-based JSA.[17]

7. Retirement pensions and bereavement benefits

The rules for Category A, B, C and D retirement pensions, bereavement payment, widowed parent's allowance and bereavement allowance are the same as those for British citizens (see p184). If you are not entitled to a full pension because part of your working life was spent abroad you may be able to rely on a reciprocal agreement (see Chapter 28) to increase your pension. People with exceptional leave cannot rely on European Community law to aggregate periods of insurance unless they are married to a European Economic Area national.

8. Industrial injuries benefits

The rules for disablement benefit, reduced earnings allowance, retirement allowance, constant attendance allowance and exceptionally severe disablement allowance are the same as those for British citizens (see p188). These benefits do not have any immigration test.

9. Disability benefits

The rules for disability living allowance (DLA), attendance allowance (AA), invalid care allowance (ICA) and severe disablement allowance are broadly the same as those for British citizens (see p191).

If your exceptional leave to enter or remain (ELR) was given on the understanding that you would not have recourse to public funds, you will count as a 'person subject to immigration control' and so not entitled. Also, any claim to these benefits could affect your immigration status (see p92).

For how long benefit is awarded

Where a medical condition is permanent, awards of DLA and AA are often made for life. DWP guidance suggests that people with limited ELR should not get life awards. We believe this may be wrong in the case of people who are granted ELR under the failed asylum seeker policy (see below). In other cases, unless the Home Office has stated in writing the circumstances in which leave will be extended, it will be difficult to argue that the award should not be limited.

When a person is given ELR under the policy for asylum seekers whose applications are rejected, or under the European Convention on Human Rights, s/he is normally given leave for a period of four years, and then becomes eligible to apply for indefinite leave to remain. DWP guidance states that any award of DLA, AA or ICA should be limited to the date your current immigration leave is due to run out.[18] If your award is limited in this manner, you will need to claim that benefit again at the end of the award, and again show that you meet all the benefit conditions, including those about disability. This places you in a worse position than a British citizen who would have been given an indefinite award (or one longer than your period of leave), especially since her/his benefit could only be withdrawn if the DWP showed that the disability conditions were no longer satisfied.

We believe the DWP approach is wrong because:
- there will only be a change of circumstance at the end of the leave if you do not apply for an extension in time, which is unlikely, or if an extension is refused, and otherwise you continue to have ELR. Home Office practice in the case of failed asylum seekers is almost always to grant indefinite leave, or to extend the exceptional leave. In the rare cases where extensions have been refused it is usually because the person has visited her/his own country in the meantime. Even in these cases there will be a right of appeal, and you should argue that you remain eligible for benefit at least until your appeal has been finished. Unless this applies to you, the end of your present period of leave is not a future change of circumstances because your leave will, in practice, be extended;
- the DWP can easily supersede your award if leave is not extended, so there is no good reason to limit the award to the end of your existing leave;
- a time-limited award may mean that you cannot qualify for Motability (see CPAG's *Welfare Benefits Handbook*). In which case there may be discrimination which possibly could be challenged by reliance on the Human Rights Act 1998.[19]

If a limited award is made because of your limited leave, consider appealing that decision. You should not wait until the award runs out.

10. Statutory sick pay, statutory maternity pay and maternity allowance

The rules for statutory sick pay, statutory maternity pay and maternity allowance are the same as for British citizens (see p194). There are no immigration conditions to these benefits and they are not public funds.

11. The social fund

There is no special treatment for people with exceptional leave to remain in the social fund rules. The rules are the same as those for British citizens (see p195).

You are not a 'person subject to immigration control' (see p157) unless you have a public funds restriction attached to your stay, in which case you are not eligible for benefit.

Notes

1 Refugees and stateless persons can rely on EC Reg 1408/71 in order to aggregate contributions, satisfy residence requirements, export certain benefits and override discriminatory provisions within the benefit rules. However this only applies to refugees and stateless persons who have moved within the EEA.
2 Sch 1B para 18 IS Regs
3 Such claims must be made within 28 days of notification of refugee status. Reg 21ZB IS Regs
4 Reg 21(3)(c) IS Regs
5 As amended in 2000 by s3 IAA 1999
6 s115(9)(d) and Sch 4 para 17 IAA 1999
7 For example, 070975 DMG

1. IS
8 s115(9) IAA 1999
9 s115(9)(b) IAA 1999
10 Reg 21(3)(c) IS Regs 'person from abroad'

2. Income-based JSA
11 s115(9) IAA 1999
12 Reg 85(4)(c) JSA Regs 'person from abroad'

3. HB and CTB
13 HB/CTB Circular A1/96 para 4

4. Child benefit and guardian's allowance
14 Reg 2(3) SS (IA)CA Regs

5. WFTC and DPTC
15 s115(1) IAA 1999
16 Although WFTC and DPTC are not listed as public funds their predecessors FC and DWA are. WFTC and DPTC are somewhat unique in that they are not new benefits but simply a renaming of their predecessors to the extent that the regulations retain their original name of FC and DWA. The legislation also makes clear that any claim for WFTC is to be treated as a claim for FC and DPTC as DWA. Therefore any claim for the renamed benefits does mean that a claim for a public funds benefit has been made.

6. Contribution-based JSA
17 JSA Regs: the amount of contribution-based JSA is set by reg 79 and not reg 83 which refers to the 'persons from abroad' rule in reg 85(4).

9. Disability benefits
18 Memo AOG Vol 2/40 para 3
19 Art 14 of the Human Rights Act 1998 prohibits discrimination but only in respect of any of the rights contained within the Act (Convention Rights). In order for a case to be successful it is necessary to show that the benefit involved is covered by the Act, for example as a property right. This in itself may prove difficult, although not impossible, as the courts have tended to view property rights very much as applying only to contributory benefits. However, there is scope to challenge this and it may well be that the benefit may be within another of the Convention rights.

Chapter 18

....

Limited leave to remain

The benefits covered in this chapter are:
1. Income support (p233)
2. Income-based jobseeker's allowance (p239)
3. Housing benefit and council tax benefit (p244)
4. Child benefit and guardian's allowance (p245)
5. Working families' tax credit and disabled person's tax credit (p247)
6. Contribution based jobseeker's allowance and incapacity benefit (p249)
7. Retirement pensions and bereavement benefits (p250)
8. Industrial injuries benefits (p251)
9. Disability benefits (p251)
10. Statutory sick pay, statutory maternity pay and maternity allowance (p253)
11. The social fund (p253)

This chapter covers the rights of people who have limited leave to remain in the UK under the immigration rules. The most common types of leave to remain are for spouses and other family members of people settled here, for students, visitors and overseas workers. Refugees, asylum seekers and people with exceptional leave all have special rules and are not dealt with in this chapter. If you have temporary admission you do not have limited leave (see p113).

In general, if you have limited leave, you will only be entitled to benefit if you have no public funds condition attached to your leave or you are able to rely on European Community law. If you have limited leave and a public funds restriction attached you are excluded from entitlement to most means-tested and non-contributory benefits. Rules differ according to the benefit involved.

What is limited leave?

You have limited leave to remain if you are in the UK and your right to stay here is subject to a time limit in one of the following ways:
- as a condition placed on your visa or entry clearance;
- by an immigration officer on arrival in the UK; *or*
- by the Home Office if your leave to remain has been varied or extended.

Your limited leave may be shown by an entry clearance sticker, by a stamp in your passport or by a letter issued by the Home Office. For details, see Chapter 9. In most cases a person with limited leave will also be subject to a condition or requirement that s/he does not have recourse to public funds. If you have limited leave which is not subject to a public funds condition you will not be excluded from any benefits provided you satisfy the normal rules of entitlement. If the benefit is dependent on contributions or being in work you must not be debarred from taking employment as a condition of stay.

Temporary admission or temporary release do *not* count as leave to remain. Both are given by way of a standard immigration service form indicating that the holder remains liable to detention. If you are in the UK because you have temporary admission or temporary release you do not have limited leave to remain and the provisions set out in this chapter do not apply to you (see Chapter 19 for details of relevant provisions).

Even if your original leave has expired, you still have limited leave to remain if you applied for an extension of leave before or on the date it was due to expire. This leave continues until the Home Office grants your application, or, if it is refused, until the time allowed for bringing an appeal against that decision has expired. If the application is granted and you are given further leave, the new leave, and any conditions attached to it, is effective from the date it is given. Any conditions of your original leave continue to apply as long as you have statutory leave,[2] since this period is treated simply as an automatic extension of your original period of leave.

If your application for an extension was made after the date your leave expired, then you do not have leave to remain. You are an overstayer (see Chapter 19 for details of the provisions which apply).

If the time limit on your leave to remain has been removed in writing, you have indefinite leave to remain (see Chapter 15). Any other condition on your permission to be here also ends when the time limit ceases. The only restrictions on your right to benefit concern sponsorship undertakings (see p104) and habitual residence (see p135).

If you are a European Union (EU) or European Economic Area (EEA) national you are very unlikely to have limited leave to remain. That is because EU or EEA nationals arriving in the UK normally have a direct right to enter the UK and do not need leave to enter or remain,[3] so immigration officers do not give EU or EEA nationals leave to enter.[4] Since June 2002 the rights of free movement have been extended to Swiss nationals.

Some EEA nationals will have been issued with residence permits, but these merely record a right they already have, and do not amount to a grant of permission by the Home Office. EEA nationals and members of their families can apply for and may be granted indefinite leave to remain under the immigration rules,[5] but they are not required to do so. For the rules concerning EU and EEA nationals, see Part 4.

Your leave to enter or remain does not end when you leave the UK, unless it was granted for a period of six months or less. This is the result of a change in the law in 2000.[6] Any leave to enter or remain in the UK for longer than six months, whether given abroad by an entry clearance officer, or by an immigration officer on arrival in the UK, or at the Home Office as an extension or variation of stay by the Secretary of State, continues in force while you are abroad.[7] This includes indefinite leave to remain (see Chapter 15). So long as you return to the UK before the expiry of that period of leave you do not require fresh leave.

1. Income support

Most people with limited leave are not entitled to income support (IS) because of the rules concerning 'persons subject to immigration control' (PSIC).

A 'person subject to immigration control'

You are a PSIC if:[8]
* you need leave to be in the UK but have not been given it (see Chapters 3 and 4); or
* your leave was given under an immigration rule which requires no recourse to public funds (see p92); or
* you are a sponsored immigrant (see p105); or
* you only have leave to remain in the UK because you are allowed to stay awaiting an appeal under the immigration rules (see p83).

However, some people with limited leave can qualify for benefit. There are two types of IS that you may be entitled to:
* **ordinary rate IS** if you satisfy the general conditions for entitlement and are within one of the groups who can claim IS such as lone parent, pensioner or because of incapacity for work; or
* **urgent cases IS**, paid at a lower rate than ordinary IS. The rules on income and capital are different to ordinary rate IS.

In order to qualify if you have limited leave you must fall within one of the groups below that are exempt from the definition of PSIC as well as satisfying the following general conditions:
* be in Great Britain (GB) or only temporarily absent from GB;
* satisfy, or be exempt from, the habitual residence test;
* satisfy all the other general conditions of entitlement to IS.

Your entitlement might also be affected if you are considered to be part of the same household as a person living abroad.

Groups with limited leave that can qualify for income support

- A person from a country that has ratified the European Social Chapter of 1961 or the European Convention on Social and Medical Assistance and who is lawfully present. (This applies to all European Economic Area (EEA) countries, Cyprus, Czech Republic, Hungary, Latvia, Malta, Poland, Slovakia and Turkey.) Benefit is paid at the ordinary rate. For details on the meaning of 'lawful presence', see p131.
- A person who has been given limited leave as a sponsored immigrant (see p105) and whose sponsor has died. Benefit is at the urgent cases rate.
- A student or other person whose funding from abroad is temporarily interrupted and there is a reasonable expectation that her/his supply of funds will be resumed. Payment is at the urgent cases rate and is for a maximum for 42 days (whether in one or more spells) within a period of leave.
- An asylum seeker who has a right to benefit under the transitional rules (see Chapter 20 for details). Payment is at the urgent cases rate.
- A person who is lawfully employed and is a national or a family member of a national of Algeria, Morocco, Slovenia, Tunisia or Turkey. This is because there are European Community (EC) agreements with these countries, which provide for equal treatment within social security. These rights stem from EC law but have not been incorporated into UK law, therefore the DWP is unlikely to accept that IS is covered by these agreements. Seek specialist advice on this issue. Benefit would be paid at the ordinary rate.[9]

Even if you are not a PSIC you will not qualify for IS if you fail the habitual residence test (see p135).

No recourse to public funds

You are a PSIC for IS purposes if your leave was given under an immigration rule which requires you not to have recourse to public funds (see p235) and none of the exceptions to that rule apply (see p92).[10]

When deciding whether a person's permission counts as leave 'subject to a condition that he does not have recourse to public funds', it is the type of leave that was given that matters, not what the Home Office or the DWP says about the status later.

Limited leave given to adults normally requires that there be no recourse to public funds. The most important exception is family members of a recognised refugee who are given leave in line with that person, and are not made subject to a 'no recourse' condition. This may not apply if the refugee had already had indefinite leave for a long period by the time the family member is granted leave, as the Home Office may then treat the application as one made under the immigration rules. The family member could then be treated in the same way as a person applying to join a UK resident, without the advantages usually given to refugees. If you are applying for family reunion and you believe you should qualify as a refugee, you should seek advice about your family's status in the UK.

For full details of exceptions, see p92. If your permission to be in the UK comes within one of the exceptions, your limited leave does not make you a PSIC. This remains the case if you apply for an extension before this leave runs out. However, you will still need to pass the habitual residence test (see p135).

Even if you are not a PSIC, claiming IS may still affect your immigration status (see p156). In particular, if the leave stamp states that you must not have recourse to public funds you will break the terms of your leave and commit a criminal offence even if that condition ought not to have been attached to your category of permission.[11] If this condition has been attached, you may want to ask the Home Office to remove it, but you should seek expert advice before making such a request.

Arguing that your leave was not given under the immigration rules

If you have permission given for a limited period, and are not within one of the exceptions (see p157), you will be a PSIC. Until the changes that came into effect in April 2000 you could argue that you were not given leave under the immigration rules. Because of the wording of the IS rules, even if you seemed to have leave subject to a condition that you would have 'no recourse to public funds', this may not have applied for IS purposes. The IS rules previously referred to leave given in accordance with the immigration rules, so if you did not meet any one of the requirements of the relevant rules, you could argue that your leave was not given in accordance with them. This could mean you were also exempt from the habitual residence test as a person with exceptional leave to remain (see p92) and from the sponsored immigrant rule (see p105).

The rules have been changed and the old definition of 'persons whose right to benefits were restricted' has been replaced. You will no longer be able to use this exception, even if you had received benefits in this way before 3 April 2000. You only become entitled again once you cease to be a PSIC when the conditions on your stay are lifted.

Sponsored immigrants

Most of the people who have this status will have indefinite leave to remain (see Chapter 15), but some children between the ages of 16 and 18, and most of the small number of people admitted under the immigration rules as 'other relatives' (that is, to join a relative other than a spouse, parent or child), may be admitted with limited leave and will only be permitted to join parents or other relatives if their sponsors have signed undertakings.

Waiting for an immigration appeal

When a person has been given leave to enter or remain in the UK and then applies in time to vary or extend that stay there will, in most cases, be a right of appeal against refusal of that application. If you lodge an appeal you will have the right to remain in the UK to attend the hearing of that appeal. This applies also if you lodge an appeal against a refusal of leave to enter the UK at a time when you held a valid visa or still had a period of leave to remain. These provisions of immigration law were introduced during 2000. In these cases your right to stay is a form of statutory leave,[12] but it is not like the statutory leave you have while you are waiting for the Home Office to make a decision on an application made while you have leave to remain. While you wait for the Home Office to decide, any conditions attached to your previous leave, apart from the time limit, continue to apply. This means that if your leave was not subject to a condition that you have no recourse to public funds, so that you were able to claim certain benefits, you remain entitled while you wait for a decision.

While you wait for an appeal, on the other hand, that entitlement will not apply, because the Home Office has taken a decision to end your leave. You still have leave to be here as long as the appeal is treated as pending, but no entitlement[13] to IS, unless you can show that one of the exceptions set out in the regulations[14] applies. The regulations specifically exclude from entitlement asylum seekers with transitional protection because transitional protection ends when the Home Office decides to refuse you asylum, and is not extended to cover an appeal.[15]

Temporary disruption of funds

If you are a PSIC with limited leave which is subject to a condition that you do not have 'recourse to public funds', you are entitled to urgent cases IS if:[16]
- you were expecting to be sent money from abroad but those remittances have been temporarily disrupted; *and*
- there is a reasonable expectation that money will be sent in the future; *and*
- since you were last given leave to remain in the UK you have supported yourself without receiving public funds (see p92) except where those public funds were paid because of this rule.

The maximum period during which IS can be paid under this rule is 42 days in any one period of leave.[17] This does not have to be a continuous claim, but could, for example, be for seven separate weeks. The exact effect of the wording of this rule is uncertain. Most of the people who can make use of it are in the UK as overseas students. Before the changes introduced in 2000 they would generally be given leave for one year at a time, and then have to apply for extensions. A period of leave would run from the last grant of leave to remain (or leave to enter if this was your first period since entering the UK), and end with the grant of the

· ·

n spouses

uestion of whether it is wise for a person to claim benefit often arises in the
xt of those who have been joined from abroad by a foreign spouse. The
e will be allowed to work but will have limited leave with a public funds
tion attached to her/his stay.

these circumstances the person with limited leave is generally not entitled
im benefits because s/he is a PSIC but the partner who s/he has joined can
benefit. Some benefits allow the amount of benefit to be reduced so that
ent is made only for the person who is free from immigration control or
d. Other benefits, however, do not make this provision. The problem,
fore, is that the partner with limited leave could have recourse to public
s *indirectly*. If as a result of making that claim the partner who is eligible for
fit receives more benefit than s/he would have done if the PSIC had not been
nt in the household then there is 'additional recourse to public funds' (see
or more details).

the spouse from abroad is joining a person who is an EEA national or a British
n who is able to rely on EC rights these rules may not apply (see Part 4 on the
s of EEA nationals).

n fiancé(e)s

same problems apply as for spouses (see above).

se abroad

same rules apply as for British citizens if you have been living with your
se abroad before you came to the UK – see p169.

r people in your family with a different status

ur spouse has a more favourable immigration status s/he should claim
ead. Check the chapter that deals with that person's status. If you count as a
for IS, and do not come under any of the exemptions, your spouse will not
ble to include you in her/his applicable amount unless s/he is getting IS paid
e urgent cases rate (see p162).

t of claiming public funds on immigration status

treated as public funds under the immigration rules.[21] If you have claimed
um, then claiming any public funds is very unlikely to affect your immigration
tion. In other situations, whether or not you are a PSIC for IS purposes,
ning public funds may mean that:

e Home Office may refuse you further leave to remain, if that leave would
equire 'no recourse to public funds'. Even though short periods of reliance on

next period of leave to remain. Leave would also end v
the Common Travel Area (CTA) (comprising the UK, Ir
the Channel Islands). Students now will generally be g
cover the whole of their intended studies, and any lea
more than six months duration will not end when you t

The benefit rule still refers to 'any one period . . .
extended'. But leave will not generally now be 'extende
others coming for a period of time will usually be given
and it will continue throughout that time, without the n
of leave from an immigration officer on return to the UI
have only one period of leave to cover the whole of you
you can, in most cases, have supported yourself during
order to claim an urgent cases payment in another perio
and seems intended to cover situations similar to those i
2000.

Examples of the kinds of situations when this rule may

- a disruption to the banking system in your home coun
- a collapse in exchange rates which means that your
  immediately buy hard currency; or
- if your sponsor abroad has unexpected financial difficu

You can only use this rule if you were expecting to receive
if your only sponsor or potential sponsor is in the UK you
her/his support stops. However, the rule does not say that
now expect to receive in the future, also has to be from
qualify because a person in the UK will give you financial s

Home Office policy is that reliance on public funds for
no fault of the person concerned will not be used to
However, even a claim for IS for a short period may mear
will look much more closely at any application for an ext
particular, your ability to support yourself.

Habitual residence test

A person who claims IS must satisfy the habitual residence
is because you are deemed by the DWP to be a 'person fro
of your nationality or immigration status. This applies
remain is not subject to a condition that you have 'no recou
a sponsorship undertaking. It is not necessary to be here fo
in order to be habitually resident.

The habitual residence test only applies to the IS claima
to any partner or child for whom IS is being claimed. If you
have a partner who is more likely to pass, s/he could claim
may be disadvantages to this (see CPAG's *Welfare Benefits H*

Foreig

The c
cont
spou
cone

In
to ch
clair
pay
settl
ther
func
ben
pres
p96

I
citi
righ

Forei

The

Spou

The
spo

Othe

If y
ins
PS
be
at

Effe

IS
asy
po
cla

•

public funds should not lead to refusal of further leave, it may affect the Home Office's attitude towards you. For example, if you claim public funds during your one year's leave as the spouse of a person settled in the UK, at the end of that year you may be given a further year's leave before indefinite leave is considered, instead of immediate indefinite leave;

- if your leave was given after 1 November 1996 and the stamp states that you must not have recourse to public funds, you break the terms of your leave and commit a criminal offence by claiming IS. Any action is very unlikely, especially if your claim is covered by the Home Office policy.[22]

Because of these problems, you should weigh up the risks and advantages of claiming.

If you are one of a couple and your partner does not have limited leave s/he may claim benefit and be paid at the single person rate. For IS no payment can be made for you if you are a PSIC (unless you come under one of the exemptions) and therefore there is no recourse to public funds if your partner claims. However, it may not be wise for that person to claim because it could demonstrate that s/he could not maintain you, and your immigration position could be affected. To claim benefit implies that you cannot maintain yourself, let alone your spouse. This could affect the application for indefinite leave made by a foreign spouse, as it would be clear that contrary to the claimant's statement to the Home Office s/he could not maintain her/him.

2. Income-based jobseeker's allowance

For the rules concerning contribution-based jobseeker's allowance (JSA), see p249.

It is difficult for people with limited leave to meet the normal rules for income-based JSA, so you should always check to see if you may be entitled to income support (IS) instead (see p233).

Income-based JSA counts as public funds under the immigration rules.[23] The possible effects of claiming income-based JSA on your immigration position are the same as those for IS (see p233).

The rules about who is a 'person subject to immigration control' (PSIC) or 'person from abroad' are the same as for IS (see p233).[24] If you are a PSIC you are not entitled to income-based JSA unless you can fit within one of the exemptions of the PSIC definitions.

Groups with limited leave that can qualify for income-based jobseeker's allowance

- Asylum seekers who have transitional protection (see Chapter 20). Payment is at the urgent cases rate. It would be easier to claim IS instead as there is no requirement to satisfy the labour market conditions for getting the urgent cases payment of IS.

- A national of a country that has ratified the 1961 European Social Chapter or the European Convention on Social and Medical Assistance and who is lawfully present. See p131 for details of lawful presence. (This applies to all European Economic Area countries, Cyprus, Czech Republic, Hungary, Latvia, Malta, Poland, Slovakia and Turkey.) Benefit is paid at the ordinary rate.
- A person who has been sponsored but whose sponsor has died (see p105 on meaning of sponsor). The urgent cases rate is payable.
- A person whose funding is temporarily disrupted and there is a reasonable expectation that it will be reinstated. Benefit is paid at the urgent cases rate. In general it would be easier to claim IS rather than income-based JSA as there is no condition to be available for work in order to qualify for an urgent cases payment of IS. See temporary disruption of funds above.
- A person who is lawfully employed and is a national or a family member of a national of Algeria, Morocco, Slovenia, Tunisia or Turkey. This is because the European Community (EC) has agreements with these countries, which provide for equal treatment within social security. These rights have not been incorporated into UK law for income-based JSA and therefore the DWP may not accept that there is entitlement. However, the agreements apply to benefits that provide for 'unemployment' and there is developing caselaw that income-based JSA is a benefit for 'unemployment' in EC terms (see p418 for further details of these association agreements).[25]

If you are not a PSIC, your entitlement to income-based JSA depends on whether or not your leave has a prohibition or restriction on employment (an employment condition).

Leave with an employment condition

Your limited leave may have a prohibition or restriction on working (see below). This may have been superseded by the Home Office.

If you have a prohibition or restriction on working which has not been superseded, you cannot meet the usual JSA condition that you are immediately able to work as an employed earner.[26] This means that you can only be entitled to JSA if:

- you are treated as available for work (see p241). This is very unlikely to be useful for people with an employment condition; *or*
- you are entitled to hardship payments (see p242). This is different from urgent cases rate.

Who has leave with an employment condition?

Conditions of your immigration leave can only be imposed in writing, except in specified circumstances.[27] If you do not have a written employment condition as part of your current leave (or your last leave, if the permission you have now is statutory leave while you wait for a Home Office decision on whether to grant an extension), then there is no employment condition on your stay. This applies even if an employment condition is normally imposed with the type of leave that you have. The only exceptions to these rules are if:

- you were given an unreadable leave stamp by an immigration officer. If this applies, you are treated as having been given leave to enter for six months with a prohibition on taking employment;[28]
- you entered the UK as a member of a tour group or other party, and the terms of your entry were given in writing to the person leading the group;[29]
- you entered the UK from another part of the Common Travel Area (UK, Ireland, the Channel Islands and Isle of Man) without being given written leave. If this applies, you may be treated as having been given limited leave to enter for a limited period with a prohibition on taking employment.[30]

There are two types of employment condition:

- prohibition – the stamp reads 'employment prohibited' or 'condition that holder does not enter employment paid or unpaid'. This is usually imposed on visitors (including visitors in transit) and prospective students (see Chapter 9); *and*
- restriction – the stamp reads 'condition that holder does not enter or change employment paid or unpaid without the consent of the Secretary of State for Employment'. There are two groups affected:
  - people who have a work permit or permit for training and work experience who have permission to work in the job referred to in the permit; *and*
  - students, au pairs, seasonal workers, working holidaymakers and others (see Chapter 9). Seasonal workers are restricted to a particular short-term job; the others are generally treated as having been given the necessary consent without having to apply for permission to take a particular job.

A person who is here without a restriction on taking employment may qualify for income-based JSA. However most people who are in the UK with limited leave and who are allowed to work are subject to a public funds condition.

Note that a hardship payment is a payment of income-based JSA. See CPAG's *Welfare Benefits Handbook* for who can get one and in what circumstances.

Treated as available for work

Under JSA rules, certain people are treated as available for work for short periods. In theory, you can use these rules even though your immigration leave means that you cannot take employment. In practice, because a jobseeker's agreement is normally required, these rules are very unlikely to help anyone who has a condition on employment. Even if you have a restriction, rather than a prohibition, on working, and are 'deemed' to have the necessary consent without a specific application it will be difficult to meet the requirement for an agreement. It may be possible to be entitled for a few weeks before the agreement interview by using the rules that treat some people as available for work, actively seeking work and as exempt from needing an agreement.[31] For details of these rules, see CPAG's *Welfare Benefits Handbook*.

Leave with no employment condition

The most important types of leave with no condition on employment are:
- spouse of a person settled in the UK;
- spouse of a person with limited leave (eg, of a student, if the period of study is long enough, or of a work permit holder);
- private servant in a diplomatic household; *and*
- Commonwealth citizen with UK ancestry.

If you are not a PSIC (see p157) and your leave has no condition on employment, you are entitled to income-based JSA as long as you meet the normal rules for entitlement. The most important of these are that you:[32]
- are not in full-time employment (ie, working 16 hours or more a week);
- are available for and actively seeking employment; *and*
- have made a jobseeker's agreement.

For full details of these and the other rules, see CPAG's *Welfare Benefits Handbook*.
Claiming JSA may break the conditions of your immigration leave and have other effects on your immigration status (see p93).

Hardship payments

Hardship payments of JSA are different from urgent cases income-based JSA. If you are entitled to a hardship payment, you do not have to be available for and actively seeking work or have signed a jobseeker's agreement.[33] This means that someone who has limited leave with an employment condition, but who is not a PSIC, can be entitled to a hardship payment of JSA. For details of hardship payments and how to claim them, see CPAG's *Welfare Benefits Handbook*.
To qualify as a person in hardship you must satisfy both of the following conditions.[34] First, you must come within one of the following groups:
- you are pregnant or your partner is pregnant (claim IS if you are more than 29 weeks pregnant); *or*
- you are a lone parent of a child aged 17-18 (claim IS if you care for a child aged 16 or under); *or*
- you have limited capacity because of a chronic medical condition and that condition has lasted or is likely to last for at least 26 weeks (claim IS if you are incapable of work); *or*

- you or your partner devotes a considerable portion of the week to caring for a person who:
  - receives attendance allowance (AA) or the higher or middle rate care component of disability living allowance (DLA); *or*
  - has claimed AA or DLA but has not had that claim determined (in either of these cases claim IS if you are regularly or substantially engaged in caring for such a person); *or*
- you are one of a couple responsible for a child or young person; *or*
- you qualify for a disability premium as part of your JSA; *or*
- you are under age 18; *or*
- you are under age 21 and were in the care of the local authority under the Children Act 1989 within the last three years.

Secondly, the DWP must be satisfied that unless JSA is paid:
- in the case of a person who has claimed or is receiving AA or DLA, the carer would not be able to continue caring; *or*
- the vulnerable person will suffer hardship.[35] The vulnerable person is the pregnant woman, child, young person, person who would qualify for the disability premium, or chronically sick person mentioned above. In the case of a chronically sick person, that person's health would decline further within two weeks.

When considering whether a person would suffer hardship, the rules require the decision maker to take into account:
- the potential entitlement you or any partner would have to the disability premium, if the other conditions for JSA were met (for disability premium, see CPAG's *Welfare Benefits Handbook*);
- your potential entitlement to a disabled child premium for a child living with you if the other conditions for JSA were met (for disabled child premium, see CPAG's *Welfare Benefits Handbook*);
- the resources available to you or any partner, including resources available (to either of you) from other members of the household;
- the shortfall of those resources below the amount of any hardship payment which would be made;
- any substantial risk that essential items, including food, clothing, heating and accommodation, will cease to be available (or will only be available at considerably reduced levels) to you or any partner or children living with you;
- the length of time the above situation will continue.

Claiming JSA, including hardship payments, may break the conditions of your immigration leave and have other effects on your immigration status (see p93).

Amount of hardship payments

Hardship payments are worked out in the same way as normal income-based JSA (see CPAG's *Welfare Benefits Handbook*) except that the applicable amount is reduced by:[36]

- 20 per cent of the appropriate personal allowance for a single person of your age, if you, any partner or any child you are responsible for is pregnant or seriously ill; *or*
- otherwise, 40 per cent of that allowance.

Habitual residence

The rules are as for IS (see p237).

Spouse abroad

The rules are the same as for IS (see p238).

Partner here with a different status

The rules are the same as for IS (see p238). Note that there are special rules for certain couples without children who claim income-based JSA. Such couples are usually required to claim 'joint-claim JSA' (see CPAG's *Welfare Benefits Handbook*) as a condition of getting an award of income-based JSA. The rules recognise that this is not possible in the case of a partner who is a PSIC and excluded from benefit and simply restates under the joint-claim rules that benefit will be paid at the single person rate to the person who can claim.

Recourse to public funds

As for IS (see p234).

3. Housing benefit and council tax benefit

Most people with limited leave will not be eligible for housing benefit (HB) or council tax benefit (CTB) as they are likely to fall within the definition of a 'person subject to immigration control' (PSIC) because they have a public funds restriction attached to their stay. The HB and CTB rules are very like the income support (IS) rules, but with some differences. There is no urgent cases rate for HB or CTB; the categories of people covered by urgent cases rate get normal HB and/or CTB.

If you are being paid IS or income-based jobseeker's allowance (JSA) the local authority dealing with your HB or CTB claim should not make enquiries about your immigration status or habitual residence.[37] If you are not being paid IS or income-based JSA the following rules apply.

You are only entitled to HB or CTB if:

- you are not a PSIC unless you come under any of the exemptions (see below); *and*
- for HB, you have accommodation in Great Britain, which you normally occupy as your home (which can include temporary absences – see p302),[38] or for CTB, you are liable to pay council tax for accommodation in which you reside (see p303).[39]

If you do not meet these rules, you are not entitled to HB or CTB.

HB and CTB are public funds under the immigration rules.[40] The possible effects of claiming HB or CTB on your immigration position are the same as those for IS (see p238).

Persons subject to immigration control

The rules about who is a PSIC are the same as for IS (see p233). The exemptions from the definition are also the same as for IS apart from the fact that you cannot rely on European Community association agreements for either HB or CTB.

Habitual residence test

Even if you are not a PSIC you will not qualify for HB or CTB if you fail the habitual residence test. The rules on the habitual residence test for HB and CTB are the same as for IS (see p237).

Spouse abroad

The rules are the same as for IS (see p238).

Partner here with different status

The rules for HB and CTB are different to IS and income-based JSA as there is no provision within the regulations requiring the claim to be assessed only at the single person's rate. Both benefits will be assessed at the couple rate.

Recourse to public funds

As there is no provision to pay at a lower rate for couples with different immigration statuses any claim for benefit may mean that the spouse will have indirectly had recourse to public funds and her/his immigration position may be put at risk.

4. **Child benefit and guardian's allowance**

Child benefit counts as public funds under the immigration rules.[41] If your leave requires you to have no recourse to public funds (see Chapter 8), claiming or receiving child benefit can affect your immigration position (see p93). Guardian's allowance is not public funds, but cannot be paid without a current award of child benefit.

Child benefit

People with limited leave are generally excluded from entitlement to child benefit if they have a public funds restriction attached to their stay. They are therefore defined as 'persons subject to immigration control' (PSIC) and ineligible for benefit. However, as with the benefits above, there are exemptions.

If you are exempt or have transitional protection, you must still meet the other residence rules to be entitled to child benefit (see p247).

General rules

You qualify if:
- you are responsible for a child or paying a contribution towards the cost of the child, (see Chapter 12);
- you and your child both satisfy the presence test (see p177);
- you satisfy the immigration status test (see below);
- you are liable to pay UK income tax.

The rules are the same as for British nationals (see p177).

Immigration status test

If you are a PSIC you are excluded from entitlement to child benefit.[42] However there are many exemptions to this rule. A number of people are entitled to child benefit despite being here with limited leave and some people can still claim as a result of transitional rules introduced in 1996 when immigration status first became a factor limiting access to child benefit.

You are exempt from the PSIC rules if:
- you are a European Union (EU) or European Economic Area (EEA) national;
- you are the family member of an EU or EEA national, including a British citizen. This certainly includes a partner and probably also includes adult children, parents and other relatives (see p347). This means that the parent of a British citizen child is entitled to claim child benefit for any child, even if the child is subject to immigration conditions;
- you have leave given to you after another person gave a written sponsorship undertaking (see p104);
- you are a national, or a family member of (and living with) a national, of Algeria, Morocco, Slovenia, Tunisia or Turkey and that national is lawfully working in Great Britain.[43] 'Lawfully working' is not defined in the benefit rules. We consider that you are working lawfully if your work is not in breach of a condition attached to your leave to remain. The DWP is likely to take

the view that working while you have temporary admission will not be enough, even if you have been given permission to work. This should be challenged;[44]
- in the past you have lived in a country to which a reciprocal agreement about child benefit applies (see Chapter 28). This can apply regardless of your nationality;
- you are entitled to child benefit because of transitional rules. This applies if you were being paid child benefit on 6 October 1996. Transitional protection continues until the award of child benefit is revised or superseded. If you have subsequent children you remain eligible for child benefit for your existing children as this does not constitute grounds for a revision or supersession.

If you are a PSIC and there is another person who could claim child benefit, it would be advisable for that other person to make the claim.

Child's status is different

The child normally takes the status of the parents. Where there are parents of different status and the child is here with limited leave and subject to a public funds condition, a claim for child benefit would be recourse to public funds. It would probably be unwise to claim unless the child comes within one of the above groups who are exempt from the PSIC rules.

Transitional protection for pre-1996 claimants

If you were in receipt of child benefit on 6 October 1996 you retain entitlement until the claim is revised or superseded by a decision maker. This can only be done if there are grounds for a revision or supersession – eg, a relevant change of circumstances. If you were in receipt of child benefit on 6 October 1996 and you claim child benefit for another child after that date, for example following the birth of the child or the arrival of a child to join the household, the existing claim for child benefit should not be revised or superseded. Entitlement to that child benefit should continue to be paid. This is because the claim for 'additional child benefit' is in fact a new and separate claim for benefit.[45]

Guardian's allowance

The rules are the same as for British citizens (see p180). There is no immigration test for this benefit, but you are not entitled to guardian's allowance unless you are entitled to child benefit.[46]

5. **Working families' tax credit and disabled person's tax credit**

Most people with limited leave will not qualify for tax credits because 'persons subject to immigration control' (PSIC) are excluded from entitlement.

Furthermore, these benefits are linked to work and as people with limited leave they are likely to have a condition preventing them working while in the UK and consequently could not qualify for a work-based benefit. There are some important exceptions.

General rules

You are entitled to working families' tax credit (WFTC) and disabled person's tax credit (DPTC) if:

- you are in full-time work (at least 16 hours a week);
- you and your partner satisfy the residence test (see below). This includes a rule about the source of your and your partner's earnings;
- you satisfy the immigration status test (see below).

Residence test

The rules are the same as for British nationals (see p175). To be ordinarily resident you do not have to be here indefinitely (see p132). Your spouse/partner also has to satisfy the residence and earnings from work rules.

Immigration status test

You are exempt from the PSIC rules for WFTC or DPTC if:[47]

- you are the family member of a European Union or European Economic Area national, including a British citizen. This includes a partner and may also include adult children, parents and other relatives (see p347). This means that the parent of a British citizen child is exempt for WFTC and DPTC purposes;
- you are a national or a family member of (and living with) a national of Algeria, Morocco, Slovenia, Tunisia or Turkey and that national is lawfully working in Great Britain (GB).[48] 'Lawfully working' is not defined in the benefit rules. We consider that you are working lawfully if your work is not in breach of a condition attached to your leave to remain;
- you had leave given to you under a sponsorship agreement and the sponsor has died.

If you are a national of a country which is a party to the Fifth ACP (Africa, Caribbean, Pacific) EEC Convention (see p419) and you are lawfully working in the UK and none of these exemptions apply, you may be exempt from the immigration condition under European Community law.[49] See p419 for further details of this agreement.

Family abroad

If your spouse is abroad, you were living with your spouse abroad (ie, you established a household together there) and you intend to live together again you will not be entitled to claim tax credits. This is an indefinite prohibition. This is because you cannot satisfy the residence test for tax credits. However, the meaning of 'ordinary residence' is fairly flexible so it is possible for a spouse to be abroad for a part of the year and still be treated as 'ordinarily resident' in GB.

Family member with different immigration status

If your spouse is not excluded from claiming because of her/his immigration status then s/he should make a claim for WFTC instead of you. Either member of the couple can qualify if one is in full-time work. However, if the benefit in question is DPTC the person who claims must be the disabled worker (see CPAG's *Welfare Benefits Handbook* for details of entitlement).

Recourse to public funds

WFTC and DPTC are not listed as 'public funds' under the immigration rules because those rules have not been amended since the introduction of the tax credits.[50] However, these two credits are essentially the same benefits as the previous benefits of family credit and disability working allowance, which *are* listed, and in any case both tax credits are named in the Immigration and Asylum Act 1999.[51] The Home Office considers that this is enough for the tax credits to be treated as public funds for the purposes of the rules.

> If your leave requires you to have no recourse to public funds (see Chapter 8), claiming or receiving WFTC or DPTC can affect your immigration position.

Because claiming WFTC or DPTC means that you are working as well as claiming public funds, a claim is likely to lead to close Home Office attention to any request for further leave. For other effects of claiming public funds, see p93.

If you are one of a couple where one of the couple is subject to a public funds restriction you can argue that you have not had recourse to any additional public funds. This is because the amount of WFTC for a couple is the same as for a single parent, so membership of the family does not lead to additional recourse to public funds. If, however, your child has a public funds restriction attached to her/his stay any claim could have immigration implications because any award of benefit will be calculated on the basis of the number of children for whom you are responsible.

6. **Contribution-based jobseeker's allowance and incapacity benefit**

A claim for these benefits may lead to the Home Office being told that you have been working. If you have worked in breach of your immigration conditions, there is a risk of prosecution for that breach.[52]

These are not listed in the benefits from which people can be excluded on grounds of immigration status. Nor do they count as public funds.[53] However, to be entitled to these benefits you must have paid a sufficient amount of national insurance contributions and/or have sufficient credits. This means that you must have been able to take up employment. Some people with limited leave have the right to take employment and they may be able to qualify for these benefits, but only if they have been in Great Britain for a period of approximately two years, during which time they have been able to work and paid/been credited with contributions. For details of the contribution conditions see CPAG's *Welfare Benefits Handbook*. Even if you had permission to work, a claim may cause problems if the Home Office is informed. Any request for further leave may be looked at more closely to see if you can support yourself without recourse to public funds. If you were a student when you worked, the Home Office may check that your work was only vacation or part-time work. If it was not, further leave as a student could be refused.

Note that incapacity benefit can be paid on a non-contributory basis (see p251).

Dependency additions

- **Contribution-based jobseeker's allowance**: There are no dependency additions paid.
- **Incapacity benefit:** Dependency additions are payable for both adults and children. For details of when these can be paid, see CPAG's *Welfare Benefits Handbook*. A person with limited leave and subject to a public funds condition may be an adult dependant. Your spouse who is the claimant for incapacity benefit can claim an addition for you regardless of your immigration status. Child dependency additions are generally only paid for children for whom child benefit is paid. Some children if paid child benefit would be having recourse to public funds.

7. Retirement pensions and bereavement benefits

The rules for Category A, B, C and D retirement pensions, bereavement payment, widowed parent's allowance and bereavement allowance are the same as those for British citizens (see p184). There are no special rules for people with limited leave.

These benefits are not treated as public funds for the purposes of the immigration rules.[54] However, to be entitled to these benefits you (or your spouse) must have paid national insurance contributions (for details, see CPAG's *Welfare Benefits Handbook*). If this means that you have worked in the UK, a claim may affect your immigration status, in the same way as a claim for contribution-based jobseeker's allowance or incapacity benefit (see p239).

You may be a dependant of a person claiming one of these benefits. Your spouse may be entitled to claim the adult dependency addition for you. You cannot generally claim for a child dependant unless child benefit is payable.

8. Industrial injuries benefits

The rules for disablement benefit, reduced earnings allowance, retirement allowance, constant attendance allowance and exceptionally severe disablement allowance are the same as those for British citizens (see p188). There are no special rules for people with limited leave.

These benefits are not treated as public funds for the purposes of the immigration rules.[55] However, to be entitled to these benefits you must normally have worked in the UK. This means a claim may affect your immigration status, in the same way as a claim for contribution-based jobseeker's allowance or incapacity benefit.

9. Disability benefits

These benefits are disability living allowance (DLA), attendance allowance (AA), invalid care allowance (ICA) and non-contributory incapacity benefit. Anyone who is a 'person subject to immigration control' (PSIC) under the benefit rules is excluded. The definition of PSIC is the same as for income support (IS) (see p233). However, there are some exceptions to this rule and some people will have transitional protection dating back to 1996.

Even if you are exempt or have transitional protection, you must still meet the other residence rules for these benefits.

Disability living allowance, AA and ICA are treated as public funds under the immigration rules.[56] If your leave requires you to have no recourse to public funds (see p92), claiming or receiving these benefits can affect your immigration position, in the same way as a claim for IS (see p238).

Exemptions from immigration condition

You are exempt from the immigration condition for DLA, AA, and ICA if:[57]
- you are the family member of an European Union or European Economic Area national. This would apply whatever the nationality or immigration status of the family member. Furthermore, there is no necessity for the EEA national to

be a 'worker'. The exemption applies simply because of nationality including a British citizen. This exemption clearly includes a partner and children but in many cases will also include adult children, parents and other relatives (see p347);

- you are a national of Algeria, Morocco, Slovenia, Tunisia or Turkey and you are lawfully working in Great Britain (GB);[58]
- you are a family member (see p347) of a person who is:
  - a national of Algeria, Morocco, Slovenia, Tunisia or Turkey and lawfully working in GB; *and*
  - you are living with that person;[59]
- you are a 'sponsored immigrant' who has been given leave to remain in the UK after your sponsor made a written undertaking (see p104);[60] *or*
- for DLA and AA, in the past you have lived in the Isle of Man, Jersey or Guernsey (or, for AA only, Norway) and a reciprocal agreement about DLA or AA applies to you (see Chapter 28). This can apply regardless of your nationality.

Transitional protection for pre-February 1996 claimants

If none of the above exceptions applies, but you were being paid one of these benefits before 5 February 1996, the immigration condition does not apply to you for that benefit until that award is revised or superseded by a decision maker.[61]

The Court of Appeal ruled that transitional protection should end with the period of an award, and could not be renewed by another claim after that. The House of Lords has upheld the Court of Appeal's ruling.[62] Therefore, if there is a gap in claim or at the end of a time limited award, transitional protection will end. Transitional protection ends when a revision or supersession is carried out.

A request for a higher rate of one of the components of DLA or AA will allow a revision or supersession to be carried out, and this will end your transitional protection. If you do ask for a revision or supersession and you are not exempt, you will lose all that benefit.

If you are claiming and you are not a family member of an EEA national or of a refugee then you may need to consider whether it is wise to claim. Under the immigration rules DLA, AA and ICA are defined as public funds.

Residence test

You have to satisfy a residence and past presence test. The rules are the same as for British citizens (see p192).

10. **Statutory sick pay, statutory maternity pay and maternity allowance**

The rules for **statutory sick pay (SSP)** and **statutory maternity pay (SMP)** are the same as those for British citizens (see p194). There are no special rules for people with limited leave. However, these benefits are only paid to people who have worked and if you have limited leave you may not be in a position to take up work. They are not public funds under the immigration rules.[63]

Both SSP and SMP are social security benefits where responsibility for the administration and payment of the benefit has been devolved to employers. Because of this, it is very unlikely that a claim for these benefits will lead to the Home Office being informed. The DWP will only become involved if there is a dispute about entitlement, but even then, because your immigration status is irrelevant, it is very unlikely that the Home Office will be advised.

Maternity allowance is not listed as public funds. It is payable based on your past work record. To qualify you must be a person who has been in legal employment and who has no employment prohibition attached to your leave.

You are entitled to claim extra benefit for an adult dependant (see CPAG's *Welfare Benefits Handbook*).

11. **The social fund**

Most people with limited leave will not be eligible for social fund payments. This is because 'persons subject to immigration control (PSIC) are excluded from entitlement. However, there are some exemptions.

Groups who are not excluded from social fund payments

- A person from a country that has ratified the European Social Chapter of 1961 or the European Convention on Social and Medical Assistance and who is lawfully present. This applies to all European Economic Area (EEA) countries, Cyprus, Czech Republic, Hungary, Latvia, Malta, Poland, Slovakia and Turkey. For details on the meaning of 'lawful presence', see p131.
- A person who has been given limited leave as a sponsored immigrant (see p104).
- A student or other person whose funding from abroad is temporarily interrupted and there is a reasonable expectation that her/his supply of funds will be resumed.
- An asylum seeker who has a right to benefit under the transitional rules (see p275).
- A person who is lawfully employed and is a national or a family member of a national (and is living with her/him) of Algeria, Morocco, Slovenia, Tunisia or Turkey.

- A European Union (EU) or EEA national.
- A family member of an EU or EEA national. This would apply whatever the nationality or immigration status of the family member. Furthermore there is no necessity for the EEA national to be a 'worker'. The exemption applies simply because of nationality including a British citizen. This exemption will certainly include a partner and children, but in many cases will also include adult children, parents and other relatives (see p347).

General rules

If you fall within one of the above exemptions you may be able to get a social fund payment, but you will also have to satisfy the general conditions of entitlement. See p195, for details of the main conditions for entitlement and different types of payment from the social fund.

You cannot get a budgeting loan or a community care grant from the discretionary social fund unless you are in receipt of, or about to be in receipt of, a means-tested benefit. This is referred to as a qualifying benefit. You must also be in receipt of a qualifying benefit in order to receive a maternity or funeral payment and cold weather payments. These rules mean that if you are not entitled to these benefits because of your immigration status, you cannot be given a social fund payment. You do not have to be in receipt of a means-tested benefit to qualify for a crisis loan or a winter fuel payment. However, any loans from the social fund have to be repaid and therefore a person must be seen to have income and the possibility of being able to repay before an award can be made.

Residence rules

The residence conditions for the regulated social fund are the same as for British citizens (see p198). There are no specific residence conditions for the discretionary social fund, but there are special rules which relate to 'persons from abroad'. If you are a 'person from abroad' under the income support or income-based jobseeker's allowance rules then a crisis loan can only be awarded in order to alleviate the consequences of a disaster.[64] A 'person from abroad' is a person who has failed the habitual residence test and is not the same as a PSIC.

Notes

1 s3C IA 1971
2 This is a new provision of law, amended in 1999.
3 s7 IA 1988
4 See also reg 14 I(EEA) Regs
5 para 255 HC 395 (the last complete statement of the Immigration Rules, 23 May 1994)
6 ss3A and 3B IA 1971, and the I(LER) O
7 Art 13 I(LER)O

1. IS

8 s115(9) IAA 1999
9 The EC association agreements all differ but are largely based on the rights contained in EC Reg 1408/71. The agreements provide equal treatment in social security. The term social security has the meaning laid down in EC Reg 1408/71 which since June 1992 includes IS. See Chapter 28 for further details of the agreements.
10 s115(9) IAA 1999
11 s24(1)(b)(ii) IA 1971
12 Sch 4 para 17 IAA 1999
13 s115(9)(d) IAA 1999
14 Reg 2 SS(IA)CA Regs
15 Reg 12(5) SS(IA)CA Regs
16 Sch Part I para 1 SS(IA)CA Regs; reg 70(2A) IS Regs
17 Reg 71(2) IS Regs
18 Letter from Home Office Minister David Waddington to Max Madden MP in December 1985.
19 Reg 21(3) IS Regs 'person from abroad': habitual residence
20 Reg 21(3) IS Regs 'person from abroad': habitual residence
21 para 6(c) HC 395 'public funds'
22 s24(1)(b)(ii) IA 1971

2. Income-based JSA

23 para 6(c) HC 395 'public funds'
24 s115 IAA 1999; reg 85(4) JSA Regs 'person from abroad'
25 In *Hockenjos v Secretary of State for Social Security* [2001] EWCA Civ 624 it was held that JSA came within the scope of EC Directive 79/7.
26 ss1(2)(a) and 6(1) JSA 1995
27 s4(1) IA 1971

28 Sch 2 para 6 to IA 1971. This only applies to people whose examination began on or after 10 July 1988. A person whose examination began before that has indefinite leave. For details, see Macdonald, pp66-69
29 Immigration (Leave to Enter and Remain) Order 2000 art 9. This is likely only to be used to grant entry to visitors anyway, and so can be expected to mean that all those who enter in this way are prohibited from working.
30 s9(4)-(6) IA 1971; (CERI)O. For details see Macdonald, pp158-59.
31 Regs 14(1), 19(1) and 34 JSA Regs
32 s1(2) JSA 1995
33 Reg 141(4) JSA Regs
34 Reg 140(1) JSA Regs
35 Reg 140(1) JSA Regs
36 Reg 145(1) JSA Regs

3. HB and CTB

37 HB/CTB Circular A1/96 para 4
38 s130(1)(a) SSCBA 1992; reg 5 HB Regs
39 s131(3)(a) SSCBA 1992
40 para 6(c) HC 395 'public funds'

4. Child benefit and guardian's allowance

41 s115(1) IAA 1999; and see also para 6(b) HC 395) 'public funds'
42 S115(9) IAA 99
43 Sch Part II para 2 SS(IA)CA Regs. This exemption is included because of the UK's obligations under EC agreements with these countries.
44 In R(FC) 1/01 a commissioner held that a Turkish asylum seeker who was working as a minicab driver would have been able to rely on the Turkish Association Agreement to claim family credit even if UK rules had excluded him from entitlement. In EC law both family credit and child benefit are 'family benefits' therefore the caselaw has equal application to child benefit.
45 CF/1015/1995
46 s77(1)(a) SSCBA 1992

5. WFTC and DPTC

47 Reg 3(1A) FC Regs; reg 5(1A) DWA Regs

48 Reg 3(1A)(d)(i) FC Regs; reg 5(1A)(a)(i) DWA Regs. This exemption is included because of EC agreements with these countries which provides that there be equal treatment in matters of social security. In R(FC) 1/01 a commissioner held that a Turkish asylum seeker would have been able to rely on the EC Association Agreement with Turkey and claim family credit as a 'family benefit' even if not entitled under this rule. This judgment would apply equally to WFTC.

49 This is because you may be entitled under EC law to social security benefits linked to employment on the same basis as UK nationals: para 2 Annex VI Council & Commission Decision 91/400/ECSC, EEC: OJ No. L 229, 17 August 1991, p249

50 para 6(c) HC 395 'public funds'

51 s115(1) IAA 1999

6. Contribution-based JSA and IB

52 s24(1)(b)(ii) IA 1971. Any prosecution must be brought within six months of the last breach of conditions: s127 Magistrates Court Act 1980

53 s115(1) IAA 1999; and see also para 6(c) HC 395

7. Retirement pensions and bereavement benefits

54 s115(1) IAA 1999; and see also para 6(c) HC 395

8. Industrial injuries benefits

55 s115(1) IAA 1999; and see also para 6(c) HC 395

9. Disability benefits

56 s115(1) IAA 1999; and see also para 6(d) HC 395

57 Sch Part 11 to SS(IA)CA Regs

58 This exemption is included because of the UK's obligations under EC agreements with these countries (see Chapter 28).

59 Sch Part II para 3 to SS(IA)CA Regs

60 Sch Part II para 4 to SS(IA)CA Regs

61 Reg 12(10) SS(IA)CA Regs

62 *M (a child) v Secretary of State for Social Security* [2001] UKHL 35

10. SSP, SMP and MA

63 para 6(c) HC 395 'public funds'

64 SF Dir 16(b)

Chapter 19

∙∙

No leave to remain

The benefits covered in this chapter are:
1. Income support (p263)
2. Income-based jobseeker's allowance (p265)
3. Housing benefit and council tax benefit (p267)
4. Child benefit and guardian's allowance (p267)
5. Working families' tax credit and disabled person's tax credit (p268)
6. Contribution-based jobseeker's allowance and incapacity benefit (p269)
7. Retirement pensions and bereavement benefits (p269)
8. Industrial injuries benefits (p270)
9. Disability benefits (p270)
10. Statutory sick pay, statutory maternity pay and maternity allowance (p270)
11. The social fund (p271)

This chapter deals with people who need leave to enter or remain in the UK, but who do not have that leave. If you do not need leave to enter or remain in the UK because you have the right of abode (which includes British citizens) or you are a European Union (EU) or European Economic Area (EEA) national or the family member of an EU or EEA national, see the chapter relevant to your immigration status.

The types of immigration status covered by this chapter can be confusing. In particular, many people – including DWP and Home Office staff – misunderstand the differences between 'deportation' and 'removal', or 'decision to deport' and 'deportation order'. Each term used in this book has a special meaning and only applies to that situation. You should make sure you understand the terms that are being used (see Part 1 for further details).

Effect of claiming benefit on immigration position

Most people who have no leave to remain will not be eligible for benefits. However, should a claim be made, the DWP or local authority may notify the Home Office. This is more likely if the claim is for income support, jobseeker's allowance, housing benefit or council tax benefit than other benefits, but is possible for any benefit. *Because of this you should always seek immigration advice before approaching the benefits authorities.* The only group of people whose immigration status will not be affected by a claim is asylum seekers who can claim under the transitional arrangements, and who are in touch with the immigration authorities. Even for these people there may be difficulties both with the Home Office and the DWP, and if you believe this exception applies to you, you should still seek advice.

The possible effects of a benefit claim are:

- If the Home Office has lost touch with you, information about a benefit claim, including your address and details of family members, may be passed to the Home Office. This may lead to deportation or removal action being taken against you quickly, and includes the risk that you may be detained.
- If the Home Office knows your address but has taken no action for a long time on your case, a benefit claim may lead to your file being acted on by the Home Office, which may lead to an unfavourable decision more quickly than if you do not claim.
- If you are waiting for a decision on an application for leave to remain in the UK a benefit claim may harm the chances of you being accepted.

In any case covered by this chapter there will be serious issues to be considered. You will need to weigh carefully the advantages and disadvantages of making a claim, and should always take expert advice. There are circumstances such as unexpected illness, a serious accident, or responsibilities as a carer when you may have no alternative but to make a claim.

Who does not have leave to remain?

Not all of those who are here without leave are in the country illegally; many are here with the express permission of the immigration authorities. You may be in the UK without leave to remain if:

- you had leave to remain until a deportation order was made (see p261);
- you have been given temporary admission by an immigration officer (see p259);
- you have been granted bail, either by a chief immigration officer or by the Immigration Appeal Tribunal;
- you had permission to be in the UK, but have remained here in breach of the time limit (overstayers) (see p260);
- you made an unsuccessful application for asylum, and have remained in the UK after the case is completed;
- you have lost your immigration appeal, but remain in the UK while you try for a judicial review or while the Home Office considers representations about your case;
- you have entered the UK without obtaining leave to enter (see p262).

Temporary admission

A person who has temporary admission has been given permission to be in the UK outside the immigration rules. However, although you have permission to be here you do not have any type of leave to remain. Temporary admission is most commonly given to asylum seekers who are awaiting a decision on their asylum application. A person who applies for asylum at the port of entry or who enters illegally and then asks for asylum can be detained or given temporary admission.

If you have already been refused entry you are only likely to be admitted to the UK, whether on temporary admission or on bail, if your application was made under the 1951 Refugee Convention or the European Convention on Human Rights (see p61).

You will also have a right to remain here for your hearing against refusal of entry if you arrived with a valid visa (or other entry clearance), or if you were returning after a short absence and still had leave to remain. In these circumstances you are considered to be in the same position as someone who has remained here and applied to vary the terms of leave to remain. An immigration officer will have suspended your leave to enter or to remain when the decision to refuse you entry was made, but your permission is still effective for the purpose of your appeal. The Immigration Acts give you the right to remain on the conditions set out in your leave to remain or on the entry clearance sticker in your passport. You will not be in the UK without leave, and you should look at the chapter dealing with your immigration status as indicated there.

Someone with temporary admission has never had leave to enter the UK. However, as long as you comply with the terms of your temporary admission or bail (see below) you are in the UK legally. You are not an overstayer, nor are you subject to a deportation order, nor are you an illegal entrant.

If you are given leave, your immigration status changes and you should see the chapter relevant to your status. If you are refused leave, the rules covered by this chapter continue to apply to you until *either*:

- you are given leave to enter by an immigration officer; *or*
- you leave the UK.

If an immigration officer decides that you are an illegal entrant, then different rules apply (see p262).

If you break the terms of your temporary admission or bail, or escape from immigration detention, an immigration officer may decide that you are an 'absconder', and that you should be treated as an illegal entrant. If this happens, different rules apply – see p262.

If you are not given temporary admission, but the Home Office is investigating whether you are a British citizen or have the right of abode, it may inform the DWP of this situation, although this is unlikely. If the DWP is aware that you are being investigated, you may be treated as a 'person subject to immigration control' (PSIC) (see p157). If this happens, you can argue that you are not restricted because you are free from immigration control, as a person with the right of abode who does not require leave.

Overstayers

You are an overstayer if you had limited leave to enter or remain in the UK, but have remained in the UK beyond the date that leave expired, without applying for or being granted any other permission.

You become an overstayer on the day after your leave runs out. However, if you applied for leave to remain before your leave runs out, you may still have limited leave to remain, even if there is no stamp in your passport. This is a special form of statutory leave.

Overstayers can be removed from the UK without the need for deportation proceedings, but will be able to appeal against that decision under the 1951 Refugee Convention or the Human Rights Act 1998 before they are removed. The only exception to this rule might arise where someone has already had an opportunity to appeal under these provisions and cannot show any relevant change of circumstances in the meantime.[1] Before a decision is made on whether to order removal, an overstayer can be detained by the police. This is usually only for long enough for an immigration officer to conduct an interview, after which the officer will decide whether to detain the person or to release her/him temporarily.

Most of the overstayers who are in the UK at any time have not been traced by the authorities, and are simply at liberty. Overstaying your leave is a criminal offence,[2] although prosecutions are rare.

Former asylum seekers

If you have made an application for asylum in the UK, and have had the application refused, you will generally have had a right of appeal against that decision while you remain in the country. Unless you win your appeal, and are granted asylum, that right will eventually run out. If you did not keep in touch with the immigration authorities at the time of the decision you might have lost the right to appeal, or, if you failed to turn up for the hearing, your case may have been rejected without hearing from you.

You will have had a right to remain as long as the appeal process has continued. If there was a hearing of your case, and the appeal has been dismissed, that right will have ended, and if you have not left and re-entered the UK since, you will have no permission to be here. The point at which your right of appeal ended, and the right it gave you to stay here, will depend on the circumstances of your case:

- if the appeal was 'certified' the immigration laws will only have given you a right to appeal once to an adjudicator;
- if it was not, you may have been able to appeal again, to the Immigration Appeal Tribunal;

- if you were not given permission to appeal to the Tribunal you only had the right to bring a further challenge by judicial review, in the High Court;
- if you had a full hearing at the Immigration Appeal Tribunal there will have been an opportunity to apply for permission to appeal against its decision to the Court of Appeal.

Staying on here will not always mean that you have made your stay illegal because you may not have committed any offence under the immigration laws, but it will always mean that you are liable to be detained. The attitude of the immigration authorities may depend on whether they think you chose to keep out of contact with them, or whether they have simply taken no action to remove you from the UK.

Former asylum seekers in this situation will not be entitled to benefits.

Applications to remain outside of the immigration rules

Some people may be present in the UK while they try to persuade the Home Office to allow them to stay, even though they do not have any rights to stay under the immigration rules and have no right of appeal against a decision by the Home Office. This may happen because you have never had a right of appeal in this country; if you had no claim to asylum; if you never made an application to stay on longer; or – in some circumstances – if you were unable to meet one of the special requirements of the immigration rules because of your age or nationality or because you did not have the correct papers. In the last case your only option to stay on will be outside the appeals system. Similarly, if you had a right of appeal under the Immigration Acts but it has now run out, any further application to stay will have to be made outside the framework of the immigration rules and the appeals system.

This can take two forms. You may make written representations to stay, often on compassionate grounds, either directly to the Home Office, or perhaps through a Member of Parliament. But if a decision has been taken that you should leave, and you no longer have a right of appeal, your only option is likely to be to challenge that decision by an application for judicial review. This will not count as an appeal, since it is not provided for under the immigration laws but under general rules of public, or administrative, law. In either of these cases you are very unlikely to be here unlawfully, in the sense that you will not be committing any offence under immigration law while you wait for the result of your application, even if you have previously overstayed or entered the UK illegally.

Deportation order made while in UK with leave

A deportation order may be made as a way of removing you from the UK and prohibiting your re-entry, if you have leave to remain. The most common circumstance in which you are likely to be deported is if you commit a criminal offence, and it is considered sufficiently serious. People who have the right of abode and Commonwealth citizens who have been settled here since before 1973 cannot be deported. Anyone else can but, of course, the greater your ties to this country and the less serious the offence, the less likely you are to be deported.

This procedure has the effect of ending your leave from the date the deportation order is signed. If you have leave to remain, a decision to make a deportation order (this is different from the deportation order itself) does not affect your benefit entitlement. For details about deportation orders and when they can be made, see Chapter 7.

If you do not appeal the decision to deport or you lose your appeal and a deportation order is made, a restriction order may be made. You cannot be given temporary admission or bail.

Once a deportation order is signed, removal directions are usually made straightaway or as soon as your whereabouts are known to the Home Office. If you are not going to be removed immediately, the Home Office will normally notify you in writing that your removal has been deferred.

Illegal entrants

You are only an illegal entrant for benefit purposes if an immigration officer has told you in writing that you are an illegal entrant.[3]

You remain an illegal entrant until you are given leave to enter or remain in the UK, or you are removed. If you lose benefit because of an immigration officer's decision that you are an illegal entrant and the High Court or Court of Appeal overrules that decision,[4] you may be able to argue that the benefit decisions were wrong because they relied on an invalid decision. If this applies you should take expert advice.

Until an immigration officer decides that you are an illegal entrant, you are not one for benefit purposes, even if you obviously entered the UK illegally. Until an immigration officer decides that you are an illegal entrant, the following rules apply:

- *either* you were given leave to enter the UK – eg, as a visitor; *or*
- you entered the UK without leave. This may be because:
  - you were not seen by an immigration officer – eg, you were hidden in a lorry; *or*
  - you presented a travel document which the immigration officer did not stamp – eg, a passport issued to a British citizen or EU or EEA national.

If you were given leave, that leave counts under the benefit rules until it runs out, at which point, if you are still here and have not applied for an extension of stay, you become an 'overstayer' (see p260). If that leave carried a condition that you should not have 'recourse to public funds' (see p92) you are a PSIC,[5] but if it does not, you are not. If you have not been given leave to enter by an immigration officer you are a PSIC if the law required you to have leave.[6] Any leave to enter given to you ends on the date of a decision by an immigration officer that you are an illegal entrant.[7]

---

1. Income support

Claiming income support may seriously affect your immigration position (see p93).

Most people who have no leave to remain are 'persons subject to immigration control' (PSIC) and are therefore excluded from entitlement to income support (IS). However, some people are exempted and others may have transitional protection.

You are a PSIC if:[8]
- you need leave to be in the UK but have not been given it (see Chapter 4); *or*
- your leave was given under an immigration rule which requires no recourse to public funds (see p92); *or*
- you are a sponsored immigrant under the benefit rules (see p104); *or*
- you only have leave to remain in the UK because you are allowed to stay awaiting an appeal under the immigration rules (see p83).

This would apply where:
- you have temporary admission (see p259); *or*
- your conditions on entry clearance or a previous unexpired leave make you subject to a condition that you should not have 'recourse to public funds'; *or*
- you are an overstayer (see p260); *or*
- you have remained in the UK after your asylum case has ended (see p260); *or*
- you are only able to stay here because you have a judicial review pending, or are waiting for the Home Office to make a decision on further written representations about your case; *or*
- a deportation order has been made against you (see p261); *or*
- an immigration officer has decided that you are an illegal entrant (see p262).

Groups that can qualify for income support
- A person from a country that has ratified the European Social Chapter of 1961 or the European Convention on Social and Medical Assistance and who is lawfully present. (This applies to all European Economic Area countries, Cyprus, Czech Republic, Hungary, Latvia, Malta, Poland, Slovakia and Turkey.) Benefit is paid at the ordinary rate. For details on the meaning of 'lawful presence' (see p131).
- A person who has been given limited leave as a sponsored immigrant (see p104) and whose sponsor has died. Benefit is at the urgent cases rate (see p162).

- A student or other person whose funding from abroad is temporarily interrupted and there is a reasonable expectation that her/his supply of funds will be resumed. Payment is at the urgent cases rate and is for a maximum for 42 days, whether in one or more spells, within a period of leave.
- An asylum seeker who has a right to benefit under the transitional rules (see Chapter 20). Payment is at the urgent cases rate.
- A person who is lawfully employed and is a national or a family member of a national of Algeria, Morocco, Slovenia, Tunisia or Turkey. This is because there are European Community (EC) agreements with these countries, which provide for equal treatment within social security. These rights stem from EC law but have not been incorporated into UK law, therefore the DWP is unlikely to accept that IS is covered by these agreements. Seek specialist advice on this issue. Benefit would be paid at the ordinary rate.

If you have no entitlement to benefits under these rules but you are later recognised as a refugee, you may be able to claim backdated benefit. You must make a claim within 28 days of being notified of your refugee status (see Chapter 16).

If you are not entitled to IS, your partner may be able to claim instead.

Urgent cases payments and transitional protection

If you are a PSIC with no leave to remain you may be entitled to an urgent cases payment of IS if you are covered by transitional protection.[9] This would mainly apply to asylum seekers (see Chapter 20).

If there is a break in your claim, transitional protection continues as long as one of the old urgent cases rules applies to you. It also continues if your immigration status changes but you still count as a PSIC – eg, if you were an overstayer and then an immigration officer decides that you are an illegal entrant.

Because you are entitled to an urgent cases payment, you do not have to claim income-based jobseeker's allowance, so you do not have to be available for work.[10]

Urgent cases payment is paid at a different rate from ordinary IS (see p162).

Habitual residence test

The rules are the same as those for British citizens – see p166.

2. Income-based jobseeker's allowance

Claiming income-based jobseeker's allowance may seriously affect your immigration position (see p93).

For contribution-based jobseeker's allowance (JSA), see p269.

The rules about who is a 'person subject to immigration control' (PSIC) are the same as for income support (see p263). You are only entitled to income-based JSA if you are not a PSIC and there is no written prohibition on taking work (see p240) and you are *either*:

- available for work – you are entitled to full rate income-based JSA; *or*
- not available for work and you qualify as a person in hardship (see p266) – you are entitled to hardship rate income-based JSA.

Written permission to work

Under British law no one needs government permission to work. Only if you have written permission to be at liberty in the UK, can a prohibition on taking work be attached to that permission. If you have no permission to be at liberty in the UK, no prohibition can be attached. If you have overstayed your leave to remain, or that leave has been ended by a deportation order, any work condition attached to that leave ended when the leave ended. In practice, Home Office and DWP staff do not understand this and wrongly assume that anyone without leave cannot work without permission to work.

An employer may commit a criminal offence by employing a person in the UK without leave who does not have Home Office permission to work.[11] But if you take work when you have no permission to do so, you do not commit any offence.

If you have applied for asylum, the Home Office will normally give you permission to take work if you ask for it, once six months have gone by without a decision on your application. This is done by stamping your application registration card/standard acknowledgement letter with the words 'there are no restrictions on the person named above taking employment and s/he does not need to get permission from the DWP before taking work,' or something similar. Permission can also be given on a notice of temporary admission (or temporary release). If you have been detained and are released on bail you will be entitled to work unless a restriction on employment has been imposed on you, and that will be very unusual.

Varying your temporary leave by stamping your documents with permission overrides any restriction or prohibition on working on your temporary admission. Sometimes this permission may be refused or withdrawn, particularly if you are detained.

In theory, this kind of permission to work may be given to other people who have applied to stay for exceptional reasons – eg, statelessness, but this is not common.

Even if you can work legally without permission, you may need written permission to work from the Home Office to get urgent cases JSA. This would be very unusual, but will apply if you:

- have bail with no prohibition on taking work; *or*
- have been released by a court after an application for *habeas corpus*.

If this applies, the Home Office may be prepared to give you written permission to work, even though you do not need it. You should seek expert advice before approaching the Home Office. Some people in this situation will not be PSICs (see below).

People who are not 'persons subject to immigration control'

Some people covered by this chapter, for example asylum seekers with transitional protection, are not PSICs under the benefit rules. It will be difficult to have your claim accepted, however, unless you can produce written evidence from the immigration authorities. However, even if the definition does not apply, you will still have to pass the habitual residence test (see p135).

Availability for work

You will only be entitled to full rate or urgent cases income-based JSA if you are available for work. You can only meet that rule if:

- you are exempted from the PSIC rules because of your nationality (see p263); *or*
- you entered the UK without being given leave to enter, but an immigration officer has not yet decided that you are an illegal entrant (see p262).

You do not need Home Office permission to work to be available for work.

Hardship payments

Hardship payments of JSA are different from urgent cases payments of income-based JSA. They are intended for people who are not available for work, but who are vulnerable and who would suffer hardship if JSA were not paid. For details, see p242. You cannot receive hardship payments if you are a PSIC, unless you come under one of the exemptions.

Habitual residence test

The rules are the same as those for British citizens (see p166).

3. **Housing benefit and council tax benefit**

Claiming housing benefit or council tax benefit may seriously affect your immigration position (see p93).

Most people with no leave to remain will not be eligible to claim housing benefit (HB) or council tax benefit (CTB). This is because they are likely to be defined as a 'person subject to immigration control (PSIC) and as such are excluded from entitlement. The HB and CTB rules concerning PSICs are very like the income support (IS) rules, but with some differences. There is no urgent cases rate for HB or CTB; the types of cases covered by urgent cases rate get normal HB and CTB.

You are only entitled to HB or CTB if:

- you are not a PSIC (see below); *and*
- for HB, you have accommodation in Great Britain which you normally occupy as your home (which can include certain temporary absences) (see p302);[12] *or*
- for CTB, you are liable to pay council tax for accommodation in which you reside (see p303).

If you do not meet these rules, you are not entitled to HB or CTB.

'Persons subject to immigration control'

The rules about who is a PSIC are the same as for IS. The exemptions from the definition are also the same as for IS apart from the fact that you cannot rely on European Community association agreements for either HB or CTB (see p263).

4. **Child benefit and guardian's allowance**

Claiming child benefit or guardian's allowance may seriously affect your immigration position (see p93).

Generally if you have no leave to remain you are a 'person subject to immigration control' (PSIC) and excluded from child benefit. The rules about who is a PSIC and the exemptions are the same as those for people with limited leave (see p246).

Some people who are PSICs receive child benefit under transitional rules, which date back to 1996. If you are receiving child benefit under these transitional rules you can continue to receive it until the claim is revised or superseded by a decision maker. This can only be done if there are grounds for a revision or supersession – eg, if there has been a relevant change of circumstances since the award of child benefit.

If you were in receipt of child benefit on 6 October 1996 and you claim child benefit for another child after that date, for example following the birth of the child or the arrival of a child to join the household, the existing claim for child benefit should not be revised or superseded. Entitlement to your existing award of child benefit should continue to be paid. This is because the claim for 'additional child benefit' is in fact a new and separate claim for benefit and therefore there are no grounds upon which to revise or supersede your award.[13]

If you are a family member of a European Economic Area national you are not a PSIC and will be eligible for benefit. If you are a national of a country with which the UK has a reciprocal agreement you may be eligible for benefit under the agreement.

5. Working families' tax credit and disabled person's tax credit

Claiming working families' tax credit or disabled person's tax credit may seriously affect your immigration position (see p93).

Most people with no leave to remain will not be eligible for tax credits because 'persons subject to immigration control' are excluded from entitlement. Furthermore to be entitled to these benefits you must be working. A claim for these benefits may lead to the Home Office being told that you are working. If you have written permission to work, this will not affect you. If you are prohibited from working by the conditions of your temporary admission, there is a risk that you will be arrested for breach of those conditions.[14] You may be refused further temporary admission, and it is possible that you will be prosecuted for the breach.[15] If you have been released on bail and there is a condition prohibiting you from taking employment you could face similar risks, but this is unlikely as it is rare to place an employment condition on immigration bail, at least where it is granted by an Immigration Appeal Tribunal. If you are found to be working in breach of your bail conditions and you have sureties who have signed in support of your bail, they may forfeit the money they have pledged.[16]

The rules are the same as for people with limited leave (see p247).

6. **Contribution-based jobseeker's allowance and incapacity benefit**

Claiming contribution-based jobseeker's allowance or incapacity benefit may seriously affect your immigration position (see p93).

There are no special rules for people with no leave to remain. The rules are the same as for British citizens (see p181), though the conditions of any temporary admission, bail or detention may mean that you do not meet those rules for contribution-based jobseeker's allowance (see below).

To be entitled to these benefits you must have paid national insurance contributions as an employed or self-employed person (see CPAG's *Welfare Benefits Handbook*). A claim for these benefits may lead to the Home Office being told that you have been working. For possible effects if you worked in breach of the conditions of your temporary admission or bail immigration, see p49.

Special rules for contribution-based jobseeker's allowance

The 'persons subject to immigration control' rules (see p157) do not apply to contribution-based jobseeker's allowance (JSA). However, because of the normal rules for JSA:
- you are only entitled to contribution-based JSA if there is no written prohibition on taking work (see p240) and you are available for work;
- otherwise, check whether you qualify for income-based JSA, paid at the hardship rate (see p266).

7. **Retirement pensions and bereavement benefits**

The benefits included are Category A, B, C and D retirement pensions, bereavement payment, widowed parent's allowance and bereavement allowance.

The rules for entitlement are the same as those for British citizens (see p184). There are no special rules for people with no leave and these benefits are not public funds benefits. In theory, therefore, a person with no leave to remain may claim. However, in order to receive a full pension a person must have worked and paid national insurance contributions for most of her/his working life. Furthermore, any claim may bring the person to the attention of the Home Office, which could lead to removal or deportation.

8. **Industrial injuries benefits**

These are disablement benefit, reduced earnings allowance, retirement allowance, constant attendance allowance and exceptionally severe disablement allowance.

Although these benefits are not included within the definition of public funds for the purposes of the immigration rules, claiming them may seriously affect your immigration position (see p93).

The rules for entitlement are the same as those for British citizens (see p188). There are no special rules for people with no leave.

9. **Disability benefits**

These benefits are disability living allowance, attendance allowance, invalid care allowance and non-contributory incapacity benefit.

These benefits are treated as public funds for the purposes of the immigration rules, and claiming them may seriously affect your immigration position (see p93).

People with no leave to remain are not normally entitled to these benefits because of the 'persons subject to immigration control' rule. The rules for these benefits and the exceptions are the same as for people here with limited leave (see p251).

10. **Statutory sick pay, statutory maternity pay and maternity allowance**

The rules for statutory sick pay (SSP), statutory maternity pay (SMP) and maternity allowance are the same as those for British citizens (see p194). There are no special rules for people with no leave.

These benefits are not public funds under the immigration rules.[17] Furthermore, both SSP and SMP are benefits, which are paid by your employer; therefore, it is very unlikely that a request for them or payment of them will come to the attention of the Home Office. The DWP will only be involved if there is a dispute about entitlement, but even then, because your immigration status is irrelevant, it is very unlikely that the Home Office will be advised. If the Home Office is informed, your immigration position may be affected (see p93), and if you have worked in breach of conditions that may have effects (see p49).

Maternity allowance is a benefit paid by the DWP, therefore any claim is likely to bring you to the attention of the immigration authorities. There is no specific immigration test, but it is payable based on your past work record. Therefore to qualify, you must be a person who has been in legal employment and who has no employment prohibition.

11. **The social fund**

Most people with no leave are unable to get social fund payments. This is because people who are 'persons subject to immigration control' (PSIC) are excluded from entitlement (see p157).[18]

Groups who are not excluded from social fund payments

- A European Union (EU) or European Economic Area (EEA) national.
- A person from a country that has ratified the European Social Chapter of 1961 or the European Convention on Social and Medical Assistance and who is lawfully present (this applies to all EEA countries, Cyprus, Czech Republic, Hungary, Latvia, Malta, Poland, Slovakia and Turkey). For details on the meaning of 'lawful presence', see p131.
- A person who has been given no leave as a sponsored immigrant (see p104).
- A student or other person whose funding from abroad is temporarily interrupted and there is a reasonable expectation that her/his supply of funds will be resumed.
- An asylum seeker who can qualify for benefit under the transitional rules (see p275).
- A person who is lawfully employed and is a national or a family member of a national (and is living with her/him) of Algeria, Morocco, Slovenia, Tunisia or Turkey.
- A family member of an EU or EEA national. This would apply whatever the nationality or immigration status of the family member. Furthermore there is no necessity for the EEA national to be a 'worker'. The exemption applies simply because of nationality including a British citizen. This exemption will certainly include a partner and children, but in many cases will also include adult children, parents and other relatives (see p347).

General rules

If you fall within one of the exemptions above you may be able to get a social fund payment but you will also have to satisfy the general conditions of entitlement. See p195 for details of the main conditions of entitlement and different types of payment from the social fund.

You cannot get a budgeting loan or a community care grant from the discretionary social fund unless you are in receipt of, or about to be in receipt of, a means-tested benefit. This is referred to as a qualifying benefit. You also must be in receipt of a qualifying benefit in order to receive a maternity or funeral payment and cold weather payments. These rules mean that if you are not entitled to these benefits because of your immigration status, you cannot be given a social fund payment. You do not have to be in receipt of a means-tested benefit to qualify for a crisis loan or a winter fuel payment. However, any loans from the social fund have to be repaid and therefore a person must be seen to have income and the possibility of being able to repay before an award can be made.

Residence rules

The residence conditions for the regulated social fund are the same as for British citizens (see p195). There are no specific residence conditions for the discretionary social fund, although there are special rules, which relate to 'persons from abroad'. If you are a 'person from abroad' under the income support or income-based jobseeker's allowance rules then a crisis loan can only be awarded in order to alleviate the consequences of a disaster.[19] A person from abroad is a person who has failed the habitual residence test and is not the same as a PSIC (see p157).

Notes

1 s73 IAA 1999
2 s24(1)(b) IA 1971
3 Only immigration officers make illegal entry decisions. Adjudicators and the Immigration Appeal Tribunal have no power to decide that a person is an illegal entrant: *Khawaja v SSHD* [1984] AC 74; [1983] 1 All ER 765.
4 By quashing it.
5 s115(9)(b) IAA 1999
6 s115(9)(a) IAA 1999
7 *Khawaja*. Any statutory leave also ends.

1. IS
8 s115(9) IAA 1999
9 Reg 12 SS(IA)CA Regs; reg 70(2A) IS Regs
10 Reg 4ZA and Sch 1B para 21 to IS Regs

2. Income-based JSA
11 s8 AIA 1996

3. HB and CTB
12 s130(1)(a) SSCBA 1992

4. Child benefit and guardian's allowance
13 CF/1015/1995

5. WFTC and DPTC
14 Sch 2 para 21(1) IA 1971 'temporary admission'; Sch 2 paras 24 and 33 IA 1971 'bail'
15 s24(1)(e) IA 1971. Any prosecution must be brought within six months of the last breach of conditions: s127 Magistrates Court Act 1980. It is not clear if breach of bail conditions is an offence.
16 Sch 2 paras 23 and 33 IA 1971

10. SSP and SMP
17 s115(1) IAA 1999; and see also para 6(c) HC 395 (the last complete statement of the immigration rules, 23 May 1994)

11. The social fund
18 S115(9) IAA 1999
19 SF Dir 16(b)

Chapter 20

∙∙∙

Asylum seekers

This chapter covers:
1. Transitional arrangements from 2000 (p275)
2. When entitlement ends (p281)
3. Asylum seekers and European agreements (p282)
4. Income support (p286)
5. Income-based jobseeker's allowance (p286)
6. Housing benefit and council tax benefit (p287)

This chapter deals with the rights to benefits of certain people who have claimed asylum in the UK but who have not yet been recognised as refugees or given exceptional leave to remain. The term 'asylum seeker' does not refer to a distinct immigration status, but simply describes an application someone has made. That person's status in immigration law may vary depending on how and when the application is made (see Chapter 5 for more details).

But 'asylum seeker' is, in effect, a 'benefit status', since the introduction of the scheme of asylum support (see Chapter 5). Under the current law an application to the Home Office or an immigration officer to be allowed to remain in the UK on the ground that being required to return would amount to a breach of the European Convention on Human Rights (ECHR) is also treated as an asylum application. If you have applied for asylum either under the 1951 Refugee Convention, or (since October 2000) under Article 3 of the ECHR, you are entitled to be supported under the asylum support scheme.[1] This does not apply if you have applied to be allowed to remain under any other Article of the ECHR.

This extension of the definition of asylum, for the purposes of benefit or support, did not apply until the Human Rights Act 1998 came into force on 2 October 2000,[2] and the benefit rules had already been changed as a result of the Immigration and Asylum Act 1999, by April 2000. Between April and October 2000 only an application under the 1951 Refugee Convention carried an entitlement. The changes in April meant that anyone who applied for asylum from then on would not be able to claim benefits but, with a few exceptions (see p275), would have to rely on asylum support. The only asylum seekers who could claim benefits were those who had already applied for asylum when the rules changed in April. The rules covered in this chapter deal mainly with people who were asylum seekers before the rules changed, and those rules probably cannot be

∙∙∙∙
273

extended to include anyone whose claim is made under the ECHR. Exceptions to this might arise:

- where people who are covered by transitional provisions make an extra claim under the ECHR (see p278); *or*
- in the case of family members who become separated after the changes took effect (see p279).

When you make an application for asylum in the UK it is generally referred to as a claim. You claim asylum, or you make a claim to be a refugee, under the 1951 Refugee Convention. In this chapter, when the process of seeking asylum is referred to, it is described as an application, to make clear the difference between seeking asylum and claiming benefit.

Prohibiting benefit claims

Nearly everyone who applies for asylum after the introduction of the new scheme, in Part VI of the Immigration and Asylum Act 1999, is barred from access to benefits.[3] Only two groups of asylum seekers are still permitted to claim benefits under the benefit rules in force since April 2000. They are people who:

- were asylum seekers when the scheme was introduced, who remain entitled under the transitional provisions (see p275); *or*
- come from a country whose nationals are outside the general prohibition because of a European agreement (see p282).

The benefits covered in this chapter are income support (IS), income-based jobseeker's allowance, housing benefit (HB) and council tax benefit (CTB). These are the only benefits with special rules concerning asylum seekers, the only ones which permit asylum seekers to be treated differently from other people with the same immigration status. This chapter covers those special rules, as they apply to the two broad groups of asylum seekers who can still receive benefit payments.

The Immigration and Asylum Act 1999 introduced two main changes to the social security system. It created the new scheme of asylum support (see Chapter 5), and it introduced the new definition of 'persons subject to immigration control', who would be ineligible for benefit. The categories of people excluded from benefit are defined broadly by the Act,[4] and a number of exceptions are set out in Regulations.[5] The combined effect of the changes, for asylum seekers, is that they are expected to depend on asylum support, not social security benefits.

There is one possible alternative to applying for asylum support. This is to apply for local authority support under the National Assistance Act 1948 (see p285). This is not strictly a question of entitlement to social security benefits, and only an outline of that scheme is given here.

There is one other restriction on claiming benefits that is connected with a person's immigration status. If you are a 'person from abroad' who is not habitually resident in the UK you will not be able to receive IS, income-based JSA, HB or CTB (see p135). Asylum seekers and refugees are exempt from this restriction.

1. **Transitional arrangements from 2000**

You remain entitled to benefit from 3 April 2000 despite the changes in the rules from that date if you were an asylum seeker *and*:

- you applied for asylum on arrival on any date up to and including 2 April 2000 (see below); *or*
- you were in receipt of benefits before the last set of benefit changes affecting asylum seekers, in 1996 (see p276); *or*
- you are a national of one of the 'upheaval countries' (Sierra Leone and the Democratic Republic of Congo), who applied for asylum in the UK within three months of the declaration (see p280).

These different categories stem from the previous overhaul of the benefit system, affecting the eligibility of people entering the UK, in 1996. The cut-off dates reflect both changes from 1996 and 2000, protecting the rights of those who were receiving benefits under the arrangements in force at the time of either change.

Asylum claimed on arrival before 3 April 2000

The benefit rules define an asylum seeker who can still qualify for benefits as someone who:[6]

'submits on his arrival (other than on his re-entry) in the UK from a country outside the Common Travel Area a claim for asylum on or before 2 April 2000 to the Secretary of State ... and that claim is recorded by the Secretary of State as having been made before that date.'

To qualify under this rule you must have:

- made an application for asylum; *and*
- made that application to the Home Office; *and*
- made that application on your arrival in the UK; *and*
- arrived from a country outside the Common Travel Area; *and*
- not be re-entering the UK when you arrive; *and*
- had that asylum application recorded by the Secretary of State.

The exact legal meaning of making your application 'on arrival' is still a matter of dispute. You should argue that it applies to you if you made your application while you were still within the airport or seaport at which you arrived in the UK, whether or not you had already passed through immigration control.

The most important document that was issued to new asylum seekers was the standard acknowledgment letter (SAL). There were two sorts of SAL in use, with different colours:

- SAL1 (blue/orange) was issued to on-arrival applicants. These documents were issued by immigration officers at ports.
- SAL2 (red/grey) was for in-country applicants. These were issued by the Asylum Screening Unit and by immigration officers who are not based at ports.

DWP and local authority staff are instructed to treat a person with a SAL1 as an on-arrival applicant and a person with a SAL2 as an in-country applicant.[7]

Many asylum seekers still hold a SAL, which remains valid, but since the beginning of 2002 these papers are being replaced by a small identity card known as an application registration card (ARC).

In practice, the SAL is not always a good guide to whether an application was made on arrival. For example, a claimant attending the Asylum Screening Unit to add dependants to her/his asylum application may have had her/his SAL1 taken away and replaced with a SAL2, and on occasion the ports simply ran out of copies of the SAL1 form, and used the SAL2 instead. Some existing asylum seekers will have had their SAL replaced by an ARC. If you only have a SAL2 but sought asylum 'on arrival' you will need to have explained the circumstances to the DWP. The Home Office does not make the decision whether the application was made on arrival. This decision is no different from any other concerning benefit, though it may be based upon information from the Home Office.

As long as you applied for asylum 'on arrival', as defined in the rules, before 3 April 2000, you will have been entitled[8] to receive income support (IS), housing benefit (HB), and council tax benefit (CTB). Income support and income-based JSA will have been paid at the urgent cases rate, but HB and CTB have no urgent cases rate, and they will have been paid at the full rate. To qualify for income-based jobseeker's allowance you must also have been given permission to work by the Home office.[9]

Your right to receive benefit did not end with the change in the Regulations. Once you have been assessed as entitled to benefit in this way your entitlement continues until the next 'relevant decision' (see p281) on your asylum application.

Asylum applications pending since February 1996

The second group covered by transitional arrangements is made up of people who still have rights under the rules in force before the previous change in the law. The number of people concerned is small, as the only people who can qualify under this rule are people whose asylum applications and first benefit claims were made before 4 February 1996.

Until 4 February 1996 under the old rules all asylum seekers could qualify for benefit, whether or not the application was made 'on arrival'.

The benefit rules introduced in February 1996 were declared unlawful by the Court of Appeal on 21 June 1996.[10] But the rules were altered again in a lawful way from 24 July 1996, and these changes were backdated to 5 February 1996, so that anyone who first claimed between 5 February and 23 July lost their entitlement according to the previous rules as soon as the alteration took effect. They could still qualify, and could continue to receive benefit, under the new rules, if they had applied for asylum on arrival during that period. But if they had applied in-country, after entering the UK, they lost entitlement to benefit from 24 July.

Anyone still receiving benefit as an asylum seeker who had first claimed before 5 February remained entitled under transitional provisions.[11] This applied even if the asylum application had already been refused before 5 February 1996, but you had appealed against that decision. So long as you were entitled to benefit immediately before the changes your entitlement continued, in accordance with the previous rules. Entitlement ended when a 'relevant decision' (see p281) was made. This rule about the ending of entitlement was a part of the new scheme introduced in July 1996, but it was applied to everyone, with no transitional provisions.

The new arrangements brought in by the Immigration and Asylum Act 1999 maintained these transitional arrangements from the 1996 scheme. Anyone who on 2 April 2000 still remained entitled because they were eligible under the benefit rules that applied until February 1996 is still eligible to receive any of the benefits, until a relevant decision is made.[12] The benefits covered are IS, a social fund payment, HB and CTB. Income-bed JSA is not covered because it did not exist in 1996.

It is still not clear whether this transitional protection is limited to the benefits you were entitled to before 5 February 1996, or whether entitlement to, say, only HB, also gives transitional protection for IS and CTB.

Under the rules in force before 5 February 1996 you only stopped being an asylum seeker when:[13]
- the asylum application was finally determined, including any appeal or further appeal, or was abandoned; *and*
- the Home Office recorded that final determination or abandonment.

Although the rule for entitlement to asylum support is similar to this, it does not apply in the case of benefit entitlement. You will stop being entitled to benefit when the next relevant decision is made on your application, and in many cases that will be before your asylum application is finally finished if you then go on to appeal.

You only have protection if your asylum application was made and recorded by the Home Office before 5 February 1996. Remember, there are no rules about how an asylum application is made: a verbal request or a letter may be enough. It is for the benefits authority, not the Home Office, to decide whether an asylum claim was made and whether, for benefit purposes, a record of it counts as having been made by the Home Office.

Broken claims

For many years there was legal dispute about the effect of a break in your claim on your entitlement to transitional protection. The Court of Appeal has now decided[14] that you do not have to have remained entitled to benefit throughout the period since 4 February 1996 to be entitled now. This decision overturns decisions in earlier cases by social security commissioners, and it upholds the view that CPAG has taken since the Regulations were introduced.

This means that, if your benefit entitlement ends after 5 February 1996 because, for example, you get a job, the transitional protection does not end. The protection continues until you stop being an asylum seeker, so if you need to claim benefit again you are still an asylum seeker under benefit rules.

Human rights applications

Because the definition of an asylum application, for asylum support and benefits purposes, has been extended as a result of the Immigration and Asylum Act 1999, it is possible to have an entitlement to support through an application under the European Convention on Human Rights (ECHR) (incorporated into the Human Rights Act 1998). Since 2 October 2000, if you claim that removing you from the country would amount to a breach of the UK's obligations under the ECHR, you are treated as an asylum seeker. This claim can be made at any point between arrival at a UK port and final removal from this country, and it will serve to stop any action by the immigration authorities to send you away, in the same way as an application for asylum under the 1951 Refugee Convention. The Home Office must consider the circumstances before you can be lawfully removed. If the application is rejected there will, in most cases, be a right of appeal against that decision before removal. (see the Law Society's *Guide to Immigration and Asylum Law* for more details).

At the same time as this was introduced, the rules on immigration and asylum appeals were changed. The new appeals rules brought in the notion of the 'one-stop' appeal, in which all the possible grounds you might have for challenging a Home office decision must be put forward at the earliest opportunity, and heard together. The effect of these rules is that you will not normally be allowed to have an asylum appeal, arguing about protection under the 1951 Refugee Convention, and then, if that fails, later make a separate application and appeal under the Human Rights Act 1998.

But when the new appeals rules came into force, the Human Rights Act was only applied to decisions of the immigration authorities made after 2 October 2000.[15] If you had been refused asylum before that date, and you were waiting for an appeal to be heard, you could not argue Human Rights Act points in the appeal.[16] The new 'one-stop' arrangements would not apply, and, if you lost your asylum appeal, you would get a fresh chance to make your human rights claim, when the Home Office later tried to remove you from the UK. For the purpose of benefits this would be a fresh application, because in the meantime you would have received a 'relevant decision' (see p281), ending your benefit claim. So if you were still receiving benefit while you were waiting for an appeal, making an extra application under the Human Rights Act would not prolong the period for which you could claim benefit.

It may be different if you were still waiting for a first decision on your asylum application by 2 October 2000, rather than an appeal. If you lodge an application under the Human Rights Act after that date but before you lose benefit, you should continue to receive benefit for any further time it takes the Home Office to deal with your case as a result of the new application. The same will apply to a family member who makes a separate claim after 2 October 2000 (see below). In each case your entitlement to benefit under these rules will end when the Home Office makes a decision on your application (see p281).

Family members of asylum seekers

The transitional protection for asylum seekers also applies to members of an asylum seeker's family.[17] These rules were brought in on 26 July 1996, but the DWP accepts that they apply from 5 February 1996.[18] You are protected if on 5 February 1996:

- you were *either*:
  - included as a dependant of an asylum seeker on her/his asylum application;[19] *or*
  - you had an application for asylum in your own right and were a family member of an asylum seeker;[20] *and*
- that asylum seeker had transitional protection (see p275).

This protection applies not only to members of the family for the purposes of a single benefits claim, but also former family members who subsequently claim benefits in their own name. This means that where a couple separate or a child leaves school, the former family member can claim benefit in their own name under the transitional rules.

Such protection lasts as long as the asylum seeker whose family member you are or were has protection, and also continues if you then apply for asylum in your own right (see example on p280).

In this case, transitional protection continues until you stop being an asylum seeker for benefit purposes (see p281), or if the person whose dependant you were has stopped being entitled by the time you make your separate application. This applies even though your asylum application was not made 'on arrival'. This is because your transitional protection means that the old rules apply to your asylum application and, because that application would have counted as an asylum application under the old rules, it counts as long as you have transitional protection.

Since 2 October 2000, when the Human Rights Act 1998 came into force, it has been possible to make asylum applications to the Home Office under the ECHR as well as the 1951 Refugee Convention. A former family member who would be entitled to benefit because of the transitional rules would be eligible to apply under whichever of these two conventions s/he relies on (see Chapter 5).

Example

Metin and Hanim are a married couple from Turkish Kurdistan who were both active there in an illegal left-wing organisation. They enter the UK illegally in 1995 and Metin applies for asylum asking for Hanim, his wife, to be recorded as his dependant. Metin is awarded IS urgent cases rate for the couple. On 5 February 1996, Metin qualifies for protection because he was entitled before that date to IS as an asylum seeker. Hanim also qualifies for protection because she is a member of Metin's family, but it does not matter at this time because she is not claiming benefit in her own right.

In July 2000 the couple separate. Because Hanim is protected and Metin's asylum application has not been decided, she is entitled to urgent cases IS. In August 2000 Hanim applies for asylum in her own right, and in October makes a further application, that removing her would be a breach of the ECHR. In November 2000 the Home Office finally refuses Metin's asylum application. Hanim remains protected until her application is decided because she is still an asylum seeker.

Upheaval countries

One other group of asylum seekers can qualify under the new rules.[21] Between February 1996 and April 2000, the Secretary of State had the power to make a declaration that a country was subject to such a fundamental change in circumstances that he would not normally order the return of a person to that country. This is also known as an 'upheaval declaration'.

Only two declarations were ever made. The first was for the former Zaire (now the Democratic Republic of Congo), and the other was for Sierra Leone. The power to make these declarations has been removed from 3 April 2000. The effect of the declaration was to put in-country applicants in the same position, as far as their eligibility for benefits was concerned, as on-arrival applicants, and since the introduction of the asylum support scheme there is no longer any difference in the entitlement of the two groups.

When a declaration was made about a country, you became an asylum seeker for benefit purposes:
- if you were a national of that country when the declaration was made; *and*
- if you applied for asylum within three months following the date of the declaration.

You became an asylum seeker for benefit purposes from the date the Home Office recorded that application as having been made.

You can only use this rule if you are a national of the country for which the declaration was made. If you have no nationality, if you are stateless, or if, like a number of people from Sierra Leone, you hold another form of British nationality, you can apply for asylum as a refugee from your country of former habitual residence but, even though that country is named in a declaration, an asylum claim would not make you an asylum seeker under benefit rules.

A declaration was made on 16 May 1997 that the former Zaire (now known as the Democratic Republic of Congo) was subject to a fundamental change.[22] This meant that, as a national of the Democratic Republic of Congo, you needed to make your asylum application made on or before 16 August 1997 to be eligible for benefit. The declaration about Sierra Leone was made on 1 July 1997, and your asylum application had to be made to the Home Office by 30 September 1997.

2. **When entitlement ends**

Under the transitional rules you are only eligible until the Home Office makes a decision on your application. These rules do not apply to people who can claim because of the European agreements (see p282), who should be able to receive benefit throughout the process of application and appeal, including any court challenges against refusal.

Under any of the three transitional arrangements, for people with benefit entitlement made before 5 February 1996, or on-arrival asylum applications before April 2000, or upheaval countries (see p280), you are entitled to benefit until the Home Office makes a decision. When it does, there will be one of five possible results, *either*:

- to accept your application and grant you asylum; *or*
- to refuse you asylum but grant exceptional leave, and this also applies to cases accepted under the Human Rights Act 1998; *or*
- to refuse you outright and give you no status, but to give you a right of appeal; *or*
- to grant you some other kind of status, most often because you have married in the meantime, and are permitted to stay with your spouse; *or*
- if you had previously applied for asylum, had appealed and lost, and have tried to make a fresh application with new evidence, the Home Office may refuse you outright, and if it considers that the evidence is not enough to amount to a new application, it will deny you a further appeal.

Your entitlement to benefit after the decision has been made depends on what that decision is. If it is a positive decision, and you are granted leave to remain your entitlement depends on the status granted. It makes no difference under which arrangement you were previously entitled.

Until 4 February 1996 you stopped being an asylum seeker for benefit purposes when your claim was finally determined.[23] A claim was not finally determined while on appeal or while a judicial review was pending. When the rules were changed in 1996 a new rule ending benefit entitlement from the date of the Home Office decision was introduced, in order not to pay benefit during the appeal process. That rule applied both to people who were still receiving benefit under the transitional arrangements because they had claimed before February 1996, and to new 'on-arrival' claimants. The same rule was applied to asylum seekers entitled to benefit under the arrangements for 'upheaval countries' (see p280). This rule has been maintained under the new transitional scheme from April 2000.

For all the transitional schemes, then, you stop being an asylum seeker for benefit purposes when the next decision after that date is taken on the asylum application (even if you have transitional protection). Your right to benefit will end *either*:

- on the date of the decision by the Home Office on your asylum application;[24] *or*
- on the date of the dismissal of your appeal against the Home Office refusal,[25]

whichever happens first. This will depend on the stage your asylum application had reached when you became entitled under the transitional rules. If you claimed benefit after 5 February 1996, the next decision will be the Home Office decision on your asylum application. If you claimed benefit before 5 February 1996 but the Home Office was still considering that application on 5 February 1996, the next decision will be the Home Office decision on your asylum application. If you were refused asylum before 5 February 1996 and had an appeal pending on that date, DWP guidance says that the next decision is that made at the end of that stage of the appeal process.

Most asylum seekers who lose entitlement to benefit will be entitled to claim asylum support during the appeal process.

3. **Asylum seekers and European agreements**

One group of asylum seekers will not be excluded from benefits and will be able to make claims for benefits, even if their asylum applications are made after the changes to the benefits rules. Their eligibility depends on their nationality. All asylum seekers are included within the definition of 'persons subject to immigration control' set out in the law,[26] but this broad exclusion is subject to exceptions,[27] each of which describes a group of people who are entitled to certain benefits. Among the groups listed are nationals of those countries which have ratified either the European Convention on Social and Medical Assistance (ECSMA) or the Council of Europe Social Chapter.[28] For more details, see Chapter 28. If you are a national of one of these countries and you are 'lawfully present' in the UK you will be able to claim:

- income support (IS);
- income-based jobseeker's allowance (JSA);
- a social fund payment;
- housing benefit (HB); *or*
- council tax benefit (CTB).

This leaves two questions, neither of which is easy to answer. First, which countries are included? and second, who is 'lawfully present'?

The countries covered

The process of acceding to international agreements like these usually involved two steps, signature and then ratification. Only countries that have ratified one or the other of the agreements are covered; signature alone is not enough. These two agreements come from the Council of Europe rather than the European Union (EU), so they are open to a much wider group of countries. It appears that one country, Estonia, has signed but not yet ratified the ECSMA, but it has signed and ratified the Social Chapter.

The problem is that there are two versions of the Social Chapter. The original form was agreed in Turin in 1961, and a revised version, with new additions, agreed in Strasbourg in 1996. This second version includes all the old provisions about social security contained in the first version. Since the new version was finalised, there has been no real point in signing up to an old version of the Chapter, and it seems to be only this second version that has attracted signatures in recent years. Because it contains all the provisions from the older version, it may be that all the states that have ratified the revised Chapter should be treated as having ratified the original version.

The UK Government signed and ratified the old version of the Chapter, but so far has only signed, and not ratified, the revised version. This may be why the benefit Regulations refer to countries that have ratified the Chapter as signed in Turin in 1961. But a list of countries that have ratified the Chapter, issued by the (then) Department for the Environment Transport and the Regions (DETR) in guidance circulated in April 2000 includes some, such as Romania, that have ratified only the revised, not the original, version. The purpose of the DETR guidance is to advise local authorities on who is eligible for HB and CTB, among other things.

But the DETR list does not include Bulgaria, Estonia or Slovenia, all of which have ratified the revised Chapter. The complete list of non-EEA states which have ratified one or other of the agreements is:

Bulgaria (revised)

Cyprus (original)

Czech Republic (original and revised)

Estonia (revised)

Hungary (original)

Latvia (original)

Malta (original *and* ECSMA)

Poland (original)

Romania (revised)

Slovakia (original)

Slovenia (revised)

Turkey (original *and* ECSMA)

This list includes some countries that have produced numbers of asylum seekers in recent years.

The DWP has also issued guidance in 2000.[29] Unlike the DETR list, this suggests that only the Republic of Cyprus, Czech Republic, Hungary, Latvia, Malta, Poland, Slovakia and Turkey are included. This leaves out the countries which have only ratified the second version of the Chapter.

The DWP list also says that Turkish Cypriots, people from the 'Turkish Republic of Northern Cyprus' cannot be included either as Cypriot or as Turkish citizens for the purpose of the benefit rules, but this can be argued, because many Turkish Cypriots are treated by the Turkish authorities as entitled to dual nationality with Turkey. Besides, older people born on the island will have been born before partition, and so were certainly Cypriot citizens until then. The breakaway state of the Turkish Republic of Northern Cyprus is not a recognised country and cannot give citizenship, so these people will not have acquired a new citizenship to replace their Cypriot citizenship.

Lawfully present

Being a citizen of one of these countries is not enough. You must also be 'lawfully present' in the UK. This condition may mean few asylum seekers can qualify. The scope of this requirement is still not entirely certain. Some appeals to tribunals against decisions of the former DSS early in 2001 were allowed, agreeing that an asylum seeker given permission to stay while an application was considered is lawfully present. But the DWP is likely to appeal against these rulings.

Meanwhile, an appeal was heard in the Court of Appeal on entitlement to housing as a homeless person. Although this was not about benefit entitlement, the same rules would apply. The Court decided[30] that you are not entitled if you are on temporary admission (see Chapter 5), because this does not mean you are 'lawfully present'. There was no appeal against this decision, and the tribunal decisions allowing appeals seem to be wrong.

The Court of Appeal decided the case on UK law alone, deciding what 'temporary admission' amounts to, but its decision is similar to judgments from the European Court of Justice (ECJ) on the effect of other agreements,[31] and it seems likely that if these cases were referred to the European Court, as they probably could be, the result would be the same.

If this is right, the only asylum seekers who can use these agreements are people who seek asylum while they are already in the country lawfully on some other basis, for example, as a visitor or student. They can count as lawfully present while the Home Office is dealing with their application, and can receive benefit if they qualify under the normal rules so long as they remain here as asylum seekers. They will not be bound by the rules about the ending of entitlement that apply to the transitional schemes (p275), and can still be entitled to benefit if they are applying for judicial review.

DWP Guidance indicates[32] that 'people who have come to the UK to seek asylum are not 'lawfully present''. If this Guidance is used to refuse benefit to any asylum seeker from one of the states which have ratified the Conventions, it could be wrong. The judgment of the ECJ only excludes people who are on temporary admission conditions, not those who have applied to the Home Office to vary their immigration status from one category to another.

National Assistance Act 1948

The scheme that was introduced from 5 February 1996 denied benefit to any asylum seeker who did not make an application 'on arrival'. Once the law had been amended to allow this to happen, in July 1996, asylum seekers who had applied after entering the UK were barred from receiving IS, HB and CTB, and they were left with no support. Court cases later established [33]that they could not be left to starve, and that there was a way for them to be supported by local authorities under the National Assistance Act 1948.[34] The changes to the law after 1999 have removed most asylum seekers from this provision,[35] but only if the need for support arises 'because he is destitute, or because of the physical effects, or anticipated physical effects, of his being destitute'. So an asylum seeker who would have been able to receive help from a local authority under this provision soley because s/he had no income can no longer do so. All of the asylum seekers who were being supported in this way now come under the asylum support scheme.

But if an asylum seeker has needs for other reasons, s/he may still be entitled to support under the National Assistance Act instead of through the National Asylum Support Service (NASS). This is likely to be important to those who have a disability, as well as to those who are elderly. If an asylum seeker needs special care, or accommodation with adaptations because of a disability, the local social services department has a duty to help rather than NASS.[36] An asylum seeker who might be covered by these arrangements is likely to need a community care assessment by social workers as a first step. This is a complicated area of the law, depending partly on important decisions taken by the courts. If you think you may have a claim under this legislation you should take specialist advice.

4. Income support

Asylum seekers are all treated as 'persons subject to immigration control' (see p157) for income support (IS) purposes, but the Regulations allow two groups to claim benefit.[37] They are:
- people covered by one of the transitional schemes (see p275); *and*
- nationals of countries which have ratified one of the European agreements (see p282) or who applied for asylum while in the UK with leave.

Urgent cases payment of income support

You can qualify for urgent cases payment of IS under transitional rules if a sponsorship undertaking (verbal or written) was given for you before 5 February 1996 and you were entitled to IS before that date (see p276). This can be used if your asylum application is refused (after 5 February 1996) and as a result you are no longer an asylum seeker for benefit purposes.

For how urgent cases payment of IS is worked out, see Chapter 13.

5. Income-based jobseeker's allowance

An asylum seeker who would be entitled to urgent cases income-based jobseeker's allowance (JSA) is always entitled to income support (IS) instead. The only advantage of claiming JSA is that your national insurance contribution record is maintained (see CPAG's *Welfare Benefits Handbook*).

The rules for 'persons subject to immigration control' (PSIC) and 'persons from abroad' are the same as for IS (see above). If you are not a PSIC (or 'person from abroad') for JSA you may have to satisfy the usual rules for JSA – see the chapter relevant to your immigration status.

If you are claiming under the transitional rules you will only be entitled to urgent rate income-based JSA if you have written permission from the Home Office to take work. [38]

6. **Housing benefit and council tax benefit**

Transitional provisions

If you are being paid income support (IS) or income-based jobseeker's allowance (JSA) (including urgent cases payments) the local authority that deals with your HB or CTB claim should not make enquiries about your immigration status or habitual residence.[39]

If you are covered by the transitional arrangements because you were assessed as eligible for IS purposes as an 'on-arrival' asylum seeker you will automatically also have qualified as eligible for HB and CTB. But you may have qualified for HB and CTB without receiving IS. Before April 2000 definitions of people who were barred because of their immigration status from receiving benefits, were written in separately to the Regulations for each benefit. This has been changed, by having a single definition,[40] covering all the relevant benefits.[41]

Under the rules in force before April 2000 discrepancies emerged, because the various definitions in the previous rules were not identical. In particular, the HB and CTB Regulations failed to make any reference to any disqualification of people who had been given temporary admission or temporary release (see Chapter 5). This meant that asylum seekers and others who had not been given leave to remain, and were present on temporary admission, were not barred from claiming HB or CTB.

The transitional arrangements set out in Regulations do not allow for this group of claimants, so if you received HB or CTB because you were on temporary admission conditions, you will have lost your entitlement to benefit when the rules changed in April 2000, and will not be able to re-claim unless you are granted permission to stay by the Home Office.

The only conditions under which asylum seekers can receive HB or CTB are the same as those for IS.[42]

Notes

1 s94(1) IAA 1999
2 Human Rights Act 1998 (Commencement No.2) Order 2000
3 s115 IAA 1999
4 s115(9) IAA 1999
5 SS(IA)CA Regs

1. Transitional arrangements from 2000

6 Reg 12(4)(a) SS(IA)CA Regs
7 HB/CTB Circular A1/96 pp22-3
8 Reg 2(5) and (6) SS(IA)CA Regs
9 Reg 12(4)(c) SS(IA) CA Regs
10 *R v Secretary of State for Social Security ex parte JCWI*, [1996] 4 All ER 385
11 Reg 12(1) SS(PFA)MA Regs
12 Reg 2(4)(a) SS(IA)CA Regs
13 Reg 70(3A)(a) IS Regs before amendment by reg 8(3)(c) SS(PFA)MA Regs; reg 7A(5)(a) HB Regs before amendment by reg 7(b) SS(PFA)MA Regs; reg 4A(5)(a) CTB Regs before amendment by reg 3(b) SS(PFA)MA Regs
14 *Mustafa Yildiz v Secretary of State for Social Security*, case C/2001 3093, 28 February 2001, CA
15 IAA 1999 (Commencement (No.6) Transitional and Consequential Provisions) Order 2000
16 *Selvaratnam Pardeepan* 00/TH/2414, IAT
17 Reg 12(1) SS(PFA)MA Regs as amended by Sch 1 para 5 AIA 1996
18 HEO(AO) 16/96
19 See HEO(AO) 16/96
20 The guidance states that only family members who have not claimed asylum in their own right qualify: HEO(AO) 16/96. This seems to be wrong because, eg, it would treat separated partners differently depending upon whether each had claimed asylum in their own name.
21 Reg 12(4)(b) SS(IC)CA Regs
22 IS Bulletin 47/97

2. When entitlement ends

23 Reg 70(3A)(b) IS Regs before amendment by reg 8(3)(c) SS(PFA)MA Regs; reg 7A(5)(a) HB Regs before amendment by reg 7(b) SS(PFA)MA Regs; reg 4A(5)(a) CTB Regs before amendment by reg 3(b) SS(PFA)MA Regs
24 Reg 12(5) SS(IA)CA Regs
25 Reg 2(4) SS(IA)CA Regs

3. Asylum seekers and European agreements

26 s115(9) IAA 1999
27 Reg 2 SS(IA)CA Regs
28 Sch para 1 part 4 SS(IA)CA Regs
29 Memo DMG vol 2 2/00
30 *Kaya v Haringey LB*, 1 May 2001
31 For eaxample, *Kazim Kus v Landeshaupstadt Wiesbaden*, Case C-237/91, [1992] ECR I-6781
32 Memo DMG vol2 2/00
33 For example, *R v LB Hammersmith and Fulham ex parte M* [1997] 9 Admin LR 504
34 s21 National Assistance Act 1948
35 s116 IAA 1999
36 *Westminster City Council v NASS* [2001]

4. IS

37 Reg 2 SS(IA)CA Regs

5. Income-based JSA

38 Reg 12(4)(c) SS(IA)CA Regs

6. HB and CTB

39 HB/CTB Circular A1/96 para 4
40 s115(9) IAA 1999 and see SS(IA)CA Regs
41 s115(1) IAA 1999
42 SSIACAR reg 12(7)

Part 3

Going abroad

Chapter 21

· ·

Going abroad

This chapter explains the effect on your benefit entitlement of spending time
out of the UK. It covers:
1. Considerations which affect benefit entitlement (below)
2. Temporary absence (see p293)

The rules concerning who may come to and go from the UK, the conditions that
apply to them, and the procedures applied are explained in Part 1 of this book.
Those rules are part of immigration law, and that is set at the level of the UK.
There are no significant differences depending on which part of the UK you live
in or return to. Most benefits, on the other hand, are set at the level of Great
Britain (GB), with slightly different arrangements for Northern Ireland.[1] The
differences are largely administrative, and most benefits are extended to cover
Northern Ireland by various Acts and regulations.[2] This Part deals with the main
scheme of benefits, and follows the regulations in referring to GB. Most of these
provisions can be applied to Northern Ireland in a similar way, but if you live in
Northern Ireland you should take further advice on how, if at all, the differences
in administration will affect your entitlements.

1. Considerations which affect benefit entitlement

There are two main considerations which may affect your benefit entitlement if
you travel:
* the standard rules for Great Britain (GB) and Northern Ireland which
determine the effect of your absence on entitlement to the various benefits.
There are important distinctions to be made depending on whether your
absence is considered to be only 'temporary' or not (see p293);
* the reciprocal agreements existing between the UK Government and other
governments under which you may qualify for benefits while abroad (see
Chapter 28).

If you are travelling to or from a European Economic Area (EEA) member state
and you are:

- a citizen of the European Union (EU) – ie, a national of one of the member states of the EU; *or*
- a citizen of one of the additional EEA states; *or*
- a member of the family of an EU or EEA citizen; *or*
- a national of one of the countries outside the EEA which has concluded an association agreement with the EU,

you may be entitled to certain benefit payments by virtue of European rules.

Benefit may be payable on account of being insured under the social security scheme of the other state while you are in the UK, or because you are covered under the UK schemes, or by combining cover under the two schemes. Certain benefits payable to you in the UK can continue to be paid while in the other country. Arrangements under the association agreements are essentially a special class of reciprocal agreements, covered by European Community law, rather than bilateral accords between two governments. All of these rights are covered in detail in Part 4.

In describing the effects of going abroad on your benefit entitlement, this book uses a number of phrases which carry specific legal meaning, and which need to be defined. These include:

- presence;
- absence;
- temporary absence;
- permanent absence;
- residence; *and*
- ordinary residence.

Generally speaking, the meaning given to these phrases is easy enough to grasp, but in law they require a precise rather than a general meaning because you can be entitled to or refused benefit depending on whether your circumstances fall one side or the other of a dividing line. Some of these are defined in Chapter 11. For the meaning of temporary and permanent absence, see p293.

This Chapter and the rest of Part 3 should be read in conjunction with Part 2, which sets out the residence and presence conditions for the various benefits, and also deals with the absence abroad of partners and children.

If you are, or expect to be, receiving benefits you should bear in mind certain general concerns when you are considering spending time outside the UK. In particular you should remember that for:

- **contributory benefits** even where there are no specific residence conditions, the contributions system itself acts as a residence test, since you have to have paid a certain number of national insurance (NI) contributions within a particular period before you can qualify for payment. This means that you must generally have been present in the UK, although if you work abroad for an employer based in the UK you may pay NI contributions, and may qualify. For the contribution conditions, see CPAG's *Welfare Benefits Handbook*;

- **means-tested benefits** you may be subject to the habitual residence test, and your absence from the UK may have an effect on whether or not you can meet this test. The effect of this rule has been significantly relaxed in recent times,[3] but if you are not considered to be 'habitually resident' in the UK, and do not come within one of the exceptions to the rule, you will be considered a 'person from abroad'[4] for the purposes of the relevant benefits. This may have serious implications for your entitlement to the four benefits covered, income support, income-based jobseeker's allowance, housing benefit and council tax benefit. For details of the habitual residence test, see p130;
- **other benefits** your entitlement may be affected by periods of absence, depending on the particular rules of entitlement applying to ordinary residence and past presence for those benefits.

2. **Temporary absence**

The term 'temporary absence' is important in determining whether you can remain entitled to particular benefits when you go abroad.

For many benefits, the fact that your absence abroad is temporary is a precondition for retaining entitlement, but for certain benefits there are also additional requirements that relate primarily to the purpose and length of time you are away. For certain benefits, absences from Great Britain (GB) – temporary or otherwise – are of very little importance. For details, see Chapter 22 (for benefit rules for Northern Ireland, see CPAG's *Welfare Benefits Handbook)*.

What is temporary absence?

'Temporary absence' is not defined in the legislation and there are no clear rules determining whether your absence will be treated as being temporary. The only guidance available is the caselaw of the courts and the social security commissioners, which sets out the factors the DWP must consider in determining whether the absence is temporary. It also provides examples of situations that will lead to a finding that your absence is not temporary. Every absence is unique and distinct, and accordingly, your case will be given individual consideration, so it is important that you provide full details of:

- why you wish to go abroad;
- how long you intend to be abroad; *and*
- what you intend to do while you are abroad.

Each of these considerations needs to be taken into account, and it is your responsibility to demonstrate that your absence is a temporary one.[5]

In the case of *Javed Akbar,* the Court of Appeal overruled the view previously taken by the High Court that a temporary absence was the opposite of a permanent absence.[6] The High Court had decided that an absence was temporary in any case where it was 'not permanent'. Following the decision by the Court of Appeal, a temporary absence, for benefits purposes, will not mean every absence that can be described as being 'not permanent'. Even so, any absence which is shown to be permanent cannot be considered temporary in any circumstances.

Both the High Court and Court of Appeal agreed that a person can still be temporarily absent even though s/he has not fixed the date for her/his return. In addition, the Court of Appeal agreed that in the particular case of *Javed Akbar* the overall conclusion that the claimant's absence was temporary was correct, and the circumstances serve as a useful example.

Example

Javed Akbar advised his local benefit office that he was going to Pakistan for three months in order to get over a bout of depression. It was accepted this would be temporary, and invalidity benefit continued to be paid. After three months he said he was unsure when he would return, and it would depend on the treatment he was receiving. The absence continued to be treated as temporary for seven months more, but after that benefit was stopped. Soon after this he returned to GB and appealed. Throughout the absence he had submitted medical certificates. It was accepted that he had always made clear his intention to return, as well as the temporary purpose of his absence, even though he could not say clearly when he would return. The fact of his return was taken as confirming his expressed intentions, and this circumstance, even though it arose after the date of the adjudicating officer's decision, was a relevant matter which should be taken into account.

The three most important factors in determining whether your absence is temporary are:[7]

- your intention for going abroad;
- the length of your absence; *and*
- the purpose of your absence.

Intention will always be an important factor but will never, on its own, be conclusive.[8] For example, a person may wish to return but find there are obstacles, such as an unexpected change in family responsibilities, which prevent her/him from returning for the foreseeable future. This may mean that her/his absence ceases to be temporary, despite intentions to the contrary.

Example

Momin returns to visit his family in Bangladesh for a three-month period. While he is there his father suffers an accident, and dies, leaving his disabled mother alone. As the only child of the family without other immediate dependants it falls on Momin to care for his mother until suitable long-term arrangements can be made. There are no nursing homes or similar institutions to care for his mother, and by the time he returns to the UK it is more than two years since he left.

There is no set period for a temporary or non-temporary absence, although commissioners have tended to treat a period of 12 months or more as demonstrating a non-temporary absence.[9] There is no reason in principle why an absence of several years cannot still be considered temporary, but the circumstances would need to be exceptional.[10] The number and lengths of other absences (past and intended) may also be taken into account in determining whether the immediate absence is temporary.[11]

If the purpose of the trip abroad is obviously temporary (eg, for a holiday or to visit friends or relatives or for a particular course of treatment) and you buy a return ticket, then your absence will be viewed as temporary.

The nature of an absence can change over time. If an absence, after the factors mentioned above have been considered, is found to be temporary at the beginning of the period, that does not mean that it will always remain temporary.[12] If circumstances change while you are abroad (eg, you go abroad for one reason and decide to stay abroad for a different purpose) then your absence may in time come to be regarded as no longer temporary.

Example
Zeinab receives incapacity benefit, housing benefit and council tax benefit. When she travels to visit family she leaves her council flat, and the absence is accepted as temporary by both the DWP and the local authority. Two months later she writes to say she intends to stay four months longer, as she is receiving medical treatment which is helping her. This is accepted as still temporary, and benefit continues to be paid. After six months her incapacity benefit stops, as she has received the maximum payment of 26 weeks' benefit. A further two months later she writes again to say her new partner has work locally and she intends to remain there with him for a year or more before returning to the UK. Both the DWP and the local authority decide that her absence is no longer temporary, and payments of housing benefit and council tax benefit are stopped.

For more details about how the temporary absence rules apply to the benefits mentioned in this example, see Chapter 22.

Where the rules for the different benefits (see Chapter 22) refer to 'temporary absence' and 'temporarily absent', you should take care to note that the absence is often qualified by other specific conditions which vary from benefit to benefit. For some benefits, you must 'intend' to return to GB within a specific period and for others you must 'intend' the absence to be temporary as well as it actually being temporary. In many cases, these differences should not affect the outcome.

Finally, it is important to note that in calculating the period over which you are temporarily absent from the UK, the day you leave and the day you return are counted as days in the UK.[13] This is a general rule which will apply unless the regulations dealing with a particular benefit specify otherwise. The rules for child benefit, for instance, provide that what counts is where you are on midnight of the day in question,[14] so that the day you travel out of the UK will be a day of absence (so long as you leave the territory – see p131 for definition – by midnight).

Notes

1 See R(S) 5/85
2 See for example, Social Security (Northern Ireland Reciprocal Arrangements) Regulations 1976 SI No.1003

1. Considerations which affect benefit entitlement
3 *Swaddling v Adjudication Officer* C-90/97 [1999] *The Times* 4 March, ECJ; *Nessa v Chief Adjudication Officer* [1999] 4 All ER 677, HL
4 Reg 21(3) IS Regs; reg 85 JSA Regs; reg 7A(4)(e) HB Regs; reg 7A(4)(3) CTB Regs

2. Temporary absence
5 *Chief Adjudication Officer v Ahmed and others* CA, 16 March 1994, *The Guardian*, 15 April 1994 per Neill LJ
6 *R v Social Security Commissioners ex parte Javed Akbar* [1992] *The Times* 6 November
7 para 070859 DMG
8 *Ahmed and others*
9 R(U) 16/62
10 *Ahmed and others*
11 R(I) 73/54
12 R(S) 1/85
13 R(S) 1/66
14 Reg 1(3) CB(RPA)Regs

Chapter 22

··

Entitlement to benefit when going abroad

This chapter deals with the effect of going abroad on your entitlement to benefits. The following benefits are covered:
1. Income support (below)
2. Income-based jobseeker's allowance (p299)
3. Housing benefit and council tax benefit (p301)
4. The social fund (p303)
5. Working families' tax credit and disabled person's tax credit (p306)
6. Short-term contributory benefits (p307)
7. Benefits for children (p310)
8. Retirement pensions (p312)
9. Bereavement benefits (p314)
10. Industrial injuries benefits (p315)
11. Disability and carers' benefits (p316)
12. Statutory sick pay and statutory maternity pay (p319)
13. Premiums and absence abroad (p319).

This chapter does not help you to determine if you are entitled to benefit in the first place. It deals with the *effect* of going abroad on your entitlement to benefits. For details of entitlement to both means-tested and non-means-tested benefits, see CPAG's *Welfare Benefits Handbook*. To determine your immigration status, see Part 1 of this book. For the effect of your immigration status on your right to claim benefit, see the appropriate chapter in Part 2.

For many benefits an important consideration for entitlement is whether you are going abroad on a temporary or permanent basis. For the meaning of 'temporary absence', see Chapter 21. For the meaning of other terms relating to absence and residence, see Chapter 11.

1. Income support

For people required to sign on as available for work, income support (IS) was replaced by income-based jobseeker's allowance on 7 October 1996.[1] To be

····
297

entitled to IS you must be present in Great Britain (GB).[2] If you have become entitled to IS while in GB during a temporary absence you may remain entitled for a period of either four or eight weeks. It is not necessary for any IS payments to be *received* prior to any temporary absence, but you must have claimed and satisfied the conditions of entitlement.

Regardless of the other reasons for your absence from GB, you only remain entitled to IS if:[3]

- you leave temporarily; *and*
- the period of your absence is unlikely to exceed 52 weeks; *and*
- you continue to satisfy all other conditions of entitlement to IS (ie, you do not work, you remain incapable of work, etc).

Housing benefit and council tax benefit may continue to be paid in addition to any IS you are paid during such an absence (see p301).

You will remain entitled for a period of eight weeks if you satisfy the above three requirements *and*:[4]

- you are accompanying abroad a child or young person who is a member of your family solely in order for that person to be treated for a disease or physical or mental disablement; *and*
- those arrangements relate to treatment outside GB which is provided by or under the supervision of an appropriately qualified person while you are abroad.

You will remain entitled for a period of four weeks if you satisfy the above three requirements *and*:[5]

- the reason you are exempt from the requirement to be available for work is *not* one of the following:
  - you are incapable of work – but see below for qualification for benefit when you are incapable of work;
  - you are in education;
  - you are involved in a trade dispute or are within a period of 15 days of returning to work following a trade dispute;
  - you are a 'person subject to immigration control' who is entitled to urgent cases payments of IS (see Chapter 13 – but in these cases you are unlikely to be allowed to travel and then return to continue with your asylum application);
  - you are a person who is appealing against a decision that you are not incapable of work; *or*
- you are incapable of work and the only reason you are absent from GB is to get treatment related to your incapacity from an appropriately qualified person; *or*
- you are in Northern Ireland; *or*
- you have a partner who is also absent from GB and who is entitled to a pensioner, enhanced pensioner, higher pensioner, disability or severe disability

premium. It is only necessary for you to be entitled to the premium. It is not necessary for you to be be paid it; *or*

- on the day you leave GB you have been incapable of work for a period of:
  - 196 days (28 weeks) if you are either terminally ill or you are entitled to the highest rate of the care component of disability living allowance; *or*
  - 364 days in any other case.

Breaks in periods of incapacity of eight weeks or less are disregarded in both instances.

2. **Income-based jobseeker's allowance**

Jobseeker's allowance (JSA) was introduced on 7 October 1996 to replace unemployment benefit and (for people who have to look for work in order to qualify for benefit) income support. For full details see CPAG's *Welfare Benefits Handbook*.

Presence in Great Britain

To be entitled to income-based JSA you must be present in Great Britain (GB).[6] If you have become entitled to income-based JSA while in GB, during a temporary absence you may be treated as still in GB and therefore remain entitled for a period of up to one, four, or eight weeks, provided that your absence is unlikely to exceed 52 weeks.[7] It is necessary that you satisfy all the other conditions of entitlement for income-based JSA,[8] the most important of which is that you are available for and actively seeking employment. Unless you go to Northern Ireland (in which case you may remain entitled for up to four weeks), there are certain other conditions you need to satisfy in order to be treated as present in GB[9] and these overlap with the circumstances in which you can be treated as available for and actively seeking work despite your absence (see below).

Available for and actively seeking employment

To get income-based JSA you must be available for and actively seeking employment.[10] You could cease to satisfy these conditions if you go abroad. However, when you go abroad you will still be treated as available for and actively seeking employment for:[11]

- **a maximum of one week** if you are temporarily absent from GB to attend a job interview (but you must notify an employment officer of your absence);[12] *or*
- **a maximum of four weeks** of your absence if you are part of a couple and you are getting the pensioner, enhanced pensioner, higher pensioner, disability or

severe disability premium for your partner and both you *and* your partner are absent from GB; *or*

- **a maximum of eight weeks'** temporary absence if you take your child abroad for medical treatment by an appropriately qualified person; *or*
- **a maximum of three months** if your absence is within another European Economic Area state (see Part 4).

In addition, in order to be treated as actively seeking work in any of these four circumstances you (and in the case of the fourth condition, your partner) must be absent from GB for at least three days for each week you wish to be treated as available for work.[13] In all cases, in order to remain entitled to benefit, the temporary absence must be unlikely to exceed 52 weeks.[14]

Even if you satisfy the above requirement, you will not be treated as still present in GB unless:
- if you are going abroad in order to attend an interview, you are:[15]
  - not actually absent from GB for more than seven continuous days; *and*
  - able to demonstrate to your employment officer on your return that you attended the interview;
- if you are taking your child abroad for medical treatment, the treatment is:[16]
  - for a disease or physical or mental disablement;
  - performed outside GB;
  - performed while you are temporarily absent from GB and is by or under the supervision of a suitably qualified person.

You are also treated as available for and actively seeking employment where someone else is abroad if you are:[17]
- part of a couple and you are looking after your child while your partner is temporarily absent from the UK;
- temporarily looking after a child on a full-time basis because the person who normally looks after the child is ill, temporarily absent from the home or is looking after another family member who is ill.

Entitlement will be for a maximum of eight weeks in both cases. In addition, you must look after the child at least three days in every week you wish to be treated as actively seeking employment.[18]

People in receipt of a training allowance

People in receipt of a training allowance from the Learning and Skills Council for England, the National Council for Education and Training for Wales, Scottish Enterprise or Highlands and Islands Enterprise but not receiving training can get income-based JSA without being available for or actively seeking employment and do not require a jobseeker's agreement.[19] In these circumstances, you can still get JSA for four weeks if you are temporarily absent from GB and entitled to a training allowance, without having to show that your absence is unlikely to exceed 52 weeks.[20]

Holidays from jobseeking

You can take a holiday from jobseeking and still remain entitled to JSA. You may spend a maximum of two weeks in any one period of 12 months (not calendar years) not actively seeking employment and living away from home.[21] You must:

- tell your employment officer about your holiday – in writing, if requested; *and*
- fill out a holiday form so you can be contacted if employment becomes available.

Although you are exempt from *looking* for work during this period, you still have to be *available* and willing to return to start work during the holiday. In practice, therefore, absences abroad during this period are unlikely to be allowed.

Housing costs

During your four or eight-week temporary absence from GB you remain entitled to any housing costs paid as part of income support[22] or income-based JSA[23], provided:

- your home is not let or sub-let to anyone else;
- you intend to return to live in it;
- the period of your absence is unlikely to exceed 13 weeks.

If you do not go abroad but:

- are absent from your home; *and*
- satisfy the above conditions; *and*
- continue to be entitled to some income-based JSA,

you remain entitled to your housing costs for a period of 13 weeks. In certain circumstances you may remain entitled to your housing costs for a period of 52 weeks.[24] See CPAG's *Welfare Benefits Handbook* for details of these circumstances. The rules are similar to those for housing benefit and council tax benefit (see below).

Back-to-work bonus

Back-to-work bonus can be paid whether you are in GB or abroad. So if you stop claiming JSA and are going abroad to start work, you should ensure that you make your claim.[25]

3. **Housing benefit and council tax benefit**

For the basic rules about who can get housing benefit (HB) and council tax benefit (CTB), see Part 2.

Housing benefit

During a temporary absence abroad you can remain entitled to HB for a period of either 13 or 52 weeks.

You remain entitled to HB for the first 13 weeks of any period of temporary absence from your home provided that:[26]

- you intend to return to occupy the dwelling as your home; *and*
- the property is not let or sub-let while you are away; *and*
- you are unlikely to be away for more than 13 weeks; *and*
- you meet the other conditions of entitlement to benefit.

You remain entitled to HB for the first 52 weeks of any period of temporary absence from your home provided:[27]

- you intend to return to occupy the dwelling as your home; *and*
- the property is not let or sub-let while you are away; *and*
- you are unlikely to be absent from the property for longer than 52 weeks (although, under exceptional circumstances, you may be permitted to extend the period for which you remain away by a short amount,[28] which DWP guidance interprets as meaning a maximum of a further three months); *and*
- you fall into one of the following categories:[29]
  - you are sick and in hospital; *or*
  - you or your partner or child are undergoing medically approved treatment or convalescence in the UK or abroad; *or*
  - you are on a training course in the UK or abroad approved by or on behalf of a government department, a local authority, any Secretary of State, Scottish Enterprise or Highlands and Enterprise or operated on their behalf by a local authority;[30] *or*
  - you are caring for someone who is sick in the UK or abroad and the care you are providing is medically approved; *or*
  - you are caring for a child whose parent or guardian is temporarily absent from her/his home because s/he is receiving medical treatment; *or*
  - you are receiving medically approved care not in residential accommodation in the UK or abroad; *or*
  - you are a student eligible for HB – see CPAG's *Welfare Benefits Handbook*; *or*
  - you left your home as a result of fear of violence and you are not entitled to HB for the accommodation you now occupy.[31]

In determining whether you intend to return home, account will be taken of whether you have left your personal belongings in the dwelling.[32]

With both durations of HB entitlement during a temporary absence the entitlement period begins on the first day that you are absent from the home[33] and the period of temporary absence begins again each time you leave, even if you only return for a very brief period.[34] However, you will not necessarily remain entitled by returning to your home for short periods and leaving again. You are only entitled to HB/CTB to help you pay for accommodation which you and your family (if any) *normally* occupy as your home.[35] If you have another home abroad which you or members of your family also occupy,[36] then your absences from the UK could affect your entitlement to benefit if your absences are long enough or regular enough to mean that your 'main' home ceases to be in the UK. However, you will not lose benefit on these grounds if members or your family normally occupy a home abroad, but are not part of your household.[37]

Council tax benefit

To be able to claim CTB you must first be liable to pay council tax for the accommodation in which you live.[38] If your main home is abroad you may avoid liability for the council tax altogether.[39] This carries a risk, though, since demonstrating that your main home is abroad would adversely affect your HB entitlement (see p302), and could have a negative effect on other benefits you may wish to claim.

If you are temporarily absent from GB you can continue to get CTB for a period of either 13 weeks or 52 weeks. The rules are almost the same as for HB (see p302).[40] The only variation relates to the transitional provision that applies to CTB, which is important. If you have been absent from your accommodation prior to 1 April 1995 you continue to be entitled to CTB for as long as that period of absence lasts (provided you satisfy the other entitlement conditions).[41]

You may also avoid liability for the council tax itself by showing that your dwelling is exempt.[42] Absences abroad may mean this is the case where the property is left unoccupied. The following are the most likely circumstances where this would apply:
- the property will be substantially unfurnished for a period of less than six months; *or*
- the previous resident is either receiving personal care other than in a hospital or home; *or*
- the previous resident is providing someone else with personal care; *or*
- the property is substantially unfurnished and requires or is undergoing major repairs or structural alterations to make it habitable; *or*
- such major repairs or alterations have only been completed within the past six months.

For more details see CPAG's *Council Tax Handbook*.

4. **The social fund**

The social fund is divided into two parts:
- **the regulated social fund** from which three benefits are payable:

- payments for maternity expenses;
- funeral expenses; *and*
- winter fuel payments;
- **the discretionary social fund** from which there are three types of payment:
  - budgeting loans;
  - community care grants; *and*
  - crisis loans.

For details of when you are entitled to payments from the social fund, see CPAGs *Welfare Benefits Handbook.*

Regulated social fund

Maternity and funeral expenses

Entitlement to payments from the social fund for maternity expenses, known as Sure Start maternity grants, is restricted to claimants who have been awarded income support (IS), income-based jobseeker's allowance (JSA), working families' tax credit and disabled person's tax credit, and, in some circumstances, council tax benefit (CTB) (see CPAG's *Welfare Benefits Handbook* for more details).[43] There is an additional requirement, which is that the parents must have received medical advice concerning the child, or the mother concerning the pregnancy, from a health professional.[44] Entitlement to a maternity grant during any absence from the UK is subject to the same rules as those other benefits.

All of these claimants and anyone in receipt of housing benefit or CTB can also claim funeral expenses,[45] but without the extra condition of having had to receive medical advice. The deceased must have been ordinarily resident in the UK at the date of death, and the burial or cremation must take place in the UK. But for people treated as workers for the purposes of European Community law (see p390) the rules concerning ordinary residence and the place of funeral are both extended to the European Economic Area.[46] There are no special rules concerning temporary absence, but since the claimant or her/his partner must be in receipt of one of the qualifying benefits on the date of claim, payment is governed by the same rules as those benefits.

Cold weather payments

Cold weather payments are payable only to people in receipt of IS, incapacity benefit or JSA on at least one of the days during the qualifying week of cold weather.[47]

You must be ordinarily resident in GB, but otherwise the presence and residence tests for the regulated social fund are dictated by the presence and residence conditions attached to the various means-tested benefits identified above. You should refer to the section in this chapter dealing with the relevant benefit to identify the effect of absences from GB on your entitlement to benefits from the regulated social fund.

Winter fuel payments

Winter fuel payments are available to anyone aged 60 or over to help towards the cost of the largest of the year's fuel bills. The only condition apart from age is that you are ordinarily resident in GB in the qualifying week,[48] a week which is set by the DWP and announced in advance of the winter. Eligibility does not depend on receiving any other benefits. For special conditions applying to people in certain kinds of accommodation, see CPAG's *Welfare Benefits Handbook*. Temporary absence will not affect your entitlement as long as you remain ordinarily resident (see p132). You will not usually need to make a claim if you have received a winter fuel payment before, but if this will be the first year in which you become entitled to a payment, or if you have been away from GB for long enough to have lost your entitlement in the meantime, you should contact your local office to make a claim. Claims can also be made for any of the past three years, if you have not received payment when you believe you should have been entitled. You will also be entitled to claim a backdated payment if at the time of the qualifying week you were a 'person subject to immigration control' (see p157) but have since been granted leave, usually by recognition as a refugee, which covers the relevant week.[49]

Discretionary social fund

Payments from the discretionary social fund can only be paid to meet needs which occur in the UK.[50] It is only necessary, therefore, to show that you are in the UK for a sufficient period to allow your particular need to be established here.

Budgeting loans

In order to get a budgeting loan, you need to be receiving IS or income-based JSA when the decision is made on your application and you or your partner must have been receiving either qualifying benefit for 26 weeks before that date.[51] It is likely, however, that if it is your partner who is the claimant, then your partner must also apply for the loan, and you would not qualify independently.[52] You should in any case check the rules relating to absence for the qualifying benefit – see p297 for IS or p299 for income-based JSA.

Community care grants

You can get a community care grant if, when you make your application, you are receiving IS or income-based JSA.[53]

If you have been staying in institutional or residential care, and it is likely that you will receive IS or income-based JSA when discharged, you should also be able to receive a grant. This is a long-standing concession, which applies to those 're–establishing' themselves in the community.[54] A claim should be made within six weeks of the date you expect to be discharged. The High Court has decided that in these cases the 'community' refers only to GB, so you can only claim successfully on this basis if you lived in GB before the time you made your application.[55] If your claim is made in any other circumstances, and providing you are in receipt of a qualifying benefit, there is no other presence or residence test to satisfy.

Crisis loans

You do not need to be entitled to or receiving any other benefit in order to get a crisis loan. The qualifying criteria set out in the Social Fund Directions[56] are not restricted. 'Persons subject to immigration control' (see p157) who are not entitled to IS or income-based JSA are excluded from claiming a crisis loan, unless this is the only way of alleviating the consequences of a disaster.[57] Even in this situation, it will be necessary to show the social fund officer that you are able to repay the loan.[58]

---

5. **Working families' tax credit and disabled person's tax credit**

The rules relating to absences for working families' tax credit (WFTC) and disabled person's tax credit (DPTC) are the same.

Both benefits are paid weekly for periods of 26 weeks. Benefit entitlement is determined by your circumstances at the start of the 26-week period. There are only certain special changes in your circumstances that can affect your benefit within the 26-week period.[59] None of these changes relate to absence abroad. For details see CPAG's *Welfare Benefits Handbook*. You should bear in mind that if a child or young person is provided for in your award of WFTC/DPTC your entitlement will cease if the child leaves your household, and is covered by another award of WFTC/DPTC or income support, from the date the entitlement arises under the other award.[60]

In order to be entitled to WFTC[61] or DPTC[62] you must be 'in' GB. This means that you must be present and ordinarily resident in GB (and your partner, if you have one, must be ordinarily resident in GB) when you make your claim. If your partner is not ordinarily resident in GB and you previously lived together abroad, you can claim WFTC as a lone parent if you and your partner do not intend to resume living together. For details of these tests, see p132. For other details about dependants, see Chapter 12.

So if you go abroad there is no direct effect on your current award of benefit. However, in order to be entitled to WFTC or DPTC on your return you once again need to satisfy the presence and residence rules. Your absence from GB can affect whether or not you are ordinarily resident when you return. You may be refused benefit if you are regularly absent from GB and, as a result, the DWP believes that you no longer normally live in GB as part of the regular order of your life.[63] Under these circumstances you would need to re-establish yourself in GB before becoming entitled to WFTC or DPTC again.

For all claims of DPTC you also need to be in receipt of a qualifying benefit.[64] The qualifying benefits are disability living allowance, attendance allowance, disablement benefit (with constant attendance allowance), war disablement pension (with war pensioner's constant attendance allowance or mobility supplement), or recent payments (in the past 182 days) of higher rate or long-term incapacity benefit, severe disablement allowance or a disability or higher pensioner premium with any of the following: income support, income-based jobseeker's allowance, housing benefit or council tax benefit. These benefits have presence and residence tests, so you may lose your entitlement following a temporary absence abroad. For more details see Chapter 11. In addition, second and subsequent claims for DPTC are linked either to entitlement to certain benefits or to satisfying certain disability tests. Your absences may therefore affect your entitlement to these benefits and, in turn, your entitlement to DPTC.

If you go abroad to work and then on your return need to make a new claim (see above), you may lose entitlement to WFTC or DPTC unless you are immediately re-employed in this country. This is because, in order to get WFTC or DPTC:

- your earnings and those of any partner must derive at least in part from work in the UK and not wholly from work done outside the UK;[65] *and*
- you must be employed at the date of the claim;[66] *and*
- you must be employed in your 'normal' work which is likely to last for a period of five weeks or more beginning with the date of the claim;[67] *and*
- you must work for 16 or more hours in the week of your claim or in one of the two preceding weeks or, if you have been on holiday from work, be expected to work for 16 hours or more in the week after you return.[68]

You should get specialist advice in relation to a claim for either of the tax credits if:

- you are intending to go abroad, other than during a period of holiday from your work; *or*
- your absences are likely to be prolonged or frequent; *or*
- you are giving up work to go abroad or intending to work while abroad.

6. **Short-term contributory benefits**

These benefits are contribution-based jobseeker's allowance (JSA), incapacity benefit and maternity allowance (MA). For details of the presence and residence conditions for these benefits, see Chapter 11.

Contribution-based jobseeker's allowance

The rules relating to absences for contribution-based JSA are the same as for income-based JSA (see p299).[69]

However, like other contributory benefits, you need to satisfy the contribution conditions[70] which means that you are unlikely to qualify unless you have lived and worked in the UK for several years. For the contribution conditions, see CPAG's *Welfare Benefits Handbook*.

For contribution-based JSA, you are still treated as present in Great Britain (GB) if you are outside GB because you are an offshore worker[71] *or* because you are a mariner and you are left outside GB, provided you report to a consular officer or chief officer of customs within 14 days or as soon as reasonably practicable.[72] For what counts as an offshore worker for these purposes, see p189. If you fall into one of these categories, then you remain entitled to benefit despite your absence from GB provided you fulfil all the other entitlement conditions.

In order to allow you to look for work elsewhere in the European Economic Area (EEA), you will be able to continue to receive contribution-based JSA for a period of up to three months, paid to you in another EEA country (see p376).

Incapacity benefit

If you are temporarily absent (see p293) from GB then you can remain entitled to benefit. Unless you are receiving either attendance allowance (AA) or disability living allowance or you are a member of the family of a serving member of the forces and are temporarily absent because you are living with that person,[73] then you can only remain entitled to benefit for the first 26 weeks of any such absence[74] and unless either of these conditions applies to you, the Secretary of State must certify that it would be consistent with the proper administration of the benefits scheme for you to qualify for benefit despite your absence.[75]

You *also* need to satisfy one of the following conditions:[76]

- you are going abroad for treatment for an incapacity which began before you go abroad. This must be the reason why you go abroad. You cannot simply decide to receive such treatment while you are abroad.[77] The treatment itself must be carried out by some other person[78] and must usually be of a medical nature: convalescence or a trip abroad for a change in environment will not qualify;[79] *or*
- your incapacity is the result of an industrial injury[80] (see CPAG's *Welfare Benefits Handbook*) and you go abroad in order to receive treatment which is appropriate to that injury; *or*
- at the time you go abroad you have been continuously incapable of work for six months and you remain continuously incapable of work for the time that you are abroad and claiming benefit. In this case it is not necessary for your absence to be for the purpose of receiving treatment.

You can also get benefit for the whole of the period of the temporary absence if one of the above three conditions applies to you and you have been continuously absent from GB since 8 March 1994.[81]

You are also treated as present in GB and entitled to benefit if you are outside GB because you are an offshore worker[82] *or* because you are a mariner.[83] For what counts as an offshore worker for these purposes, see p189. If you fall into this category then you remain entitled to benefit despite your absence from GB provided you fulfil all other entitlement conditions.

Maternity allowance

In order to get MA you need to have been in employment either as an employed or a self-employed person for at least 26 weeks in the 66 weeks before the week in which your baby is due. Until August 2000 you also needed to have paid Class 1 or Class 2 national insurance (NI) contributions during each of the these 26 weeks.[84] This has now been replaced by an earnings condition,[85] so that you receive standard rate MA if your earnings in any 13 weeks of the 66-week period are at the level of the lower earnings limit (see CPAG's *Welfare Benefits Handbook* for details of this). If they are not, then if your earnings have at least reached the 'threshold' level (which in 2002/03 is £30 a week) you will be entitled to the variable rate of MA, payable at the lower of either the standard rate or 90 per cent of your weekly earnings. Maternity allowance is payable for a period of 18 weeks starting at any time from the beginning of the 11th week before the week in which your baby is due to the week following the week in which you actually give birth to your baby.[86]

However, in order to satisfy the 'recent work' test you have to have been employed or self-employed in GB.[87] As a result, a lengthy recent absence abroad may mean that you fail to establish your entitlement to MA. You may, however, still be able to claim MA if you:[88]

• have been working abroad and you return to GB; *and*
• remained ordinarily resident in GB during your period of absence; *and*
• have received earnings at least equal to the threshold figure.

If you think this applies to you then you should get help from your local advice centre.

The rules dealing with whether you remain entitled to MA when you are temporarily absent from GB are nearly the same as for incapacity benefit (see p308). The only differences are that the test of treatment for an incapacity arising as the result of an industrial injury does not apply and that MA is only payable for a period of 18 weeks.

Your pregnancy alone will not be sufficient for the purposes of remaining entitled to benefit during your period of temporary absence. You need to show a further specific incapacity.[89] It would be advisable to obtain backdated medical certificates before going abroad.

7. **Benefits for children**

The benefits covered here are child benefit and guardian's allowance.

Child benefit

For presence and residence conditions, see p177. Both the parent who will receive the benefit and the child in respect of whom the benefit is paid must satisfy past residence tests, and since 7 October 1996 entitlement also depends upon immigration status.[90] The rules concerning absence from GB are different from those for other benefits, as the legislation specifies when a period of absence shall be counted, both by day and by week (see p177 for details). In order to qualify for payment for any child for whom you are responsible, you must[91] be present in GB at the beginning of the week in which payment is due, or be treated as present. You can be considered as present and eligible to receive child benefit for up to eight weeks[92] beginning with the first week of absence (a week is counted as one of absence if you are out of GB by midnight on the night of Sunday/Monday[93]), so long as your absence from the UK is intended to be temporary. If you have a child born abroad during a temporary absence you will be eligible for child benefit up to the eighth week of your absence, providing benefit would be payable if the child had been born in GB.[94]

You can also be treated as present in GB even though you are working abroad if you are:[95]

- employed as a civil servant for a UK government department; *or*
- a serving member of the forces; *or*
- temporarily employed outside GB, so long as you are liable to pay UK income tax on at least half of your earnings in that year; *or*
- living with your spouse who is within one of the three groups above; *or*
- living as the unmarried partner of a person who is within the three groups above, providing you were living together before you went abroad.

There are exceptions to the presence test for child benefit (see p177 for details) which mean that you can be eligible for payment if:[96]

- you are temporarily absent for a period of up to 28 days; *and*
- the benefit week is within a period of 183 consecutive days when you are likely to be in the UK; *and*
- you were, within that period of 183 days, but before the benefit week in question, an employed or self-employed earner.

The residence conditions for the child mean that s/he must generally be present in the UK, but child benefit may still be payable during absences of up to eight weeks, or up to 156 weeks (three years).

Benefit is payable for up to eight weeks of absence if:

- you were entitled to child benefit for the child in the week before s/he left GB; *and*
- the absence is intended to be temporary.[97]

Benefit is payable for up to 156 weeks of a child's absence if:
- s/he is absent only[98] because s/he is receiving full-time education at a recognised educational establishment;[99] *or*
- s/he is absent for the purpose of receiving treatment for an illness or disability of body or mind which began before leaving the UK, and the Secretary of State has determined the period of absence.[100] In both these periods of absence of the child, eight weeks and 156 weeks, the past presence condition is treated as met for a child born outside UK, if the mother satisfies the residence conditions.[101]

If you are treated as present even though you or your spouse are working abroad as a UK civil servant, while paying income tax in the UK, or as a member of the forces (see p180), your child will also be treated as being present for child benefit purposes, however long you are abroad, provided s/he is living with you.

Child dependency increases are subject to the rules of entitlement to child benefit. You are eligible for increases of other benefits in respect of a child so long as you are entitled to child benefit.[102] There are no additional rules concerning presence, residence or absence.

Guardian's allowance

There are no special residence and presence tests for guardian's allowance. To be entitled to guardian's allowance:[103]
- you must be entitled or treated as entitled to child benefit; *and*
- one of the child's parents must satisfy residence conditions (see p180 for details).

Generally the residence and absence conditions for child benefit will apply to guardian's allowance, but entitlement can continue during a temporary absence abroad if:[104]
- you have been in a country, including a European Economic Area country, where there is a reciprocal agreement under which you would have been entitled to guardian's allowance except for the fact that you are not receiving child benefit; *or*
- you are treated as being present because of your employment as a civil servant or member of the forces (see p180).

In addition you will remain entitled to guardian's allowance during a temporary absence if:[105]
- the child in respect of whom the benefit is paid remains in GB; *and*

- you continue to contribute to her/his maintenance by at least the amount of the total of child benefit and guardian's allowance; *and*
- no one else is entitled to receive child benefit during that period.

Guardian's allowance can continue to be paid while you are absent from GB, but it will not be uprated during any absence. The rules are the same as for retirement pensions.

8. Retirement pensions

For the presence and residence requirements of retirement pensions and for further entitlement details, see p184. There are residence requirements for Categories C and D retirement pensions. Category C pension is not dealt with here because the qualifying conditions mean that you must now be well over 100 years of age to be entitled, and very few people any longer qualify.[106] For details see 15th edn of CPAG's *National Welfare Benefits Handbook*, and take specialist advice if necessary.

Both Category A and B retirement pensions are contributory benefits. Category A pensions depend on either your own or your spouse's contribution record. For the contribution conditions, see CPAG's *Welfare Benefits Handbook*. There are no residence or presence rules for either category, but you are unlikely to qualify unless you or your late spouse lived and worked in Great Britain (GB) for several years. Special rules apply if you have worked for all or part of your working life in other European Economic Area countries, allowing you to add together periods of insurance under the schemes of the different countries in which you have worked (see p356). It is possible to qualify for a reduced rate Category A or B pension where insufficient national insurance (NI) contributions have been paid to satisfy the contribution conditions in full. Reduced rate pensions are frequently paid to people who have arrived in GB part way through their working lives, and to people who have spent periods of their working lives abroad and not paid sufficient contributions to maintain their pension entitlement. In certain cases where people have worked abroad, contribution records from the two countries can either be aggregated to build up an entitlement to a pension based on the combined totals, or part pensions from both countries can be paid – for details see Chapter 26.

If you are relying on your spouse's contribution record, you may be entitled to a pension even if you have never worked in or been to the UK and you still remain abroad. You can also claim a retirement pension based on your own or your spouse's contributions even if you are not living in GB when you reach pensionable age.

Example

When Muhith came to work in the UK he always intended only to stay a few years to earn enough to support his family at home. His wife Sumena never travelled here. The years passed, the family came to depend on Muhith's UK earnings, and he never found work back home. Some years before he reached pensionable age he became ill and returned home, where he later suffered a heart attack and died. Sumena will be able to claim a retirement pension based on his contribution record as soon as the age conditions are met.

Category D pensions are for those people who are aged over 80 years. You must satisfy the following residence and presence requirement:[107]
- you were resident in GB for at least 10 years in any continuous period of 20 years ending on or after your 80th birthday; *and*
- you were ordinarily resident in GB on:
  - your 80th birthday; *or*
  - a later date on which you claimed Category D pension.

A Category D pension is generally worth less than a Category A or B pension. The pensions 'overlap', which means that if you will be entitled to a Category A or B pension, the above residence and presence conditions are not important. Absences from GB during the 20-year period prior to your 80th birthday could, therefore, affect your entitlement to benefit, as could absences around the time of your 80th birthday or the date of your claim. If you wish to spend time abroad or live abroad after you are 80 then it is important to carefully plan any such absences because you will be unlikely to qualify for any other benefit which you will be able to claim while you are abroad. Dependants' additions are not paid with a Category D pension.

After establishing entitlement to any retirement pension, you will continue to be entitled to it regardless of any absences from GB.[108] However, absences abroad can still have an effect on the *amount* of benefit you receive. If you spend a sufficient amount of time abroad so that you cease to be ordinarily resident (see p132) in GB, the amount of benefit you receive is frozen for any day on which you are absent. This means that benefit for those days will be paid at the rate when you stopped being ordinarily resident or the rate at which it was first paid if that was later.[109] Your benefit is not up-rated along with everyone else's benefit. These rules do not apply in countries with which the UK has reciprocal agreements allowing for continued up-rating of pensions payments (see p411). The difference between these two groups of countries is not a breach of the Human Right Act 1998.[110]

However, you will still be entitled to an up-rated benefit, even if you are not ordinarily resident, if your entitlement is based on the contributions of your spouse and that person is ordinarily resident in GB on the day before the benefit is up-rated.[111]

You remain entitled to up-rated Category B pension even though you are not ordinarily resident in GB if:[112]

- the spouse on whose contributions the Category B pension is based has died or you are divorced from her/him; *and*
- you have married again; *and*
- your new spouse was not entitled to a Category A pension before the up-rating date; *and*
  - *either* you were still married to your new spouse on the day before the up-rating date;
  - *or* you married on or after that date.

In all of these cases you will be entitled to the up-rated amount of benefit again after your return to GB *provided* you are once again ordinarily resident. You should therefore try to time any permanent retirement abroad so that you can take the maximum benefit with you.

You are only entitled to the age addition of 25p payable with your pension when you are 80 for any day you are absent from GB if you:[113]

- are ordinarily resident in GB; *or*
- were entitled to the age addition before you stopped being ordinarily resident in GB; *or*
- are entitled to an increased rate of any category of retirement pension under a reciprocal agreement (see Chapter 28).

9. **Bereavement benefits**

The three payments of benefit for widows, widow's payment, widow's pension and widowed mother's allowance, were replaced, with effect from 9 April 2001, by new bereavement benefits.[114] The old system of widows' benefits were shown to discriminate, in that they were only available to women and not to men. The new benefits scheme closely follows the existing scheme, but a surviving spouse of either sex is entitled. All of these are contributory benefits and the contribution conditions must be satisfied in relation to your late spouse's contribution record – see CPAG's *Welfare Benefits Handbook*.[115] Bereavement benefits comprise bereavement payment, widowed parent's allowance and bereavement allowance. Entitlement to widowed parent's allowance and bereavement allowance is subject to a work-focused interview,[116] although in the case of bereavement allowance it is possible to have the interview deferred.[117] Failure to attend may affect your claim or the amount of benefit paid unless you can show 'good cause' (see CPAG's *Welfare Benefits Handbook*).

The only presence and residence conditions that apply to these benefits are those which relate to bereavement payment:[118]
- you or your late spouse were in GB at the time of her/his death; *or*
- you returned to GB within four weeks of your late spouse's death; *or*
- you meet the contribution conditions for widowed parent's allowance or bereavement allowance.

Absences from GB are only significant for people who wish to claim the lump-sum bereavement payment who, if they or their spouse were not in GB at the time of her/his death, have to come to GB within four weeks of the death in order to claim the payment.

It is therefore important for widows/widowers whose late spouse has worked and paid national insurance contributions in GB, but who themselves are living abroad, to check their benefit entitlement. The time limit for claiming bereavement benefits is three months[119] and this can be extended when the widow/widower was unaware of her/his spouse's death.[120] Therefore, it is always worth checking for these benefits. Once entitlement to bereavement benefits has been established, the rules governing entitlement to benefit while abroad are as for retirement pension (see p312).

10. **Industrial injuries benefits**

The relevant benefits are disablement benefit, reduced earnings allowance, retirement allowance, constant attendance allowance and exceptionally severe disablement allowance.

You are only entitled to these benefits if you:
- have an accident which 'arises out of and in the course of' employed earner's employment or a disease which is 'prescribed in relation to' employed earner's employment[121] – for details, see CPAG's *Welfare Benefits Handbook*. An employed earner is defined as a person employed in Great Britain (GB);[122] *and*
- were in GB when the accident happened[123] or engaged in GB in the employment which caused the disease.

For details concerning when you may be treated as being in or employed in GB, when your accident or disease may be treated as if it arose in GB, and when your employment may count as employed earner's employment (including mariners, airmen and women, volunteer development workers, and offshore workers) see p189.

To get **disablement benefit** or **retirement allowance** you do not have to satisfy any presence or residence conditions.[124] As a result, your absences from GB do not affect your entitlement to these benefits provided you are able to satisfy the requirements relating to your work and your accident or disease.

In order to get **reduced earnings allowance (REA)**, **constant attendance allowance** or **exceptionally severe disablement allowance** you must be present in GB when you claim.[125]

You remain entitled to constant attendance allowance and exceptionally severe disablement allowance for a period of six months (beginning with the first date on which you are absent) during which you are temporarily absent (see p293) from GB.[126] If your period of temporary absence is longer than six months the Secretary of State has a discretion to allow you to continue to receive benefit.[127]

You remain entitled to REA for a period of three months (beginning with the first date on which you are absent) during which you are temporarily absent from GB.[128] If your period of temporary absence is longer than three months, then the Secretary of State has a discretion to allow you to continue to receive benefit.[129] For constant attendance allowance or exceptionally severe disablement allowance, as well as for REA, the Secretary of State in exercising this discretion will consider the reasons for your absence and any other relevant matters. To be entitled to REA:[130]

- your absence from GB must *not* be in order to work or engage in any other economic activity; *and*
- your claim must have been made before you leave GB; *and*
- you must have been entitled to REA before going abroad.

You count as present in GB for the purposes of REA while you are employed as a mariner or airman or woman.[131] It has not been possible to make new claims for REA since 1990, unless the accident or illness to which the claim refers occurred before then. This means that if you lose your entitlement to your current claim by a longer period of absence abroad you will lose this benefit and not be able to re-claim it on your return.

11. **Disability and carers' benefits**

These benefits are disability living allowance (DLA), attendance allowance (AA), invalid care allowance (ICA) and severe disablement allowance (SDA). For details of the presence and residence conditions in relation to these benefits and for the circumstances in which you may be treated as present because of either your occupation or that of another member of your family, see Chapter 11. Your absences abroad are likely to affect your ability to satisfy the initial and past presence requirements for these benefits. The position for SDA, however, is slightly different (see p318).

Disability living allowance and attendance allowance

If you are coming to Great Britain (GB) and are unable to satisfy the residence rule that you have been present in GB for a total of 26 weeks in the last 52 weeks (13 weeks for children under six months of age), you will only be able to get these benefits if you are terminally ill.[132] If you are terminally ill, you still need to be present and ordinarily resident in GB in order to be entitled to these benefits.[133] However, if your earnings or those of your spouse are exempt from UK income tax you are subject to an extra test of having been present in GB for a total of at least 156 weeks in the last four years. This residence condition is not waived if you are terminally ill.[134]

If you have been abroad it may be difficult for you to show that you satisfy the criteria for the mobility and/or the care component for the necessary three months prior to the claim. If you experience difficulties with this you should seek advice.

If you go abroad then you are still treated as present in GB and therefore entitled to benefit if you are:

- temporarily absent from GB and have not been absent for a period of more than 26 weeks *provided* the absence was intended to be temporary at the outset;[135] *or*
- temporarily absent from GB for the purpose of being treated for an incapacity or a disabling condition which began before you left GB *provided* the Secretary of State certifies that it is consistent with the proper administration of the system that you should continue to receive benefit;[136] *or*
- abroad as a serving member of the forces, an airman or woman or mariner, or a continental shelf worker, or if you are living with a close relative (see p192) who is a serving member of the forces.[137]

If you satisfy any of the above requirements for any particular day, then you are also treated as present in GB for the purpose of the past presence requirement for DLA and AA. This requirement is that you have been present in GB for a period of 26 weeks in the last 52 weeks before your claim to benefit.[138]

If by the time you wish to go abroad you have reached 66 years of age and are receiving the lower rate care component or the lower rate mobility component of DLA you should be aware that if you break your claim you may not re-qualify for benefit when you return.[139] This is because claims must be made by the age of 65, and an absence longer than the period for which benefit can continue to be paid will mean you will be too old to meet the qualifying conditions for DLA, and may be unable to satisfy the stricter tests which apply to AA.

Invalid care allowance

The residence and presence conditions for ICA are the same as for DLA and AA *except* that:[140]

- there is no waiver of the 26-week rule for the terminally ill; *and*
- those who receive UK tax exempt earnings are not treated differently from those who do not.

For details of these rules, see Chapter 14.

If you go abroad you will remain entitled to ICA (and you will still be treated as present in GB for the purposes of the 26-week rule) if your absence is **temporary**[141] and;

- the absence is for a continuous period that does not exceed four weeks and was always intended to be temporary (in practice the disabled person would need to travel with you or you would fail to satisfy the ordinary conditions of entitlement, but see below); *or*
- the absence is for the specific purpose of caring for the disabled person who is also absent from GB and who remains entitled while absent to AA, DLA at the highest or middle rate, or constant attendance allowance. 'Specific' here does not have to mean sole purpose but the major purpose of the absence.[142]

You will also remain entitled to benefit if you go abroad without the person for whom you care provided:[143]

- the absence is for a continuous period that does not exceed four weeks and was always intended to be temporary; *and*
- you have only temporarily stopped providing care of at least 35 hours a week; *and*
- you have provided the necessary amount of care for at least 14 weeks in the period of 26 weeks before you go abroad *and* you would have provided that care for at least 22 weeks in that period but were unable to because either yourself or the person for whom you care had to go into a hospital or a similar institution for medical treatment. However, you will lose your benefit if the person for whom you care loses her/his entitlement to AA or DLA after s/he has been in hospital, residential or nursing care for four weeks, or 12 weeks if s/he is under 16 years of age and in receipt of DLA.

You are therefore able to take a four-week temporary holiday from caring every six months in which either you or the person for whom you care is abroad and you will still be able to receive benefit for this period.

Severe disablement allowance

Severe disablement allowance is being phased out.[144] It has not been possible to make a new claim for SDA since April 2001, but if you were entitled to the benefit before then you can continue to receive it on the same conditions as before. The rules dealing with whether you remain entitled to SDA when you are temporarily absent from GB are nearly the same as for incapacity benefit (see p308). The only differences are:[145]

- the test of treatment for an incapacity arising as the result of an industrial injury does not apply; *and*
- if you are a member of the family of a serving member of the forces, you are still only entitled for the first 26 weeks of the period of your temporary absence.

The initial presence and residence rules are similar to those for DLA and AA (see p316) – that is, you must be present, ordinarily resident and present for 26 weeks in the 52 weeks preceding the claim.[146] However, if you return from an absence abroad within the same period of incapacity (for an explanation of 'period of incapacity' see CPAG's *Welfare Benefits Handbook*) then you do not have to satisfy the presence and residence requirements again when you return.[147]

12. **Statutory sick pay and statutory maternity pay**

From 6 April 1996 there are no longer any requirements of presence or residence for statutory sick pay or statutory maternity pay. You remain entitled to these benefits wherever you are based, provided you meet the normal entitlement rules – see p194 for details.[148]

13. **Premiums and absence abroad**

Premiums are paid as part of your weekly entitlement to income support, income-based jobseeker's allowance, housing benefit and council tax benefit. Many of these premiums are dependent on your receipt of another benefit – eg, disability living allowance, attendance allowance or invalid care allowance. If your absence abroad means that you will lose entitlement to the qualifying benefit, you will also lose the relevant premium, although carer's premium continues to be paid for a further eight weeks. You may not be entitled to the premium as soon as you return, since you may need to satisfy again the presence test for the qualifying benefit. You may lose entitlement to a bereavement premium unless you make a fresh claim within eight weeks of the end of your previous claim.[149]

If you are receiving premiums, it is important to consider the full implications of your absence abroad on your benefit entitlement. It may be possible for you to time your absences in such a way that your premiums are not affected. For more information, consult your local advice agency.

Notes

1. **IS**
   1 See CPAG's *Migration and Social Security Handbook* 2nd edition
   2 s124(1) SSCBA 1992
   3 Regs 4(1), (2)(a) and (b) and 3(a) and (b) IS Regs
   4 Reg 4(3)(c) and (d) IS Regs
   5 Reg 4(1)(a) and (2)(a)-(c) IS Regs as amended

2. **Income-based JSA**
   6 s1(2)(l) JSA 1995
   7 Reg 50 JSA Regs
   8 Reg 50(2)(a), (3)(c) and (5)(c) JSA Regs
   9 Reg 50(2)-(6) JSA Regs
   10 s1(2)(a) and (c) JSA 1995
   11 Regs 14, 19 and 50 JSA Regs, as amended by the Social Security (Jobseeker's Allowance and Mariners' Benefits) (Miscellaneous Amendment) Regulations 1997 SI No. 563;
   12 Regs 14(1)(m), 19(1)(m) and 50(6)(c) JSA Regs
   13 Reg 19 JSA Regs
   14 Reg 50(2)(c), (3)(b) and (5)(b) JSA Regs
   15 Reg 50(6)(b) and (d) JSA Regs
   16 Reg 50(5)(d) and (e) JSA Regs
   17 Reg 14(1)(e) and (g) and 19(1)(e) and (g) JSA Regs
   18 Reg 19(1)(e) and (g) JSA Regs
   19 Reg 170 JSA Regs
   20 Reg 50(1) and (4) JSA Regs
   21 Reg 19(1)(p)(ii) JSA Regs
   22 Sch 3 para 3(10) IS Regs
   23 Sch 2 para 3(10) JSA Regs
   24 Sch 3 para 3(11) IS Regs; Sch 2 para 3(10) and (11) JSA Regs
   25 s26 JSA 1995, Social Security (Back to Work Bonus) (No.2) Regulations 1996

3. **HB and CTB**
   26 Reg 5(8) HB Regs
   27 Reg 5(8B) and (8C) HB Regs
   28 Reg 5(8B)(d) HB Regs
   29 Reg 5(8B) and (8C) HB Regs
   30 See also paras 3.39-3.41 GM and reg 5(9) HB Regs
   31 For further details of who is treated as occupying a dwelling see CPAG's *Welfare Benefits Handbook*.
   32 *R v HBRB ex parte Robertson* [1988] *The Independent,* 5 March 1988

   33 Reg 5(8) and (8C) HB Regs
   34 *R v Penwith DC ex parte Burt* 22 HLR 292
   35 s130(1) SSCBA 1992 and reg 5(1), (2) HB Regs
   36 See reg 5(2) HB Regs
   37 See para A3.15 GM
   38 s131(3)(a) SSCBA 1992
   39 s6(5) Local Government Finance Act 1992; s99(1) Local Government Finance (Scotland) Act 1992
   40 Reg 4C CTB Regs as amended
   41 Reg 6 HBCTBIS (Amdts) Regs
   42 Art 3 Council Tax (Exempt Dwellings) Order 1992 (SI No. 558)

4. **The social fund**
   43 Reg 5(1)(a) SFM&FE Regs as amended by SFM&FE (Amdt) Regs
   44 Reg 3 SFM&FE (Amdt) Regs
   45 Reg 7 SFM&FE Regs as substituted by Social Security (Jobseeker's Allowance and Mariners' Benefits) (Miscellaneous Amendments) Regulations 1997 SI No. 563
   46 Reg 7(1A) SFM&FE Regs
   47 Reg 1A SFCWP Regs
   48 Reg 2(a) SFWP regs
   49 Reg 4(2) SFWP Regs
   50 SF Dirs 23(1)(a) and 29
   51 SF Dir 8
   52 *R v Social Fund Inspector and Secretary of State for Social Security ex parte Davey* (CO/1418/97), unreported, QBD
   53 SF Dir 25
   54 SF Dir 4(a)(l)
   55 *R v SFI ex parte Amina Mohammed* [1992] *The Times,* 25 November 1992
   56 SF Dirs 14-17
   57 SF Dir 16(b)
   58 SF Dir 22

5. **WFTC and DPTC**
   59 For WFTC see s128(3) and (4) SSCBA 1992; regs 49-51A FC Regs; for DPTC see s129(6) and (7) SSCBA 1992; regs 54-56A DWA Regs. The names of the benefits have been changed, but the references in the Act and the names of the Regulations have remained unchanged.
   60 Reg 50 FC Regs; reg 55 DWA Regs

61 Reg 50 FC Regs; reg 55 DWA Regs both as amended by Tax Credits Schemes (Miscellaneous Amendments) Regulations 1999 (SI No. 2487)
62 s128 SSCBA 1992; reg 3 FC Regs; R(FC) 2/93
63 *R v Barnet London Borough Council ex parte Shah* [1983] 2 AC 309
64 s129(1), (2) and (4) SSCBA 1992; reg 7 DWA Regs
65 Reg 3(1)(c) and (d) FC Regs; reg 5(1)(c) and (d) DWA Regs
66 Reg 4(1)(c) FC Regs; reg 6(1)(c) DWA Regs
67 Reg 4(6)(a) FC Regs; reg 6(6)(a) DWA Regs
68 Reg 4(5) FC Regs; reg 6(5) DWA Regs

6. Short-term contributory benefits
69 s21 and Sch 1 para 11 JSA 1995; regs 14, 19 and 50 JSA Regs as amended by Social Security (New Deal) Regulations 1998 (SI No. 1274) and Jobseeker's Allowance (Amendment) (No. 2) Regulations 1999 (SI No. 3087)
70 ss1(2)(d)(i) and 2 JSA 1995
71 Reg 11(1A) SSB(PA) Regs as amended
72 Reg 4A SS(MB) Regs as amended
73 In order to qualify as a member of the family you must be the spouse, son, daughter, step-son, step-daughter, father, father-in-law, step-father, mother, mother-in-law or step-mother of the person serving in the forces – see reg 2(5)(b) SSB(PA) Regs
74 Reg 2(1), (1A), (1B) SSB(PA) Regs
75 Reg 2(1)(a) SSB(PA) Regs
76 Reg 2(1) SSB(PA) Regs
77 R(S) 2/86 and R(S) 1/90
78 R(S) 10/51
79 R(S) 1/69; R(S) 2/69; R(S) 4/80; R(S) 6/81
80 s94(1) SSCBA 1992
81 Reg 3 SSB(PA) (Amendment) Regulations 1994 (SI No. 268)
82 Reg 11(2) SSB(PA) Regs
83 Reg 4A SS(MB) Regs
84 s35(1)(b) SSCBA 1992
85 s53 WRPA 1999
86 ss35(2) and 165 SSCBA 1992
87 s2(1)(a) and (b) SSCBA 1992
88 Reg 2 Social Security (Maternity Allowance) (Work Abroad) Regulations as amended by Social Security (Maternity Allowance)(Work Abroad)(Amendment) Regulations 2000 (SI No. 691)
89 R(S) 1/75

7. Benefits for children
90 s146A SSCBA 1992
91 Reg 2(2) CB&SS (FAR) Regs
92 Reg 4(2) CB (RPA) Regs
93 s147(1) SSCBA 1992; R(F) 1/82
94 Reg 4(3) CB (RPA) Regs
95 Regs 6 and 7(1) CB (RPA) Regs
96 Reg 5(2)(b) CB (RPA) Regs
97 Reg 2(2)(b) CB (RPA) Regs
98 CF/7146/1995
99 R(F) 2/83
100 Reg 3(2)(c)(iii) CB (RPA) Regs
101 Reg 2(3) CB (RPA) Regs
102 s80(1) SSCBA 1992
103 s77 SSCBA 1992
104 Reg 13(1)(a) SSB(PA) Regs
105 Reg 13A(3) SSB(PA) Regs

8. Retirement pensions
106 For the residence rules see s78 SSCBA 1992, regs 9, 11 and 12 SS(WB&RP) Regs, and regs 4 and 5(3)(c) SSB(PA) Regs
107 Reg 10 SS(WB&RP) Regs
108 Reg 4(1) SSB(PA) Regs
109 Reg 4(3), (4), (5)(c) and(6) SSB(PA) Regs
110 See *Rotao Annette Carson v Secretary of State for Work and Pensions* [2002] EWHC 978
111 Reg 5(3)(a), (aa) and (6) SSB(PA) Regs
112 Reg 5(7) SSB(PA) Regs
113 Reg 8(1) SSB(PA) Regs

9. Bereavement benefits
114 See ss54-56 WRPA 1999, amending SSCBA 1992
115 For widows' benefits see s36(1)(b) (substituted by s54(1) WRPA 1999), 37(1) and 38(1) SSCBA 1992
116 s2A(2)(d) SSAA 1992, as amended by WRPA 1999
117 s2A(6)(c) SSAA 1992
118 Reg 4(a) SSB(PA) Regs
119 s1(2)(a) SSAA 1992 as amended by s 70 WRPA 1999, reg 19(2), (3) SS(C&P) Regs
120 ss3, 4 SSAA 1992 as amended by s70 and Sch 8 WRPA 1999

10. Industrial injuries benefits
121 ss94(1), 108 and 109 SSCBA 1992 as amended by s65 Social Security Act 1998
122 s2(1)(a) SSCBA 1992
123 s94(5) SSCBA 1992
124 Reg 9(3) and (7) SSB(PA) Regs
125 s113 SSCBA 1992
126 Reg 9(4) SSB(PA) Regs

127 Reg 9(4) SSB(PA) Regs
128 Reg 9(5) SSB(PA) Regs
129 Reg 9(5) SSB(PA) Regs
130 Reg 9(5)(a)-(c) SSB(PA) Regs
131 Reg 5(b) SS(IIMB) Regs; for the meaning
     of 'mariner' and 'airman' see regs 4-7
     and Sch II of SS(EEEIIP) Regs

11. **Disability and carers' benefits**
132 Reg 2(4) SS(DLA) Regs; reg 2(3) SS(AA)
     Regs
133 Reg 2(1) SS(DLA) Regs; reg 2(1) SS(AA)
     Regs
134 Reg 2(1)(b) SS(DLA) Regs; reg 2(1)(b)
     SS(AA) Regs as amended by Social
     Security (Immigration and Asylum)
     Consequential Amendment Regulations
     2000 (SI No. 636)
135 Reg 2(2)(d) SS(DLA) Regs; reg 2(2)(d)
     SS(AA) Regs; reg 10 SSB(PA) Regs
136 Reg 2(2)(e) SS(DLA) Regs; reg 2(2)(e)
     SS(AA) Regs; reg 10 SSB(PA) Regs
137 Reg 2(2)(a)-(c) SS(DLA) Regs; reg
     2(2)(a)-(c) SS(AA) Regs
138 Regs 2(1)(a)(iii), (2) SS(DLA) Regs; regs
     1(a), 2(1)(a)(iii), (2) SS(AA) Regs
139 Reg 3 SS(DLA) Regs as amended by
     Social Security (DLA) Amendment
     Regualtions 1997 (SI No. 349)
140 Reg 9 SS(ICA) Regs as amended by
     Social Security (Immigration and
     Asylum) (Consequential Amendment)
     Regulations 2000
141 Reg 9(2) SS(ICA) Regs; reg 10B SSB(PA)
     Regs
142 CG/15/1993
143 Regs 4(2) and 9(2) SS(ICA) Regs
144 s65 WRPA 1999
145 Regs 2(1)(bb) and (1B)(a) SSB(PA) Regs
146 Reg 3 SS(SDA) Regs as amended by
     Social Security (Immigration and
     Asylum) Consequential Amendment
     Regulations 2000
147 Reg 3(3) SS(SDA) Regs

12. **SSP and SMP**
148 Reg 10 SSP(MAPA) Regs; reg 2A
     SMP(PAM) Regs

13. **Premiums and absence abroad**
149 Sch 2 para 8A(3) IS Regs, and similar
     provisions in JSA, HB and CTB Regs, all as
     amended by Social Security
     (Amendment) Bereavement Benefits
     Regulations 2000 (SI No. 2239)

Chapter 23

∙∙

Getting paid while abroad

This chapter covers:
1. General rules (below)
2. Receiving benefit while abroad (below)
3. Paying national insurance contributions while abroad (p327)

1. General rules

This chapter deals with how to get your benefit paid to you when you go abroad. Because some benefits require national insurance (NI) contributions, the chapter also covers how to make voluntary NI contributions in Great Britain or Northern Ireland when you go abroad. For further details about NI contributions, see CPAG's *Welfare Benefits Handbook*.

In order to find out whether you are entitled to benefit see the chapter relevant to your immigration status in Part 2 of this book. In order to find out how your absence or absences abroad affect your benefit entitlement, see Chapter 22. If a number of benefits are paid, the temporary absence rules will apply separately to each benefit.

For all benefits, if you delay for a year in cashing or collecting your benefit after it has been issued to you (whether or not this is because you have gone abroad), you will lose your right to have it paid to you even though you are strictly 'entitled' to the benefit.[1] The only exceptions to this rule are if:[2]

- you apply in writing to the DWP or Inland Revenue for the benefit to be paid to you and you have good cause for not asking for the money earlier (for the meaning of 'good cause' see CPAG's *Welfare Benefits Handbook*); *or*
- the Secretary of State is satisfied that no payment was issued either by girocheque, order book or direct credit transfer; *or*
- payment was issued and returned and no duplicate payment has been issued.

2. Receiving benefit while abroad

If you go abroad and remain entitled to benefit there are a number of ways in which you can be paid while you are abroad. You should tell your local office of your preference at the time you notify them of your absence. You can:

- keep your order book and simply cash the orders when you return to Great Britain (GB); *or*
- authorise a person in GB to cash your order book; *or*
- ask for your benefits to be paid directly into a bank or building society account in GB;[3] *or*
- ask the DWP to pay your benefits directly into a bank account abroad, although in some countries you will have to open an account with a specific bank in order to be paid in this way.

Contact your local office to get more details about the procedures.

There are specific considerations relating to particular benefits which are described below.

Income support and income-based jobseeker's allowance

If you are going abroad, you should inform your local benefits office. If you are claiming income-based jobseeker's allowance (JSA) and you are going abroad in order to attend a job interview, you should notify your employment officer (EO) who may also ask you to explain your absence in writing. Similarly, if you are taking a two-week holiday from jobseeking (see p301) you must notify your EO in writing and you will be asked to fill out a holiday form so you can be contacted if a job becomes available.

It is normal practice for the DWP to ask you to return your order book when you go abroad for a temporary absence, even if you retain your benefit entitlement. If this happens you should contact the DWP as soon as you return and ask to be paid the arrears you are owed. If you are paid by giro you will normally be told to claim after you have returned. If you remain abroad longer than the period for which you are entitled to benefit, or if you are not entitled to these benefits while abroad, you will need to make fresh claims for housing benefit (HB) and council tax benefit (CTB).

Working families' tax credit and disabled person's tax credit

If you are in receipt of either of these benefits and you are going abroad for up to three months, you can cash your order book up to the date of your departure and then cash the remaining orders upon your return. This is because each order is valid for three months. If you are going abroad for more than three months you will need to arrange another method of payment for working families' tax credit or disabled person's tax credit due while you are abroad. You should contact the Tax Credits Office (see Appendix 2).

Housing benefit and council tax benefit

If you are going abroad you should tell your local authority about your absence and notify it of any reduction in income that may occur, for instance if your part-time earnings are going to cease. This is because such a reduction may affect the amount of benefit to which you are entitled. Housing benefit is awarded for a maximum 'benefit period' of 60 weeks, but benefit is often awarded for a shorter period. Your claim will still be treated as continuous if you re-apply for benefit either 13 weeks before your claim runs out or four weeks afterwards.[4] So before going abroad check when your benefit period is due to end and, if necessary, re-apply before you leave or immediately after you come back. If your claim on your return will be more than four weeks late you will need to argue that you have good cause for a late claim.[5] If you have any difficulties getting such a claim accepted, you should contact your local advice centre.

In some circumstances (eg, where you will lose most of your benefits when going abroad) you may become entitled to HB or CTB while abroad, even if you were not entitled while in the UK. If you are in this situation you should try to work out the date from which you will become entitled. You should then make a claim before you go abroad, covering you from the date in question and providing details of the anticipated reduction in income. If there will be no one checking your post who can provide any further details that might be requested while you are away, you should authorise the local authority to check the details directly with the relevant benefits office and/or with your employer.

If you are going abroad for longer than you will be able to claim HB and CTB, and there is someone living in your home while you are away, then, depending on that person's circumstances, it may be possible for her/him to argue that s/he is responsible for paying the housing costs and so claim HB and CTB in her/his own right.

If you are a private or housing association tenant and your HB is paid directly to you, while you are away you may need to make arrangements with your local authority to request that the benefit is paid directly to your landlord.

Incapacity benefit, severe disablement allowance, maternity allowance and contribution-based jobseeker's allowance

Incapacity benefit (IB), severe disablement allowance (SDA), maternity allowance and contribution-based JSA can be paid to you while you are abroad. Before going abroad you should inform your local office of your trip and the reasons for it. You will be asked to fill out a form giving the reasons for your absence and when you intend to return to the UK. You should tell your office well in advance of your trip abroad otherwise it may not be possible to reach a decision on your claim before you go abroad.

If you have claimed IB or SDA and you are due a medical examination when you go abroad you should ask if this can be arranged abroad. If this is not agreed you will run a greater risk that the Secretary of State will refuse to pay these benefits during your absence.

Retirement pensions and bereavement benefits

Both retirement pensions and bereavement benefits can be paid to you while you are abroad. If the DWP thinks that you are entitled to retirement pension and it has an address at which to contact you, it will write to you a few months before you reach state pension age to determine whether or not you wish to claim. If you do not receive a letter but you think that you may be entitled, you should contact the DWP yourself (for address see Appendix 2).

If you are happy for your benefit to be paid in the UK or to cash your order book on your return you do not need to tell your local office that you are going abroad if you will not be away for more than three months. If, however, you are going abroad for more than three months, you should tell your local office so that arrangements can be made to pay your benefit to you abroad. If benefit is paid to your address abroad, it will be paid either every four weeks or every 13 weeks. If you are going abroad and are going to return within two years you can choose to have the benefit paid as a lump sum when you return. If you need to get your benefit paid into a bank account while you are abroad, you should give the DWP as much notice as possible as it is often very slow in making these arrangements. If you have not resolved this before you leave, ask a friend, relative or advice agency in the UK to complete the arrangements.

Attendance allowance and disability living allowance

If you are going abroad and you are in receipt of attendance allowance (AA) or disability living allowance (DLA) you should contact your local benefits office or the Disability Benefits Unit (see Appendix 2). If you are in receipt of SDA or extra premiums paid with your HB or CTB, remember that you may lose these allowances if your absence means that you will lose entitlement to DLA or AA. It may be possible for you to time your absence to avoid this situation and to ensure that you can continue to claim on your return.

Invalid care allowance

If you are going abroad and are in receipt of invalid care allowance (ICA) you should contact your local office.

If you lose your entitlement to ICA you should still be eligible for a carer's premium paid with your income support, IB JSA, HB or CTB for a further period of eight weeks, provided you are entitled to these benefits while you are away.[6] If you lose your entitlement to ICA while you are abroad and the disabled person for whom you care is staying in the UK, s/he may be able to claim a severe disability premium during your absence instead. For further information see CPAG's *Welfare Benefits Handbook*.

3. Paying national insurance contributions while abroad

Entitlement to many benefits (the 'contributory benefits') depends on the national insurance (NI) contributions you have made. When you go abroad you can generally decide whether or not to continue to pay NI contributions voluntarily here, in order to protect your entitlement to certain benefits. The contribution rates if you go abroad are the same as if you pay in the UK.

For pensions you can obtain a 'pension forecast' by writing to the Inland Revenue. You should receive a reply which may help you to decide whether to make voluntary contributions or not. If your pension will be so low that you will always need to claim a means-tested benefit to top it up and you are planning to stay in this country when you retire, it is probably not worth making voluntary contributions. For further details see CPAG's *Welfare Benefits Handbook*.

Payments may be made in any of the following ways:

- by direct debit every month in arrears;
- once a year at the end of the year for which the contributions are due;
- by a person you nominate to make the payments for you in the UK in either of the above two ways.

For further information about whether or not to make voluntary contributions and how to make them you can contact the Pensions and Overseas Benefits Directorate (see Appendix 2) and obtain leaflet NI 38. With this leaflet you will also be sent Form CF 38 which you should fill in and return if you decide to make contributions while you are abroad.

Notes

1. General rules

1 Reg 38(1) SS(C&P) Regs as amended by Tax Credits (Claims and Payments) (Amendment) Regulations 1999 (SI No. 2572)

2. Receiving benefit while abroad

2 Reg 38(2A) SS(C&P) Regs
3 Reg 21 SS(C&P) Regs as amended by SS(C&P) Amendment Regulations 1999 (SI No. 2358) and Tax Credits (Claims and Payments) Amendment Regulations 1999 (SI No. 2572)

4 Reg 72(12) and (13) HB Regs; reg 62 (13) and (14) CTB Regs
5 Reg 72(15) HB Regs; reg 62(16) CTB Regs
6 Sch 2 para 14(ZA) HB Regs; Sch 1 para 16 CTB Regs; Sch 1 para 17 JSA Regs – all as amended by Social Security (Miscellaneous Amendments) Regulations 2000 (SI No. 681)

Part 4

European Community social security law

Chapter 24

. . . .

European Community social security law: introduction

This chapter covers:
1. Who needs to use this section (below)
2. The foundations of the European Union (p332)
3. Using European Community law (p334)
4. Immigration outline for European Economic Area nationals (p336)
5. The two routes for claiming social security benefits (p337)
6. Remedies (p340)

This part of the book concerns the rights and benefits to which you may be entitled if you are travelling to, from or around the European Economic Area (EEA). It describes the rights you may have as a citizen of a country within the EEA including the European Union, or as a dependant of one of these citizens.

Because this book is about benefit entitlement for migrants, this section only covers European law in respect of migrants. For information about European Community law on the equal treatment between men and women, see CPAG's *Welfare Benefits Handbook*.

---

1. **Who needs to use this section**

If you are a European Economic Area (EEA) national (see p332) you are never a 'person subject to immigration control' for benefit purposes (see p157). This is because as an EEA national you do not require leave to enter and are not subject to the 'no recourse to public funds restriction'. This applies equally to any family members who enter the UK with you, whatever their nationality.[1] However EEA nationals may have to satisfy the habitual residence test for certain benefits (see p135). If you fail the habitual residence test you will be classified as a 'person from abroad' for benefit purposes. This means that you are not entitled to certain benefits. However, the habitual residence test only applies if you have been in the Common Travel Area for less than two years. Furthermore, certain EEA nationals are exempt from the habitual residence test.

People for whom this section will be particularly relevant are as follows:
- EEA nationals who are subject to the habitual residence test;
- EEA nationals who have failed the contributions conditions for contributory benefits but who have worked in another member state;
- EEA nationals who do not meet the residence conditions for a particular benefit but who have worked or resided elsewhere in the EEA;
- EEA nationals who have family members living in other EEA states;
- spouses and family members of EEA nationals who are not themselves EEA nationals and who wish to claim benefit;
- nationals of states which have association agreements with the European Union;
- refugees and stateless persons.

2. The foundations of the European Union

The European Union (EU) was established in 1957. It began as an economic body and this is reflected in its original name, the European Economic Community (EEC). The EU now has 15 members as follows:

Austria	Germany	The Netherlands
Belgium	Greece	Portugal
Denmark	Ireland	Spain
Finland	Italy	Sweden
France	Luxembourg	The UK

European Community (EC) law has been extended to countries outside the EU who are covered by the European Economic Area (EEA) Agreement. EEA nationals are covered by EC law to the same extent as nationals of EU states. The EEA Agreement came into force in January 1994 when the EU joined another trading group, the European Free Trade Area. The EEA consists of the EU countries plus:

Iceland

Liechtenstein

Norway

From 1 June 2002, the right to freedom of movement also applies to Switzerland. Any further references in this part to EEA nationals should be interpreted as including Switzerland.

EC law applies in all 19 of these countries but it extends beyond the actual territory of the member states. It also applies to countries 'for whose external relations a member state is responsible'. Therefore Spain not only includes the mainland but also the Balearic and the Canary Islands. Portugal includes Madeira and the Azores.[2] However, there are certain exceptions to this general rule. In particular, in the UK Gibraltar is covered, whereas the Isle of Man and the Channel Islands are not.

The institutions of the European Community

The main EC institutions are:

The Commission

The Commission,[3] which is based in Brussels, is effectively the EU's civil service. There are 20 commissioners in charge of the various 'Directorate Generals', and they are European officials, not representatives of their states of origin. It is the Commission that makes proposals for European legislation; it therefore, has quite a different role to the UK civil service, which is supposed to have a non-political role.

The Council

The Council[4] decides whether to pass community legislation after consultation with the European Parliament (see below). It is based in Brussels. It is made up of the representative minister from each member state with domestic responsibility for a particular policy area. In the field of social security the Council consists of the minister for social affairs from each member state. In the UK this is the minister for social security.

Some EC measures require the Council to vote unanimously to pass them before they become law. However, most measures need a 'qualified majority' vote of ministers. This means that ministers cast votes according to the size of their member state. Therefore, the UK has ten votes, whereas the Republic of Ireland, with a much smaller population, has only three votes. Under this system, a proposal needs 62 votes out of 87 to pass, so if the UK wants to block such a proposal, it would need the support of two other large member states, or a number of small member states, to be successful.

The European Parliament

The European Parliament, which is based in Strasbourg, does have some participation in the adoption of EC legislation but its role is very much one of an advisory and supervisory body. Unlike the British Parliament, it cannot pass laws itself, although it can require the Council to consider its representations. Members of the European Parliament are directly elected by people of the member states and sit in political groups reflecting their political opinions rather than their nationalities. For some types of EC law, the European Parliament is only entitled to be consulted, but in many areas, it has the right to a co-decision with the Council. This gives it considerable influence over the final legislation. For example, both Articles 39 and 42 of the EC Treaty give the Parliament 'co-decision' power.

The European Court of Justice

This is the main institution you need to know about for the purposes of this book. There is more information about its procedure on p341. The European Court of Justice (ECJ) is based in Luxembourg. It has responsibility for making sure EC law is observed and applied in the same way throughout the EU. Its decisions are binding on all member states. It should not be confused with the European Court of Human Rights, which operates from Strasburg and hears cases based on the European Convention on Human Rights (see CPAG's *Welfare Benefits Handbook* for more information).

Judgments of the ECJ are brief and do not offer the type of reasoning found in UK judgments, and this can often present difficulties for those seeking to interpret a case.

3. **Using European Community law**

The European Union (EU) is the product of a number of international treaties. The Treaty of Rome (the European Community (EC) Treaty) was the founding treaty and it remains in force today. However, it has been amended by a number of subsequent treaties. The important ones for this book are; the Single European Act 1986, the Treaty of European Union ('Maastricht') 1993 and the Treaty of Amsterdam 1999.

The objects of the EC Treaty as amended include:

- the promotion of economic and social cohesion through the creation of an area without frontiers;
- the prohibition of discrimination on grounds of nationality;
- the introduction of a concept of European citizenship.

Since the UK joined the EU in 1973 the EC's legal system has had an important effect on English law. There are two important principles:

- The supremacy of EC law over domestic law – EC law has higher standing than the law of the member state. If domestic law is not consistent with EC law a court or tribunal should not apply it.[5]
- 'Direct effect' (see below).

'Direct effect' means that EC law forms a part of our national legal system, as if it had been adopted by the UK Parliament. As a result, individuals can claim rights under that law in national courts or tribunals. Not all EC measures have direct effect. In order to have 'direct effect', an EC law must be:

- clear;
- precise; *and*
- unconditional.

The European Court of Justice (ECJ) applies this test generously, with the consequence that many provisions of EC law are directly effective. Most EC law relevant to this book is directly effective.

Purposive interpretation of European Community law

The European legal system and its terminology differ from domestic law. The relationship between EC law and the domestic law of member states is complex. This is inevitable, as EC law has to deal with many different legal systems. There are different principles of interpretation for EC law and UK law. This causes problems as the UK judiciary does not always apply the European principles where appropriate.

Interpretation of European law takes a 'purposive' approach. That means you interpret a legal instrument by establishing its objective. It is therefore important to interpret any EU provisions in the light of the objectives of EC law as a whole.

By contrast, UK law is interpreted by taking the literal meaning of the words and phrases used. Only if this is ambiguous, is the purpose of the legislation examined.

European legislative instruments

Most EC law relevant to social security is in the form of treaty articles or regulations (see below).

Treaties

Treaties are the constitutional framework of the EC and they have a higher status than other EC legislation. The ECJ (see p341) regularly returns to the fundamental principles of the treaties when considering cases. Individual parts of the treaty are divided into Articles.

Regulations

'Regulation' has a different meaning in EC law to that in UK law. In UK law a 'regulation' is secondary legislation made by a minister using powers given by statute. Courts and commissioners can consider the validity of a set of regulations and in some circumstances declare them unlawful and strike them down.

In EC law a 'regulation' is not secondary legislation. It is more like UK primary legislation. It has direct effect and it overrides conflicting domestic legislation. This will be the case even if an EC regulation is in conflict with a UK statute.

Where a regulation is the legal instrument used, it lays down the content of the law itself and it is unnecessary for a member state to legislate in the same field. Therefore, unlike a directive there is no need for a member state to transpose regulations in domestic law.

Directives

A directive is an instrument of EC law which is addressed to the governments of member states. It is akin to an instruction to member states to change the law in a particular area. For example, there is a new race directive that requires member states to remove race discrimination in areas such as access to social security. The directive is binding upon the member state as to the result to be achieved, but it leaves the individual member states with discretion as to how to achieve it.[6] Directives are transposed into domestic law via a statute or statutory instrument (confusingly also called a 'regulation' in the UK). Member states are usually given a period of two years to incorporate the directive into domestic legislation.

The relationship between directives and national law is quite complex. In particular, member states do not always interpret directives accurately. Therefore although a directive has been adopted you may still find some areas that appear to be incompatible with EC law. If there is any doubt it is important to compare the directive with the domestic law to see whether the directive has been properly implemented.

Decisions

Decisions are in some ways similar to directives. It is an individual act designed to be addressed to a specified person(s) or state. A decision does not require any further measures to be taken to implement it. It is a binding act with the force of law. However, it is only binding on the parties to whom it is addressed.[7]

Recommendations

Recommendations and opinions form part of what is known as 'soft law'. They are not binding on anybody, but courts and tribunals should take them into account in reaching their decisions.[8]

---

4. Immigration outline for European Economic Area nationals

UK immigration law is governed by a series of Acts of Parliament,[9] which provides a framework under which secondary legislation, in the form of immigration rules, set out the specific detail.[10] However, these Acts and rules cannot be applied to people entitled to rely on rights of entry and residence in the UK under European Community (EC) law.[11]

If you have a right to enter and live in the UK under EC law, you cannot be prevented from doing so by national law. Three categories of people have rights of entry, residence and to engage in economic activities in the UK as a result of EC law. They are:

• European Union (EU)/European Economic Area (EEA) nationals;

Chapter 24: European Community social security law: introduction
5. The two routes for claiming social security benefits

24

- family members, *of any nationality*, of EU/EEA nationals;
- nationals of states outside the EU/EEA to whom rights are granted by agreements between their state and the EU/EEA (see Part 5).

If EC law gives you a right to enter and reside in the UK, national law cannot affect that right by requiring, for instance, that you ask for permission to enter the UK or to reside here.[12] However, you can be required to let the UK authorities know that you have taken up residence here. If you are exercising your EC rights you are able to enter and reside in another member state freely. You are not admitted subject to a period of leave and consequently you can remain in that state for as long as you choose. These rights apply equally to your family whatever their nationality. For example, an EEA national who is married to a Nigerian citizen will not have to get entry clearance for her/his spouse. S/he does not have to fulfil the UK immigration conditions for a spouse and s/he will not be given limited leave. This applies to all EEA nationals, including UK nationals. However, in order for a UK national to bring in a spouse avoiding UK immigration rules the UK national must first engage EC law. S/he will, therefore, need to have moved within the EEA exercising EC rights.

Your right of residence in the UK can only come to an end if you cease to qualify under EC law, or your personal activities constitute a threat to public policy, public security or public health.[13] You cannot be removed for claiming benefits. If the UK authorities wish to expel you from the UK, you are entitled to a right of appeal against that decision.[14]

5. **The two routes for claiming social security benefits**

Freedom of movement

It is a fundamental principle of European Community (EC) social security law that nationals of member states should be able to move freely from one member state to another in order to seek work. The right to mobility is not absolute, but is generally confined to economically active groups. If you are a citizen of a European Economic Area (EEA) member state you and your dependants will have rights under EC law, and therefore under UK law to enter and reside in the UK.

EC law does not set out to make social security provisions the same in each member state. The national systems and standards of living are too different for that to be feasible. Instead EC law aims to ensure there is continuity of social protection for people who move between member states. Although the objective is clear, often the law is not.

The legislation which sets out these principles is as follows.

24

Chapter 24: European Community social security law: introduction
5. The two routes for claiming social security benefits

- Article 39 of the EC Treaty. This gives workers a right to free movement between member states.
- Article 43 of the EC Treaty. This gives the self-employed a right to 'freedom of establishment'.

The aim of the Treaty is to achieve economic as well as social integration, and the rules are based on the general rule against discrimination in Article 12:

'Within the scope of application of this Treaty, and without prejudice to any social provision contained therein, any discrimination on grounds of nationality shall be prohibited.'

EC law recognises that there is more to removing barriers to free movement than the abolition of immigration controls. The objective of free movement would in practice be frustrated if a migrant were to lose out on social security benefits guaranteed under the law of a member state.

Examples

A British woman may be deterred from taking up a job in France if she cannot rely on national insurance contributions made in both countries when she comes to receive her pension, whether she returns to England, or retires in France.

An Italian man may decide not to seek work in the UK if he cannot get child benefit for children living in Italy.

The two methods developed under EC law designed to overcome social barriers to freedom of movement are:

The co-ordination rule: Regulation 1408/71

The rules to co-ordinate social security under EC law are mainly set out in Regulation 1408/71, although this must be read together with EC Regulation 574/72 which implemented it. The provisions are intended to co-ordinate the social security systems of member states so that neither workers nor their families lose out on social security protection by moving within the European Union (EU) or EEA.

The social advantage rule: Regulation 1612/68

This rule was developed under the freedom of movement provisions of EC law. The aim is to ensure that certain people moving from one member state to another are not financially disadvantaged as a result, and that they acquire the same rights of access to social security and social assistance as citizens of the host state. In other words, after moving they should have access to the same 'social advantages' which they receive in their state of residence as citizens of that state.

Chapter 24: European Community social security law: introduction
5. The two routes for claiming social security benefits

24

Unlike the co-ordination provisions Regulation 1612/68 does not even mention social security. Its connection with social security is that a 'social advantage' includes social security benefits. This brief reference in the regulation to social advantage means that unlike the co-ordination provisions there are no specific benefits mentioned and there are no detailed rules as to how to apply the social advantage rule.[15]

Deciding which rule to use

The social advantage rule and the co-ordination rule both have the same objectives: to make it easier for workers to move freely from member state to member state. But the **personal scope** (the range of people covered) and the **material scope** (the range of benefits covered) are not the same, although they may overlap.

This means that some groups of people come within the personal scope of Regulation 1408/71, but not within the personal scope of Regulation 1612/68, or *vice versa*. Some people come within the personal scope of both Regulations. Similarly, the European Court of Justice (ECJ) has said that some benefits, such as a benefit for the support of young work-seekers, are within the scope of both the social advantages and co-ordination rules. Other benefits may come within the scope of one or neither of the rules.

The route you choose will depend on which benefit is involved and what you want to achieve. For example in the *O'Flynn* case,[16] it was successfully argued that restricting funeral payments to funerals within the UK was contrary to EC law. This case was argued using the social advantage rule, because the social fund is not within the material scope of EC Regulation 1408/71. Equally neither housing benefit nor council tax benefit are covered by the co-ordination rule but they would be considered to be a social advantage (see Chapter 25). On the other hand if you want to take a benefit abroad, you would have to rely on the co-ordination rule (see Chapter 26). The following questions should establish which route you should follow.

- Do I come within the personal scope of the co-ordination rule?
- Does this benefit come within the material scope of the co-ordination rule?
- Can the co-ordination rule help?
- Do I come within the personal scope of the social advantage rule?
- Does this benefit come within the material scope of the social advantage rule?
- Can the social advantage rule help?

6. Remedies

Appeal tribunals and social security commissioners

Remedies

If a person believes that s/he has rights under European Community (EC) law s/he can assert those rights in the appropriate tribunal or court. A social security claimant should raise the matter with the DWP when making a claim or when s/he receives a decision by the DWP. EC law binds UK courts and tribunals, it also binds the DWP. This means that you can rely on EC law in applications for revisions and supersessions and in appeals to tribunals and social security commissioners in the same way as you would use UK law. See CPAG's *Welfare Benefits Handbook* for details of how to challenge social security decisions.

It is an error of law for a tribunal to fail to address a point of European law raised in the course of an appeal.[17] If a case involves a European Economic Area (EEA) national the tribunal should make enquiries to determine whether that person can be assisted by EC law.[18]

The claimant can ask the tribunal or commissioner to refer the matter to the European Court of Justice (ECJ) (see p341) but should seek specialist help before doing so. Legal help (formerly legal aid) is available for references to the ECJ if legal assistance would have been available before the domestic court or tribunal. Although it is possible to refer cases to the ECJ from a tribunal it is probably more sensible to refer matters from the commissioner or higher courts.[19]

In some very limited circumstances national time limits in which to lodge an appeal or to bring a judicial review do not apply as they may act as a bar to you asserting EC rights. The circumstances in which this would apply is when a member state has not fully transposed a directive into domestic legislation.[20] The time limit runs only from the time the directive is fully transposed. This would not apply to EC regulations which do not require transposing legislation by the member state. Furthermore, a national limit which restricts the backdating of benefit is not contrary to EC law.[21]

Legal help

Legal help is available for assistance with preparation for tribunals and commissioners' appeals. Public funding for representation is not generally available for hearings before tribunals and commissioners. However, solicitors with contracts for welfare benefits can get public funding for representation for claimants under section 6(8)(b) Access to Justice Act.[22] This gives the Lord Chancellor discretion to award public funding for representation in proceedings which are otherwise excluded. You have to show in addition to the usual tests, that legal representation is the only adequate way of establishing the facts and presenting the case.

The European Court of Justice

How cases get to the court

The ECJ has the power to make preliminary rulings concerning:

* interpretation; *and*
* validity.

Actions in the ECJ refer to questions on the interpretation or validity of EC law only. The ECJ has no power to interpret national legislation. Some are direct actions – eg, an action brought by the Commission against a member state for failure to fulfil a Treaty obligation[23] or an action brought by one member state against another.[24]

More significantly for this book, the other way in which cases reach the ECJ is on a reference from a national court under Article 234 of the EC Treaty. Where a question of interpretation of EC law arises in any court or tribunal of a member state, that court or tribunal may request a ruling on that question if it considers that a decision on the question is necessary to enable it to give judgment.

A reference under Article 234 is not an appeal. It merely provides a means for national courts to obtain a ruling on the interpretation of an EC provision. The national court then applies the ruling to national law and decides the case itself.

A reference can be made by any 'court or tribunal' which would clearly include both social security commissioners and tribunals, and the domestic proceedings are then adjourned pending the outcome of the reference.

There is no absolute right to have your case referred to the ECJ unless you have no further judicial remedy. A final court of appeal must make a reference in relation to a question of EC law. In the UK, this is generally taken to mean the House of Lords. However, there is some authority to suggest that if leave to appeal cannot be obtained by a higher court that a reference should be made by the lower court or tribunal.[25] Once judgment has been given by the ECJ, the member state must act to give effect to it.[26]

There is also no right to a reference to the ECJ if the matter is *'acte clair'*.[27] This means that if a provision is clear, for example because the ECJ has already ruled on the question, there is no need for the court to refer.

The ECJ has held[28] that it is *not* necessary for a national court to make a reference if:

* the question of EC law is irrelevant; *or*
* the provision has already been interpreted by the Court of Justice; *or*
* the correct application is so obvious as to leave no room for doubt.

The Court of Appeal[29] has also ruled on this issue. The Court held that a reference would not be necessary if the Court of Justice had already ruled on the question, or the matter was reasonably clear and free from doubt.

Individuals cannot apply to the ECJ direct. You can ask a tribunal or commissioner to refer a question to the ECJ, but you should seek specialist advice before doing so. In view of the complexity of the law it may be more sensible to seek a referral from a commissioner than from a tribunal.

The procedure

The UK court, commissioner or tribunal drafts the question and submits it to the ECJ. It is then served on the parties, who have two months to make written submissions. There is usually an oral hearing.

The UK proceedings are adjourned pending the outcome of the reference. The ECJ often takes a very long time to give its judgments so a reference is likely to cause a considerable delay. It may be appropriate to ask the DWP to make interim payments while awaiting a decision.[30]

The advocate general's opinion

The judges of the Court are assisted by nine advocate generals (AG). The AG's are not judges but they do have something of a judicial function. Once all the parties to a case have made their submissions and before the judges consider the case the AG gives an opinion. The AG's opinion offers an analysis of the legal position, much more akin to a UK judgment, and thus reading the AG's opinion often illuminates the reasoning of the ECJ. However, the opinion is not binding and it may or may not be followed by the ECJ. Where the ECJ choose not to follow the opinion, which happens increasingly in social security law, the applicants and their advisers are often left somewhat bemused as to how the ECJ arrived at its decision.[31] The AG's opinion is given to all parties to the proceedings and is published in the *Official Journal*.

The judgment and after

Once the judgment has been given, the member state must act to give effect to it, if necessary. The UK proceedings will be re-listed for hearing in the light of the judgment.

Damages

If a member state breaches EC law by denying an individual rights to which s/he is entitled under EC rules, it may be liable to pay damages. In order to claim damages in such cases, the individual must show three things. First, the EC law at issue must have intended to confer rights on individuals. Second, there must be a link between the damage, which the person suffered, and the breach of EC law by the member state. Finally, the breach must have been 'sufficiently serious'. The ECJ can award damages if the following can be shown:

- the EC law at issue intended to confer rights on individuals; *and*
- there is a link between the damage the person suffered and the breach of EC law by the member state; *and*
- the breach was 'sufficiently serious'.

In other words, not every breach of EC law by a member state will give individuals the right to claim damages. If a member state was diligent about attempting to apply EC law correctly it will not be liable.[32]

The precise scope of this doctrine has not yet been worked out but it has recently been held that damages can only be awarded where the state's failure was 'manifest and serious'.[33]

Costs and legal help

Generally legal help (formerly legal aid) is available if it would have been available for proceedings before the domestic courts. This includes the High Court, Court of Appeal, the House of Lords and some cases before the commissioners and tribunals.[34] The ECJ does not rule on costs. The ECJ can grant legal help itself where a party is unable to meet all or part of the costs of the case.

Notes

1. **Who needs to use this section**
   1 EEA nationals have the right to enter another member state under EC Reg 1612/68 and have the right to bring members of their family with them. They are not subject to any periods of limited leave and therefore do not fall within the UK definition of 'person subject to immigration control' as set out in s115 IAA 1999. Furthermore the spouse of an EEA national does not lose EC law rights simply because they separate. See *Diatta*. Case C–267/83.
   2 Art 227(1) of the Treaty. For a full list of countries covered see para 070040 DMG

2. **The foundations of the EU**
   3 Art 155-163 EC Treaty
   4 Arts 145-154 EC Treaty
   5 *Costa v ENEL* [1964] ECR 585; *Administrazione della Finanze delle State v Simmenthal* [1978] ECR 629
   6 Art 189 EC Treaty
   7 Art 189 EC Treaty
   8 *Grimaldi v Fonds de maladies Professionelles* [1989] ECR 4407; see *Wadman v Carpenter Farrer Partnership* [1993] IRLR 374

4. **Immigration outline for EEA nationals**
   9 IA 1971; Immigration (Carriers' Liability) Act 1987; IA 1988; AIAA 1993; AIA 1996
   10 The principle rules are found in HC 395 (the last complete statement of the immigration rules, 23 May 1994)
   11 s2 European Communities Act 1972
   12 C-157/79 *Pieck* [1981] ECR 21711, [1980] 3 CMLR 378
   13 Arts 39(3) and 56 Treaty of Rome
   14 Art 15 I(EEA)O; Art 8 Dir 64/221

5. **The two routes for claiming social security benefits**
   15 Most of the definitions and rules relating to social advantage come from caselaw. For example the definition of worker in *Lair* Case C-39/86 and entitlement to social advantage in *Lebon* Case C-316/85
   16 Case C–237/94 *O'Flynn v Chief Adjudication Officer*

6. **Remedies**
   17 R(SB) 6/91 and R(S) 2/93
   18 CIS/771/1997

19 Traditionally legal aid has been excluded
from representation before the
commissioners and tribunals. However,
it was successfully argued in CF/3662/
1999 that the Lord Chancellor did have
the power to award legal aid under
s6(8)(b) of the Access to Justice Act. This
has now happened several times. In
theory it should also be possible to
secure legal aid for a hearing before a
tribunal.

20 Case C-208/90 *Emmott*

21 Cases C-410/92 *Johnson* and Case C–
338/91 *Steenhorst-Neerings*

22 See note 19

23 Art 169 EC Treaty

24 Art 170 EC Treaty

25 *Hagen v Fratelli* [1980] 3 CMLR 253

26 Arts 5 and 170 EC Treaty

27 *Acte clair* is a doctrine originating in
French administrative law, whereby if
the meaning of a provision is clear no
'question' of interpretation arises. It was
first introduced into EC law by the
Advocate General in Cases C-28/30/62
Van Gend en Loos. It was later applied in
CILFIT /srl Case C-283/81.

28 *CILFIT /srl* Case C-283/81

29 Lord Denning in *Bulmer Ltd v Bollinger SA*
[1974] Court of Appeal see also *R v ILEA
(ex parte Hinde)* [1985] 1 CMLR 716

30 There is a general view that interim
payments should be available pending
EC cases but the DWP is rarely asked to
do so. A refusal may be challengeable by
judicial review but you should seek
specialist advice before proceeding.

31 See for example, *Graham* Case C-92/94
involving discrimination in invalidity
benefit.

32 *Francovich v Italian State* [1993] 2 CMLR
66; [1991] ECR I 5357; [1992] IRLR 84

33 *R v HM Treasury ex parte British
Telecommunications plc* [1996] 3 WLR
203; *Brasserie du Pecheurs SA v Federal
Republic of Germany* [1996] QBD 404;
[1996] 2 WLR 506

34 See note 19

Chapter 25

••

The co-ordination of social security: general rules and principles

This chapter covers:
1. The legal basis for the co-ordination of social security (below)
2. The personal scope of Regulation 1408/71 (p346)
3. The material scope of Regulation 1408/71 (p349)
4. The single state principle (p353)
5. The principle of non-discrimination (p355)
6. The principle of aggregation and apportionment (p356)
7. The principle of exportability (p357)
8. Overlapping benefits (p357)

1. The legal basis for the co-ordination of social security

The co-ordination rules secure and promote freedom of movement by co-ordinating the many different social security schemes within the European Economic Area (EEA). The intention is that people should not lose out on social security protection simply because they move to another member state.

The legal basis for the co-ordination of social security can be found both in Treaty Articles and Regulations. It stems from the following fundamental principle as set out in Article 39 of the Treaty.

- Freedom of movement for workers shall be secured within the Community.
- Such freedom of movement shall entail the abolition of any discrimination based on nationality between workers of the member states as regards employment, remuneration and other conditions of work and employment.

Article 42 of the Treaty is designed to secure the following safeguards for migrant workers and their dependants:

25

Chapter 25: The co-ordination of social security: general rules and principles
1. The legal basis for the co-ordination of social security

- the aggregation of all qualifying periods taken into account under the laws of the different countries, for the purpose of acquiring, retaining and calculating benefit entitlement; *and*
- payment of benefits to people resident in the territories of member states other than their state of origin.

The mechanism adopted by the European Community (EC) to achieve this is Council Regulation (EEC) 1408/71.[1] However, this regulation has to be read together with EC Regulation 574/72, which sets out the procedure for implementing EC Regulation 1408/71. The regulations are divided into three parts:
- the general rules applying to all benefits;
- the applicable law – eg, which member state is responsible for paying you benefit;
- the special rules for each individual category of benefit.

The precise rights of people, under the co-ordination rule, vary according to the status of the particular claimant and according to the benefit claimed. It is therefore important to check the individual rules for each category of benefit. These are covered in Chapter 26. However, there are general principles that apply. In particular the regulations have four main principles:
- the single state (see p353);
- non-discrimination (see p355);
- aggregation and apportionment (p356);
- exportability (see p357).

2. The personal scope of Regulation 1408/71

The term **'personal scope'** relates to who can rely on the Regulation. You fall within the personal scope of the Regulation if you are an employed or self-employed person who is, or has been, subject to the legislation of one or more member states and:
- you are a national of one of the member states; *or*
- you are a refugee; *or*
- you are a stateless person; *or*
- you are a family member or a survivor of an European Economic Area (EEA) national, a refugee or a stateless person who has been employed or self-employed.

Chapter 25: The co-ordination of social security: general rules and principles
2. The personal scope of EC Regulation 1408/71

25

Insured people

The concept of an employed or self-employed person for European Community (EC) social security purposes has an EC law meaning which overrides any definition in the national legislation.[2] An employed or self-employed person is defined as:

> 'any person who is insured compulsorily or on an optional basis, for one or more of the contingencies covered by the branches of a social security scheme for employed or self-employed persons'.[3]

The personal scope of Regulation 1408/71 is therefore defined in relation to people insured under national legislation rather than in relation to the definitions of free movement. The term 'worker' is not used in this Regulation and indeed the European Court of Justice (ECJ) has ruled that the two terms are not the same.[4]

You are included under this definition if:

- you are currently paying national insurance contributions; *or*
- you ought to be paying national insurance contributions (because you fulfil the statutory criteria) even if your contributions have not in fact been paid;[5]*or*
- you have, in the past, been insured under the relevant scheme of insurance;[6]*or*
- you have worked but are no longer economically active;[7]*or*
- you are a student[8] who has previously been subject to the legislation of at least one member state.[9]

If you are a part-time worker you will still be covered under the co-ordination rule, no matter how much or how little time you devote to your activities.[10] However, you must still satisfy the insurance definition (see above). If you earn less than the lower earnings limit, then you are probably not covered.[11]

Family members of an insured person

The definitions of **'family member'** are slightly different under the co-ordination rule and the ' rule. Under the social advantage rule, for example, children are considered to be children until the age of 21 rather than 18 as with UK law. Equally under the social advantage rule your 'partner' generally means your spouse. Under the co-ordination rule a member of the family is any person defined or designated as a member of the household by the legislation under which benefits are provided. This means that the decision as to whether or not you count as the family member of an insured person is largely a matter of national law. Under UK law, you are a 'member of the family' if you are a dependant.[12] This would include unmarried couples and children up to the age of 18 for whom you are treated as responsible. UK rules define the family as largely being those who are members of your household. However, EC law specifically allows for a family member to be included under the co-ordination rule even if

25

Chapter 25: The co-ordination of social security: general rules and principles
2. The personal scope of EC Regulation 1408/71

s/he is not living in your household as long as they are mainly dependent on you.[13]

The rights that you gain as a family member are often referred to, particularly by the DWP, as 'derived rights'.[14] Until recently, EC law drew a clear distinction between those rights which you could obtain yourself as an insured person under the co-ordination rule and the more limited rights which could be claimed as derived rights. However, a recent decision of the European Court of Justice (ECJ) suggests that the scope of derived rights may be interpreted broadly, and in favour of claimants. The reasoning for this is that an insured person is likely to also be a worker because the social security entitlement of a 'worker's' family under the co-ordination rule is a social advantage.[15] It seems that earlier decisions, which distinguished between the rights of the insured person and the rights of members of their families and survivors, are now limited to the aggregation and co-ordination rules relating to unemployment benefits[16] and that, in respect of all other social security benefits, family members and survivors of workers can benefit from the co-ordination rule on the same terms as workers themselves.

As a family member you can retain your derived rights even when you are not living permanently with the worker.[17] You only lose your EC rights if you divorce.

Survivors

You are defined as a **'survivor'** if you are a survivor in national law – eg, in the UK, a widow or widower is a survivor. Note that this is subject to the same proviso that you can be a dependant, and do not have to have been living under the same roof as the worker.[18] As a survivor you retain rights under the co-ordination rule when your spouse dies.

Refugees

A refugee is defined in Article 1(d) of the Regulation as being a person who is a refugee under Article 1 of the Convention on the Status of Refugees, signed at Geneva on 28 July 1951. This means a person who is unwilling or unable to return to the country of her/his nationality or former habitual residence because of a well-founded fear of persecution on specified grounds. It has been established that a person is a refugee within the meaning of the 1951 Refugee Convention as soon as s/he fulfils the criteria contained in the definition.[19] This would necessarily occur prior to the time at which her/his refugee status is formally determined. In other words a person is a refugee from the point s/he claims to have grounds for asylum not from the point that the Home Office grants her/him refugee status.

In theory, therefore, an asylum seeker who has worked in the UK can argue that current legislation which excludes asylum seekers from benefit are in breach of the equal treatment provision in Regulation 1408/71. A number of challenges have been made relying on this approach; as yet none have been successful.[20] (Although some asylum seekers have successfully claimed benefit under the EC association agreements – see p418.) The Court of Appeal rejected the argument

Chapter 25: The co-ordination of social security: general rules and principles
3. The material scope of Regulation 1408/71

25

on the basis that EC Regulation 1408/71 only comes into play once there has been some movement between member states.[21] Such an approach is odd because refugees do not have rights of free movement. The reasoning by the Court of Appeal would, therefore, mean that the Regulation would rarely apply to refugees. Since that decision a number of similar cases have arisen in Germany and the German courts have chosen to refer the cases to the ECJ.[22] In the light of these references two further cases were brought to the social security commissioner with a view to a reference to the ECJ. The commissioner chose not to refer the UK cases even though the German cases do not address all the relevant questions for UK benefits. The ECJ has recently decided these cases and held that in order for a refugee to rely on EC Regulation 1408/71 s/he must have moved with the European Economic Area (EEA).[23]

Applying the existing caselaw a refugee or an asylum seeker who has moved within the EEA should be able to rely on EC Regulation 1408/71 to override the UK exclusions from benefit. They must have worked in at least one EEA member state.

Stateless persons

A stateless person is someone who does not have any nationality.

3. **The material scope of Regulation 1408/71**

The 'material scope' of the Regulation refers to the matters covered or the range of benefits that are within its scope. Individual social security benefits are not directly referred to. Instead the Regulation refers to any social security designed to protect against certain risks. The risks are listed in Article 4(1) of the Regulation as those for:
- sickness and maternity benefits;
- invalidity benefits;
- old age benefits;
- survivors' benefits;
- benefits for accidents at work and occupational diseases;
- death grants;
- unemployment benefits;
- family benefits.[24]

In addition, the regulation specifies that 'special non-contributory benefits' are within the scope of the Regulation if they are intended either:
- to provide supplementary, substitute or ancillary cover against the risks above;
  or
- solely as specific protection for the disabled.

25

Chapter 25: The co-ordination of social security: general rules and principles
3. The material scope of Regulation 1408/71

The Regulation specifically excludes from its scope 'social assistance'.

Therefore EC Regulation 1408/71 categorises benefits into one of three groups. These are:

- social security;
- special non-contributory benefits;
- social and medical assistance.

It is important to establish which category a particular benefit falls within because your rights under the Regulation vary according to this. For a detailed list of which benefits fall within each category, see Chapter 26.

Social security benefits

Social security benefits are those benefits from each member state provided for the risks listed above. It does not matter whether these benefits are created under a general or a special social security scheme, nor whether the scheme under which they arise is contributory or non-contributory.[25] The co-ordination rule also applies to schemes where employers are liable to pay benefit.[26] Therefore schemes such as statutory maternity pay and statutory sick pay fall under the scope of the Regulation and are social security. Equally working families' tax credit (WFTC) and disabled person's tax credit which are administered by the Inland Revenue but essentially remain social security within the scope of the Regulation.

Special non-contributory benefits

Since 1992, the co-ordination rule also covers a new category of benefits described as special non-contributory benefits. These are benefits provided under legislation or schemes other than those provided in Article 4(1) where such benefits are intended:

- to provide supplementary, substitute or ancillary cover to the risks catered for by the branches of social security; *or*
- solely as specific protection for the disabled.[27]

The main distinction between special non-contributory benefits and social security benefits listed under Article 4(1) is that special non-contributory benefits cannot be exported.

Social and medical assistance

The categories of risks listed as being covered by social security benefits and special non-contributory benefits[28] are exhaustive. Any branch of social security not mentioned in the list is not covered by the co-ordination rule.[29] In addition, the co-ordination rule is specifically said not to apply to:

- social and medical assistance;
- benefit schemes for victims of war or its consequences;
- special schemes for civil servants or persons treated as such.[30]

Chapter 25: The co-ordination of social security: general rules and principles
3. The material scope of Regulation 1408/71

25

In the past the European Court of Justice (ECJ) has ruled that benefits such as income support are social assistance and not covered by European Community (EC) rules.

How to distinguish between benefits

Working out whether a particular type of benefit is 'social security', 'social assistance' or a 'special non-contributory benefit' is an important exercise because establishing the right category enables you to work out whether, and how the co-ordination rule applies to it.

The category into which a benefit falls depends upon factors relating to each benefit, in particular its purpose and the conditions for eligibility,[31] rather than whether or not it is described as 'social security' by the national legal system.[32]

Under EC law, a social security benefit is one which confers upon an individual a legally defined position entitling her/him to benefits in particular circumstances without any individual or discretionary assessment.[33] By contrast social assistance is a benefit or measure which makes the claimant's need one of the essential criteria for eligibility. It is usually a means-tested benefit rather than one where entitlement is linked to a particular risk.

The ECJ used to struggle with what it called 'hybrid' benefits which are those with the characteristics both of social security (ie, giving a legally defined right in the event of a defined risk occurring), and social assistance (ie, being generally available to the population as a whole provided they satisfy the 'need' criterion). However, it often tended to offer a generous interpretation to the term social security and held such hybrid benefits to be social security. For example, the ECJ had ruled that attendance allowance (AA) and mobility allowance (the predecessor to disability living allowance (DLA)) were invalidity benefits for the purpose of Regulation 1408/71.[34]

The introduction of the category of 'special non-contributory benefits' was a response to the difficulties of the Court. This is reflected in subsequent caselaw from the ECJ which held that AA and DLA are no longer invalidity benefits but fall within the category of special non-contributory benefits (see p350).

Member states' declarations

Each member state is required to list the benefits it considers to be social security benefits and those which are treated as special non-contributory benefits.[35] They do this in special declarations which you can find in the *Compendium of European Social Security Law* and as an annex to Regulation 1408/71.[36] The ECJ has held that if a member state has listed a benefit as social security, then you are entitled to rely on the declaration to prove that the benefit is social security and, therefore, comes under the co-ordination rule.[37] However, the declarations are increasingly of little practical help because they are not updated. They contain references to

25

Chapter 25: The co-ordination of social security: general rules and principles
3. The material scope of Regulation 1408/71

out-of-date legislation and do not take account of changes to EC social security law.

For example some benefits that are listed by the UK Government as social security benefits are now also listed by the UK as special non-contributory benefits. The ECJ has considered the position for such benefits in two cases, one for AA the other for DLA, and has held that since 1992 these benefits are special non-contributory benefits and thus non-exportable.[38]

The ECJ held that the listing of AA and DLA in Annex IIa of the Regulation must be accepted as establishing that the benefits were special non-contributory benefits. The fact that the UK had not removed these benefits from its declaration on social security benefits did not prejudice this position. This is something of a bizarre judgment as it effectively allows a member state to change an EC regulation. The judgments may also have consequences for income-based jobseeker's allowance (JSA) and for WFTC.

The UK Government considers income-based JSA to be a special non-contributory benefit rather than social security. However, applying EC criteria it is difficult to see that it could be anything other than an unemployment benefit under Article 4(1) and consequently social security. Indeed a commissioner and the Court of Appeal have held that for EC purposes income-based JSA is an unemployment benefit.[39] For working families tax credit the position is slightly different. Family credit, the predecessor to WFTC is listed as a special non-contributory benefit but there is caselaw establishing that family credit is a family benefit and therefore social security. The declaration has not been updated to include WFTC. However, WFTC is in rather a unique position in that it is not a new benefit but simply family credit renamed.[40] Therefore, the rules and caselaw relating to family credit should be applied to WFTC. The current DWP position is to continue to treat WFTC as though it were a family benefit. Yet this would appear to be inconsistent with its position on AA and DLA and with the subsequent decisions of the ECJ.

If a benefit is not listed in the declaration as social security it does not necessarily mean that it is not covered. The ECJ may treat it as such if, in fact, it has the characteristics of a social security benefit.[41]

How a benefit is characterised is a matter of law, which can only finally be resolved in cases of dispute by the ECJ.[42] In practice, the DWP is not likely to treat a benefit as social security unless it is in the UK declaration, so if you want to use the co-ordination rule to claim a benefit which might be treated as social security, but could also be a hybrid benefit, or social assistance, you should take legal advice.

4. **The single state principle**

The Regulation specifies that a person is subject to the legislation of a single member state only.[43] This is called the '*lex laboris*' rule. This means that you pay contributions and you claim benefits from only one member state. The general rule[44] is that the state responsible for you is the state in which you last worked. The state that is responsible for you is called the **'competent state'**. It should be remembered that this is a general rule and there are many exceptions to the rule. The competent state's social security institution is the competent institution. The DWP is the UK's primary competent institution. You can only qualify for UK social security benefits under the co-ordination rule if the UK is the competent state.

Therefore, if you last worked in Germany and have just arrived in the UK to look for work, Germany is the competent state and the German social security department will be the competent institution responsible for paying you benefit, even though you will be required to sign on in the UK. However, if you subsequently work in the UK the competent state becomes the UK and the competent institution the DWP. You are normally subject to the legislation of the state in which you work even if you live in another member state.[45]

In some circumstances you may be subject to the legislation of more than one member state. This only arises if you are simultaneously employed in one European Economic Area (EEA) state and self-employed in another.[46]

However this would arise only rarely and in general in order to avoid duplication of benefits, only one state can be the competent state.

Exceptions to the rule that you are subject to the legislation of the state in which you last worked

The regulation contains specific situations where you will not be subject to the legislation of the member state where you last worked. These are as follows:

- You work temporarily in another European Union (EU)/EEA member state for a UK employer.
  - If the company that employs you sends you to work in another EU/EEA member state for less than a year, then you will remain subject to the legislation of the original member state. However, if you are replacing another employee whose period of posting is ending, you will be subject to the legislation of that member state.[47]
  - If you are being sent to another EEA member state from the UK to work for less than a year, you should get form E101 from the DWP before you go abroad. This certifies that you remain covered by UK legislation. If the job is extended for up to a year due to unforeseen circumstances, then you can apply for an extension using form E102. Your employer must apply for this extension before the end of the first 12-month period.[48]

- You are temporarily self-employed in another EU/EEA member state.
  - The same rules apply if you are self-employed and go to work in another EEA member state for less than 12 months.[49] If you go from the UK to take up temporary self-employment in another member state you will pay self-employed earner's contributions (Class 2 and 4) as if you were still in the UK. You will not have to contribute to the other member state's insurance scheme.[50]
  - You will normally be accepted as self-employed if you have been self-employed for at least 12 weeks during the last two tax years or since then, although it may be possible to classify you as self-employed even if you do not fully meet this condition. To clarify the position you should contact the Inland Revenue Contributions Office.
  - People working in the German construction industry have, in the past, experienced difficulties when registering as self-employed in Germany. If you go to work in the construction industry in Germany you must register at the local office of the Chamber of Handicrafts (Handwerkskammer) taking your form E101 with you. In order to register with the Handwerkskammer, you will need to prove that you are qualified in your trade. You must provide a 'certificate of experience' which you can obtain from the British Chamber of Commerce. If you do not register with the Handwerkskammer, you are not allowed to be self-employed in Germany.
- You are employed in two or more EU/EEA member states.[51] If you are employed in two or more EU/EEA member states, unless you are an international transport worker (see below), you will be insured under the UK scheme if:
  - you normally live in the UK, and the UK is one of the EU/EEA member states you work in; *or*
  - you work for several companies that are based in different EU/EEA member states; *or*
  - you do not normally live in any EU/EEA member state that you work in but your employer is based in the UK.
- If when you start work you are sent abroad immediately by an employer or agency, you will usually carry on paying UK national insurance contributions.
- If you are taken on while abroad you will normally be insured under that member state's scheme.

However, there are special rules if an agency hires you to work for a client in the Netherlands or Germany. You may have to pay UK national insurance contributions for up to nine months if you are in Germany and six months if you are in the Netherlands. After this period you will be insured in the member state in which you are working. Your employer needs to get form E101 to inform the social security authority in the other member state that you will remain insured in the UK, and then form CZ3822 to inform the UK Contributions Office.

Chapter 25: The co-ordination of social security: general rules and principles
5. The principle of non-discrimination

25

International transport workers

If you are an international transport worker and work in two or more member states, you will be insured under the UK scheme if:

- your employer's registered office is in the UK; *or*
- your employer's registered office is in another EU/EEA member state and you work for a branch office in the UK; *or*
- you live in the UK and work mainly in the UK even if your employer does not have an office here.

If none of the above applies, you are insured under the scheme of the EU/EEA member state where your employer has its main office.

Special arrangements

In some circumstances, it may be to your advantage to remain insured in the UK even if you are working in another member state.[52] If so, the UK Contributions Office and its counterpart in the other member state must agree to this. You should write to the Contributions Office to find out about your position.

Special rules also apply to mariners, civil servants, diplomatic or consular staff and people called up for service in the armed forces. You should get advice from the appropriate authority – the Contributions Office in the UK.

5. **The principle of non-discrimination**

If you are covered by the co-ordination rule, you are entitled to enjoy the same benefits under the legislation of the competent state as a national of that state. This is often referred to as the equal treatment provisions. The principle of non-discrimination prohibits any form of discrimination, direct or indirect, based on your nationality. Direct discrimination arises when one person is treated less favourably than another. Indirect forms of discrimination are not so easy to identify but arise in rules which, although apparently neutral and non-discriminatory, have, in practice, a greater adverse impact on those who are not nationals of the competent state. For example, the habitual residence test in UK law (see p135) would appear to be a rule, which applies equally to all European Economic Area (EEA) nationals. However, British and Irish citizens are far more likely to satisfy the test than other EEA nationals. Therefore the rule could be indirectly discriminatory.

The non-discrimination principle has been used to extend the rights of EU/EEA claimants and their families in relation to widows' rights,[53] disabled people's allowances,[54] allowances for large families[55] and non-contributory old age allowances.[56]

25

Chapter 25: The co-ordination of social security: general rules and principles
6. The principle of aggregation and apportionment

6. The principle of aggregation and apportionment

Aggregation and apportionment of insurance periods for the purpose of acquiring and calculating entitlement to benefit are key co-ordinating mechanisms.

Aggregation

Aggregation means adding together periods of contributions, residence or employment in all the member states in which you have lived or worked. This may be necessary if the acquisition, retention or recovery of benefits is conditional upon completion of periods of residence, employment or insurance. What constitutes a period of residence, employment or insurance is determined by the legislation of the member state in which it took place.[57]

The principle is that you should not lose out if you choose to exercise your rights to move within the European Economic Area (EEA). If you were to be at a disadvantage should you need to claim benefit this may deter you from moving. The principle of aggregation effectively lifts internal borders within the EEA in respect of residence and contribution conditions. Therefore, if necessary, you should be entitled to benefits on the basis of all of the contributions that you have made to all of the social security schemes in any member states in which you have been insured. Furthermore, it provides that, where necessary, periods of residence or employment should be taken into account as if they were completed in the member state in which you are seeking benefit.

For example, a Spanish person who has worked for many years in Spain arrives in the UK and works for two weeks. S/he may rely on the contributions paid in Spain to claim contribution-based benefits such as jobseeker's allowance or incapacity benefit. S/he may also rely on the periods of residence in Spain to meet any residence conditions – eg, for child benefit or disability living allowance. She obviously would still need to satisfy the main conditions for the particular benefit but European Community (EC) rules allow you to overcome territorial limitations in terms of access to and the calculation of benefit.

Aggregation tends to be applied to short-term benefits like unemployment, maternity, sickness and some invalidity benefits. There are no general aggregation provisions. Each type of social security benefit to which aggregation provisions are applied has its own rules and you will need to take account of these when claiming.[58] These are covered in Chapter 26.

Apportionment

Apportionment means that two, or more, European Union (EU)/EEA member states pay a proportion of your benefit. It is a technique used in relation to longer-term entitlements such as old age and survivors' benefits and some other types of invalidity benefits.

Apportionment is often coupled with aggregation. For example, if you have contributed to the state pension scheme in a number of EU/EEA member states, each state must pay a proportion of the rate to which you would have been entitled if you had spent your whole working life in that state. The proportion is calculated by dividing your working life by the length of time actually worked in each member state.

To avoid duplication of benefit entitlement, only the Competent State carries out the aggregation exercise, and you will only receive a pro rata amount of any aggregated benefit.[59]

7. The principle of exportability

The aim behind the principle of exportability is to abolish residence and presence conditions which may restrict entitlements to benefit, and to enable people to export certain social security benefits when they cease to be resident in the member state where the entitlement arose.

The portability mechanism means that, except where the co-ordination rule specifically provides otherwise, certain benefits may not be reduced, modified, suspended, withdrawn or confiscated just because you go to live in a different member state.[60] Not all benefits that fall under Regulation 1408/71 can be exported. The principle of exportability only applies to:

- invalidity benefits;
- old age benefits;
- survivors' cash benefits;
- pensions for accidents at work or occupational diseases;
- death grants.

Unemployment, sickness and maternity benefits can only be exported to a limited extent. You cannot export special non-contributory benefits; they are paid only in the state that you are resident.[61] Family benefits cannot be exported but you can claim family benefits for family members who are living apart from you in another European Union/European Economic Area member state. The rules on exporting benefits vary according to the benefit concerned and are covered in Chapter 26.

8. Overlapping benefits

The general principle of the co-ordination rule is that a claimant should not use one period of compulsory insurance to obtain a right to more than one benefit derived from that period of insurance.[62] In general, you will only be insured in one European Union (EU)/European Economic Area (EEA) member state for any one period,[63] so you cannot use insurance from that one period to obtain entitlement to benefits of the same kind from two member states. Usually, benefits will be adjusted to ensure either that only one state (the competent state) pays the benefit, taking into account periods of insurance in other EU/EEA member states; or that the benefit is paid pro rata according to the lengths of periods of insurance in different member states. Aggregation or portability provisions apply, but not both.

The co-ordination rule allows a member state to introduce provisions to prevent 'double recovery'. In the UK these are contained in the Overlapping Benefits Regulations.[64]

In certain cases, however, you may be paid both the full level of a UK benefit and a proportion of the benefit from another member state, which has been accrued as a result of insurance contributions there. Following a decision of the European Court of Justice (ECJ),[65] member states are not allowed to apply provisions preventing the overlapping of their own benefits with those of other member states where it would have the effect of reducing what you would have received from your years of contribution in the first member state alone.

This means that no adjustment can be made to your benefits under the Overlapping Benefits Regulations if the 'duplicate' benefits, which you are receiving, are:

- a UK benefit based only on years of insurance in the UK (without seeking to bring in periods of insurance from work abroad) and a benefit paid by another EU/EEA member state based only on your contribution in that member state; *or*
- a UK benefit based only on years of insurance in the UK (without seeking to bring in periods of insurance from work abroad) and a benefit paid as a result of contributions in another EU/EEA member state, where entitlement to the benefit from the second member state arises on other provisions of the co-ordination rule.

For benefits – like old age and death benefits – which are paid pro rata by different member states, depending on the length of the period of insurance in each member state, the overlapping provisions do not apply so as to 'adjust' benefits downwards. Each member state must pay you either the benefit you have earned under its system, pro rata, or the rate payable under its own legislation for the years worked, whichever is higher. In such cases the single state rule does not apply.

Example

In the UK, if you have been employed for 90 per cent of the qualifying years of your working life, you are entitled to the basic rate state retirement pension at the full rate. If you have spent the remaining 10 per cent of your working life in another member state, you can now receive your full UK pension as well as the 10 per cent pro rata pension to which you are entitled from the other member state.

There are further detailed exceptions to the overlapping provisions in relation to benefits paid for invalidity, old age, occupational disease or death.[66] Broadly speaking, a member state is not allowed to apply its overlapping provisions to reduce benefits you receive from it, which are of the same kind just because you are receiving other benefits in respect of those risks from another member state.

Notes

1. **The legal basis for the co-ordination of social security**
   1 Reg 1408/71 replaced EEC Reg 3 on 1 October 1972. The principles of both Regulations are the same and earlier caselaw which refers to Regulation 3 is still good law.

2. **The personal scope of Regulation 1408/71**
   2 *Hoekstra (ne Unger)* [1964] ECR 177; *De Cicco* [1968] ECR 473 (under Reg 3, the predecessor to Reg 1408/71)
   3 Art 2(a) Reg 1408/71
   4 Contrast *Levin v Staatssecretaris van Justitie* [1982] ECR 1035, [1982] 2 CMLR 454 with *Heissische Knappschaft v Maison Singer et fils* [1965] ECR 965
   5 *Mouthaan* [1976] ECR 1901
   6 *Hoekstra* (see note 2)
   7 *Pierik* [1979] ECR 1917
   8 Students were added to the list of persons covered by Reg 1408/71 in 1999; Reg 307/99 OJ L307/99.
   9 Although students fall within the scope of the Regulation this does not mean that they can override UK rules which exclude students from access to certain benefits. These exclusions apply to all students and therefore are not in breach of Reg 1408/71. However, exclusion of students from income-based JSA has been found to breach EC Directive 79/7 by discriminating against women. See CJSA/1920/1999 (*65/00).

10 *Kits van Heijuningen* [1990] ECR 1753
11 C-317/93 *Nolte* (ECJ judgment 14 December 1995) suggests that a lower earnings limit cannot be displaced as constituting indirect sex discrimination, contrary to Dir 79/7, because it can be justified by objectives of social policy.
12 s137 SSCBA 1992
13 Art 1(f) Reg 1408/71
14 See *Cristini*
15 *Cabanis-Issarte* Case C-308/93 ECJ
16 *Kermaschek* [1976] ECR 1669, and see paras 23-24 and 34 of *Cabanis-Issarte* (note 15)
17 *Gul v Dusseldorf* [1980] ECR 1573; [1987] 1 CMLR 501; *Echternach* [1989] ECR 723; *Diatta v Land Berlin* [1985] ECR 567; [1986] 2 CMLR 164. The inconsistent decision of the House of Lords in *Re Sandler*, *The Times*, 10 May 1985, is probably wrong and should have been referred to the ECJ.
18 Art 1(f) Reg 1408/71
19 *Khaboka v Home Secretary* [1993] Imm AR. Joined cases CIS/564/1994 and CIS/7250/1995
20 *Krasniqi v CAO and Secretary of State* CA 10 November 1998, CF/3662/1999, CFC/2613/1997(*25/00) R(FC) 1/01
21 *Krasniqi* (see note 20)

22 *Khali v Bundesanstalt für Arbeit Case* C-95/99, *Chaaban v Bundesanstalt für Arbeit* Case C-96/99, *Osseili v Bundesanstalt für Arbeit* Case C-97/99, *Basser v Landeshauptstadt Stuttgart* Case C-98/99. All four of these cases involve a stateless person and the ECJ has been asked to address the point as to whether Reg 1408/71 applies to stateless persons who have travelled to a member state from a non-member country. A fifth case from the Federal Social Court in the case of *Addou v Land Nordrhein-Westfalen* Case C-180/99 asks the question whether it is necessary for refugees to move within the EEA before they may rely on Reg 1408/71.

23 CF/3662/1999

3. The material scope of Regulation 1408/71

24 Listed in Art 4(1) Reg 1408/71
25 Art 4(2) Reg 1408/71
26 Art 4(2) Reg 1408/71
27 Art 4(2a) Reg 1408/71
28 Art 4(1)-(2a) Reg 1408/71
29 *Scrivner and Cole* [1986] I ECR 1027
30 Art 4(4) Reg 1408/71
31 *Gillard* [1978] ECR 1661 para 12; *Piscitello* [1983] ECR 1427 para 10; *Newton* C-356/89
32 *Scrivner and Cole* (see note 29)
33 *Newton* C-356/89
34 For example, *Scrivner and Cole* (the Belgian 'minimex' (like income support) and Newton (mobility allowance))
35 Art 5 Reg 1408/71. The declarations are published in the *Compendium of European Social Security Law*
36 Annex IIa Reg 1408/71
37 *Beerens* [1977] ECR 2249 and *Newton* C-356/89
38 *Partridge* Case C-297/96. A similar decision was made in respect of DLA in *Snare* Case C-20/96
39 This case involved a claim under EC Directive 79/7 on the equal treatment between men and women in social security. *Hockenjos v Secretary of State for Social Security* [2001] EWCA Civ 624(CA) and CJSA/1920/1999(*65/00)
40 The rules relating to WFTC are still to be found in the Family Credit (General) Regulation 1987 and the Tax Credits Act 1999 specifies that both FC and DWA are to be known as WFTC and DPTC respectively.

41 *Beerens* (see note 37)
42 In *Newton* (see note 37) the UK Government said that mobility allowance was not social security because it was not in its declaration and was more akin to social assistance. The ECJ said that it had more of the characteristics of social security.

4. The single state principle

43 Art 13 Reg 1408/71
44 Contained in Art 13 Reg 1408/71
45 Art 13(2)(a) and (b) Reg 1408/71
46 Art 14(c) Reg 1408/71
47 Art 14(1)(a) Reg 1408/71
48 Art 14(1)(b) Reg 1408/71
49 Art 14a(1)(a) Reg 1408/71
50 Art 14a(1)(a) Reg 1408/71
51 Art 14(2) Reg 1408/71
52 Art 17 Reg 1408/71

5. The principle of non-discrimination

53 *Vandeweghe* [1973] ECR 1329
54 *Costa* [1974] ECR 1251
55 *Palermo* [1979] ECR 2645
56 *Frascogna* [1987] ECR 3431

6. The principle of aggregation and apportionment

57 *Mura* [1977] ECR 1699, [1978] 2 CMLR 416; but see also *Frangiamore* [1978] ECR 725 and *Warmerdam-Steggerda* [1989] ECR 1203
58 Sickness and maternity (Art 18 Reg 1408/71), invalidity (Art 38), old age, death (survivors) and certain other invalidity benefits (Art 45(1) to (4)), occupational disease (Art 57), death grants (Art 64), unemployment (Art 67(1) and (2)), family benefit (Art 72).
59 The general overlapping provisions are contained in Arts 12 and 46 of Reg 1408/71.

7. The principle of exportability

60 Art 10(1) Reg 1408/71
61 Art 10a Reg 1408/71

8. Overlapping benefits

62 Arts 12 and 48 Reg 1408/71; see also specific provisions in relation to particular benefits; Arts 19(2), 25(1)(b), 34(2), 39(2) and (5), 68(2), 71(2), 76 and 76(3) Reg 1408/71
63 Art 13 Reg 1408/71
64 SS(OB) Regs
65 *Petroni* [1995] ECR 1149 C-24/75
66 Arts 46a, 46b and 46c Reg 1408/71

Chapter 26

Special rules for individual categories of benefits

This chapter covers:
1. Sickness and maternity benefits (below)
2. Invalidity benefits (p364)
3. Old age benefits (p369)
4. Survivors' benefits (p373)
5. Benefits for accidents at work and occupational diseases (p374)
6. Unemployment benefits (p376)
7. Family benefits (p381)
8. Special non-contributory benefits (p383)
9. Death grants (p387)

Chapter 25 identified the co-ordination arrangements of EC Regulation 1408/71 in very general terms. However, the Regulation also has very precise rules governing your rights under the co-ordination provisions. These vary according to your particular status and the particular benefit involved. It is therefore necessary to check the special rules that relate to each benefit.

This chapter covers the specific rules for the various categories of benefit. It lists the UK benefits that fall within Regulation 1408/71and explains how those benefits are affected by the co-ordination rule.

1. Sickness and maternity benefits

The UK benefits that fall under the co-ordination rule are:
- statutory maternity pay;
- maternity allowance;
- statutory sick pay;
- short-term incapacity benefit.

For details about the rules for entitlement to these benefits, see CPAG's *Welfare Benefits Handbook*.

Maternity and sickness benefits are co-ordinated by Articles 18-31 of EC Regulation 1408/71. The specific rules relating to sickness and maternity benefits in EC Regulation 1408/71 are lengthy and perhaps the most complex of all those in the Regulation. This is inevitable because it has to cater for a range of different benefits but also different circumstances that may arise. For example, if a person is involved in an accident while away from her/his place of residence s/he may need to claim a range of benefits or services. Therefore sickness and maternity benefits includes:

- **Benefits in kind** – these are comprised of health and welfare services so, for example, medical treatment would fall under this category. It also covers cash payments to reimburse the cost of these services if you have already been charged for them.
- **Cash benefits** – cash benefits on the other hand means benefits for compensation for loss of earnings.[1]

General rules relating to sickness and maternity benefits

There are certain general principles that can be identified.

- You claim benefit from the state in which you were last insured. This is one of the central themes of the co-ordination rule. However, there are exceptions to this general rule.
- Aggregation. The Regulation specifies that where a member state makes entitlement to a particular sickness or maternity benefit conditional upon the completion of periods of insurance, residence and employment, the member state shall to the extent necessary take into account any such periods completed in other states.[2]
- You should not be excluded from claiming cash benefits from the state in which you are insured simply because you reside elsewhere. However, if you are sick or pregnant you may also have to make use of health or welfare services, for example, antenatal care. It may be unrealistic to expect you to receive such treatment from the state of insurance if you are resident elsewhere. In such cases it is the place of residence that provides such treatment.
- It is the state with whom you were last insured that is liable to bear the cost of the benefit whether it is cash or in kind. This applies even if you receive treatment or benefit in another member state.

In addition to these general principles there are quite specific rules, which vary according to whether you are employed or unemployed and whether or not you are a pensioner.

Special rules for employed or self-employed people

If you are working in, and insured for sickness in, another European Economic Area (EEA) member state and you get sick, you may need to claim benefit for short-term sickness under that state's social security scheme. Periods of insurance contributions in the UK may be aggregated with periods of insurance in that member state and count towards your entitlement to such a benefit.[3] It is sometimes possible to claim benefit from a state other than the one in which you were last insured.

If you go temporarily to another EEA member state you can claim sickness and maternity benefits from that state if your condition 'necessitates immediate benefits'.[4] This includes both cash benefits and benefits in kind. This could include reimbursement of medical and pharmaceutical expenses, treatment or medication as well as weekly cash benefits. Your sickness or pregnancy does not of itself necessitate immediate benefit but if you require medical treatment the rule is engaged.

You may wish to go to another member state for treatment because it is more effective or to avoid a lengthy waiting list. If you are already entitled to benefit and go to another member state for treatment you can continue to receive benefit. You must get authorisation from the DWP in order to do this. Authorisation cannot be withheld because your home state provides the treatment necessary if the treatment cannot be provided within a reasonable time taking into account your current state of health. If you are going abroad you should give the DWP plenty of advance warning to enable it to advise you on procedures and make the necessary arrangements on your behalf.

If you have been working in and are insured in another EEA member state and become ill, you may wish to return to the UK. In these circumstances you may be entitled to the other member state's sickness benefit in the UK. However, in order to benefit, you should make your claim before you leave the other member state. If you are entitled to benefit and want to move to live in another member state or return to the state in which you habitually reside you can get benefit there if you are authorised by the DWP. Such authorisation can only be refused if removal would be prejudicial to health. It does not have to be obtained prior to departure but not having it is likely to lead to problems with the claim until you obtain it.

If you habitually reside in a state other than the competent state, you can nevertheless claim and receive benefit from the state in which you were last insured.[5]

Special rules for unemployed claimants

If you are unemployed and receiving exportable unemployment benefit (jobseeker's allowance for UK purposes) while looking for work in another member state and you become sick or the maternity allowance period begins, you no longer get unemployment benefit but sickness or maternity benefit. This is paid for the remainder of the unemployment benefit period of three months. However, this period can be extended if you are unable to return home.[6]

If you are eligible for one state's unemployment benefit because you are habitually resident in that state rather than having last worked there you are also eligible for that state's benefit while sick/pregnant.

Special rules for pensioners

If you receive an 'old age' benefit from more than one member state, including a pension from the state in which you reside, you receive sickness or maternity benefit from the state in which you are resident rather than the state where you were last insured.[7]

If you are entitled to a pension from more than one member state but you do not receive a pension from the state in which you reside, you can get sickness or maternity benefit from the member state that pays you a pension.[8]

If you are eligible for a pension in one state but are resident in another and you are waiting for the pension claim to be processed you are entitled to receive benefits in kind which will be paid for by the state of residence. Once the pension claim is processed and it is established who is responsible for payment of sickness benefits that state will reimburse the state which has paid for your benefits in kind.[9]

Making a claim

You generally make a claim for benefits on the usual claim form provided for that benefit by the competent institution. The competent institution is the DWP in the UK and its equivalent in any other state. If you are unsure which state you should claim from you should start your claim in the state in which you are living and it will be passed on to the competent institution. There are however some forms that may be useful to obtain. Again these are generally available from the competent institution.

If you have been working in another member state you should try to get a Form E104, which is a record of the social insurance that you have paid in that member state, before returning to the UK. This will help with any claims for benefit. It is not essential to have this form and if you provide evidence of your work to the DWP it will check your insurance record with the other member state. You should be able to obtain this from the competent institution of the state in which you have been working or you could ask for a copy from the DWP prior to going abroad.

You should use Form E119, available from the competent institution to obtain benefits in kind and submit evidence of incapacity to substantiate the claim.

2. Invalidity benefits

Invalidity benefits are co-ordinated by Articles 37-43 of EC Regulation 1408/71. The rules for invalidity benefits are virtually identical to those for old age and survivors' benefits. In European Community (EC) law sickness benefits and invalidity benefits are treated very differently. In the UK, incapacity benefit is an earnings replacement benefit for total incapacity to work. In other states however, 'invalidity benefits' are often more akin to a disability benefit paid according to the level of your disability, similar perhaps to industrial disablement benefit.

There are no provisions in EC law defining which are sickness and which are invalidity benefits. It is decided by looking at the conditions of entitlement to each benefit and the reason for, and length of, the incapacity.

Invalidity benefits available in the UK under the co-ordination rule are:
- long-term incapacity benefit (IB); a*nd*
- attendance allowance, invalid care allowance and disability living allowance but only if you were in receipt of benefit prior to 1 June 1992 (see below).[10]

Increases of long-term IB for child dependants are family benefits, not invalidity benefits.

Only long-term IB, paid after 52 weeks of incapacity is considered to be an 'invalidity benefit'. The short-term rates of IB are classified as sickness benefits for the purposes of EC regulations and cover shorter-term incapacities (see p361).

Severe disablement allowance (SDA) was considered to be an invalidity benefit but was abolished by the UK Government in April 2001. Claimants already receiving benefit will remain entitled but no fresh claims can now be made. In place of SDA, the Government has introduced a new type of non-contributory incapacity benefit. The Government has not yet stated whether this will be an invalidity benefit within EC rules, but, its similarity to SDA means that there are grounds to argue it should be treated as an invalidity benefit.

Attendance allowance, disability living allowance and invalid care allowance had all been established as 'invalidity benefits'. However, on 1 June 1992 these benefits were reclassified as 'special non-contributory benefits' (see p383).

For further details on the UK rules of entitlement to all of these benefits, see CPAG's *Welfare Benefits Handbook*.

General rules
- The main principles of aggregation and exportation apply to invalidity benefits. Therefore, periods of insurance in any member state must be taken into account if necessary in order for you to qualify for benefit. Once you are entitled to an invalidity benefit you can export that benefit to another member state whatever your reason for going there.[11]
- Adult dependency increases can be paid for family members even if they are living in another member state. Although you should note that such increases are family benefits rather than invalidity benefits.
- The state from which you claim benefit is the one that determines your degree of invalidity but medical reports from other states must be taken into account. In some circumstances a state can insist on having the claimant examined by a

doctor of its own choice. This is rare, however, and the general rule is that any checks and medical take place in the state in which you are living rather than the one that pays you benefit. The reports are then sent back to the paying state.[12] There are special rules relating to the aggravation of an invalidity.[13] The precise rules vary according to your situation and your status. But in general if your condition gets worse the aggravation of your condition should be taken into account in the assessment of your benefit. You should raise this with the competent institution or the relevant social security department of the state in which you are living.

- If an invalidity benefit is suspended, for example by the DWP because you failed to attend a medical, but then resumed, the same state continues to pay. If it is withdrawn but further invalidity arises the question of who pays is decided afresh.[14]

- Some types of invalidity benefits available in the European Economic Area (EEA) are paid at different levels according to the length of time that you have been insured. Different rules apply depending on whether the amount of invalidity benefit is related to the length of insurance or not.

- Invalidity benefit may change to retirement pension at different times due to differing pension ages in the member states.

Apportionment

Although all types of invalidity benefits within the EEA are subject to the aggregation principle only some are subject to apportionment. EC Regulation 1408/71 distinguishes between Type A invalidity benefits which are subject only to aggregation and Type B which are subject to both aggregation and apportionment. The UK does not have any Type B invalidity benefits.

Type A invalidity benefit

The amount of benefit you receive does not vary according to the amount of contributions paid. It is paid at a standard rate.[15] (IB is a Type A invalidity benefit.)

If you have worked and paid insurance contributions only in member states with Type A invalidity benefits you are entitled to invalidity benefit under one member state's legislation only. Which member state is responsible depends on:

- where you became sick; *and*
- whether you worked in that member state or, if not, in which member state you were last employed.

Type B invalidity benefit

The rate of your benefit varies according to the amount of contributions that you have paid.[16] You may be able to get Type B invalidity benefit from two or more EEA member states if you have paid insurance contributions in any of the following member states: Austria, Denmark, Finland, France (but only under the French miners' insurance scheme, or if you were self-employed in France),

Germany, Greece (except under the agricultural insurance scheme), Iceland, Italy, Liechtenstein, Luxembourg, Norway, Portugal, Sweden.

How much you get from each member state is worked out according to a formula. It is calculated by two different methods and you get whichever is higher.[17]

Where you have paid contributions in member states paying Type A benefits and others paying Type B, your benefit may be calculated according to the Type B formula.

If you were paying contributions in any one of the above states and you are getting benefit from only one of those, you should ask the authorities there to send your details to the other member states where you have been subject to the legislation/paying contributions. You may be entitled to a higher level of benefit.

The co-ordination rules for invalidity benefits varies according to whether you have worked and been insured only in countries with Type A or Type B invalidity benefit or whether you have worked and been insured in states with both types of invalidity benefit.

1. A person has only worked in states where the amount of benefit is not related to length of insurance

Invalidity benefit is paid by the state where you were insured at the time incapacity began. The only exception to this, is where an unemployment benefit is being paid by the country of residence, rather than employment. In this case the state of residence pays invalidity benefits.[18] If you receive invalidity benefit from the state of residence, invalidity benefit is not paid by any other state under EC law. However, if you are not entitled under this state, there may be entitlement in one of the other states where you were insured. If you are eligible in more than one state, the state where most recently insured should pay.[19]

Adult dependency increases can be paid for family members living in another state.[20]

Claims can be made either to the competent institution, which is liable to pay you, or to the social security authority in the state of residence, which will forward it on to the competent institution. Your date of claim will be the date that it is received by either authority, or the date when entitlement to sickness benefits expired, whichever is later.[21]

If entitlement depends on incapacity for work or receiving a sickness benefit for a certain period of time account can be taken of periods in receipt of another state's benefit.[22]

2. A person has only worked in states where the amount of invalidity benefit is related to the length of time insured

Invalidity benefit from each state is worked out as follows:

Calculation 1

Assess under national law alone.

Calculation 2

a) Add up total insurance in all member states and work out the amount of benefit this would give.

b) Work out the proportion of years in each state to decide the pro rata amount which is then payable by each state.

Calculation 3

The two rates of benefit produced in 1 and 2 are compared and the claimant receives the higher of the two.

3. A person has worked and been insured in states where the amount of invalidity benefit is not related to length of insurance and in states where it is

If you were insured in a country where the amount of invalidity benefit is not dependent on insurance when incapacity begins, benefit can be paid as in 1 above as long as there is no entitlement under an insurance-related scheme and you have not yet claimed retirement pension. No account is taken of insurance periods in these countries when aggregating insurance. If this does not apply, benefit is calculated as in 2 above.[23]

Claims

Generally there are no special claim forms – you simply claim benefit on the appropriate claim form provided by the competent institution – eg, IB claim form in the UK.

Claims can be made to the competent institution or to the state in which you reside which will forward it on to the competent institution. The date of your claim is the date of receipt by either authority or the date that entitlement to sickness benefits end, whichever is the later.[24]

The date of claim is the date the claim is received at either social security office. This claim will trigger payment of invalidity benefit by all states liable to pay, as the institution receiving the claim should notify all other institutions who will then assess how much each should pay.[25]

Payment of benefit could take some time if several states are involved so the state you claim from can make an interim payment. This consists of the amount payable under its national law alone. If this amounts to nil but there is entitlement in another state, that state pays. If you are eligible in several states the state where you claim pays on behalf of the other member states. Once the true amount of invalidity benefit has been assessed it can either be paid directly to the claimant by each state in which there is entitlement, or through the institution handling the claim.[26]

3. **Old age benefits**

Old age benefits available in the UK under the co-ordination rule are:
* retirement pension;
* additional pension;
* graduated retirement benefit;
* increments;
* adult dependency increases of retirement pension;
* age addition;
* Christmas bonuses.

The co-ordination rules for old age benefits are found in Articles 44 to 51 of EC Regulation 1408/71. In the UK, retirement pensions of any category are included. There are four types of retirement pension in the UK: Categories A, B C and D. Categories A and B are contributory while Category D carries a residence test and is paid in strictly limited circumstances (Category C is no longer relevant as it applies only to people who were of pension age in 1948). For further details of the UK rules for entitlement to these benefits, see CPAG's *Welfare Benefits Handbook*.

Although incapacity benefit and child dependency increases can be paid to someone over pension age, they are not classed as old age benefits.[27]

Winter fuel payments and bus passes are not benefits listed as old age benefits for EC Regulation 1408/71. However, there have been decisions by the European Court of Justice (ECJ) which have held that these are benefits linked to old age. Therefore there are strong grounds to argue that they fall under the co-ordination rule also.[28]

Increases of retirement pension for child dependants are family benefits, not old age benefits.

General rules

The provisions in the co-ordination rule in relation to entitlement to a UK pension are most likely to be of use to people who have worked in the UK but for an insufficient period to qualify for a full pension under UK rules alone, and who have also worked in another member state.
* If you have worked in more than one member state, your insurance record is preserved in each of those states until you reach pension age. You will get a retirement pension from each member state where you have worked for a year or more, based on your insurance record in that member state or, where

residence counts for benefit purposes, the length of your residence in that member state.

- If you have worked and paid contributions in more than one member state you may be entitled to a pension under EC law, even if you do not qualify for a pension under the national legislation of the country in which you are resident. Therefore a person who has paid contributions in the UK but does not qualify for a Category A or B pension under British legislation, but who worked in another European Union (EU)/European Economic Area (EEA) state may qualify for a retirement pension when those contributions are taken into account. The retirement pension is then worked out according to a formula (see p371).

- If a pension is dependent on periods of residence to qualify you for a full pension, then any periods of residence which you have completed in other member states will be taken into account.

- Retirement pensions are fully exportable. This means that your retirement pension will be paid to you regardless of where you live or stay in the EEA without any reduction or modification.[29]

- Pensionable age in the UK for a man is 65, for a woman 60. However, from 6 April 2010 the pension age for women will increase from 60 to 65 over a 10-year period. The age at which you may be entitled to a retirement pension differs from member state to member state. Because of this you may be entitled to an old age benefit in one EEA member state before you reach retirement age in another. Correspondingly, if you have been incapable of work before you reached pension age you may be entitled to pro rata invalidity benefits in the member state where you have not yet reached pension age. In the UK this is long-term incapacity benefit.

- If you worked in a member state that only recently joined the European Community and you were entitled to a retirement pension before that country joined, you may be able to rely on any reciprocal arrangements that exist with that state (see p411).

Claims

In general you make a claim for your pension in the state in which you are resident. If you have never been insured in that state your claim will be forwarded on to the member state in which you were last insured.[30] Alternatively, when you approach pension age, you could apply directly to the competent state to claim your pension. That state will pass details of your claim to any other EEA member state where you have been insured so that each one can do its calculation. The competent state will inform you whether you can claim more under domestic law alone or with your entitlement calculated under the co-ordination rule.[31]

Each member state decides how to pay your pension and pays it itself.

Calculating your pension

The following rules apply wherever you are in the EU/EEA. If you have been subject to the legislation of more than one member state, each of them must calculate your pension entitlement as follows in accordance with EC law. This is one field where migrants may be better off than others because of an exception in the overlapping provisions.

There are three steps to calculating your pension.

1. Each member state should calculate the pension you are entitled to (if any) under its own legislation.[32] For example, if you have been insured in the UK for 20 years you would be entitled to a UK pension of approximately 50 per cent of the standard rate. On the other hand, under UK domestic legislation, if you had only worked for eight years in the UK you would have no entitlement.

2. Each member state should then calculate a theoretical pension as if your entire career in the EU/EEA had been spent in that member state.[33] This theoretical amount is then reduced in proportion to the actual time you worked in that state compared with the time worked in the EU/EEA as a whole. The resulting amount is known as your pro rata entitlement.

3. Each member state then pays you whichever is the greater of the amount you are entitled to under its own domestic legislation, and the pro rata amount of its benefit which you are entitled to from that member state calculated in accordance with the co-ordination rule.[34]

. . . .

Example

Mr Coiro from Italy has worked for 43 years in different member states:

8 years in the UK

15 years in Italy

20 years in Ireland

His entitlement in the UK based on UK domestic legislation (based on periods of insurance) amounts to nothing. However, if his entitlement to a UK pension was calculated as if his entire EU/EEA career of 43 years' work had been carried out in the UK, he would be eligible for 100 per cent of the UK standard rate (this is his 'theoretical entitlement'). He can therefore claim the pro rata amount of this entitlement in respect of his years of work in the UK.

His pro rata entitlement is worked out as follows:

$$\frac{\text{his theoretical rate} \times \text{his UK period of insurance}}{\text{his EU/EEA period of insurance}}$$

which is:

$$\frac{100\% \times 8 \text{ years}}{43 \text{ years}}$$

Answer: 19%

So Mr Coiro will be entitled to the pro rata rate of 19 per cent of the UK standard rate. Since the alternative amount which he could claim from the UK based on his eight years' contributions is nil, the pro rata amount is the higher of the two possible entitlements to a UK pension and that is what Mr Coiro can claim.

In this example, Italy and Ireland would perform similar calculations and Mr Coiro would receive a pension from each on the same basis. It could be that for either or both of these member states the calculation based on their domestic legislation turned out to be higher, and Mr Coiro would receive that larger pension.

Because of the way the calculation rules work for UK pensions, entitlement under domestic legislation alone will almost invariably be equal to or higher than the pro rata amount calculated in accordance with the co-ordination rule.[35] (For example, you may qualify for a Category D pension – see p373.) In order to be considered in this way, you must have paid sufficient contributions to qualify you for a UK pension.

If you have worked for a period of less than one year in an EU/EEA member state, your pension is calculated differently and you receive no pension from that state.[36] But the period is included in the calculation of your total period of employment in the EU/EEA.[37]

Graduated retirement benefit in the UK is not included in the pro rata rate calculation, but your UK entitlement is added on after the calculation under the co-ordination rule has been carried out.[38]

The pro rata equation is not recalculated when benefits are uprated. But the rate of retirement pension is increased.[39]

Extra retirement pension for your dependants

If you are entitled to a retirement pension from an EU/EEA member state you are also entitled to an extra amount for a dependent adult. Adult dependency increases are paid at the same pro rata rate as the basic pension.[40] You can claim this benefit even if the person who depends on you is in another EU/EEA member state.

If you are living in the EU/EEA member state that pays your pension, it will also pay any benefits to which you are entitled for your children. In the UK this would be child benefit or extra pension or both. A child dependency increase is a family benefit. It is not paid at a pro rata rate, but in full.

If you are living in a member state that does not pay you a retirement pension, then the member state that is paying your retirement pension will pay the benefits for your children.

If you are getting a retirement pension from two or more member states, then the member state where you were insured for the longest time will pay any benefits you are entitled to for your children.

Receiving your UK pension in another member state

You can be paid a UK pension in any other EU/EEA member state at the same rate as you would get if you were living in the UK or at the rate calculated in accordance with the formula in the co-ordination rule.[41] The calculation as to what you are entitled to will be carried out as on p371. Your pension may be paid directly into a bank in the member state you are living in, or in the UK. Alternatively, the pension can be paid by payable order normally issued every four weeks. Payment is always made in sterling.

Receiving income-based benefit pending payment of your pension in the UK

If you get paid arrears these will usually be sent directly to you. However, you should bear in mind that if you have claimed income support while waiting for your pension to arrive from another member state, you will have to repay that amount when your pension arrives. Similarly, if you have been getting an income support type benefit in another EU/EEA member state while waiting for your UK retirement pension, you may have to pay that amount back when your UK pension arrives.

Category D retirement pension

You may be entitled to this if you are 80 years of age or over, but it is paid only in limited circumstances. Residence in another EU/EEA member state can count towards satisfying the 10-year residence conditions for a Category D pension provided that either:
- residence in the other EU/EEA member state counts towards entitlement to old age benefits in that member state; *or*
- you were insured in the other member state and you have at some time been subject to UK legislation. For example, you have been liable to pay UK Class 1 or Class 2 national insurance contributions.

If you satisfy these conditions, the period of residence in the other EU/EEA member state is added to the periods of residence in the UK and pro rata Category D retirement pension is awarded. The UK pays the percentage of benefit which is equivalent to the number of years of residence in the UK used to satisfy the 10-year residence condition.

4. Survivors' benefits

Survivors' benefits available in the UK under the co-ordination rule are:
- bereavement benefits;
- widowed parent's allowance.

Survivors' benefits are 'death benefits' under EC Regulation 1408/71. The rules for survivors' benefits are found in Articles 44 to 51 of the Regulation which are the same as those for old age benefits. Therefore the general co-ordination arrangements for survivors' benefits are the same as those for retirement pensions. The following is a summary of the main provisions for survivors' benefits. For a more detailed explanation of the rules relating to survivors' benefits, see section on old age benefits (p369).

General rules

- You can elect whether to take the amount to which you are entitled (under the co-ordination rule) from all the European Economic Area (EEA) member states in which the deceased made contributions or to take the pro rata amount from the state in which you are living.
- Survivors' benefits can be exported to any EEA member state without reduction or modification.[42] If the deceased was insured in more than one European Union (EU)/EEA member state, the pension for the surviving spouse is calculated on the same basis as would have applied to the insured person. If the person was drawing pensions under the legislation of two or more member states, the spouse will be entitled to widows' or widowers' pensions under the legislation of these member states. The rules are the same as those for retirement pensions
- If you are bereaved and your spouse was only insured in one member state, that member state pays any benefits to which you may be entitled for your children. If your spouse was insured in more than one member state, it will normally be the member state where the child lives that will pay the benefit.

5. Benefits for accidents at work and occupational diseases

Benefits for accidents at work and occupational diseases available in the UK under the co-ordination rule are:
- disablement benefit;
- constant attendance allowance, which you may receive if you are getting 100 per cent disablement benefit and need somebody to look after you;[43]
- exceptionally severe disablement allowance, which you may receive if you are getting constant attendance allowance at one of the two highest rates, and your need for constant attendance is likely to be permanent;[44]
- reduced earnings allowance which you may receive if you are assessed at at least 1 per cent for disablement benefit and your accident occurred or your disease started before 1 October 1990, and you cannot do your normal job as a result.[45]

Chapter 26 : Special rules for individual categories of benefits
5. Benefits for accidents at work and occupational diseases

26

The rules for industrial accidents and diseases can be found in Articles 52 to 63 of EC Regulation 1408/71.

General rules

- Benefits for accidents and occupational diseases covers both cash benefits and benefits in kind. Cash benefits are earnings replacement benefits and benefits in kind can cover such things as medical treatment.
- Although EC Regulation 1408/71 applies to both employed and self-employed people you should remember that UK industrial injury benefits are only available to employed earners and not to self-employed people.[46]
- The general co-ordination rules for injury benefits are the same as those for retirement pensions.[47] Periods of insurance, residence and employment can be aggregated in order to qualify for benefit.
- Disablement benefit and related allowances are payable if you go to another European Economic Area (EEA) member state. If you are intending to travel, you should consult the office which pays you benefit well in advance so that arrangements can be made for payment in the other member state.
- A person who has suffered an industrial accident or contracted an occupational disease and who goes to stay temporarily in another member state can continue to get benefits in cash and in kind.[48] This also applies if you go to another member state for medical treatment.
- If you live in a state different to the one liable to pay you benefit you can nevertheless claim from abroad and be paid.[49]
- If you were insured in another EEA member state, you will be paid directly by the appropriate institution of that state according to its rules for determining whether or not you are eligible and how much you should be paid. That institution may arrange for the DWP to make your payments, but this will not alter the amount you receive.
- If your condition deteriorates and you are getting, or used to get, benefit from an EEA member state, then that state will be responsible for carrying out any necessary further medical examinations and paying any additional benefit.

Special rules

Accidents while travelling abroad in another member state can be deemed to have occurred in the state liable to pay industrial injury benefit. This also applies while in transit between member states.[50]

If you have worked in two or more European Union (EU)/EEA states in a job that gave you a prescribed industrial disease, you will only get benefit from the member state where you last worked in that job.

Previous accidents or diseases that arose in other member states can be taken into account in determining industrial injury benefits where this is necessary to decide the extent of the disablement. Similarly later accidents or diseases can affect the assessment of disablement but only if:

26

Chapter 26 : Special rules for individual categories of benefits
5. Benefits for accidents at work and occupational diseases

- no industrial injury benefit was payable for the original accident or disease; *and*
- there is no entitlement in the state in which the subsequent accident occurred.[51]

Claims

Generally claims for benefit should be made on the usual claim form provided by the competent institution. In all cases, benefits in kind are provided by the state where the person is staying or living. Benefits in cash are provided by the state liable to pay though it can arrange for the other state to pay on its behalf. Both benefits are financed by the state liable to pay.

Benefits in kind are secured by producing form E123. Benefits in cash can be paid when a person becomes incapable of work.

---

6. Unemployment benefits[52]

The only unemployment benefit available in the UK is jobseeker's allowance (JSA). Furthermore, the Government position is that only contribution-based JSA is an unemployment benefit. However, a commissioner and the Court of Appeal in a separate case have both held that income-based JSA is an unemployment benefit for the purposes of EC Directive 79/7.[53] This Directive specifies that there must be equal treatment in social security between men and women. (see CPAG's *Welfare Benefits Handbook* for further details). Although the decision relates to a different area of European Community (EC) law there are clearly strong grounds to argue that income-based JSA is also an unemployment benefit. The European Commission has also stated that income-based JSA is an unemployment benefit.[54]

The co-ordination rules for unemployment benefits can be found in Articles 67 to 71 of EC Regulation 1408/71. The general rule of aggregation applies to unemployment benefits but the principle of exportation applies in a much more restrictive way.

General rules

- The general rule is that you will be paid unemployment benefit by the member state in which you were last employed.[55]
- An exception to this general rule is where you reside in one member state but you are working or paying contributions in another. In this case you can claim from either the member state you reside or the member state in which you pay contributions.
- If you are potentially entitled to unemployment benefit both from the member state where you last worked and the member state in which you reside you must choose where to register for work and claim unemployment benefit.[56]

- There is a limited provision for exporting unemployment benefit. If you are receiving unemployment benefit from one member state and you go to another member state you continue to be entitled to unemployment benefit from the competent state for a period of up to three months. After three months you must return to the competent state to continue receiving unemployment benefit (see below for further details).

- The general rules of aggregation apply. Contribution-based JSA requires you to have paid contributions in the two years prior to your claim. You can use periods of insurance or employment completed as an employed person under the legislation of any other member state to satisfy the contribution conditions, provided that you were subject to UK legislation immediately before claiming contribution-based JSA. Each week of employment completed as an employed person in any other member state is treated as a contribution paid into the UK scheme on earnings of two-thirds of the present upper earnings limit for contribution purposes.

- If members of your family are living in another EEA member state and the amount of your unemployment benefit is determined by the number of people in your family, then they will be taken into account as if they were living in the member state that pays your benefit.[57] If your dependant lives in another member state you will need form E302. This form may be obtained from the employment institution of the member state in which your dependant lives.

What happens if you go to another member state

If you are going to look for work in another EU/EEA member state you will be entitled to contribution-based JSA abroad if:

- you are wholly unemployed immediately before you leave the UK. This means you are without any employment except for partial and intermittent unemployment.[58] Partial unemployment means you are short-time (not part-time) working. Intermittent unemployment means you are temporarily laid off; *and*

- you satisfy the conditions for contribution-based JSA before you leave the UK.[59] You will qualify even if you have claimed contribution-based JSA but no decision has been made yet on your entitlement, but you are getting JSA hardship payments pending the decision; *and*

- your entitlement to contribution-based JSA arises from aggregating insurance payments you made in different member states.[60] Your entitlement to contribution-based JSA must not arise as a result of a reciprocal convention between the UK and a state that is not a member of the EU/EEA (for how to determine this, see p411;[61] *and*

- you are going to the other EU/EEA member state to seek work.[62] You are not entitled to exportable contribution-based JSA if you are going on holiday, visiting a sick relative or accompanying your spouse. If you give up work to accompany your spouse or partner on a posting abroad it is very unlikely that you will be able to export your UK contribution-based JSA. In order to establish entitlement you must show that:

– there was just cause for voluntarily leaving your employment; *and*
– you were capable of, available for, and actively seeking, work.

Usually it will be accepted that if you left work to accompany your partner on a foreign posting, you had just cause as long as you left no earlier than was reasonable to organise your affairs before travelling.[63] However, you may still lose entitlement because you will find it difficult to establish that you were available for work during this time. If, on the other hand, you were already unemployed and you take the opportunity of accompanying your spouse or partner abroad to seek work, you may be accepted as satisfying this condition; *and*

- you have been registered as available for work for at least four weeks in the UK.[64] In exceptional circumstances you may be allowed to leave the UK before the four weeks is up and still qualify. You must get authority in advance to do so from Pensions and Overseas Benefits Directorate in Newcastle (see Appendix 2); *and*

- you are registered for work in another EEA member state.[65] If you are looking for work in another member state, you must register for work there within seven days of leaving the UK and comply with that member state's regulations unless there are exceptional circumstances;[66] *and*

- the employment services of that member state will pay contribution-based JSA in accordance with its own legislation. This includes the method and frequency of payment.[67] The requirement to attend at a JobCentre is satisfied if:
  – you attend at an equivalent office in the other member state; *or*
  – you comply with that member state's control procedures, showing that you are available for work as its rules require.

That member state will carry out checks on entitlement to JSA in accordance with its own procedures. If there is doubt about whether you meet the registration and availability conditions of the member state in which you are living this will be reported to the DWP in the UK. On the advice of the other EEA state, the DWP will make a decision about whether you continue to be entitled or not. While the question is referred to the DWP your benefit may be suspended by the other state. It is important that the decision is made in the UK because you have the right to appeal. In some EU/EEA states there is no right of appeal against the decision of a decision maker.

If all of the above conditions are met, you will be entitled to UK JSA abroad in an EEA member state for one of the following periods, whichever is the shortest:[68]

- three months from the date when you ceased to be available to the UK employment services;[69] *or*

- until your entitlement to UK JSA is exhausted after six months/26 weeks;[70] *or*
- if you are a seasonal worker (see below), until the end of the season.[71]

A 'seasonal worker' is a person who:
- is 'habitually resident' in one member state and goes to work in another EEA member state; *and*
- does seasonal work in that second member state for a period of up to eight months; *and*
- remains in that member state for the whole period of that season's work.[72]

Seasonal work is work which happens every year and is linked to a particular season of the year.

On request a statement will be issued to you by the Pensions and Overseas Benefits Directorate (see Appendix 2) for you to give to the employment services of the member state where you are going to look for work.[73] The statement will give:
- the rate of contribution-based JSA that is payable;
- the date from which JSA can be paid;
- the time limit for registration in the other EEA member state;
- the maximum period of entitlement;
- any other relevant facts that might affect your entitlement.

You can export JSA to more than one EU/EEA member state during the same period of absence from the UK.

But JSA can only be exported once from the UK during any one period of unemployment. You cannot return to the UK and then go abroad a second time in the same period until you have worked and paid more contributions in the UK.[74]

If you have not found a job within three months and return to the UK before the three-month period is up, you will continue to get contribution-based JSA in the UK, assuming that the six-month period for which JSA can be paid is not exhausted.[75]

If you fall sick or become pregnant while looking for work in another EU/EEA member state, you may be entitled to UK short-term incapacity benefit or maternity benefit but only for the period until your contribution-based JSA entitlement runs out.[76] For example, if you have already used up four months while in the UK, you will only be entitled to two months' contribution-based JSA abroad. To claim these benefits you will need form E119.

If you become unemployed while working abroad and are insured in that member state's unemployment insurance scheme, then that member state is responsible for paying unemployment benefit. If you were previously insured in the UK you will normally be able to use periods during which you paid national insurance and aggregate them with periods of insurance in the member state you last worked in, to enable you to get the unemployment benefit of the member state where you have been working.[77]

If you are entitled to receive JSA while in another EEA member state, you should get a letter from your local JobCentre to help register for work in the other member state.

If you are going to look for work in Austria, Belgium, Finland, France, Germany, Greece, Iceland, Italy, Norway, Portugal, Spain or Sweden, you will be given Form E303. If you are going to look for work in another EU/EEA member state, then Form E303 will be sent directly to that member state.

What happens if you come to the UK and are unemployed

If you are a returning resident or an EU/EEA national coming to the UK to work or to seek work, the following applies to you.

If you have worked and paid insurance contributions under the legislation of another EU/EEA member state the periods of insurance in that state may count towards your entitlement to contribution-based JSA on your return to the UK. This will apply if, after your return to the UK, you get employment, pay Class 1 contributions but then become unemployed again.[78] You are then subject to UK legislation (ie, the UK is the 'competent state') and the UK is responsible for paying you the appropriate amount of contribution-based JSA.

If you were not subject to another member state's legislation while abroad (because you were an exception to the rule that the competent state is the state where you work – see p353) the unemployment insurance you paid while abroad may nevertheless still be taken into account when assessing your entitlement to contribution-based JSA if it is decided that, while you were abroad, you remained 'habitually resident' (see p135) in the UK.

If you are coming to or returning to the UK to look for work and have been insured in another EU/EEA member state, you may be able to get the other member state's unemployment benefit for up to three months if:[79]

- you were getting that member state's unemployment benefit immediately before coming to the UK;[80] *and*
- you have been registered as available for work for four weeks (or less if the member state's rules allow) in the other member state;[81] *and*
- you register and claim UK JSA within seven days after you were last registered in the other member state;[82] *and*
- you satisfy the UK's availability for work rules.[83] The UK DWP will carry out checks and pay benefit where unemployment benefit has been exported from another EU/EEA member state to the UK. However, the UK DWP cannot decide whether or not there is entitlement to the other member state's unemployment benefit. If a doubt arises about your continuing entitlement, the UK DWP will inform the employment authorities of the other member state and, if appropriate, may suspend payment of your unemployment benefit while

awaiting a reply. Before you leave the other member state you must get Form E303.[84]

---

7. **Family benefits**

Family benefits available in the UK under the co-ordination rule are:
- child benefit;
- working families' tax credit;
- guardian's allowance;
- child's special allowance (transitional entitlement) (not available to new claimants);
- child dependency increases for non-means-tested benefits.

The co-ordination rules for family benefits are found in Articles 72 to 76 of EC Regulation 1408/71.

General rules
- The general principle of aggregation applies to family benefits although this is limited to aggregating periods of insurance or employment. No mention is made of aggregating periods of residence.
- The principle of exportation does *not* apply to family benefits. However, it is possible to receive benefits for family members who are not living with you but reside elsewhere in the European Economic Area (EEA). For example, a Spanish person working in the UK can claim child benefit for her/his children living in Spain or elsewhere in the Community. This is despite the fact that generally it is not possible to receive child benefit for children who do not reside with you. This is an example of how you can be put in a better position under European Community (EC) law.
- Generally you are entitled to benefit from the state in which you last worked. However there are exceptions to this.
- If you are posted to work in another European Union (EU)/EEA member state for less than 12 months you remain subject to the legislation of the member state from which you have been posted. (The 12-month period can be extended for a further 12 months in certain circumstances.) The member state from which you are posted will therefore be responsible for paying family benefits.[85] If you are a member of the armed forces serving in another EEA member state, you remain subject to UK legislation.
- If you have worked outside the EEA but remain subject to the legislation of an EEA member state (see p353), you may retain the right to family benefits.[86]

In addition to the general rules there are also special rules relating only to family benefits. These rules vary according to whether you are employed, unemployed or a pensioner.

Employed persons[87]

If you are employed in a member state you claim from the state in which you are working even if your family is living in another member state. Therefore it is possible to claim a benefit such as child benefit even though the child is not living with you.

Unemployed persons[88]

If you were previously employed or self-employed; and you are getting unemployment benefit from an EU/EEA member state you are then entitled to family benefits from that member state for members of your family who are living in any EU/EEA member state. Therefore it is possible to claim benefits even though the child does not reside with you.

If you are wholly unemployed. you are entitled to family benefits from your state of residence *only* for members of your family who are residing with you if:[89]

- you are unemployed; *but*
- you were previously employed; *and*
- during your last period of employment you were resident in a different EU/EEA member state to the one you were working in; *and*
- you are receiving unemployment benefit from the member state where you are living.

Family benefits for children of pensioners

Under EC law, family benefits are payable for the dependent children of pensioners. To qualify you must be claiming:[90]

- an old age benefit; *and*
- an invalidity benefit; *or*
- a benefit for an accident at work or an occupational disease.

If you are getting your pension from only one EU/EEA member state, family benefits are payable by that member state regardless of where in the EU/EEA you or your children are living.

If you are receiving a pension from more than one member state, family benefits are payable by the member state where you live, provided there is entitlement under that member state's scheme. If there is no entitlement under its scheme, then the member state to which you have been subject to the legislation for the longest period, and under which you have entitlement to family benefits, will be responsible for paying you.[91]

Overlapping benefit rules

Migrant workers may often be separated from family members while they search for work or establish themselves in another member state. This, combined with the fact that different member states have different conditions for benefits, some based on residence, some on employment, others on contributions, means that there is great scope for duplication of payments. Therefore, EC law has rules which seek to prevent a person being able to claim family benefits from more than one member state.

For employed and unemployed persons if there is entitlement in two different states any non-contributory benefit is suspended in preference to a contributory one. However, if a person is working in the state which pays the non-contributory benefit the other benefit is suspended. In either case if the suspended benefit is higher, that state must pay an amount equal to the difference.[92]

Claims

Claims should be made to the state liable to pay on the appropriate claim form for that benefit. A certificate proving that the children are your dependants must be obtained. There is a duty to notify any changes in the size of your family, the fact that you have moved to a different state, that your partner is working and due to get family benefits from another member state and any other change that might affect entitlement.[93]

If the family benefits are not used for the benefit of the family it can be paid to another person who will apply it to this end.[94]

8. **Special non-contributory benefits**

The UK benefits available are:[95]
- attendance allowance (AA);
- disability living allowance (DLA);
- disabled person's tax credit (DPTC);
- income support (IS);
- income-based jobseeker's allowance (JSA);
- invalid care allowance (ICA);
- working families' tax credit (WFTC).

In 1992, EC Regulation 1408/71 was amended to include a new category of benefits, that of special non-contributory benefits. There are no special rules relating to these benefits and the only Articles dealing with them are Articles 4(2a) and 10a of EC Regulation 1408/71. The absence of these detailed rules and the lack of caselaw in this area means that special non-contributory benefits remain something of an unknown, or at least unexplored, quantity. This is further exacerbated by the grouping together of benefits which have little in common but actually cover the multitude of benefits found throughout the rest of the Regulation.

The inclusion of this category was largely a response to the problems encountered by the European Court of Justice (ECJ) in making the distinction between 'social security benefits' which were within the scope of the Regulation and 'social assistance benefits' which were not. It is not clear however, that this problem is resolved. If anything it has perhaps added to the burden in that the ECJ must now distinguish social security from both social assistance and special non-contributory benefits.

General rules
- The crucial factor in determining the competent state is that of habitual residence. Habitual residence for European Community (EC) purposes is not the same as the habitual residence test in UK law. See p385 for further details.
- Article 10a(1) specifies that special non-contributory benefits shall be granted to people exclusively in the territory of the member state in which they reside, in accordance with the legislation of that state. Therefore, you can only receive special non-contributory benefits from the state in which you are habitually resident and these benefits may not be exported. (Although see p364 if you were receiving attendance allowance, disability living allowance or invalid care allowance prior to 1 June 1992.)
- Special non-contributory benefits are subject to the principle of aggregation. Article 10a(2) specifies that a member state whose legislation makes entitlement to its own special non-contributory benefits subject to the completion of periods of employment, self-employment or residence shall regard where necessary, periods of employment, self-employment or residence completed in the territory of another member state as though they were completed in its own. However, this only applies once it is established that you are habitually resident in the member state from which you seek to claim benefit.
- Special non-contributory benefits are covered where they provide supplementary, substitute or ancillary cover against the social risk set out in the Article, or are specific protection for disabled people.
- Each member state has to specify which of their national benefits falls within the category of special non-contributory benefits. The UK list currently lists these as AA, DLA, disability working allowance (DWA), family credit (FC), ICA, IS, and income-based JSA. The list has not been updated and therefore does not include WFTC and DPTC. However, as these benefits essentially are simply a renaming of FC and DWA it should be assumed that they are treated as being on the list. Family credit has been held to be a family benefit by the European Court of Justice (ECJ) but this was before the introduction of special non-contributory benefits. The DWP continues to treat WFTC as a family benefit on the basis of this decision even though it listed FC as a special non-contributory benefit.[96]
- Once it is decided that you are habitually resident in a member state you may rely on the co-ordination provisions of EC Regulation 1408/71 to satisfy any

residence or contribution conditions. Therefore, if you need to claim benefit the state in which you are habitually resident must add together periods of residence or employment in order that you can qualify for benefit.

The meaning of habitual residence under Regulation 1408/71

You are entitled to claim special non-contributory benefits from a member state in which you are habitually resident rather than the state where you last worked. In *Snares*[97] the ECJ considered the position of DLA since the introduction of special non-contributory benefits. The ECJ held that entitlement to special non-contributory benefits was not conditional on the claimant having previously been subject to the social security legislation of the state in which s/he applies for the benefit. The crucial factor for this type of benefit was the place of habitual residence.

There has been a great deal of confusion over the term 'habitual residence'. This is because it also appears in UK regulations in respect of means-tested benefits. Furthermore, the House of Lords has given a definition on habitual residence for domestic law purposes which does not follow caselaw from the ECJ. In *Nessa* the House of Lords held that in order to satisfy the habitual residence test a person must satisfy a period of residence.[98] This follows earlier caselaw that held that it was necessary to complete an appreciable period of residence before you became habitually resident.

However, the co-ordination rule in EC Regulation 1408/71 allows you to aggregate periods of residence elsewhere in the EEA in order to meet national residence conditions. The appreciable period was essentially a requirement to be resident for a particular, albeit variable, period of time. Obviously a person able to rely on EC Regulation 1408/71 could not be refused a benefit falling within the scope of the Regulation merely because s/he had not been resident for an appreciable period because it is the function of EC Regulation1408/71 to override residence tests.

There is a substantial body of caselaw as to the meaning of habitual residence in the Regulation. The leading judgment is *Di Paolo*[99] which held that the key factors in determining a person's habitual residence are:

> 'the length and continuity of residence before the person concerned moved, the length and purpose of his absence, the nature of the occupation found in the other member state and the intention of the person concerned as it appears from all the circumstances.'

This case was concerned with unemployment benefits. Later judgments of the ECJ have cited *Di Paolo* as authoritative in respect of other benefits. In the case of *Swaddling* the ECJ considered both the UK and EC term of habitual residence test. It cites the *Di Paolo* test as being authoritative for IS and found that an employed person who has gone to another member state to work, who then returns to her/

his country of origin and has no close relationships or ties in the state which s/he has left, is habitually resident in her/his country of origin. Consequently Mr Swaddling was habitually resident in the UK. Once it is established a person is habitually resident and an insured person s/he may claim special non-contributory benefit. Furthermore applying the aggregation rules of EC Regulation 1408/71 means that periods of residence or employment in any member state must be taken into account in order to satisfy any residence conditions attached to that benefit. Consequently Mr Swaddling could not be refused benefit because he failed to satisfy the appreciable period under the UK habitual residence test. The aggregation rule meant that the period spent in France went towards satisfying this residence test.

Although the *Swaddling* case involved a British citizen the decision applies equally to other EEA nationals. The most important element in establishing entitlement to special non-contributory benefits is to establish that you are habitually resident applying the *Di Paolo* criteria. Equally, the decision does not just apply to IS but would have general application to special non-contributory benefits. Therefore a person who wants to claim DLA, AA, WFTC, DPTC or ICA who is habitually resident, may rely on periods of residence spent elsewhere in the EEA in order to meet residence conditions.

For further details on the UK habitual residence test, see p135.

Entitlement to AA, DLA and ICA before 1 June 1992

If you were entitled to AA, DLA or ICA before 1 June 1992 you can export your benefit if you take up 'habitual residence' (see p385) in another EU/EEA member state, provided that:
- you satisfy all the other conditions of entitlement, except the 'residence' and 'presence' conditions; *and either*
- you are working in the UK (this counts whether or not you are paying national insurance contributions); *or*
- you have worked in the UK as an employed or self-employed person.[100]

In some circumstance if you live in the UK and you go to live in residential care you will lose your AA or DLA. Because of the wording of the UK regulations this does not apply if you go into residential care in another EEA state.

Entitlement to AA, DLA and ICA after 1 June 1992

If you became entitled to AA, DLA or ICA after 1 June 1992 the benefits are treated as special non-contributory benefits and cannot be exported. They are payable only in, and at the expense of, the member state of 'habitual residence'. You may, however, claim a similar special non-contributory benefit from the EU/EEA member state where you are 'habitually resident' if there is an equivalent benefit there.

9. Death grants

There are no UK death grants covered under the co-ordination rule.

Notes

1. Sickness and maternity benefits
1 Case C-61/85
2 Art 18 Reg 1408/71
3 Art 18 Reg 1408/71
4 Article 22 Reg 1408/71
5 Articles 19(1) and 21
6 Article 25
7 Articles 27 and 31
8 Article 28
9 Article 26

2. Invalidity benefits
10 [10]Prior to June 1992 AA and DLA were considered to be invalidity benefits and therefore exportable. However from 1 June 1992 these benefits are listed as special non-contributory benefits and are no longer exportable. *Partridge*; *Snares* CDLA /913/94. However, those eligible for benefit prior to this date will retain the right to export these benefits, Art 95 Reg1408/71.
11 Art 10(1) and Annex VI O(12) Reg 1408/71
12 Art 40(4) Reg 1408/71 and Arts 40 and 51 Reg 574/72
13 Arts 40(4) and 41
14 Art 42
15 Vol 3 paras 22416 and 22419 AOG; Art 37 Reg 1408/71
16 Vol 3 paras 22467 and 22471 AOG; Art 45(1) Reg 1408/71
17 Art 46(3) Reg 1408/71
18 Art 39 Reg 1408/71
19 Art 39(2) and (3) Reg 1408/71
20 Art 39(4)
21 Art 35(1) Reg 574/72
22 Art 40(3)
23 Art 40(1) and (2) Reg 1408/71
24 Art 35(1) Reg 574/72
25 Arts 36, 41 and 43 Reg 574/72
26 Arts 45, 47 and 53 Reg 1408/71

3. Old age benefits
27 Art 77 Reg 1408/71
28 Case C-382/98 *R v Secretary of State for Social Security ex parte Taylor*
29 Arts 1(h) and (i), 10(1) and Annex VI O(12) Reg 1408/71
30 Art 36(1) Reg 574/72
31 Arts 36 and 41 and Annex 3 (O) Reg 574/72; C-108/75 *Balsamo Institut National d'Assurance Maladie Invalidite* [1976] ECR 375; R(S) 3/82
32 Art 46(1) Reg 1408/71
33 Art 46(2) Reg 1408/71
34 Art 46(2) Reg 1408/71; Vol 3 para 23863 AOG
35 Art 46(1) and (2) Reg 1408/71
36 Art 48 Reg 1408/71
37 Art 46(2) Reg 1408/71
38 Annex VI O(8) Reg 1408/71
39 Art 51(1) Reg 1408/71
40 Art 47(3) Reg 1408/71
41 Art 10(1) and Annex VI O(12) Reg 1408/71

4. Survivors' benefits
42 Arts 1(h) and (i) and 10(1) and Annex VI O(12) Reg 1408/71

5. Benefits for accidents at work and occupational diseases
43 s104(1) and (2) SSCBA 1992
44 s105 SSCBA 1992
45 Sch 7 para 11(1) SSCBA 1992
46 s95(1)-(4) SSCBA 1992
47 Art 10(1) Reg 1408/71
48 Art 55(1) Reg 1408/71
49 Arts 52 and 63 Reg 1408/71
50 Art 56 Reg 1408/71
51 Arts 61(5) and (6)

6. Unemployment benefits

52 Arts 67-71 Reg 1408/71
53 *Hockenjos v Secretary of State for Social Security* [2001] EWCA Civ 624(CA) and CJSA/1920/1999 (*65/00)
54 s1(2)(i) JSA 1995. In a letter to the TUC, November 1996, Mr Allan Larsson of the EC said that both contribution-based and income-based JSA would be treated as falling within the scope of Regs 1408/71 and 574/72. Income-based JSA is a special non-contributory benefit under Arts 4(2a) and 10(a) and Annex IIa Reg 1408/71 although, given current domestic caselaw, this probably has little significance.
55 Art 13 Reg 1408/71; C-128/83 *Caisse Primaire d'Assurance Maladie de Rouen v Guyot*; C-20/75 *Gaetano d'Amico v Landesversicherungs-anstalt Rheinland-Pfalz* [1975] ECHR 891; R(U) 4/84
56 C-227/81 *Francis Aubin v ASSEDIC and UNEDIC* [1982] ECR 1991
57 Art 68(2) Reg 1408/71
58 Art 69(1) Reg 1408/71
59 Art 69(1) Reg 1408/71
60 Arts 67(1)-(3) and 71(1)(a)(ii) and (b)(ii) Reg 1408/71
61 Annex VI section O point 7 Reg 1408/71
62 Art 69(1) Reg 1408/71
63 R(U) 2/90
64 Art 69(1)(a) Reg 1408/71
65 Art 69(1)(b) Reg 1408/71
66 Art 69(1)(b) Reg 1408/71; C-20/75 *d'Amico* (see note 55). Some EU/EEA member states have more stringent conditions than the UK and may require people with children to have formal childminding arrangements in place, including a contract, before the unemployed person is treated as available for work.
67 Art 83(3) Reg 574/72
68 Art 69(1)(c) Reg 1408/71
69 Art 69(1)(c) Reg 1408/71
70 s5(1) JSA 1995; Art 69(1)(c) Reg 1408/71
71 Art 69(1)(c) Reg 1408/71
72 Art 69(1)(c)
73 Art 83(1) Reg 574/72; R(U) 5/78
74 Art 69(3) Reg 1408/71
75 Art 69(2) Reg 1408/71; s5 JSA 1995
76 Art 25 Reg 1408/71
77 Art 67 Reg 1408/71
78 Art 67 Reg 1408/71
79 Art 69(1)(a) Reg 1408/71
80 Art 69(1) Reg 1408/71
81 Art 69(1)(a) Reg 1408/71
82 Art 69(1)(b) Reg 1408/71; C-20/75 *d'Amico* (see note 55)
83 Art 69(1) Reg 1408/71
84 Art 69(1)(c) Reg 1408/71

7. Family benefits

85 Art 14(a) and (b) Reg 1408/71
86 C-300/84 *Van Roosmalen* [1986] ECR 3095
87 Art 73 Reg 1408/71
88 Art 74 Reg 1408/71
89 Art 72a Reg 1408/71
90 Art 77 and 77(1)(t) Reg 1408/71
91 Arts 77(2)(b)(i) and (ii) and 79(2) Reg 1408/71
92 Art 10 Reg 574/72
93 Arts 86, 88, 90 and 91 Reg 574/72
94 Art 75(2) Reg 1408/71

8. Special non-contributory benefits

95 Annexe IIa Reg 1408/71
96 In *Snares*, Case C-20/96 the ECJ considered the position of DLA. An earlier decision by the ECJ had held that mobility allowance was an invalidity benefit under the Regulation. DLA was essentially the same benefit as mobility allowance, but the ECJ ruled that the fact that DLA was listed in Annexe IIa to the Regulation as a special non-contributory benefit meant that it was such a benefit. A similar decision was made in *Partridge*. .
97 *Snares* Case C-20/96
98 *Nessa v CAO* [1999], WLR 1937 (reported as R(IS) 2/00)
99 *Di Paolo* Case C-76/76
100 Art 95b(8) Reg 1408/71; R(A) 5/92

Chapter 27

∙∙∙

Using the social advantage route to claim benefits

This chapter covers

---

1. **What is a social advantage**

If you are an European Economic Area (EEA) national you are *never* a 'person subject to immigration control' for benefits purposes (see p157).[1] This applies whether or not you are here as a 'worker'. It also applies regardless of any right to reside in the UK and regardless of whether any immigration condition has been imposed or an immigration action is being taken against you. For example, even if a deportation order is made against you, you do not become subject to immigration control for benefit purposes. If you are an EEA national and you have lived in the UK for more than two years you are entitled to benefits on the same basis as UK nationals.

The right to the same 'social advantage' stems from the basic 'freedom of movement' principles laid down in Article 39 of the Treaty of Rome.

The principles set out in the Treaty are given further effect by a number of regulations and directives.

- Regulation 1612/68: which covers employed people;
- Regulation 1251/70: which covers retired and incapacitated workers;
- Directive 68/360: which covers employed people;
- Directive 73/148: which covers self-employed people, and people who are in receipt of services;
- Directive 75/34: which covers retired self-employed people and retired recipients of services.

Article 7(2) of Regulation 1612/68 gives people who have taken up work in another EEA state the right to the same tax and social advantage as nationals of that state. In other words, EEA nationals who have worked in a particular EEA state are entitled to equal treatment with nationals of the state in which they have worked. Although social advantage is only expressly articulated in EC Regulation 1612/68 in respect of people who are or have been employed, the same rights are extended to the self-employed and those receiving or providing services and to certain retired or incapacitated workers. These rights are also given to the family members of these workers.[2]

The term social advantage has been interpreted widely by the European Court of Justice (ECJ). It certainly covers all types of social security benefits but could also include items such as fare reduction cards, education grants and hospital treatment.

2. The personal scope

In order to rely on the social advantage route you must be a European Economic Area (EEA) national or a national of a dependent territory of an EEA state (see p332). You must also be able to show that you are, or have been in the past, one of the classes of person covered by the free movement provisions. These are:

- employed people;
- self-employed people;
- people providing services;
- people receiving service.

These are often collectively referred to as 'workers'. The term worker is one that causes a great deal of confusion. This is because sometimes for European Community (EC) purposes it is used as a generic term applied as a type of shorthand to describe people who are economically active. Other times it is used only to describe people who are employees. The wider definition applies not only to people who are actually employed but also to self-employed people and those receiving or providing services. If you are no longer economically active you can still be a 'worker' if you have worked in a member state but are now incapacitated, have suffered an industrial injury or if you are retired.

Your rights as a worker are extended to your spouse and other family members, whatever their nationality. If you die your family continues to have rights as survivors of an EEA worker.

The essential factor to remember when trying to establish whether someone can rely on the social advantage route is whether or not s/he has been involved in some economic activity.

UK nationals who can rely on the social advantage route

You count as a UK national under EEA law if you are:[3]
- a British citizen;
- a British subject with the right of abode in the UK;
- a British dependent territories citizen because of your connection with Gibraltar;
- a British overseas citizen – these may also count as UK nationals under EEA law.[4]

However, even if you are a UK national under EEA law, you do not always have EC law rights. You can only use the social advantage rule if:[5]
- you have travelled to another EEA state; *and*
- you went to that member state to use an EC right there; *and*
- you later returned to the UK to exercise an EC right here.

If you are a dual national with the nationality of another EEA state (eg, Ireland), you can use these exemptions even if you have never moved within the EEA.[6]

If you worked in another EEA state but remained living in the UK, you may count as a 'frontier worker' and so have EC law rights.[7]

The EC rights which carry the right to free movement and social advantage are:
- the right to work, including the right to seek work;
- the right to establish yourself as self-employed, including the right to seek to do that;
- the right to receive and provide services.

The DWP often takes the view that you have not exercised your right to free movement if you claimed income-based jobseeker's allowance on your return to the UK. This is because you have not returned to the UK 'to work'. This is wrong. If you return to the UK to seek work, you have exercised your right to free movement, regardless of any claim for benefit.[8]

If you are treated as an EEA national under these rules, then the habitual residence exemptions apply to you as they apply to other EEA nationals (see p135).

---

3. **The substantive scope**

People who are covered by EC Regulation 1612/68

If you are a European Economic Area (EEA) national and you are working in the UK, you are a worker covered by Regulation 1612/68. The UK does not include the Channel Islands and Isle of Man for this purpose.[9]

The meaning of the term worker has now been considered on numerous occasions by the European Court of Justice (ECJ) and the following principles have been established. For the purposes of Regulation 1612/68 a worker is anyone who pursues 'effective and genuine work'. That is services for another under their direction and in return for remuneration.[10] This includes part-time work, even if topped up with benefits. Anyone who loses a job involuntarily will still have rights as a worker (see p390). Someone looking for work has certain rights under 1612/98 but does not have the right to the same social advantage.[11]

The caselaw does *not* say that for an activity to count as work there must be:
- a minimum period of work;
- a minimum number of hours per week; *or*
- minimum pay.

It does not matter if you are paid in kind rather than cash.[12] It is irrelevant that the income from the work is not enough to support you.[13] Voluntary work from which you can expect no benefit is not 'work'. However, a person who works for nothing for a period of time, under an agreement that is intended to lead to payment, may qualify as a worker. Work for your rehabilitation may not count as work under this rule.

The following activities have been considered as work:
- teaching music for 12 hours a week;[14]
- work for 60 hours over 16 weeks under a contract with no fixed hours but which requires the person to be available to work;[15]
- training over the summer in a hotel school;[16]
- working as an au pair 13 hours a week for £35 and board and lodging.[17]

Voluntary and involuntary unemployment

If you are voluntarily unemployed you may lose your right of residence in a member state and the right to a social advantage. The question of whether someone is voluntarily or involuntarily unemployed is one that is decided by the JobCentre. This is likely to cause problems for people claiming benefit. Voluntary unemployment is a familiar term in UK social security rules and is applied harshly. However, European Community (EC) law allows a much more generous approach to whether you are voluntarily unemployed. If you were dismissed or resigned from your job you can still be treated as involuntarily unemployed if you are looking for work.

If you are an EEA national who has worked in the UK you still count as a worker for the purposes of Regulation 1612/68 if *either*:
- you are genuinely seeking work,[18] whether or not your employment ceased voluntarily or involuntarily;[19] *or*
- you are studying or training and your employment ended involuntarily, *or* there is a link between your present training/studies and your previous employment.[20]

People who have worked elsewhere in the European Economic Area

People who have not worked in the UK but have worked elsewhere in the EEA do have some rights under EC law but they are limited. For example, they have the right to enter a member state and to look for work and to reside. They also have the right to install family members whatever their nationality. However, they do not have the right to the same tax and social advantage as members of the national state. In order to rely on the social advantage route you must actually have worked in the state in which you wish to claim the social advantage.[21] A social security commissioner has decided that work in the EEA outside the UK cannot exempt a person from the habitual residence test as a worker for the purposes of Regulation 1612/68.[22] This is important for British citizens returning here after working in the EEA. The commissioner followed earlier caselaw that a person only has rights as a worker under EC law in the UK once that person has worked in the UK.[23] If the British person has worked in the UK prior to going to another EEA state s/he can argue that s/he is covered by EC Regulation 1612/68 as the work is not limited to the period since they last entered the UK. A person who has not worked in the UK but has worked elsewhere in the EEA may be able to rely on EC Regulation 1408/71 to override any residence tests (see p131).

People who are covered by Directive 68/360 – right of residence for employees

Directive 68/360 deals with the right of residence for employed people. As proof of your right of residence under EC law this Directive says that a residence permit should be issued. Your rights to reside come from EC law and you do not need to have a permit in order to be resident. The permit is merely confirmation of your status as an EEA national with the right to reside.[24] However, it is usually best to obtain a residence permit if you can because if you need to claim benefit and you do not have a permit, the DWP will have to decide whether or not you are a 'worker' and/or have a 'right to reside'. This often leads to refusal of benefit.

The permit must state that it has been issued pursuant to Regulation 1612/68. The Directive, therefore, operates as a companion legal provision to 1612/68 and is only available to those considered to fall under Regulation 1612/68.

The Directive provides that member states shall grant the right of residence to workers able to produce:
- the document with which they entered the member state; *and*
- a confirmation of engagement from an employer, or a certificate of employment.

In the case of your spouse or children aged under 21 the right of residence is acquired upon production of:
- the document with which they entered the member state; *and*

- a document proving their relationship, issued by their state of origin, or the state they have move from.

For dependent children over the age of 21 or other dependent relatives of the worker or worker's spouse, in addition to the above you must also provide evidence that they are dependent on you or your spouse.

A family member who is not an EEA national must be issued with a residence document having the same validity as that issued to the worker on whom s/he is dependent.[25]

A permit issued by the Home Office is usually valid for five years and is automatically renewable. However, some people are given temporary residence permits. The length of the permit is:

- up to three months where your work is expected to last for three months or less;
- up to a year where your work is expected to last for more than three months but less than a year; *or*
- five years where the employment is expected to last for more than one year.

If you worked in a job that was not for a fixed period, you should try to get your old employer to confirm that your job was for an indefinite period. The DWP should then treat your case as if a permit lasting five years had been issued.

If you worked in a job on a fixed length contract of more than three months, you should be treated as if you had been issued with a permit lasting until the expected end of the contract, even if your employment ended earlier – for example, you were made redundant.[26]

British citizens and the right to reside

British citizens do not normally rely on this Directive to reside in the UK. Their right to reside stems from UK law and a British citizen cannot be refused entry or deported from the UK. However, a UK national can invoke the right of free movement and residence in her/his own state if s/he has exercised free movement rights in another member state. In the *Singh*[27] case a British woman whose husband was an Indian national had gone to work in another member state. She was able to take her husband to that member state under EC Regulation 1612/68 and Directive 68/360. However, when she returned to the UK her husband was admitted as a spouse under UK law and was given limited leave. The European Court of Justice (ECJ) held that a national of a member state might be deterred from leaving that state to work in the territory of another member state if, on returning to work in her/his state of nationality, the conditions of her/his entry and stay, and that of her/his spouse and children, were not at least equivalent to those enjoyed under the Treaty and secondary legislation in that other member state. Consequently, an EEA national who goes to another member state to work there as an employed person and who returns to work in her/his own member state has the right to be accompanied by her/his spouse under the conditions laid down by Regulation 1612/68 and Directives 68/360 and 73/148.

Expiry, withdrawal and renewal of residence permit

A five-year residence permit is automatically renewable for a further five years. Furthermore, although in order to acquire a permit you must provide confirmation of your employment, you do not lose your right of residence if you are involuntarily unemployed (see p392). Temporary residence permits are not automatically renewable, therefore on expiry you would need to present the documents required to acquire a permit.

Your right of residence, and therefore the residence permit, can only be removed on very limited grounds:

- the grounds of public policy, public security or public health as set out in the Treaty;
- in cases of prolonged absence. A residence permit is unaffected by either breaks in residence not exceeding six consecutive months, or absence on military service;[28]
- where you become 'voluntarily unemployed'. However, this is much more narrowly defined than you might imagine (see p392) and it does not apply if you are currently temporarily incapable of work as a result of an accident or illness.[29] Arguably it also does not apply if you are temporarily unable to work due to pregnancy or the fact you have just given birth.

The DWP often make decisions as to your right of residence in respect of benefits. We consider that only the Home Office can do this (whether or not a permit has been issued).[30] This is because EC law does not state that the right of residence ends automatically, but that the residence permit may only be withdrawn for the reasons above.[31] This means that a decision to end the right to reside is a discretionary one, which must take into account all the circumstances of your case. Only the Home Office is in a position to make that decision. If the DWP decides that you have lost the right to reside, seek specialist advice.

People who are covered by Regulation 1251/70 – retired or incapacitated people

This Regulation is important as it gives you and also your family the right of residence in a member state even though you are no longer working. These rights extend to your survivors and therefore can be crucial, for example, if your spouse is not an EEA national. You have a right to remain under Regulation 1251/70 if:

- you have reached retirement pension age in that member state. In the UK this is currently 60 for women, 65 for men,[32] *and either*:[33]
  - you had worked in the UK for at least the last 12 months before retirement and resided continuously in the UK for more than three years; *or*

– your spouse is a British citizen (or lost that citizenship because s/he married you);[34] *or*
- stopped working because of permanent incapacity *and either:*[35]
  – at the date you stopped working you had resided continuously in the UK for more than two years; *or*
  – your incapacity was caused by an industrial injury or disease; *or*
  – your spouse is a British citizen (or lost that citizenship because s/he married you).[36]

When working out your period of 'continuous residence', include:[37]
- absences from the UK of up to three months a year;
- longer absences due to your country's rules about military service.

When working out your period of employment, ignore:[38]
- days of unemployment (even if you were not paid jobseeker's allowance (JSA) – eg, because of an inadequate contribution record);
- absence from work due to illness or accident.[39]

Family members of retired or incapacitated workers

If you have a right of residence under this Regulation these rights are extended to your family members even after your death and regardless of their nationality.[40]

If a worker dies during her/his working life before having acquired the right of residence under this Regulation members of her/his family are entitled to remain, provided that:
- the worker at the date of her/his death has resided continuously in the territory of that member state for at least two years; *or*
- her/his death resulted from an accident at work or an occupational disease; *or*
- the surviving spouse is a national of the state of residence or lost the nationality of that state by marriage to the worker.[41]

The rights to equality of treatment provided by Regulation 1612/68 is extended to people covered by Regulation 1251/70. Therefore the survivors of a deceased worker who enjoy the right to remain in a member state are entitled to the same social advantages as the survivors of national workers.[42]

People covered by Directive 73/148 – self-employed and providing services

The freedoms granted to workers under Article 39 are also granted by the Treaty to the self-employed in the form of a right of establishment and a right to provide services. The principal articles are Article 52 (establishment) and Articles 59 and 60(3) (services). The difference between the right of establishment and the right to provide services is one of degree rather than of kind. Both apply to business or professional activity pursued for profit or remuneration. A right of establishment is a right to install yourself in another member state permanently or semi-permanently whether as an individual or a company for the purpose of performing a particular activity there. The right to provide services, on the other hand, connotes the provision of services in one state, on a temporary or spasmodic basis, by a person established in another state. In the latter case it is not necessary to reside, even temporarily, in the state in which the service is provided.

If you are self-employed in the UK, you have a right to reside in the UK under this Directive.[43] Self-employment includes professional activity. A person who has taken preparatory steps to offer services counts as self-employed.[44] There is no minimum period of residence or of work.

The rights and the rules relating to residence are equivalent to those for employed people under Regulation 1612/68. Those who establish themselves are entitled, like workers, to a residence permit to be valid for not less than five years from the date of issue, and automatically renewable.[45]

Your right to reside is permanent, but may be taken away if:

- you stop residing in the UK for longer than six consecutive months (ignoring any absence for military service);[46] *or*
- you stop being self-employed, unless this is because of temporary incapacity due to illness or accident.[47] Arguably this would also apply if you are temporarily unable to work due to pregnancy.

Receiving services under Directive 73/148

The freedom provided by Articles 59 and 60 is expressed in terms of the freedom to provide services. It has now been extended by the ECJ to embrace the freedom to receive services. The ECJ has held that recipients of services include tourists, people receiving medical treatment and people travelling for the purposes of education and business as long as there is a commercial aspect to the service provided. In short, if you pay for the service you are covered.[48]

If you are receiving services in the UK, you have a right to reside in the UK.[49] That right continues as long as the services are being received (see example below). Services include:

- tourism,[50] but this must be more than visiting friends;[51]
- education, except for education provided as part of the national education system;[52] *and*
- medical treatment.[53]

Example

Ettore, an Italian man, came to Manchester to study languages part time at a private college. He paid the annual college fees and intended to support himself by working part time. He is unable to find any part-time work and claims income-based JSA. He is exempt from the habitual residence test because he has a right to reside in Manchester to receive the services provided by the college.

Directive 75/34 – right to remain permanently in a member state after having been self-employed there (equivalent to Regulation 1251/70)

If you have retired from self-employment because of old age or incapacity, you may have a right to reside under Directive 75/34.[54] The rules are the same as those for retired workers (see p395),[55] except that your self-employment in the UK counts as work. Even though you have a right to reside, this does not exempt you from the habitual residence test because the benefit exemptions do not refer to Directive 75/34. However, the equal treatment rule in this Directive has direct effect and so can override the habitual residence test.[56] If you fail the habitual residence test seek specialist advice.

4. The material scope

Unlike EC Regulation 1408/71 (the co-ordination rule) there is no list of benefits that fall under the term 'social advantage'. Anything that can be construed as a social advantage will be covered. The European Court of Justice (ECJ) has given a wide interpretation to this term and it would seem to be clear that all social security benefits will be covered by the social advantage rule.

The main hurdle that European Economic Area (EEA) nationals now face in claiming benefits is that of the habitual residence test and it is here that UK regulations specifically refer to the social advantage rule in European Community (EC) law. However, there are still some other areas where the social advantage route may assist claimants. What follows are the main areas for potential use of the social advantage rule. This includes:

- the habitual residence test;
- the social fund;
- tax credits.

This list is not exhaustive, there may be other areas that you can think of. In order to judge whether the social advantage route is appropriate you should ask the following questions.

- Does the domestic legislation exclude me from the particular benefit because of my nationality?
- Does the rule disproportionately affect or favour one nationality?

If the answer is yes to either of these questions there may be scope to use the equal treatment provisions.

The habitual residence test

The habitual residence test only applies to income support (IS), income-based jobseeker's allowance (JSA), housing benefit (HB) and council tax benefit (CTB).[57]

Furthermore, it applies only to the person claiming the benefit,[58] not to any partner or child for whom benefit is being claimed. If you have a partner who is more likely to pass the test than you, s/he could claim instead, though there may be disadvantages to this (see CPAG's *Welfare Benefits Handbook*).

You pass the habitual residence test if you are habitually resident (see p135) in the UK, Ireland, the Channel Islands or the Isle of Man. If you are an EEA national who is not habitually resident, and you are not exempt, you are a 'person from abroad' and are not entitled to IS, income-based JSA, HB or CTB. If you have just entered the UK the general rule is that you cannot be habitually resident until you have resided for an appreciable period. However, European Community (EC) law allows you to override this. If you are an EEA worker under Regulations 1612/68 or 1251/70, or Directives 68/360 or 73/148 you are exempt from the test.[59] Even if you are not exempt under the social advantage rule you may be able to rely on the co-ordination rule so that you do not have to be resident for an appreciable period before claiming these benefits.

The DWP should accept that you are exempt if you hold a current EEA residence permit issued by the Home Office. However, the DWP considers that it can decide that the right of residence has been lost, even if you have a current residence permit. This is highly questionable and should be challenged.

You may be covered by more than one exemption so you should check each one. If the DWP decides that you are not habitually resident and not exempt, you should appeal and take independent advice. You should also continue to make further claims because at some point you will become habitually resident but the tribunal will only be able to consider the matter at the date the decision was made (see CPAG's *Welfare Benefits Handbook*).

Lawfulness of the habitual residence test under EC law

The habitual residence test discriminates in favour of Irish nationals and against nationals of other EEA states because it applies to people who are habitually resident in the Republic of Ireland, even though that is outside the UK. Irish nationals, therefore, are more likely to be habitually resident in Ireland than nationals of other EEA states.

In *Sarwar* the Court of Appeal decided that this discrimination is not unlawful under EC law because it only affects work-seekers (not workers - who are exempt from the test) and such discrimination in relation to IS, HB and CTB entitlement is not prohibited by the EC Treaty.[60]

However, since *Sarwar*, the ECJ has ruled that discrimination in benefits on national grounds against a person who is *not* a worker is contrary to the EC Treaty.[61] This means that *Sarwar* may no longer be good law.

It is also arguable that since the introduction of JSA there are stronger grounds to argue that the habitual residence test breaches EC law. EC law requires the DWP to give EEA workseekers the same assistance as British citizens.[62] Income-based JSA may count as assistance under EC law because it is an essential and inseparable part of a co-ordinated programme of assistance to help the unemployed find work – including advice, training and jobclubs. On this basis, provision which discriminates on nationality grounds is in breach of EC law. This assistance applies to workseekers as well as workers, while the EC rule considered in *Sarwar* only applied to workers.[63]

The social fund

Funeral payments

Two rules for funeral payments particularly affect EEA nationals:

- the deceased person must have been ordinarily resident (see p132) in the UK at the date of death (see below);[64]
- the funeral must take place within the UK, unless one of the special EEA rules applies to the claimant (see below).

See CPAG's *Welfare Benefits Handbook* for the other rules about funeral payments.

Ordinary residence

The deceased must have been ordinarily resident in the UK at the date of death. S/he does not need to have died in the UK, so where a person's body is brought to the UK for burial here a payment can be made. For example, a payment can be made for a person buried here who died on holiday abroad.

Payments for funerals in another European Economic Area state

The normal rule is that a social fund payment cannot be made for a funeral outside the UK.[65] However, you are eligible for a payment for a funeral in an EEA state if you are the responsible person (see CPAG's *Welfare Benefits Handbook*) and you are:[66]

- a worker for the purposes of Regulation 1612/68 (see p390);
- a family member of a worker for the purposes of Regulation 1612/68 (see p347);
- a person with a right to reside in the UK under either Directive 68/360 (see p393) or Directive 73/148 (see p396); *or*
- a member of the family of a deceased worker for the purposes of Reg 1251/70 (see p395).

You may qualify under more than one of these exceptions. If you have an EEA residence permit the DWP should accept that these exceptions apply to you, but you do not need to have a permit.

The funeral does not have to take place in the deceased person's country of nationality, but can be in any EEA country.

The deceased does not need to have died in the UK – eg, where a person dies in France on a visit and is buried there, if a person here accepts responsibility for the funeral expenses. The expenses of transporting the deceased to the funeral directors are only covered to the extent that the transporting is done in the UK.[67] All other travelling outside the UK can be met under the usual rules.

A family member of a deceased worker for the purposes of Regulation 1251/70 can claim a payment for a funeral outside the UK in the EEA. You count as the family member of a worker for the purposes of Regulation 1251/70 if:[68]

- before s/he died the worker gained the right of permanent residence in the UK under Regulation 1251/70 (see p395) *and* you were a member of her/his family (for the purposes of Regulation 1612/68 – see p391) when s/he gained that right. You do not need to have been residing with the deceased worker when s/he gained that right.[69] For example, the spouse of a retired worker will qualify even if s/he separated before s/he gained the right to permanent residence;
- the worker died before gaining the right of permanent residence in the UK *and* you were a member of her/his family (for the purposes of Regulation 1612/68 – see p391) *and:*
  - the worker had resided continuously in the UK for two years at the date of death; *or*
  - her/his death resulted from an industrial accident or industrial disease; *or*
  - the surviving spouse of the worker is a British citizen or gave up British citizenship to marry the worker. This applies even if that spouse later died.

The exemption for a family member of a deceased worker applies to the claimant and not only to a claim for the funeral of the deceased worker her/himself.[70] So, for example, a British citizen daughter of an Italian couple would qualify for a funeral payment for her mother's funeral in Italy if her late father counted as a worker, even if her mother did not.

Lawfulness of the new funeral payment rules

These rules were made because the blanket refusal to make payments for funerals outside the UK in the old rules breached EC equal treatment law.[71] While the new rules cover most cases where there is an EC law right to equal treatment, they do not cover all those rights. If you are not covered by the new rules, then the rule that the funeral must be in the UK may still breach EC law if:

- the funeral took place in the EEA and the deceased had a right to equal treatment under EC law, but you do not have that right (see below);
- the funeral took place in the EEA and you have a right to reside under Directive 75/34 (retired self-employed and recipients of services) (see below);
- the funeral took place outside the EEA and you or the deceased had a right to equal treatment under EC law (see below).

These EC law rights have direct effect (see p334).[72] This means that where one of these rights applies, EC law overrides the rule that the funeral must take place in the UK.

If the deceased had an EC right to equal treatment then a refusal to pay for a funeral outside the UK may breach EC equal treatment rights. A migrant worker who wishes to be buried in the country of her/his birth but lacks the funds to pay for a funeral is detrimentally affected by this rule. Unlike a person who wishes to be buried in the UK, her/his wish can only be respected if the responsible person has an EC right to reside.[73]

If you have a right to reside under Directive 75/34 (see p398) you have an EC right to equal treatment in respect of social advantages.[74]

If the funeral takes place outside the EEA then no payment is made, even if you are within one of the exceptions for people with EEA rights. If this rule may detrimentally affect non-British EEA nationals it may breach EC equal treatment rights.[75]

Examples

Peter, an Irish national and a widower, died and was buried in Ireland. He has three children all of whom are receiving means-tested benefits.

His daughter, Oonagh is not an Irish national and has never exercised EC law free movement rights, but her husband, Colum, is Irish. Colum worked in the UK but was made redundant and so is a worker for the purposes of Regulation 1612/68. As his wife, Oonagh, is a family member and so can claim a payment for the funeral.

His other daughter, Mary, is an Irish national and was aged 20 when he died. At the date of his death Peter had been working in the UK for more than two years. Because of that and because Mary was aged under 21 she is a family member for the purposes of Regulation 1251/70 and so can also claim a payment for the funeral.

His son, John, is also an Irish national. He was aged 25 and living alone when Peter died. He has never worked in the UK and is single. He is not a worker for the purposes of Regulation 1612/68, nor the family member of such a person, nor does he have a right to reside as a self-employed person. He was not a family member when Peter died because he was aged over 21 and independent. Therefore none of the exceptions apply to him. If he were in fact the only immediate family member he could argue that Peter's right to equal treatment (under Regulation 1612/68) had been infringed.

Other social fund payments

Some of the other social fund rules may be unlawful under the social advantage rule, in particular:

- a crisis loan or community care grant can only be made for a need which occurs in the UK;[76]
- a grant or budgeting loan cannot be made for travelling expenses or accommodation outside the UK.[77]

These rules may be discriminatory in the case of an EEA national, because it is a condition which s/he is less likely to be able to meet than a UK national.[78] For

Chapter 27: Using the social advantage route to claim benefits
5. Family members of European Economic Area nationals

27

example, if a French retired worker living in Kent wishes to visit his sick mother, he may be given a grant if s/he lives in Belfast, but not if s/he lives in Boulogne, even though it would be cheaper for her/him to get to Boulogne.[79] This absolute rule is difficult to justify objectively especially since there is a discretion about the amount.[80] If any of these apply to you, you should ask for an internal social fund review and quickly seek specialist advice.

Tax credits

Disabled person's tax credit and working families' tax credit require that both the claimant and her/his partner to be 'ordinarily resident in the UK and that you or your partner's earnings do not wholly derive from earnings outside of the UK'. If you are refused benefit because of these conditions you may be able to use the co-ordination rule (see p345) or the social advantage rule to get benefit. Arguably the condition that your partner must be ordinarily resident in the UK may be discriminatory because it is more likely to affect migrant workers than British citizens.[81] Tax credits are clearly a social advantage so discrimination on grounds of nationality is unlawful.[82]

---

5. Family members of European Economic Area nationals

European Community (EC) law can be particularly helpful for family members who are not European Economic Area (EEA) nationals themselves. If you are a non-EEA national and you have an EC right to remain in the UK as a member of the family of an EEA national (see p346), then you do not require leave to remain[83] so you are *not* a 'person who is subject to immigration control' for benefits purposes.[84] This applies whether or not you have an EEA residence document.

If you are a non-EEA national and you do *not* have an EC right to remain in the UK, your entitlement to benefit depends upon your immigration status.

Remember that the definition of 'family member' includes not only spouse and children aged up to 21, but also other relatives – eg, a separated spouse, parents and adult children (see p346).

Family members and residence documents

A stamp in your passport or on a Home Office letter confirming your right to reside is called a 'residence document'. If you have a residence document then the DWP must accept that you do not require leave to remain.

If you do not have a residence document, then you can still count as a person who does not require leave to remain. Your right to remain comes from EC law so you do not need to have a residence document.[85] A decision on whether you are

27

Chapter 27: Using the social advantage route to claim benefits
5. Family members of European Economic Area nationals

subject to immigration control for benefit purposes is a DWP decision, not a Home Office one, and can be appealed to an appeal tribunal.

A person with an EC right to remain does not *require* leave to enter or remain, but can still be given it. For example, the right of permanent residence is shown by the grant of indefinite *leave* to remain. Also where a non-EEA family member seeks admission but does not have an EEA family permit, it is practice to give six months' leave to enter subject to a public funds condition.[86]

You may have leave subject to a condition that you do not have recourse to public funds or given as a result of a maintenance undertaking. Normally, a person with such leave would be subject to immigration control for benefits purposes.[87] However this rule can only apply to a person who *requires* leave to remain. If you have an EEA right to reside, for example because you are married to someone who is a 'worker' then you do not require leave to remain.[88] Your rights to remain are through the EC rules set out above and these override any UK provisions.

If you do not have permission to be in the UK, or you have limited leave to be in the UK, a claim for benefit may affect your immigration position (see p92). You should seek immigration advice before claiming.

Example 1

Lola is a Portuguese national. She arrives at Heathrow Airport with her 18-year-old son Joao who has a Mozambican passport but no EEA family permit. Lola is admitted as an EEA national exercising Treaty rights, but Joao is given six months' leave to enter subject to a public funds condition. Lola finds permanent work. Four months later her employer goes bankrupt and she loses her job. She is awarded income-based jobseeker's allowance (JSA). Joao also claims JSA. Because he has an EC law right to reside as Lola's son he is not 'subject to immigration control' despite the stamp in his passport. He is exempt from the habitual residence test because he has a right to reside under Directive 68/360 as the son of a worker with that right to reside (see below).

Example 2

Noor is a British citizen, but his mother, Shafla, is an elderly Indian national living abroad. Noor signs an undertaking to maintain and accommodate Shafla in the UK. Shafla is given indefinite leave to enter the UK as Noor's mother. She lives with Noor who works and maintains her. After a year, Noor moves to Germany. He works there for one year while Shafla remains in the UK, maintained by Noor. Noor returns to the UK and again finds work but is made redundant six months later. He claims JSA (both income and contribution-based) and Shafla claims income support. Because Noor has exercised his EC law right of free movement to work in Germany, he now has an EC law right to live in the UK. This includes the right to have his mother living with him as an elderly dependent relative. Shafla can argue that the sponsored immigrant rule no longer applies to her because her EC law right to reside with her son means that she no longer requires leave to remain in the UK.

Chapter 27: Using the social advantage route to claim benefits
5. Family members of European Economic Area nationals

27

Habitual residence and family members

The habitual residence test applies only to the person claiming the benefit.[89] It does not apply to any partner or child for whom benefit is being claimed. If you have a partner who is more likely to pass the test than you, s/he could claim instead, though there may be disadvantages to this (see *Welfare Benefits Handbook*).

Family members of an EEA national are exempt from the habitual residence test if:

- you have a residence document showing that you are the family member of an EEA national. This proves that you have a right to reside in the UK under Directive 68/360 or 73/148;[90] *or*
- you do not have a residence document, but are the family member of an EEA national who has a right to reside in the UK under Directive 68/360 or 73/148. This is because you have the same right to reside as the EEA national of whom you are a family member.[91]

Working families' tax credit/disabled person's tax credit for family members

If you are an EEA family member but are not an EEA national, you are entitled to working families' tax credit (WFTC) or disabled person's tax credit (DPTC) on the same basis as a British citizen (see p175). This is because EEA family members are exempt from the WFTC/DPTC immigration condition.[92]

'Family member of an EEA national' is not defined in WFTC/DPTC rules. If you have a residence document showing that you are an EEA family member, you ought to be accepted as one by the DWP.

If you do not have a residence document, the DWP will decide whether or not you are an EEA family member. If you do not have permission to be in the UK, or you have limited leave to be in the UK, a claim for benefit may affect your immigration position (see p92). You should seek immigration advice before claiming.

DWP advice is that a 'family member of an EEA national' for WFTC/DPTC is limited to the WFTC/DPTC definition of family, which is:[93]

- a married or unmarried couple and any child or young person in the household for whom one or both are responsible;
- a single person and any child or young person in the household for whom s/he is responsible.

This may be accurate in respect of benefits that fall under EC Regulation 1408/71 (see p349) because that Regulation says that the definition of family member is that used in the particular member state. However, the position is different with benefits that fall under the social advantage rule because the definition of family is different. Under the social advantage rule your family includes your spouse and children up to age 21 and any other dependent relatives in the ascending line. If

27

Chapter 27: Using the social advantage route to claim benefits
5. Family members of European Economic Area nationals

you are refused WFTC/DPTC on the grounds that you are not an EEA family member, you should seek specialist advice.

Notes

1. What is a social advantage

1 S115(9) IAA 1999 specifically states that EEA nationals are not persons subject to immigration control. This came into force on 3 Aprol 2000.
2 Case C-32/75 *Cristini*; Case C-63/76 *Inzirillo*; Case C-157/84 *Frascogna*; Case C-249/83 *Hoeckx*

2. The personal scope

3 UK Declaration dated 1 January 1983: OJ C23 28 January 1983 p1
4 The ECJ has been asked to decide this question: Case C-192/99 *Kaur*
5 Case C-370/90 *Surinder Singh* [1992] ECR I-4265
6 Case C-369/90 *Micheletti* [1992] ECR I-4239; Case C-292/86 *Gullung* [1988] ECR 111
7 The ECJ has been asked to decide whether a British citizen who travels on business to other EEA states but retains his home in the UK has acquired an EC right of residence in the UK (so he can benefit from EEA rules to have his wife stay here): Case C-60/00 *Carpenter*.
8 Art 39(3) EC Treaty (formerly Art 48(3)

3. The substantive scope

9 Art 299(6)(c) EC Treaty (formerly Art 227(6)(c); Protocol 3 to Treaty of Accession; Case C-355/89 *Barr & Montrose* [1991] I-3479
10 Case C-53/81 *Levin*; Case C-66/85 *Lawrie-Blum*
11 Case C-316/85 *Lebon*
12 Case C-196/87 *Steymann* [1988] ECR 6159

13 Case C-139/85 *Kempf* [1986] ECR 1741. Earning more than approx £2 on any one day ought to count as work, because under the rules for unemployment benefit (UB) those earnings were too high for you to count as unemployed: reg 7(1)(g)(i) Social Security (Unemployment, Sickness and Invalidity Benefit) Regulations 1983 (SI No.1598). On 7 October 1996 UB was replaced by JSA which has no equivalent rule.
14 Case C-139/85 *Kempf* [1986] ECR 1741
15 Case C-357/89 *Raulin*
16 C-27/91 *Le Manoir*
17 Case CIS/12909/1996 paras 14-15
18 Case C-85/96 *Martinez Sala* para 32
19 CIS/12909/1996 paras 21 and 23
20 Case C-39/86 *Lair* [1988] ECR 3161 para 37; Case C-357/89 *Raulin* [1992] ECR I-1027
21 Case C-316/85 *Lebon*
22 CIS/4521/1995 para 15
23 CIS/4521/1995 para 14; *Lair* and *Raulin* (see note 20)
24 Case C-48/95 *Royer* [1976] ECR 497
25 Art 4(4) Dir 68/360
26 Art 6(3) Dir 68/360
27 Case C-370/90 *Singh*
28 This refers to Art 6(2) Dir 68/360
29 This refers to Art 7 Dir 68/360. We consider that this also applies to a woman who cannot work because of pregnancy.
30 Art 16(2) I(EEA)O. If a residence permit is withdrawn by the Home Office there is a right of appeal to an immigration adjudicator: Art 18 I(EEA)O.
31 Arts 6(2) and 7 Dir 68/360
32 s122(1) SSCBA 1992 'pensionable age'
33 Art 2(1)(a) Reg 1251/70
34 Art 2(2) Reg 1251/70
35 Art 2(1)(b) Reg 1251/70
36 Art 2(2) Reg 1251/70
37 Art 4(1) Reg 1251/70

38 Art 4(2) Reg 1251/70
39 We consider that this also applies to a woman who cannot work because of pregnancy.
40 Article 3(1) Reg 1251/70
41 Article 3(2) Reg 1251/70
42 Case C-32/75 *Fiorini* and C-261/83 *Castelli*
43 Art 4(1) para 1 Dir 73/148
44 CIS/3559/1997
45 Dir 73/148, Art 4(2)
46 Art 4(1) para 3 Dir 73/148
47 Art 4(1) para 4 Dir 73/148. We consider that this also applies to a woman who cannot work because of pregnancy.
48 The point was originally raised in *Watson and Belmann* where the Commission suggested that the freedom to move within the Community to receive services was the necessary corollary to the freedom to provide services. This was approved by the ECJ in *Luisi v Ministero del Tesoro* where it was held that recipients of services included tourists, persons receiving medical treatment and persons travelling for the purposes of education and business, so far as there is a commercial aspect to the service provided.
49 Art 4(2) Dir 73/148
50 Case C-186/87 *Cowan* [1989] ECR 195
51 *Tisseyre*, IAT (6052)
52 Case C-263/86 *Humbel* [1988] ECR 5365
53 Cases C-286/82 and C-26/83 *Luisi and Carbone* [1988] ECR 5365
54 Art 1 Dir 75/34
55 Art 2(1) Reg 1251/70
56 Art 7 Dir 75/34

4. The material scope
57 Reg 21(3) IS Regs 'person from abroad'; reg 85(4) JSA Regs 'person from abroad'; reg 7A(4)(e) HB Regs; reg 4A(4)(e) CTB Regs
58 Reg 21(3) IS Regs 'person from abroad' and reg 85(4) JSA Regs 'person from abroad' use the words 'means a claimant who is not habitually resident . . .': Under HB/CTB rules the status of a partner and children does not affect entitlement.
59 Reg 21(3) (a) IS Regs 'person from abroad'; reg 85(4) (a) JSA Regs 'person from abroad' reg 7A(4)(e)(i) HB Regs; reg 4A(4)(e)(i) CTB Regs

60 *R v Secretary of State for Social Security ex parte Sarwar & Getachew* [1997] 3 CMLR 647, CA. The Court held that the claimants could not rely upon Art 6 (now Art 12) EC Treaty because that was displaced by Art 7(2) Reg 1612/68 which applies only to workers.
61 Under Art 6 (now Art 12) EC Treaty: Case C-85/96 *Martinez Sala*. The effects of *Martinez Sala* are to be considered by the ECJ in Case C-184/99 *Grzelczyk*.
62 Art 5 Reg 1612/68
63 Art 5 Reg 1612/68 refers to 'nationals', unlike Art 7 which refers to 'workers'.
64 Reg 7(1)(c) SFM&FE Regs
65 Reg 7(1)(b)(ii) SFM&FE Regs
66 Reg 7(1)(b)(i) and (1A) SFM&FE Regs
67 Reg 7A(2)(d) SFM&FE Regs
68 Art 3 Reg 1251/70
69 Even though Art 3(1) says 'who are residing with him', that limitation cannot stand with Case C-267/83 *Diatta* ECR [1985] 567: see Martin & Guild, *Free Movement of Persons in the EU*, 1996, para 8.213
70 Reg 7(1A)(c) SFM&FE Regs says 'in the case of a worker who has died' and not 'where the deceased was a worker'.
71 Art 7(2) Reg 1612/68: Case C-273/94 *O'Flynn v Adjudication Officer* [1996] I-2617; [1996] All ER (EC) 54; R(IS) 4/98
72 Art 7(2) Reg 1612/68 has direct effect (*eg O'Flynn*). Art 7 Dir 75/34 simply extends Art 7(2), and so is sufficiently precise and unconditional to have direct effect.
73 The rule is 'intrinsically liable to affect migrant workers more than national workers'.
74 Art 7 extends the right of equal treatment given by Art 7(1) Dir 75/34 to persons with a right to reside under that Directive.
75 Including under Art 12 EC Treaty (formerly Art 6)
76 SF Dirs 23(1)(a)(i) and 29
77 SF Dirs 2, 4(a) and (b)
78 Such grants and loans are clearly social advantages under Art 7(2) Reg 1612/68.
79 Unless it is *his* need to visit which counts in which case it would arise in the UK.
80 See *O'Flynn*, para 29

81 Case C-273/94 *O'Flynn v Adjudication Officer* [1996] ECR I-2617; [1996] All ER (EC) 54. A residence test for partners may be discriminatory on those grounds; *Schmid* [1993] I-2011.

82 Under Art 7(2) Reg 1612/68. If you are habitually resident in the UK under EC law then discrimination would also breach Art 3(1) Reg 1408/71 as well, if DPTC counts as a disability benefit.

5. Family members of EEA nationals

83 s7 IA 1988

84 s115(9) IAA 1999

85 Case C-48/95 *Royer* [1976] ECR 497

86 This practice may be unlawful because the terms on which leave is granted (in particular the prohibition on employment) is inconsistent with the EC law rights of the family member.

87 s115(9)(b) and (c) IAA 1999

88 This argument has succeeded under the pre-April 2000 income support rules for persons from abroad: *Tue-Bi,* Sutton Appeal Tribunal, 14 September 2000.

89 Reg 21(3) IS Regs 'person from abroad' and reg 85(4) JSA Regs 'person from abroad' use the words 'means a claimant who is not habitually resident . . .' Under HB/CTB rules the status of a partner and children does not affect entitlement.

90 Reg 21(3) IS Regs 'person from abroad', habitual residence para (a); reg 85(4) JSA Regs 'person from abroad', habitual residence para (a); reg 7A(4)(e)(i) HB Regs; reg 4A(4)(e)(i) CTB Regs

91 Art 4(4) Dir 68/360; Art 4(3) Dir 73/148; HEO(AO) 13/96 App 1 paras 6.33 and 6.41

92 Schedule Part 2 Immigration and Asylum (Consequential Amendment) Regulations

93 s137(1) SSCBA 1992; Memo Vol 2/40 paras 21-23 AOG

Part 5

International agreements

Chapter 28

• •

International agreements

This chapter covers:
1. Reciprocal agreements (below)
2. Council of Europe conventions and agreements (p416)
3. European Community agreements with non-European Economic Area countries (p418)

---

1. **Reciprocal agreements**

Reciprocal agreements are bilateral agreements made between the UK and one other country. They are part of UK law[1] and their purpose is to protect your entitlement to benefits if you move from one country which is a party to the agreement to the other. Like European Community (EC) law a reciprocal agreement can help you to qualify for certain benefits by allowing periods of residence and contributions paid in each of the two states to be aggregated. Furthermore they often specify that you must receive equal treatment with nationals of the state to which you have moved.

The scope of reciprocal agreements differs greatly, not only in terms of which benefits are covered and the provisions made but also in respect of which people are covered. It is therefore crucial to check the individual agreement at issue.

The UK has reciprocal agreements with European Economic Area (EEA) member states and with countries outside the EEA (see Appendix 7). However, EC social security provisions are more generous and therefore have largely replaced the reciprocal agreements. The general principle is that you look to EC law first and only if EC law does not assist do you go to the reciprocal agreement.

The agreements vary as to who is covered and which benefits are covered. It is therefore important to check each individual agreement. What follows is an outline of the benefits covered and the general principles relating to the agreements. You can find a list of all the countries and the benefits covered in Appendix 7. The following benefits are not covered by any of the agreements:
• disabled person's tax credit (DPTC);
• severe disability allowance (SDA);
• working families' tax credit (WFTC);
• social fund payments;

- income-based jobseeker's allowance (JSA); *and*
- income support (IS).

Reciprocal agreements with European Union/European Economic Area member states

The UK has reciprocal agreements with all European Union (EU)/EEA member states except Greece. Reciprocal agreements may only be relied on by EEA nationals where EC provisions do not apply.[2]

You cannot qualify for benefits using reciprocal agreements if you:
- fall within the 'personal scope' of the co-ordination rule (see p346);[3] *and*
- acquired your right to benefit on, or after, EC provisions applied.[4]

If you are not covered by the co-ordination rule, you may be able to get benefits using the reciprocal agreements. Appendix 7 shows the countries with which Great Britain has social security agreements, and the benefits covered by each. Agreements between EEA member states continue to apply if you do not fall within the personal scope of the co-ordination rule but you do fall within the scope of the reciprocal agreement.[5]

Agreements between EU/EEA member states can also continue to apply if:
- the provisions of an agreement are more beneficial to you than the EC provisions; *and*
- your right to use the reciprocal agreement was acquired before:
  - EC provisions applied to the UK on 1 April 1973; *or*
  - the other member state joined the EU/EEA.[6]

This is likely to help nationals of member states that joined the EU/EEA only recently.

The UK's agreement with Denmark continues to apply in both the Faroes and Greenland as they are not part of the EU/EEA. Greenland left the EC on 1 February 1985.

People covered by the agreements

Some of the agreements cover nationals of the contracting parties, while others apply to 'people going from one member state to another'. This may be particularly significant if you are a non-EU/EEA national who has worked in two or more EU/EEA member states but cannot benefit under the co-ordination rule (see p346). Of the member states which now form the EU/EEA, the agreements with Belgium, Denmark, France, Italy, Luxembourg are confined to nationals only.[7] The convention with the Netherlands has recently been re-negotiated and now extends to all people moving from one member state to the other who fall within its scope.

The reciprocal agreements define who is counted as a national for the purpose of the reciprocal agreement where nationality is an issue. In all of these, a UK national is defined as a 'citizen of the United Kingdom and colonies' (see Chapter 2 for further details on nationality).[8]

The category of people termed 'citizens of the United Kingdom and Colonies' disappeared on 1 January 1983 when the new British Nationality Act 1981 came into force. From that date on, a person who had previously held citizenship of the UK and colonies became:

- a British citizen;
- a British dependent territories citizen;
- a British overseas citizen; *or*
- a British subject.

For the purposes of the UK social security 'nationals only' conventions with Belgium, Denmark, France, Italy and Luxembourg a national in relation to the UK now includes anyone in one of t,he above four categories.

The definition of nationality contained in the agreements with Denmark, Italy and Luxembourg is simply that of a 'Danish' or 'Italian' or 'Luxemburger' national.[9] These agreements confer no rights if you are not a national of one of these member states. The agreement with Belgium, however, covers a 'person having Belgian nationality or a native of the Belgian Congo or Ruanda-Urundi'. The agreement with France refers to 'a person having French nationality' and 'any French-protected person belonging to French Togoland or the French Cameroons'.

When these agreements came into force in 1958, the Belgian Congo and Ruanda-Urundi and French Togoland and the French Cameroons were Belgian and French territories respectively. The question concerning who is presently covered by these agreements, insofar as Belgian and French nationals are concerned, is a matter for the Belgian and French authorities. If you come from one of these countries you should enquire of the Belgian or French authorities whether you are covered by these agreements.

The agreements confer equal treatment on the nationals of the contracting countries, stating that a 'national of one contracting party shall be entitled to receive the benefits of the legislation of the other contracting party under the same conditions as if he were a national of the latter contracting party'.[10]

The agreements with Finland, Iceland, Ireland, Portugal, Spain and Sweden are not confined to nationals but confer rights on:

- 'people who go from one country to another' (Ireland);
- 'a person subject to the legislation of one contracting party who becomes resident in the territory of the other party' (Portugal);
- 'a national of one contracting party, or a person subject to the legislation of that party, who becomes resident in the territory of the other contracting party' (Spain); *and*

- 'a national of the state and person deriving their rights from such nationals and other people who are, or have been, covered by the legislation of either of the states and people deriving their rights from such a person' (Sweden).

The agreements with Austria and Norway have nationality restrictions which apply to the protocol on benefits in kind (eg, medical treatment) but not to social security contributions and benefits. A national of the UK is defined as anyone who is recognised by the UK government as a UK national, provided that s/he is 'ordinarily resident' in the UK. A person can be treated as ordinarily resident from the first day of her/his stay in the UK.

The agreement with Germany is not restricted to nationals of either agreement member state insofar as social security benefits are concerned. However a nationality provision applies to the Articles relating to contribution liability.

Even if you are not a national of one of the contracting parties to these agreements you may still be able to benefit from their provisions.

Benefits covered by the agreements

The following benefits are covered by some of the reciprocal agreements (see Appendix 7 for a full list of which benefits apply to which countries).

Unemployment benefits

The relevant benefit in the UK is contribution-based JSA.

None of the agreements allow you to receive unemployment benefits outside the country where you paid your insurance contributions. However, a number do provide for insurance that you have paid in one country to count towards satisfying the conditions of entitlement in the other. This is the case with the UK agreements with Austria, Cyprus, Finland, Iceland, Malta, New Zealand and Norway.

Sickness benefits

In the UK, the relevant sickness benefit is short-term incapacity benefit. If you are entitled to sickness benefits, some of the agreements allow you to receive your benefit in the other country. In other cases, contributions that you have paid under one country's scheme may be taken into account to help you satisfy the conditions of entitlement in the other.

Maternity benefits

In the UK, the relevant maternity benefit is maternity allowance (MA). If you are entitled to maternity benefits, some of the agreements allow you to receive your benefit in the other country. You may be entitled to MA, or continue to be paid MA, if absent from the UK, under the reciprocal agreements with the following non-EU/EEA countries: Barbados, Cyprus, the Isle of Man, Jersey and Guernsey, Switzerland, Turkey and the former Republic of Yugoslavia. The circumstances under which you may be able to claim or retain MA differ from agreement to agreement.

Invalidity benefits

The relevant benefit in the UK is long-term incapacity benefit (IB). A number of the agreements allow you to receive invalidity benefits in the other country. The agreements with Austria, Cyprus, Iceland, Norway and Sweden allow you to continue to receive your long-term IB in the other country – subject to medical controls being undertaken in the agreement country. Correspondingly, you are able to receive the other country's invalidity benefit in the UK. The agreement with Barbados allows a certificate of permanent incapacity to be issued, permitting you to receive long-term IB without medical controls.

Benefits for industrial injuries

The relevant benefits in the UK are disablement benefit (including any additional components of it), reduced earnings allowance and retirement allowance.

Most of the agreements include industrial injuries benefits. The arrangements determine which country's legislation will apply to new accidents or diseases depending on where you are insured at the time. Many of the agreements allow you to combine the industrial injuries suffered in each country when assessing the degree of your latest injury. Furthermore, if you work in one country and remain insured under the other country's scheme and you suffer an industrial injury you can be treated as though the injury arose in the country in which you are insured. Most agreements include arrangements to allow you to receive all three of the UK benefits for industrial injuries indefinitely in the other country.

Retirement pensions and bereavement benefits

All the agreements include retirement pensions and bereavement benefits. In the UK, the relevant benefits are retirement pensions, bereavement allowance and widowed parent's allowance. In most cases, you can receive a retirement pension or bereavement benefit in the agreement country at the same rate you would be paid in the country where you are insured. This is the case under all of the agreements except those with Australia, Canada and New Zealand, which do not permit the up-rating of these benefits. If you go to live in one of these countries, your retirement pension (and any other long-term benefit) will be 'frozen' at the rate payable either when you left the UK, or when you became entitled to your pension abroad.

If you do not qualify for a retirement pension or bereavement benefit from either country, or you qualify for a pension or bereavement benefit from one country but not the other, the agreements with the following countries allow you to be paid basic old age and bereavement benefits on a pro rata basis, with your insurance under both schemes taken into account: Austria, Barbados, Bermuda, Cyprus, Finland, Iceland, Israel, Jamaica, Malta, Mauritius, Norway, the

Philippines, Mauritius, Sweden, Switzerland, Turkey, the USA and the former Republic of Yugoslavia.

Family benefits

In the UK, the relevant family benefits are child benefit and guardian's allowance. The provisions concerning these two benefits enable periods of residence and/or presence that you may have spent in the other country to be treated as residence and/or presence spent in Great Britain. The extent to which reciprocity exists varies, however, according to the particular agreement. For example, residence or contributions paid in the following countries count towards your satisfying UK residence conditions for guardian's allowance: Cyprus, Israel, Jamaica, Jersey/Guernsey, Mauritius and Turkey.

Dependants' benefits

In the UK a dependant's benefit is an increase of benefit covered by the agreement. Dependants' increases can be paid if the dependant is in either country to the agreement.

Of the agreements with countries which are not EU/EEA member states, those with Bermuda, Cyprus, Jamaica, Mauritius, New Zealand and the USA make provision for a person 'subject to the legislation of one member state', who becomes resident or takes up employment in the other.

The agreements with Israel, Switzerland, Turkey and the former Yugoslavia refer to nationals, in each case the respective member state's nationals and citizens of the United Kingdom and colonies.

2. Council of Europe conventions and agreements

There are numerous European conventions and agreements. These are prepared and negotiated within the Council of Europe. The most famous perhaps is the European Convention on Human Rights. The purpose of these Conventions is to address issues of common concern in economic, social, cultural, scientific, legal and administrative matters and in human rights. However, such agreements and conventions are not legally binding. They are statements of intent of the individual countries that are signatories. The UK is a signatory to a number of these agreements, two of which are significant for social security.

The European Convention on Social and Medical Assistance

The European Convention on Social and Medical Assistance (ECSMA) has been in force since 1954. It requires that ratifying states provide assistance in cash and in kind to nationals of other ratifying states, who are lawfully present in their territories and without sufficient resources, on the same conditions as their own nationals. It also prevents ratifying states repatriating lawfully present nationals of other ratifying states simply because the person is in need of assistance.

The countries that have signed this agreement are all the European Economic Area (EEA) countries (see p332) plus Malta and Turkey. European Community (EC) rules are more generous than this Convention, so it would not usually apply to EEA nationals. You may only benefit from this agreement if you are lawfully present in this country. These rights are recognised in UK law and if you are a person who is covered by the Convention you are not a 'person subject to immigration control' (see p157) for means-tested benefits.[11] This therefore has potential for asylum seekers and others who would otherwise be excluded from benefit.

Lawful presence

The DWP position on asylum seekers and the ECSMA is that if you have limited leave, for example, as a student or visitor and then claim asylum you are lawfully present. If, however, you are on temporary admission or entered the UK unlawfully you are not lawfully present. The Court of Appeal recently considered this in a case involving access to housing. The Court decided that an asylum seeker who has temporary admission is not lawfully present.[12]

The ECSMA agreement is not part of EC law, therefore it cannot override any UK rules which may conflict with it.

The 1961 Council of Europe Social Chapter

This agreement is similar in nature to the ECSMA agreement. The signatory states are all EEA countries (see p332) plus Cyprus, the Czech Republic, Hungary, Latvia, Malta, Poland, Slovakia and Turkey. If you are a national of one of these states and you are lawfully present you are not a 'person subject to immigration control' for means-tested benefits.

A subsequent Council of Europe Social Chapter has been signed and the later agreement includes most of the above countries as well as Romania, Slovenia, Switzerland and the Ukraine. However, if you are a national of the later convention you are not exempt from the definition of PSIC. This is because UK regulations make reference only to the 1961 Convention.

Although the Council of Europe agreements stem from Europe they are not part of EC law. Therefore, they are of little practical use unless recognised by UK law. This is highlighted by the fact that the exemption from the definition of PSIC applies only to nationals of the signatory states to the 1961 agreement. This is because the UK regulations expressly refer to the 1961 Agreement.

It should be noted that North Cyprus is now the Turkish Republic of North Cyprus which is only recognised as a country by Turkey. The Republic of Cyprus recognises people as its nationals who were born in North Cyprus before the

Turkish invasion of 1974. The nationality of people born after 1974 in North Cyprus is unclear though some may have another nationality – eg, Turkish.

3. European Community agreements with non-European Economic Area countries

The co-operation and association agreements

The European Community (EC) Treaty provides for agreements to be made with so called third countries outside the European Union (EU).[13] The co-operation and association agreements are of far more significance than the agreements outlined in section 2 above. This is because they are part of EC law and therefore have the potential to override UK rules.

At present, the only agreements which directly affect benefits in the UK are those with Algeria, Morocco, Slovenia, Tunisia and Turkey.

All of these agreements contain provisions which specify that there must be equal treatment for those covered by the agreement in matters of 'social security'. The UK regulations go some way to recognise these rights but they do not fully recognise them and there is, therefore, scope for challenges before the commissioners and courts.

UK regulations specify that if you are a national of one of these states and you are lawfully working in the UK you are exempt from the definition of 'person subject to immigration control' but only for the purposes of attendance allowance, child benefit, disability living allowance, disabled person's tax credit, working families' tax credit (WFTC), invalid care allowance and the social fund.

However, these agreements offer equal treatment in a much wider range of benefits. In *Surul* the European Court of Justice (ECJ) equated the Turkish agreement with EC Regulation 1408/71 and held that the benefits covered were the social security benefits in EC Regulation 1408/71. Social security in this context has a distinct meaning. It refers to certain benefits intended for the risks of unemployment, sickness, maternity, old age, bereavement, industrial injury and death (see p349 for a full list of these benefits). It is clear that these benefits are covered and it has been established that income-based jobseeker's allowance (JSA) is an unemployment benefit for EC purposes.[14] It should be noted that housing benefit and council tax benefit are not covered by EC Regulation 1408/71 and consequently do not fall within the scope of the co-operation and association agreements.

Furthermore, there is caselaw to support the view that all of the benefits covered by EC Regulation 1408/71 also fall within the scope of some of the co-operation and association agreements. In *Babahenini*[15] the ECJ considered whether a disability allowance was a benefit within the scope of the Algerian agreement. As in earlier caselaw its decision was based on the principle that you look to EC Regulation 1408/71 for guidance. However, in this case the ECJ appears to extend the scope of the agreements. The effect of this judgment is that the special non-contributory benefits also fall within the agreements (see p383 for a full list of special non-contributory benefits).

The personal scope of the agreements

To be within the personal scope of the agreements you must be a national of Algeria, Morocco, Slovenia, Tunisia or Turkey and you must be lawfully working. This has been equated with being an 'insured person'. An insured person has the meaning given in EC Regulation 1408/71 (see p347). In broad terms this means that you have worked in the UK and you have, or you ought to have, paid national insurance contributions. A commissioner has held that an asylum seeker who had worked in the UK was covered by the Turkish Association Agreement and was therefore eligible for family credit as a family benefit under that agreement.[16] The same would now apply to WFTC.

Asylum seekers and the co-operation and association agreements

There is significant potential for asylum seekers under these agreements. By applying all of this caselaw an asylum seeker from Algeria, Morocco, Slovenia, Tunisia or Turkey who has worked in the UK could qualify for income-based JSA as an unemployment benefit, child benefit and WFTC as family benefits.

Furthermore, *Babahenini* would appear to have established that income support and all other special non-contributory benefits are covered by at least some of the agreements. Therefore an asylum seeker who has worked could qualify for IS despite the restriction of UK rules. As the agreement provides for equal treatment s/he would be eligible for full-rate IS rather than an urgent cases payment. It should, however, be noted that an asylum seeker who wishes to rely on the agreements would then have to satisfy the usual rules to be eligible for IS. This means they would only qualify for example if they are a lone parent or sick or a pensioner. See CPAG's *Welfare Benefits Handbook* for full details of who can get IS. It should also be noted that a commissioner has held that 'special non-contributory benefits' (see p383) such as IS are not covered by the Turkish Agreement.

The Cotonou Agreement

The EC has now concluded the Cotonou Agreement with 72 states in Africa, the Caribbean and Pacific (ACP). The agreement replaces the earlier Lomé Convention. The Agreement includes provisions about workers. It provides that the contracting states shall 'ensure through the legal or administrative measures which they have or will have adopted, that migrant workers, students and other foreign nationals legally within their territory are not subjected to discrimination on the basis of racial, religious, cultural or social difference, notably in respect of housing, education, health care, other social services and employment'.

The Agreement states that 'workers who are nationals of an ACP state legally employed in the territory of a member state, and members of their families living with them, shall, as regards social security benefits linked to employment in that member state, enjoy treatment free from any discrimination based on nationality in relation to nationals of that member state'.

The scope of this agreement and the earlier Lomé Convention have yet to be tested in the courts. The equal treatment provisions are very much linked to employment and therefore it is likely that benefits such as WFTC and possibly income-based JSA are likely to provide the greatest potential to test its scope.

European Community race directive

A new EC directive on race is due to be incorporated into UK legislation by 19 July 2003. It requires member states to make discrimination on grounds of racial or ethnic origin unlawful in the following areas:

- employment;
- training;
- education;
- access to social security and health care;
- social advantages;
- access to goods and services.

This directives is likely to provide a fruitful source for challenging discriminatory aspects of the benefits system – eg, in the provision of national insurance numbers.

Notes

1. Reciprocal agreements
1. s179(2) SSAA 1992
2. Art 6 Reg 1408/71
3. Art 2 Reg1408/71
4. Cases C-82/72 *Walder* and C-4758/93 *Thevenon*
5. Art 2 Reg 1408/71; Case C-99/80 *Galinsky*; R(P) 1/81
6. Cases C-227/89 *Ronfeldt* and C-4758/93 *Thevenon*
7. Art 3 to each of the relevant reciprocal agreements
8. Art 1 to each of the relevant reciprocal agreements
9. Art 1 to each of the relevant reciprocal agreements
10. Art1 to each of the relevant reciprocal agreements

2. Council of Europe conventions and agreements
11. Sch 1 Part 1 Immigration and Benefits (Consequential Amendment) Regulations
12. *Kaya v LB Haringey*

3. EC agreements with non-EEA countries
13. Art 310 EC Treaty
14. *Hockenjos v Secretary of State for Social Security, Times Law Report,* 17 May 2001 and CJSA/1920/1999 (*65/00)
15. Case C113/97 – in a recent commissioner's decision, however, the commissioner held that the Turkish Agreement did not apply to income support.
16. CFC/2613/1997

Appendices

Appendix 1

Getting further advice on immigration and social security

Those who need help with an immigration problem should seek advice from their local law centre, a solicitor specialising in immigration work or one of the agencies listed below. If there is no local law centre and you cannot contact any of the agencies listed below you should contact your local citizens advice bureau.

Independent advice and representation on immigration issues

Local law centres can often help with applications and appeals. In addition contact one of the following:

Joint Council for the Welfare of Immigrants
115 Old Street
London EC1V 9JR
Tel: 020 7251 8706

Immigration Advisory Service
County House
190 Dover Street
London SE1 4YB
Tel: 020 7357 7511
www.iasuk.org.uk
(There are other offices in the regions and at the ports)

Afro Asian Advisory Service
53 Addington Square
London SE5 7LB
Tel: 020 7701 0141

AIRE Centre (Advice on Individual Rights in Europe)
3rd Floor
17 Red Lion Square
London WC1R 4QH
Tel: 020 7831 3850
www.cec.org.uk/index/htm

Greater Manchester Immigration Aid Unit
400 Cheetham Hill Road
Manchester M8 9LE
Tel: 0161 740 7722
www.ein.org.uk/gmiau

Asylum Aid
28 Commercial Street
London E1 6LS
Tel: 020 7377 5123
www.asylumaid.org.uk

• •

Refugee Action
Has one-stop services throughout the
country.

Refugee Arrivals Project
Room 1116
1st Floor
Queens Building
Heathrow Airport
Hounslow TW6 1DN
Tel: 020 8759 5740

Headquarters at:
41B Cross Lances Road
Hounslow TW3 2AD
Tel: 020 8607 6888

Refugee Council
Bondway House
3-9 Bondway
London SW8 1SJ
Tel: 020 7820 3000
www.refugeecouncil.org.uk

Refugee Legal Centre
Nelson House
153-157 Commercial Road
London E7 2EB
Tel: 020 7780 3200
www.refugee-legal-centre.org.uk

(For a fuller list of agencies concerned with immigration issues including policy, race relations and civil liberties see *JCWI Immigration, Nationality and Refugee Law Handbook*, 5th edition, 2002.)

Independent advice and representation on social security

It is often difficult for unsupported individuals to get a positive response from the DWP. You may be taken more seriously if it is clear you have taken advice about your entitlement or have an adviser assisting you.

If you want advice or help with a benefit problem the following agencies may be able to assist.

- Citizens advice bureaux (CABx) and other local advice centres provide information and advice about benefits and may be able to represent you.
- Law centres can often help in a similar way to CABx/advice centres.
- Local authority welfare rights workers provide a service in many areas and some arrange advice sessions and take-up campaigns locally.
- Local organisations for particular groups of claimants may offer help. For instance, there are unemployed centres, pensioners' groups, centres for disabled people etc.
- Claimants' unions give advice in some areas.
- Some social workers and probation officers (but not all) help with benefit problems, especially if they are already working with you on another problem.
- Solicitors can give some free legal advice. This does not cover the cost of representation at an appeal hearing, but can cover the cost of preparing written

submissions and obtaining evidence such as medical reports. However, solicitors do not always have a good working knowledge of the benefit rules and you may need to shop around until you find one who does.

If you cannot find any of these agencies in the telephone book your local library should have details.

Appendix 2

Useful addresses

Immigration issues

Home Office Immigration and Nationality Directorate (IND)
Lunar House
40 Wellesley Road
Croydon CR9 2BY
Tel: 020 8696 0688/0870 606 7766

Immigration and Nationality Enquiry Bureau
Tel: 0870 606 7766
www.ind.homeoffice.gov.uk

Visa Application Forms Unit
Tel: 0870 241 0645

Home Office Immigration and Nationality Department Asylum Group
Whitgift Centre
Wellesley Road
Croydon CR9 1AT

National Asylum Support Service (NASS)
Quest House
Cross Road
Croydon CR9 6EL
Tel: 020 8633 0521
Helpline: 0845 602 1739
www.ind.homeoffice.gov.uk

Also at:
Voyager House
30 Wellesley Road

Croydon CRO 2AD
Tel: 0845 602 1739
Fax: 0845 601 1143

Asylum support adjudicators
Christopher Wren House
113 High Street
Croydon CR1 1GQ
Tel: 020 8688 3977

Sodexho Pass Ltd
Old Cambridge Military Hospital
Hospital Road
Aldershot
Hampshire GU11 2AN
Tel: 01252 369 799 (Retail helpline)

Office of the Immigration Services Commissioner (OISC)
6th Floor
Fleetbank House
2-6 Salisbury Square
London EC4Y 8JX
Tel: 020 7211 1500
www.oisc.go.uk

Passport Agency
Globe House
89 Ecclestone Square
London SW1V 1PN
Tel: 0870 521 0410
www.passport.gov.uk

Aliens Registration Office
10 Lamb's Conduit Street
London WC1X 3MX

Work Permits (UK)
The Home Office
Level 5
Moorfoot
Sheffield S1 4PQ
Tel: 0114 259 4074
www.workpermits.gov.uk

Home Office (Minister's Private Office)
Queen Anne's Gate
London SW1H 9AT
Tel: 020 7273 4604

European Commission
London Office
8 Storey's Gate
London SW1P 3AT
Tel: 020 7973 1992

Immigration Law Practitioners' Association
Lindsey House
40-42 Charterhouse Street
London EC1M 6JH
Tel: 020 7251 8363
www.ilpa.org.uk

Electronic Immigration Network
www.ein.org.uk

Social security issues
Department for Work and Pensions (benefits)
Quarry House
Quarry Hill
Leeds LS2 7UA
Tel: 0113 232 4000
www.dwp.gov.uk

Department for Work and Pensions (policy)
The Adelphi
1–11 John Adam Street
London WC2 6HT
Tel: 020 7962 8000

Benefit Enquiry Line
Victoria House
9th Floor
Ormskirk Road
Preston PR1 2QP
Tel: 0800 88 22 00

The Pensions Service
Tyneview Park
Whitley Road
Benton
Newcastle-upon-Tyne NE98 1BA
Tel: 0191 218 7878

The Decision Making and Appeal Unit
Quarry House
Quarry Hill
Leeds LS2 7UA
Tel: 0113 232 4000

Child Benefit Centre
PO Box 1
Newcastle-upon-Tyne NE88 1AA
Tel: 0870 155 5540

Disability Benefits Unit
Government Buildings
Warbreck House
Warbreck Hill
Blackpool FY2 0YJ
Tel: 0845 712 3456

Health Benefits Division
Sandyford House
Archbold Terrace
Jesmond
Newcastle upon Tyne NE2 1DB
Tel: 0191 203 5555

Department for Education and Skills
Sanctuary Buildings
Great Smith Street
London SW1P 3BT
Tel: 0870 000 2288

The Tax Credit Office Guidance Team
Room 312, Block 3
Norcross
Blackpool FY5 3TA

Under 18 Support Team (UEST)
Rockingham House
123 West Street
Sheffield S1 4ER
Tel: 0114 259 6001

National Insurance Contributions Office
Inland Revenue (NICO)
Longbenton
Newcastle-upon-Tyne NE98 1ZZ
Tel: 0191 213 5000

Department for Work and Pensions Solicitor
New Court
48 Carey Street
London WC2A 2LS
Tel: 020 7962 8000

The President of the Appeal Service
HH Judge Michael Harris
The President's Office
4th Floor, Whittington House
19–30 Alfred Place
London WC1E 7LW
Tel: 020 7712 2600

Offices of the Social Security and Child Support Commissioners
England and Wales
Harp House
83 Farringdon Street
London EC4A 4DH

Address for administration:
5th Floor, Newspaper House
8–16 Great New Street
London EC4A 3NN
Tel: 020 7353 5145

Scotland
23 Melville Street
Edinburgh EH3 7PW
Tel: 0131 225 2201

Northern Ireland
Lancashire House
5 Linenhall Street
Belfast BT2 8AA
Tel: 028 90 332344

Independent Review Service for the Social Fund
Centre City Podium
5 Hill Street
Birmingham B5 4UB
Tel: 0121 606 2100

Health Service Ombudsman
Millbank Tower
London SW1P 4QP
Tel: 0845 015 4033

Local Government Ombudsman

England
21 Queen Anne's Gate
London SW1H 9BU
Tel: 020 7915 3210

Scotland
23 Walker Street
Edinburgh EH3 7HX
Tel: 0131 225 5300

Wales
Derwen House, Court Road
Bridgend CF31 1BN
Tel: 01656 661325

Northern Ireland
Progressive House
33 Wellington Place
Belfast BT1 6HN
Tel: 028 90 233821

The Parliamentary Ombudsman
Office of the Parliamentary
Commissioner
Millbank Tower
London SW1P 4QP
Tel: 0845 015 4033

The Independent Adjudicator
Dame Barbara Mills
The Adjudicator's Office
Haymarket House
28 Haymarket
London SW1Y 4SP
Tel: 020 7930 2292
Fax: 020 7930 2298

Appendix 3
Useful publications

Many of the books listed here will be in your local public library. Stationery Office books are available from Stationery Office bookshops and also from many others. They may be ordered by post, telephone or fax from The Publications Centre, PO Box 276, London SW8 5DT (tel: 020 7873 9090, fax: 020 7873 8200; general enquiries tel: 020 7873 0011, fax: 020 7873 8247). It also has a website for further information at www.hmso.gov.uk. Many of the publications listed are available from CPAG – see below for order details, or order from www.cpag.org.uk. For social security information in electronic format see details of the *Welfare Benefits CD-ROM* given below.

1. General immigration, nationality and asylum
JCWI Immigration, Nationality and Refugee Law Handbook
5th edition, JCWI, 2002

Macdonald's Immigration Law and Practice
5th edition, Ian Macdonald and Nicholas Blake, Macdonalds, 2001

2. Nationality
Fransman: British Nationality Law
2nd edition, Butterworths, 1998

3. Refugees and asylum seekers
The Law of Refugee Status
James Hathaway, Butterworths, 1991

The Refugee in International Law
2nd edition, Guy Goodwin-Gill, Clarendon, 1996

Support for Asylum Seekers
Willman, Knafler and Pierce, Legal Action Group, 2001

4. Human rights
Blake and Fransman: Immigration and Asylum under the Human Rights Act 1998
Butterworths, 1999

European Human Rights Law
Tarmer, Legal Action Group, 1999

5. Children
Putting Children First: a guide for immigration practitioners
Coker, Finch and Stanley, Legal Action Group, 2002

6. Social security caselaw and legislation

Social Security Case Law – Digest of Commissioners' Decisions
D Neligan (Stationery Office, looseleaf in two vols). Summaries of commissioners' decisions grouped by subject. Also at www.cas.gov.uk

Welfare Benefits CD-ROM
(CPAG). Includes: all social security legislation consolidated; over 1,500 commissioners' decisions, most with commentary; guidance; the *Welfare Benefits Handbook* with links to the relevant legislation, decisions and guidance; CPAG's *Housing Benefit and Council Tax Benefit Legislation* (with commentary); significant housing benefit and council tax benefit circulars; the *Child Support Handbook* and child support regulations. Updated three times a year. Free trial disks are available from CPAG. The single user price for 2002, including updates, is £255 + VAT. Phone Liz Dawson on 020 7837 7979 ext 212 for multi-user prices.

The Law Relating to Social Security
(Stationery Office, looseleaf, 11 vols). All the legislation but without any comment. Known as the 'Blue Book'. Vols 6, 7, 8 and 11 deal with means-tested benefits.

Social Security Legislation, Volume I: Non-Means-Tested Benefits
D Bonner, I Hooker and R White (Sweet & Maxwell). Legislation with commentary. 2002/03 edition available from CPAG if you are a member, from October 2002: £63 for the main volume.

Social Security Legislation, Volume II: Income Support, Jobseeker's Allowance, Tax Credits and the Social Fund
J Mesher, P Wood, R Poynter, N Wikely and D Bonner (Sweet & Maxwell). Legislation with commentary. 2002/03 edition available from CPAG if you are a member, from October 2002: £63 for the main volume.

Social Security Legislation, Volume III: Administration, Adjudication and the European Dimension
M Rowland and R White (Sweet & Maxwell). Legislation with commentary. 2002/03 edition available from CPAG if you are a member, from October 2002: £63 for main volume.

Social Security Legislation – updating supplement to Volumes I, II and III (Sweet & Maxwell). The February 2003 update to the 2002/03 main volumes, available from CPAG if you are a member (£38).

CPAG's Housing Benefit and Council Tax Benefit Legislation
L Findlay, R Poynter, P Stagg, and M Ward (CPAG). Contains legislation with a detailed commentary. 2002/03 edition available from December 2002, priced £79 including Supplement from CPAG. The 14th edition (2001/02) is still available at £72 per set. This publication is also on the *Welfare Benefits CD-ROM* (see above).

The Social Fund: Law and Practice
T Buck (Sweet & Maxwell). Includes legislation, guidance and commentary. The 2nd edition (July

2000) is available from CPAG for £49 if you are a CPAG member.

Social Fund Directions
Available on the IRS website at www.irssf.demon.co.uk/ssdir.htm

7. Social security guidance
Decision Makers Guide
12 volumes, memos and letters available at www.dss.gov.uk/publications/dss/2000/dmg/index.htm

Benefits Agency Guide, IS for 16/17-year-olds
(Stationery Office, amended February 1996)

Handbook for Delegated Medical Practitioners
(Stationery Office, 1988)

Housing Benefit and Council Tax Benefit Guidance Manual
(Stationery Office, looseleaf)

Industrial Injuries Handbook for Adjudicating Medical Authorities
(Stationery Office, looseleaf)

Income Support Guide
(Stationery Office, looseleaf, 8 vols.)
Procedural guide issued to DWP staff.

The Social Fund Guide
(Stationery Office, looseleaf 2 vols)

8. Leaflets
The DWP publishes many leaflets covering particular benefits or groups of claimants or contributors. They are free from your local DWP office, or by calling 01253 33 22 22 (Monday-Friday 8.30am to 4.00 pm)

or downloading an order form from www.dwp.gov.uk/publications/pubsorder.htm. If you want to order larger numbers of leaflets, or receive information about new leaflets, you can join the Publicity Register by contacting the BAPR, PO Box 16, Manchester, M60 3HH, tel: 0845 602 44 44 (9am to 6pm, Monday to Friday). Free leaflets on HB/CTB are available from the relevant department of your local council. A selection of leaflets can be found at www.dwp.gov.uk

9. Periodicals
CPAG's *Welfare Rights Bulletin* is published every two months by CPAG. It covers developments in social security law, including commissioners' decisions, and updates this *Handbook* between editions. The annual subscription is £27 but it is sent automatically to CPAG Rights and Comprehensive Members. For subscription and membership details contact CPAG. Many features from the *Bulletin* are also reproduced on the *Welfare Benefits CD-ROM*.

Articles on social security and immigration can also be found in *Legal Action* (Legal Action Group, monthly magazine), and on social security in the *Journal of Social Security Law* (Sweet & Maxwell, quarterly).

10. CPAG handbooks

Welfare Benefits Handbook
£25.00 (£7 + £1 p+p for claimants)
(2002/03)

Child Support Handbook
£17.50 (10th edition, July 2002)
(£4.50 for claimants). Also available
on the *Welfare Benefits CD-ROM*.

Paying for Care Handbook
£14.95 (3rd edition, July 2002)

Council Tax Handbook
£13.95 (5th edition, late 2002)

Debt Advice Handbook
£14.95 (5th edition, late 2002)

Fuel Rights Handbook
£13.95 (12th edition, February 2002)

*A Guide to Housing Benefit and Council
Tax Benefit*
£19.95 (July 2002)

Disability Rights Handbook
£13.00 (May 2002)

*Guide to Training and Benefits for
Young People*
£7.99 (6th edition, Autumn 2002)

New Deal Handbook
£9.99 (4th edition, now
incorporating the *Unemployment and
Training Rights Handbook*, Autumn
2002)

For CPAG publications and most of those in Sections 6 and 10 contact:
CPAG, 94 White Lion Street, London N1 9PF, tel: 020 7837 7979, fax: 020 7837
6414. Order forms are also available at: www.cpag.org.uk. For postage and
packing add a flat rate charge: for orders up to £9.99 in value, add £1; order value
£10-199.99 add £3.00; for £200+ add £5.00.

Appendix 4

People admitted for temporary purposes

Category	Rule (HC 395)	Employment conditions	Additional employment requirements	Requirement that applicants and dependants are adequately maintained and accommodated without recourse to public funds	Entry clearance required for non-visa nationals
Visitor	40-46	Employment prohibited	Must not intend to take employment in the UK or produce goods/provide services within the UK	Yes, out of resources available to applicant without taking employment or will be maintained and accommodated by relatives or friends	No
Visitor in transit	47-50	Employment prohibited	None	None	No
Visitor seeking medical treatment	51-56	Employment prohibited	Must not intend to take employment in the UK or produce goods/provide services within the UK	Yes, out of resources available to applicant without taking employment or will be maintained and accommodated by relatives or friends	No

Category	Rule (HC 395)	Employment conditions	Additional employment requirements	Requirement that applicants and dependants are adequately maintained and accommodated without recourse to public funds	Entry clearance required for non-visa nationals
Student	57–62	Freedom to take employment restricted	Must not intend to engage in any business or take employment except part-time or vacation work with the consent of the Secretary of State (in practice, consent for some work is automatically granted	Yes, is able to meet the 'costs of her/his own accommodation and maintenance without taking employment or engaging in business'	No
Student re-sitting exams	69A–69F				
Student writing a thesis	69G–69L				
Student nurse	63–69	Freedom to take employment restricted	Must not intend to take employment or engage in business other than in connection with the training course	Yes, must have 'sufficient funds available' to satisfy the requirements without engaging in business or taking employment (except in connection with the training course); a Department of Health bursary may be taken into account in determining whether the requirements are met	No

Category	Rule (HC 395)	Employment conditions	Additional employment requirements	Requirement that applicants and dependants are adequately maintained and accommodated without recourse to public funds	Entry clearance required for non-visa nationals
Postgraduate doctor or dentist	70–75	None	Must *either* intend to undertake pre-registration house officer employment for up to 12 months as required for full registration with the General Medical Council; or, if a doctor or dentist eligible for full or limited registration with the General Medical Council or with the General Dental Council must intend to undertake postgraduate training in a hospital	Yes, applicant must be able to so maintain and accommodate	No

Category	Rule (HC 395)	Employment conditions	Additional employment requirements	Requirement that applicants and dependants are adequately maintained and accommodated without recourse to public funds	Entry clearance required for non-visa nationals
Spouse of student/ prospective student	76-78	Employment prohibited except where the period of leave being granted is 12 months or more, in which case there are no working restrictions	Must not intend to take work other than that permitted according to the conditions of leave	Yes, the parties must be 'able' to so maintain and accommodate	No
Child of student/ prospective student	79–81	Employment prohibited except where the period of leave being granted is 12 months or more	None	Yes, the child must show that s/he 'can and will' be so maintained and accommodated	No
Prospective student	82-87	Employment prohibited	None	Yes, must be able to meet the costs of these requirements without working	No

Category	Rule (HC 395)	Employment conditions	Additional employment requirements	Requirement that applicants and dependants are adequately maintained and accommodated without recourse to public funds	Entry clearance required for non-visa nationals
Student union sabbatical officer	87A–87F	Restricted to working in the sabbatical post	Must not intend to engage in business or take employment except in connection with the sabbatical post	Yes, applicant must be able to so maintain and accommodate	No
Au pair	88–94	Prohibited from working except as an au pair	Must intend to take up an au pair placement	Yes, must be able to so maintain and accommodate her/himself	No (although rules advise entry clearance is obtained)
Working holidaymaker	95–100	Freedom to take employment is restricted	Must intend to take employment incidental to a holiday but not to engage in business, provide services as a professional sportsman or entertainer or pursue a career in UK	Yes, must be 'able' and must 'intend' to so maintain and accommodate her/himself	Yes

Category	Rule (HC 395)	Employment conditions	Additional employment requirements	Requirement that applicants and dependants are adequately maintained and accommodated without recourse to public funds	Entry clearance required for non-visa nationals
Child of working holidaymaker	101–103	None	None	Yes, and without parent(s) engaging in business or taking employment except as permitted as incidental to the holiday. Must show that child can and will be so maintained and accommodated	Yes
Seasonal worker at agricultural camps	104–109	Condition imposed allowing the person to take employment only up until 30 November of the year in question	Must not intend to take employment other than as a seasonal worker at an agricultural camp	Yes, applicant must be able to so maintain and accommodate	Yes, in form of a valid Home Office work card issued by the operator of the scheme approved by the Secretary of State

Category	Rule (HC 395)	Employment conditions	Additional employment requirements	Employment conditions	Requirement that applicants and dependants are adequately maintained and accommodated without recourse to public funds	Entry clearance required for non-visa nationals
Teacher or language assistant under approved exchange scheme	110–115	None (or may be restricted)	Must not intend to take employment other than in an established educational establishment in the UK under an exchange scheme approved by the Department for Education and Skills, or administered by the Central Bureau for Educational Visits and Exchanges or the League for the Exchange of Commonwealth Teachers		Yes, applicant must be able to so maintain and accommodate	Yes

Category	Rule (HC 395)	Employment conditions	Additional employment requirements	Requirement that applicants and dependants are adequately maintained and accommodated without recourse to public funds	Entry clearance required for non-visa nationals
Approved training or work experience	116–121	Freedom to take or change employment restricted	Must intend to only take employment as specified in the work permit – ie, training or work experience under the scheme	Yes, applicant must be able to so maintain and accommodate	No, but must have a work permit issued under TWES (whether a visa national or not) or if applying for leave to remain was admitted or allowed to remain as a student

Category	Rule (HC 395)	Employment conditions	Additional employment requirements	Requirement that applicants and dependants are adequately maintained and accommodated without recourse to public funds	Entry clearance required for non-visa nationals
Spouse and child of someone with limited leave as teacher/ language assistant or in approved teaching or work experience	122–127	None	None	Yes, the parties must be able to so maintain and accommodate in accommodation which they own or occupy exclusively; the child must show that s/he can and will be so maintained and accommodated in accommodation which her/his parents own or occupy exclusively	Yes

Appendix 5

People admitted for purposes leading to settlement

Category	Rule (HC 395)	Employment conditions (before settlement is obtained)	Additional employment requirements	Requirement that applicants and dependants are adequately maintained and accommodated without recourse to public funds	Entry clearance required for non-visa nationals
Returning resident (immediate settlement)	18–20	None	None	None (but must show that applicant did not receive assistance from public funds towards cost of leaving the UK previously)	No, provided applicant returns to the UK within two years
Work permit employment (leads to settlement after four years)	128–135	Freedom to take employment restricted to the approved employment	Must not intend to take employment other than that specified in the work permit	Yes, applicant must be 'able' to so maintain and accommodate	No, but work permit is required whether a visa national or not

Category	Rule (HC 395)	Employment conditions (before settlement is obtained)	Additional employment requirements	Requirement that applicants and dependants are adequately maintained and accommodated without recourse to public funds	Entry clearance required for non-visa nationals
Permit-free employment – ie, representatives of overseas media or business, diplomatic, private servants, overseas government employees, ministers of religion, overseas airline ground crews (leads to settlement after four years)	136–185	Restricted to work in particular occupation for which admitted	Must intend to work only in the occupation for which admitted	Yes, applicant must show s/he 'can' so maintain and accommodate	Yes, although those in the category of 'overseas government employee' may, as an alternative, present any satisfactory evidence of their status
Commonwealth citizens with UK ancestry (leads to settlement after four years)	186–193	None	Must intend to take or seek employment	Yes, applicant must show s/he 'will be able' to so maintain and accommodate	Yes

Category	Rule (HC 395)	Employment conditions (before settlement is obtained)	Additional employment requirements	Requirement that applicants and dependants are adequately maintained and accommodated without recourse to public funds	Entry clearance required for non-visa nationals
Spouse, unmarried partner or child of person with limited leave as work permit holder, permit-free employment (as above), Commonwealth citizen with UK ancestry (leads to settlement in line with spouse/parent)	194–199 295J–295L	None	None	Yes, parties must show that they are 'able' to so maintain and that there will be such accommodation which they own or occupy exclusively; child must show s/he 'can and will' be so maintained and accommodated in accommodation owned exclusively by her/his parents	Yes
Person establishing her/himself in business (leads to settlement after four years)	200–210	Freedom to take employment restricted	Applicant must show that s/he will be actively involved full time in the business and that s/he does not intend to take or seek employment in the UK other than work for the business	Yes, applicant must show that s/he has 'sufficient additional' funds to so maintain and accommodate until such time as the business provides her/him with an income and, thereafter, that her/his share of the profits from the business will be sufficient for such maintenance and accommodation; applicant must show that this is the case without her/his recourse to employment other than work for the business	Yes

Category	Rule (HC 395)	Employment conditions (before settlement is obtained)	Additional employment requirements	Requirement that applicants and dependants are adequately maintained and accommodated without recourse to public funds	Entry clearance required for non-visa nationals
Person intending to establish her/himself in business under the provisions of an EC association agreement (leads to settlement after four years)	211–223	Freedom to take employment restricted	Applicant must show that s/he will be actively involved in promoting/managing the company or (if self-employed or in a partnership) that s/he will be actively involved in trading or providing services and must not intend to supplement her/his business activities by taking or seeking employment in the UK other than work for the business	Yes, applicant must show that s/he has 'sufficient additional' funds to so maintain and accommodate until time as the business provides her/him with an income and, thereafter, that her/his share of the profits from the business will be sufficient for such maintenance and accommodation; applicant must show that this is the case without her/his recourse to employment other than work for the business	Yes
Investor (leads to settlement after four years)	224–231	Freedom to take employment restricted	None	Yes, applicant must be 'able' to so maintain and accommodate without taking employment (other than self-employment or business)	Yes

Category	Rule (HC 395)	Employment conditions (before settlement is obtained)	Additional employment requirements	Requirement that applicants and dependants are adequately maintained and accommodated without recourse to public funds	Entry clearance required for non-visa nationals
Writer/composer/ artist (leads to settlement after four years)	232–239	Freedom to take employment restricted	Must not intend to work other than as related to self-employment as a writer, composer, artist	Yes, applicant must show that s/he has previously been so maintained and accommodated and from her/his own resources without working except as a writer/composer/artist; applicant must show that s/he 'will be able' to accommodate her/himself from her/his own resources without working except as a writer/composer/artist	Yes
Spouse, unmarried partner and child of person with limited leave as a person establishing her/ himself in business (under the provisions of an EC association agreement or not), investor/ writer/composer/ artist (leads to settlement in line with spouse/ parent concerned)	240–245 295J–295L	None	None	Yes, the parties to the marriage must show that they 'will be able' to so maintain and that there will be such accommodation owned and occupied by themselves exclusively. Child must show s/he 'can and will' be so maintained and accommodated in accommodation which her/his parents own or occupy exclusively	Yes

Category	Rule (HC 395)	Employment conditions (before settlement is obtained)	Additional employment requirements	Requirement that applicants and dependants are adequately maintained and accommodated without recourse to public funds	Entry clearance required for non-visa nationals
Person exercising rights of access to a child resident in the UK	246–248	None	None	Yes, applicant must show that s/he is able to so maintain; there must be adequate accommodation in accommodation which applicant owns or occupies exclusively	Yes
Holder of special voucher (indefinite leave granted on admission – but no more vouchers are issued after 5 March 2002)	249–254	None	None	None	Yes, or be in possession of a special voucher issued by the British overseas post (high commission/ embassy)
Spouse and/or child of special voucher holder (indefinite leave granted on admission)	252–254	None	None	Yes, applicant must show that s/he 'can and will' be maintained and accommodated by the special voucher holder	Yes

Category	Rule (HC 395)	Employment conditions (before settlement is obtained)	Additional employment requirements	Requirement that applicants and dependants are adequately maintained and accommodated without recourse to public funds	Entry clearance required for non-visa nationals
Retired person of independent means (leads to settlement after four years) and her/his spouse, unmarried partner and child (leads to settlement in line with spouse/parent)	263–276 295J–295L	Employment prohibited; there is no reference in the immigration rules to prohibiting employment for unmarried partners but it is likely that they, in line with other dependants, will be given a working prohibition	None, but applicant should be 'retired'	Yes, applicant must be 'able and willing' to so maintain and accommodate from her/his own resources with no assistance from any other person and without taking employment; if the spouse or unmarried partner is admitted, the parties must show that they 'will be able' to so maintain and accommodate in accommodation which they own or occupy exclusively; a child must show that s/he 'can and will' be so maintained and accommodated in accommodation owned or occupied exclusively by her/his parent(s)	Yes
Spouse or unmarried partner of settled person in UK (leave granted for probationary period initially, thereafter indefinite leave granted)	281–289 295A–295I	None	None	Yes, the parties must show that they 'will be able' to so maintain and that there will be such accommodation owned or occupied by themselves exclusively	Yes

Category	Rule (HC 395)	Employment conditions (before settlement is obtained)	Additional employment requirements	Requirement that applicants and dependants are adequately maintained and accommodated without recourse to public funds	Entry clearance required for non-visa nationals
Bereaved spouse or unmarried partner; death occurring during the probationary period (immediate settlement)	287–289 295M–295O	None	None	None	Only granted to those applying to stay rather than enter
Fiancé of settled person in UK (granted limited leave initially; with a view to marriage and settlement)	290–295	Employment prohibited	None	Yes, applicant must show that there will be adequate maintenance and accommodation available to her/him until the date of the marriage and that, after the marriage, the parties to the marriage 'will be able' to so maintain and that there will be such accommodation owned or occupied by themselves exclusively	Yes

Category	Rule (HC 395)	Employment conditions (before settlement is obtained)	Additional employment requirements	Requirement that applicants and dependants are adequately maintained and accommodated without recourse to public funds	Entry clearance required for non-visa nationals
Child of settled parent(s) or relatives in UK (indefinite leave granted on admission)	297–300	None	None	Yes, applicant must show that s/he 'can and will' be accommodated adequately by the 'parent, parents or relative' the child is seeking to join in accommodation which the 'parent, parents or relatives' the child is joining own or occupy exclusively; applicant must also show that s/he 'can and will' be maintained adequately by the 'parent, parents or relative' the child is seeking to join (note, this new wording was added to the immigration rules by Command Paper, CM4851)	Yes
Child of parent(s) given limited leave to enter or remain in UK with a view to settlement (given limited leave initially with a view to settlement)	301–303	None	None	Yes, applicant must show s/he 'can and will' be so maintained and accommodated in accommodation owned or occupied exclusively by the parent(s)	Yes

Category	Rule (HC 395)	Employment conditions (before settlement is obtained)	Additional employment requirements	Requirement that applicants and dependants are adequately maintained and accommodated without recourse to public funds	Entry clearance required for non-visa nationals
Child of fiancé (limited leave initially but will eventually obtain settlement when fiancé marries and obtains settlement)	303A–303E	None	None	Yes, applicant must show that s/he 'can and will' be so maintained and accommodated	Yes
Parent, grandparent and other dependent relatives of person settled in the UK (immediate settlement)	317–319	None	None	Yes, applicant must show that s/he 'can and will' be so maintained and accommodated in accommodation owned or occupied exclusively by the sponsor	Yes

Category	Rule (HC 395)	Employment conditions (before settlement is obtained)	Additional employment requirements	Requirement that applicants and dependants are adequately maintained and accommodated without recourse to public funds	Entry clearance required for non-visa nationals
Refugee and spouse and child of refugee (immediate settlement)	327–352	None	None	No	No, although if the dependant of a refugee is seeking reunion with a person who has come to the UK and been recognised as a refugee s/he must apply for entry clearance to travel to the UK

Note 1: For the requirements relating to non-British citizen children born in the UK to parent(s) given leave to enter or remain, see paras 304–309 HC 395; and for adopted children, see paras 310–316 HC 395. Non-British citizen children born in the UK do not have to satisfy any public funds requirements if they satisfy the rules relating to them, whereas adopted children do.

Note 2: For the application of the public funds requirements to those with exceptional leave, see Chapters 6 and 8.

Note 3: There are two recent schemes for people to come to the UK for work which operate outside the immigration rules: the 'Innovators' scheme (a two-year pilot launched in July 2000) and the 'Highly Skilled Migrant Programme' (HSMP) which began in January 2002. They are for highly motivated, skilled workers/business people. It is not envisaged that people falling into either category would need to have recourse to public funds.

Appendix 6

Alternative sources of help

Many migrants are excluded from means-tested benefits. Most people affected are asylum seekers, but British citizens and other European Economic Area nationals are also excluded if they fail the habitual residence test. Many people who are subject to immigration control are now excluded from local authority housing, even when they are homeless. Furthermore, since April 2000 a person who is subject to immigration control can in some circumstances be excluded from help under the National Assistance Act 1948.

The National Assistance Act 1948

Local authorities have a duty under the National Assistance Act to accommodate and support a person in need of 'care and attention'.[1] However, a 'person subject to immigration control' is excluded from this type of support if her/his need for care and attention arises solely because s/he is 'destitute'. This restriction was introduced in response to concerns by local authorities about the numbers of destitute asylum seekers receiving such support following their exclusion from the benefit system. However, this does not mean that the fact they are without funds (ie, destitute) cannot be taken into account at all. The courts have decided that if a person's experience of destitution is made significantly more acute for other relevant reasons, such as age, disability or illness, then they can qualify for National Assistance Act support even if they are 'subject to immigration control'. This applies to asylum seekers as well as non-asylum seekers who are 'subject to immigration control.[2]if the need for 'care and attention' is because of a reason other than destitution, for example, disability or ill health a person is not excluded from help. An authority can also provide help to 'nursing mothers' under the National Assistance Act.

The Children Act 1989

Local authorities must promote the welfare of 'children in need' in their area.[3] The local authority may also accommodate a child in need with her/his family.[4] There have been a series of cases in which local authorities have sought to limit their duty to accommodate the child only. In one case[5] the Court of Appeal agreed with this stance, but later cases have overturned the judgment.[6] Further developments can be expected shortly in this area as these cases are due to be heard in the House of Lords.

Disabled and mentally ill people

Local authorities must assess the needs and provide appropriate services to migrants who appear to be disabled[7] and to those who have been suffering from mental illness and who are discharged from hospital.[8]

Notes

1 s21(1)(a) National Assistance Act 1948
2 *O and Bhikha* [2001] 1 WLR 2539 CA;
    Mani, Tasci and J [2002] EWHC 735
    (Admin), 18 April 2002; *Murua* (HC)
    CO/2463/01, 25 October 2001
3 s17 Children Act 1989
4 s20 Children Act 1989
5 *G, W and A v Lambeth*
6 Both the *J v Enfield* and *W v Lambeth*
    cases cast doubt on the *A v Lambeth*
    decision and held that local authorities
    can provide support under a general
    power contained in s2 of the Local
    Government Act 2000
7 National Health Service and Community
    Care Act 1990; Chronically Sick and
    Disabled Persons Act 1970
8 s117 Mental Health Act 1983

Appendix 7

Reciprocal agreements

Benefits covered in conventions with EU/EEA member states

State	Retirement pension	Bereavement benefits	Guardian's allowance	Incapacity benefit (short-term)	Incapacity benefit (long-term)	Jobseeker's allowance	Maternity allowance	Disablement benefit	Industrial injuries benefits	Child benefit	Attendance allowance	Invalid care allowance
Austria	X	X	X	X	X	X	X	X	X	X	-	-
Belgium	X	X	X	X	X	X	X	X	X	X	-	-
Denmark		X	X	X	X	X	X	X	X	X	X	-
Finland	X	X	-	X	X	X	X	X	X	X	-	-
France	X	X	-	X	X	X	X	X	X	X	-	-
Germany		X	X	X	X	X	X	X	X	X	X	-
Iceland	X	X	X	X	X	X	-	X	X	-	-	-
Ireland	X	X	X	X	X	X	X	X	X	-	-	-
Italy	X	X	X	X	X	X	X	X	X	-	-	-
Luxembourg	X	X	X	X	X	-	X	X	X	-	-	-
Netherlands	X	X	X	X	X	X	X	X	X	-	-	-
Norway	X	X	X	X	X	X	X	X	X	X	X	-
Portugal	X	X	X	X	X	X	X	X	X	X	-	-
Spain	X	X	X	X	X	X	X	X	X	X	-	-
Sweden	X	X	X	X	X	X	X	X	X	X	-	-

There is no agreement with Greece or Liechtenstein. The agreement with Gibraltar provides that, except for child benefit, the United Kingdom and Gibraltar are treated as separate European Economic Area countries.

Although Northern Ireland is part of the United Kingdom, there is an agreement between Great Britain and Northern Ireland. This is because benefits in Northern Ireland and Great Britain are separate and administered under different social security legislation.

Benefits covered in conventions with non-EU/EEA member states

State	Retirement pension	Bereavement benefits	Guardian's allowance	Incapacity benefit (short-term)	Incapacity benefit (long-term)	Jobseeker's allowance	Maternity allowance	Disablement benefit	Industrial injuries benefits	Child benefit	Attendance allowance	Disability living allowance	Invalid care allowance
Barbados	X	X	X	X	X	-	X	X	X	X	-	-	-
Bermuda	X	X	-	-	-	-	-	X	X	-	-	-	-
Canada	X	-	-	-	-	X	-	-	-	-	X	-	-
Cyprus	X	X	X	X	X	X	X	X	X	-	-	-	-
Guernsey	X	X	X	X	X	X	X	X	X	X	X	X	-
Isle of Man	X	X	X	X	X	X	X	X	X	X	X	X	X
Israel	X	X	X	X	X	-	X	X	X	X	-	-	-
Jamaica	X	X	X	-	X	-	-	X	X	-	-	-	-
Jersey	X	X	X	X	X	-	X	X	X	X	X	X	-
Malta	X	X	X	X	X	X	-	X	X	-	-	-	-
Mauritius	X	X	X	-	-	-	-	X	X	X	-	-	-
New Zealand	X	X	X	X	-	X	-	-	-	X	-	-	-
Philippines	X	X	-	-	-	-	-	X	X	-	-	-	-
Philippines	X	X	-	-	-	-	-	X	X	-	-	-	-
*Switzerland	X	X	X	X	X	-	-	X	X	X	-	-	-
Turkey	X	X	X	X	X	-	X	X	X	-	-	-	-
USA	X	X	X	X	X	-	-	-	-	-	-	-	-
Yugoslavia	X	X	-	X	X	X	X	X	X	X	-	-	-

The agreement with Australia was terminated in April 2002.

Following the break-up of Yugoslavia the reciprocal agreement between the United Kingdom and Yugoslavia should be treated as separate agreements between the United Kingdom and: the residue of the former

Appendix 7: Reciprocal agreements

● ●

republic: Serbia and Montenegro; Bosnia-Herzegovina; Croatia; the former Yugoslav republic of Macedonia; and Slovenia.

From June 2002 an agreement with Switzerland allows Swiss nationals the right to rely on EC social security provisions, such as Regulation 1408/71 as if they were EEA nationals.

Appendix 8

Visa nationals

Afghanistan
Albania
Algeria
Angola
Armenia
Azerbaijan
Bahrain
Bangladesh
Belarus
Benin
Bhutan
Bosnia-Herzegovina
Bulgaria
Burkina Faso
Burundi
Cambodia
Cameroon
Cape Verde
Central African Republic
Chad
China (People's Republic of)
Colombia
Comoros
Congo (Democratic Republic of)
Congo (Republic of)
Croatia
Cuba
Djibouti
Dominican Republic
Ecuador
Egypt
Equatorial Guinea
Eritrea
Ethiopia
Fiji
Gabon

The Gambia
Georgia
Ghana
Guinea
Guinea Bissau
Guyana
Haiti
India
Indonesia
Iran
Iraq
Ivory Coast
Jordan
Kazakhstan
Kenya
Korea (Democratic People's Republic)
Kuwait
Kyrgyzstan
Laos
Lebanon
Liberia
Libya
Macedonia
Madagascar
Maldives
Mali
Mauritania
Mauritius
Moldova
Mongolia
Morocco
Mozambique
Myanmar
Nepal
Niger
Nigeria

Oman
Pakistan
Papua New Guinea
Peru
Philippines
Qatar
Romania
Russia
Rwanda
Sao Tome & Principe
Saudi Arabia
Senegal
Sierra Leone
Slovak Republic
Somalia
Sri Lanka
Sudan
Surinam
Syria
Taiwan
Tajikistan
Tanzania
Thailand
Togo
Tunisia
Turkey
Turkish Republic of Northern Cyprus'
Turkmenistan
Uganda
Ukraine
United Arab Emirates
Uzbekistan
Vietnam
Yemen
Federal Republic of Yugoslavia
(including documents issued by the
Former Socialist Republic of
Yugoslavia)
Zambia

Appendix 9

Passport stamps and other endorsements

Figure 1: Certificate of entitlement

Figure 2: Green uniform format visa

Figure 3: Red entry clearance

Figure 4: Date stamp

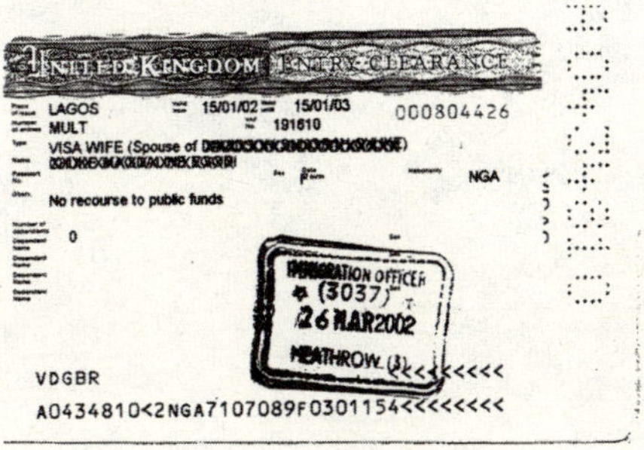

Figure 5: Limited leave to enter

Leave to enter for/until
No work or recourse to public funds

CODE 3

. . . .

Figure 6: Indefinite leave to enter

> Given indefinite leave to
> enter the United Kingdom

Figure 7: Refusal of leave to enter

Figure 8: Leave to remain with public funds restriction

> Leave to remain in the United Kingdom on
> Condition that the holder maintains and
> Accommodates himself and any dependants
> Without recourse to public funds is hereby
> Given
>
> Until...
>
> ....
>   on behalf of the Secretary of State
>   Home Office
>
> Date ....

CODE 1

Figure 9: Leave to remain date stamp

Figure 10: Indefinite leave to remain

Figure 11: Application registration card

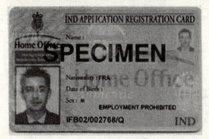
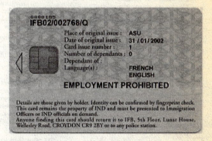

Figure 12: Letter granting refugee status

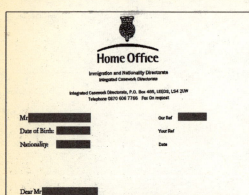

Home Office

Immigration and Nationality Directorate
Integrated Casework Directorate

Integrated Casework Directorate, P.O. Box 486, LEEDS, LS4 2UW
Telephone 0870 606 7766   Fax On request

Mr ▓▓▓▓▓▓▓   Our Ref ▓▓▓▓▓▓▓

Date of Birth: ▓▓▓▓▓▓▓   Your Ref

Nationality: ▓▓▓▓▓▓▓   Date

Dear Mr ▓▓▓▓▓▓▓

GRANT OF STATUS (ASYLUM)

I am writing to tell you that you have been granted indefinite leave to enter the United Kingdom as a refugee recognised under the 1951 United Nations Convention relating to the Status of Refugees and its 1967 Protocol. This means that you are free to stay in this country permanently. Passports of recognised refugees are not endorsed and you should keep this letter carefully as your authority to remain in the United Kingdom.

You should understand, however, that if during your stay in the United Kingdom you take part in activities involving, for example, the support or encouragement of violence, or conspiracy to cause violence, whether in the United Kingdom or abroad, so as to endanger national security or public order, the Secretary of State may deport you.

EMPLOYMENT

You are free to take a job and do not need the permission of the Department for Education and Employment, or the Home Office before doing so. The Employment Service can help you find a job or train for work—any job centre or employment office will be able to help you and you can apply for a place on a government-sponsored training scheme if you meet the conditions for these schemes. You are also free to set up in business or any professional activity within the regulations that apply to that business or profession.

If you want to live or work in the Isle of Man or one of the Channel Islands you must first ask the Island's immigration authorities.

HEALTH, SOCIAL SERVICES, AND EDUCATION

You are free to use the National Health Service and the social services, and other help provided by local authorities as you need them. You will be able to get Social Security Benefit (including Income Support) if you meet the conditions. If you want to study for a degree or other approved course you can apply for a grant from your local education

ICD.0725   1 of 2

BUILDING A SAFE, JUST AND TOLERANT SOCIETY

---

ou will be charged only home students' fees for any further or higher education
take.

any of these services, take this letter with you and show it if there is any
ut your entitlement to the service. Your local Social Security Office will give
vice on Social Security Benefits. The Refugee Council, Bond Way House, 3–9
London, SW8 1SJ (telephone 020-7582 6922) can advise on other welfare
ur local Citizens' Advice Bureau will help you with general questions.

BROAD

ational passport to travel outside the United Kingdom could affect your status
If you want to travel abroad you should apply for a Home Office Travel
rom the Travel Document Section, Immigration and Nationality Directorate,
itgift Centre, Croydon, CR9 2AT (telephone 0870-241 0645). If you leave the
dom with a Home Office Travel Document you will be allowed back into the
ny time while it is still valid.

ely

[signature]

asework Directorate

Given indefinite leave to enter the United Kingdom

IMMIGRATION OFFICER
* (254) *
31 AUG 2001
GATWICK (3)

Figure 13: Letter granting exceptional leave to remain

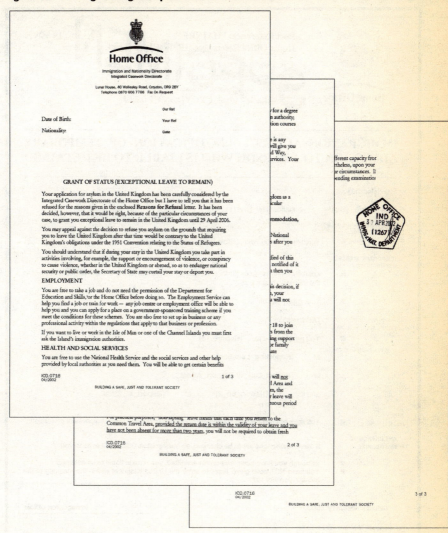

Figure 14: Notice of temporary admission

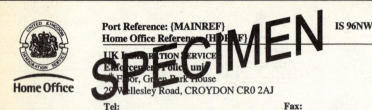

Port Reference: {MAINREF}
Home Office Reference: {HOREF}

IS 96NW

UK IMMIGRATION SERVICE
Enforcement Policy unit
4th Floor, Green Park House
29 Wellesley Road, CROYDON CR0 2AJ

Tel: Fax:

Home Office

SPECIMEN

IMMIGRATION ACT 1971 - NOTIFICATION OF TEMPORARY ADMISSION TO A PERSON WHO IS LIABLE TO BE DETAINED

To: {Name}

Date of Birth: {Bd1}   Nationality: {Nat1}

LIABILITY TO DETENTION

    A.   You are a person who is liable to be detained*.

TEMPORARY ADMISSION RESTRICTIONS

    B.   I hereby authorise your (further) temporary admission to the United Kingdom subject to the following restrictions**:

■   You **must** reside at:

    {Address1}

■   You **must** report to: {Report_To}

    at   {Reporting_Location}

    on   {Report_On} at {Report_At}hrs.

    and then on: {Report_on_2}   at   {Report_at_2}hrs.

■   You **may not** enter employment, paid or unpaid, or engage in any business or profession.

ANY CHANGE OF RESTRICTION

■   **If these restrictions are to be changed, an Immigration Officer will write to you.**

■   **Although you have been temporarily admitted, you remain liable to be detained**
■   **You have NOT been given leave to enter the United Kingdom within the meaning of the Immigration Act 1971**

Date **31 January 2002**

Immigration Officer

* Paragraph 16 of Schedule 2 to the Act
** Paragraph 21 of Schedule 2 to the Act

[IS 96NW Temporary Admission (revise) VC2]

Figure 15: Notice of illegal entry/administrative removal

Home Office	Port Reference: _____ Home Office Reference: _____ **IS 151A**

IMMIGRATION SERVICE

6th _____

29 Well _____ D _____ 30 2AJ

Tel: _____ Fax: _____

NOTICE OF DECISION

NOTICE TO A PERSON LIABLE TO REMOVAL

Under Section 33(1) of the Immigration Act 1971/Section 10(1) the Immigration and Asylum Act 1999

To

I have considered all the information available to me and I am satisfied that you are:

☐ A) an illegal entrant as defined in section 33(1) of the Immigration Act 1971;

☐ B) a person subject to administrative removal in accordance with section 10 of the Immigration and Asylum Act 1999 as:

    i) a person who has failed to observe a condition of leave to enter or remain;

    ii) a person who has obtained leave to remain by deception;

    iii) a member of the family of a person on whom directions have been served.

LIABILITY TO DETENTION

A. You are therefore a person who is liable to be detained pending the completion of arrangements for dealing with you under the Act.** I propose to give directions for your removal from the United Kingdom in due course and details will be given to you separately.

DETENTION/ TEMPORARY ADMISSION

B. I hereby authorise

☐ your detention in approved accommodation/*_____ (please see the notice below).

☐ your temporary admission in the United Kingdom*** The conditions attached to this are explained on the form IS 96 which is enclosed.

Date _____

Immigration Officer

* Delete as appropriate

** Paragraph 16 of Schedule 2 to the 1971 Act

*** Paragraph 21 of Schedule 2 to the 1971 Act

Important notice for persons detained under the Immigration Act 1971.

You may on request have one person known to you or who is likely to take an interest in your welfare informed at public expense as soon as practicable of your whereabouts.

[IS151A — VC2]

Figure 16: Removal directions for illegal entrants/those subject to administrative removal

---

| P... eference: | **IS 151B** |
| Off... Reference: | |

Home Office

~~SAMPLE~~

...IMMIGRATION... ...SERVICE
...Enforcement... ...ction
Harlington...

Tel: 0208 745 2... ...ax: 0208 745 2474

NOTICE OF DECISION

In compliance with the Immigration and Asylum Appeals (Notices) Regulations 2000... ...ragraph 1 of schedule 4 to the Immigration and Asylum Act 1999

DECISION TO ISSUE REMOVAL DIRECTIONS TO AN ILLEGAL ENTRANT/OTHER IMMIGRATION OFFENDER OR A FAMILY MEMBER OF SUCH A PERSON - APPLICATION FOR ASYLUM REFUSED

Under paragraphs 9-10 of schedule 2 to the Immigration Act 1971 & section 10(1) of the Immigration and Asylum Act 1999

To

You are:

☐ A) an illegal entrant as defined in section 33(1) of the Immigration Act 1971;

☐ B) a person subject to administrative removal in accordance with section 10 of the Immigration and Asylum Act 1999 as:

   i)   a person who has failed to observe a condition attached to leave to enter or remain; or

   ii)   a person who has obtained leave to remain by deception; or

   iii) directions have been given to a person to whose family you belong

I have therefore issued directions for your removal to

You have applied for asylum in the United Kingdom. The Secretary of State has decided to refuse your application for asylum for the reasons stated on the attached notice.

REMOVAL DIRECTIONS   A.   Directions have now been given for your removal from the United Kingdom* by flight/ship   to
at   hrs on.

RIGHT OF APPEAL   B.   You are entitled to appeal to an adjudicator against these directions on the following grounds:

■   **Before** removal on asylum grounds, that is because removal in pursuance of these directions would be contrary to the United Kingdom's obligations under the 1951 United Nations Convention relating to the Status of Refugees**

■   If you are appealing on asylum grounds, you also have a right to appeal **before** removal on the grounds that on the fact of your case there is in law no power to give them on the ground on which they are given***

■   **After** removal, if you are not also appealing on asylum grounds, that on the fact of your case there is in law no power to give them on the ground on which they are given ***

The attached notice tells you how to appeal and where advice and assistance can be obtained.

The contents of this notice have been explained to you in English/ .... by me/
.... *(name of interpreter)*

Date

Immigration Officer

*   Paragraph 9 or 10 of Schedule 2 to the 1971 Act/Section 10(8) of the 1999 Act
**   Section 69 of the 1999 Act   ***   Section 86 of the 1999 Act

[IS 151B Illegal entrant (PA) – VC3]

Figure 17: Embarkation stamp

Appendix 10

Abbreviations used in the notes

AC	Appeal Cases
All ER	All England Reports
Art(s)	Article(s)
CA	Court of Appeal
CMLR	Common Market Law Reports
Crim App R	Criminal Appeal Reports
ECJ	European Court of Justice
ECR	European Court Reports
EEA	European Economic Area
ECHR	European Convention on Human Rights
EctHR	European Court of Human Rights
EHRR	European Human Rights Reports
EWCR	England and Wales Court of Appeal
EWHC	England and Wales High Court
FLR	Family Law Reports
HL	House of Lords
HLR	Housing Law Reports
IAT	Immigration Appeal Tribunal
Imm AR	Immigration Appeal Reports
INLR	Immigration and Nationality Law Reports
IRLR	Industrial Relations Law Reports
LGR	Local Government Reports
New LJ	New Law Journal
OJ	Official Journal of the European Communities
PC	Privy Council
QB	Queen's Bench Reports
QBD	Queen's Bench Division
reg(s)	regulation(s)
s(s)	section(s)
Sch(s)	Schedule(s)
SJ	Solicitors' Journal
SLT	Scots Law Times
SSHD	Secretary of State for the Home Department
WLR	Weekly Law Reports

Appendix 10: Abbreviations used in the notes

Acts of Parliament

AIA 1996	Asylum and Immigration Act 1996
AIAA 1993	Asylum and Immigration Appeals Act 1993
BNA 1948	British Nationality Act 1948
BNA 1981	British Nationality Act 1981
FLRA 1969	Family Law Reform Act 1969
IA 1971	Immigration Act 1971
IA 1988	Immigration Act 1988
IAA 1999	Immigration and Asylum Act 1999
IntA 1978	Interpretation Act 1978
JSA 1995	Jobseekers Act 1995
SSAA 1992	Social Security Administration Act 1992
SSCBA 1992	Social Security Contributions and Benefits Act 1992

European law

Secondary legislation is made under the Treaty of Rome 1957, the Single European Act and the Maastricht Treaty in the form of Regulations (EC Reg) and Directives (EC Dir).

Regulations

Each set of regulations has a statutory instrument (SI) number and date. You ask for them by giving their date and number

AS(Amdt) Regs	The Asylum Support (Amendment) Regulations 2002 No.472
AS(IP)Amdt regs	The Asylum Support (Interim Provisions)(Amendment) Regulations 2002 No.471
CB Regs	The Child Benefit (General) Regulations 1976 No.965
CB(RPA) Regs	The Child Benefit (Residence and Persons Abroad) Regulations 1976 No.963
CB&SS(FAR) Regs	The Child Benefit and Social Security (Fixing and Adjustment of Rates) Regulations 1976 No.1267
CB&SS(FAR)Amdt Regs	The Child Benefit and Social Security (Fixing and Adjustment of Rates)(Amendment) Regulations 1998 No.1581
CF(A)O	The Consular Fees (Amendment) Order 1986 No.1881
CTB Regs	The Council Tax Benefit (General) Regulations 1992 No.1814
DWA Regs	The Disability Working Allowance (General) Regulations 1991 No.2887
FC Regs	The Family Credit (General) Regulations 1987 No.1973
HB Regs	The Housing Benefit (General) Regulations 1987 No.1971
HBCTBIS(Amdts) Regs	The Housing Benefit, Council Tax Benefit and Income Support (Amendments) Regulations 1995 No.625
I(CERI)O	The Immigration (Control of Entry through the Republic of Ireland) Order 1972 No.1610

I(EEA)O	The Immigration (European Economic Area) Order 1994 No.1895
I(EEA) Regs	The Immigration (European Economic Area) Regulations 2000
I(EC)O	The Immigration (Exemption from Control) Order 1972 No.1613
I(LER)O	The Immigration (Leave to Enter and Remain) Order 2000
IAA(N) Regs	The Immigration Appeals (Notices) Regulations 1984 No.2040
IAA(P) Rules	The Immigration Appeals (Procedure) Rules 1984 No.2041
IS Regs	The Income Support (General) Regulations 1987 No.1967
JSA Regs	The Jobseeker's Allowance Regulations 1996 No.207
SFCWP Regs	The Social Fund Cold Weather Payments (General) Regulations 1988 No.1724
SFM&FE Regs	The Social Fund Maternity and Funeral Expenses (General) Regulations 1987 No.481
SFM&FE(Amdt) Regs	The Social Fund Maternity and Funeral Expenses (General) Amendment Regulations 1996 No.1443
SS(IA)CA Regs	The Social Security (Immigration and Asylum) Consequential Amendments Regulations 2000 No.636
SMP Regs	The Statutory Maternity Pay (General) Regulations 1986 No.1960
SMP(PAM) Regs	The Statutory Maternity Pay (Persons Abroad and Mariners) Regulations 1987 No.418
SS(AA) Regs	The Social Security (Attendance Allowance) Regulations 1991 No.2740
SS(C&P) Regs	The Social Security (Claims and Payments) Regulations 1987 No.1968
SS(Con) Regs	The Social Security (Contributions) Regulations 2001
SS(DLA) Regs	The Social Security (Disability Living Allowance) Regulations 1991 No.2890
SS(EEEIIP) Regs	The Social Security (Employed Earners' Employment for Industrial Injuries Purposes) Regulations 1975 No.467
SS(GA) Regs	The Social Security (Guardian's Allowance) Regulations 1975 No.515
SS(IB) Regs	The Social Security (Incapacity Benefit) Regulations 1994 No.2946
SFWFP Regs	The Social Fund Winter Fuel Payment Regulations 2000 No.729
SS(IB-ID) Regs	The Social Security (Incapacity Benefit – Increases for Dependants) Regulations 1994 No.2945
SS(ICA) Regs	The Social Security (Invalid Care Allowance) Regulations 1976 No.409
SS(IIAB) Regs	The Social Security (Industrial Injuries) (Airmen's Benefits) Regulations 1975 No.469

SS(IIMB) Regs	The Social Security (Industrial Injuries) (Mariners' Benefits) Regulations 1975 No.470
SS(IIPD) Regs	The Social Security (Industrial Injuries) (Prescribed Diseases) Regulations 1985 No.967
SS(MB) Regs	The Social Security (Mariners' Benefits) Regulations 1975 No.529
SS(NIRA) Regs	The Social Security (Northern Ireland Reciprocal Arrangements) Regulations 1976 No.1003
SS(OB) Regs	The Social Security (Overlapping Benefits) Regulations 1979 No.597
SS(PFA)MA Regs	The Social Security (Persons from Abroad) Miscellaneous Amendments Regulations 1996 No.30
SS(SDA) Regs	The Social Security (Severe Disablement Allowance) Regulations 1984 No.1303
SS(WB&RP) Regs	The Social Security (Widow's Benefit and Retirement Pensions) Regulations 1979 No.642
SSB(Dep) Regs	The Social Security Benefit (Dependency) Regulations 1977 No.343
SSB(PA) Regs	The Social Security Benefit (Persons Abroad) Regulations 1975 No.563
SSB(PRT) Regs	The Social Security Benefit (Persons Residing Together) Regulations 1977 No.956
SSFA(PM) Regs	The Social Security and Family Allowances (Polygamous Marriages) Regulations 1975 No.561
SSP Regs	The Statutory Sick Pay (General) Regulations 1982 No.894
SSP(MAPA) Regs	The Statutory Sick Pay (Mariners, Airmen and Persons Abroad) Regulations 1982 No.1349
VOLO	The Immigration (variation of Leave) order 1976 No.1572

Other information

API	Asylum Policy Instructions, Home Office
DMG	The Decision Makers Guide
GM	The Housing Benefit and Council Tax Benefit Guidance Manual
IDI	Immigration Directorate Instructions

Note: There are many cases referred to in the notes. Some are followed by a bracketed number or similar reference – eg, (12573) – these are references to unreported decisions of the Immigration Appeal Tribunal.

Index

. . . .

How to use this Index

Entries against the bold headings direct you to the general information on the subject, or where the subject is covered most fully. Sub-entries are listed alphabetically and direct you to specific aspects of the subject.

refugees 219
see also family benefits
working holidaymakers 10
recourse to public funds 101
working restrictions
see employment conditions
writers
recourse to public funds 101

Z
Zaire
upheaval countries and asylum
seekers 280